THAILAND:
Dictatorship or Democracy?

DONALD F. COOPER

MINERVA PRESS
MONTREUX LONDON WASHINGTON

THAILAND: Dictatorship or Democracy?
Copyright © Donald F. Cooper 1995

ISBN 1 85863 416 4

First Published 1995 by
MINERVA PRESS
10 Cromwell Place
London SW7 2JN

Printed in Great Britain by
B.W.D. Printers Ltd., Northolt, Middlesex

THAILAND: Dictatorship or Democracy?

"The better the mirror, the more a man sees what he may not wish to have seen."

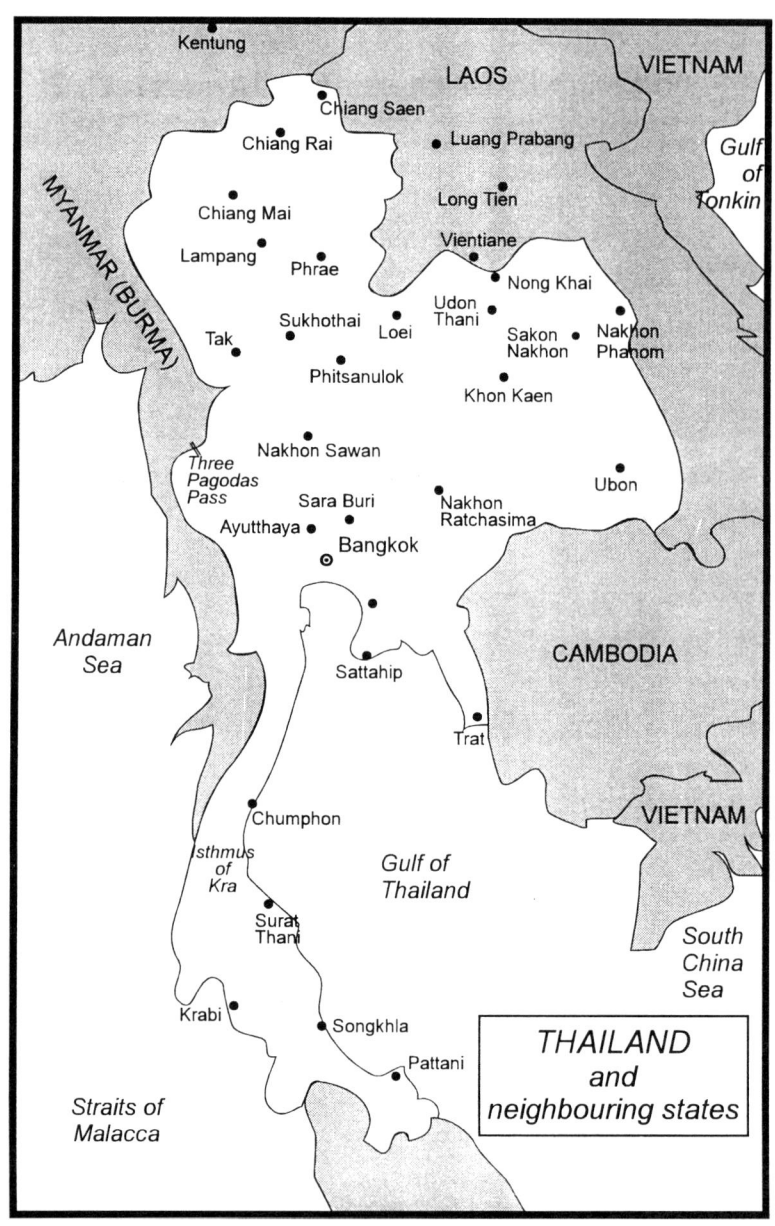

THAILAND
and
neighbouring states

Contents

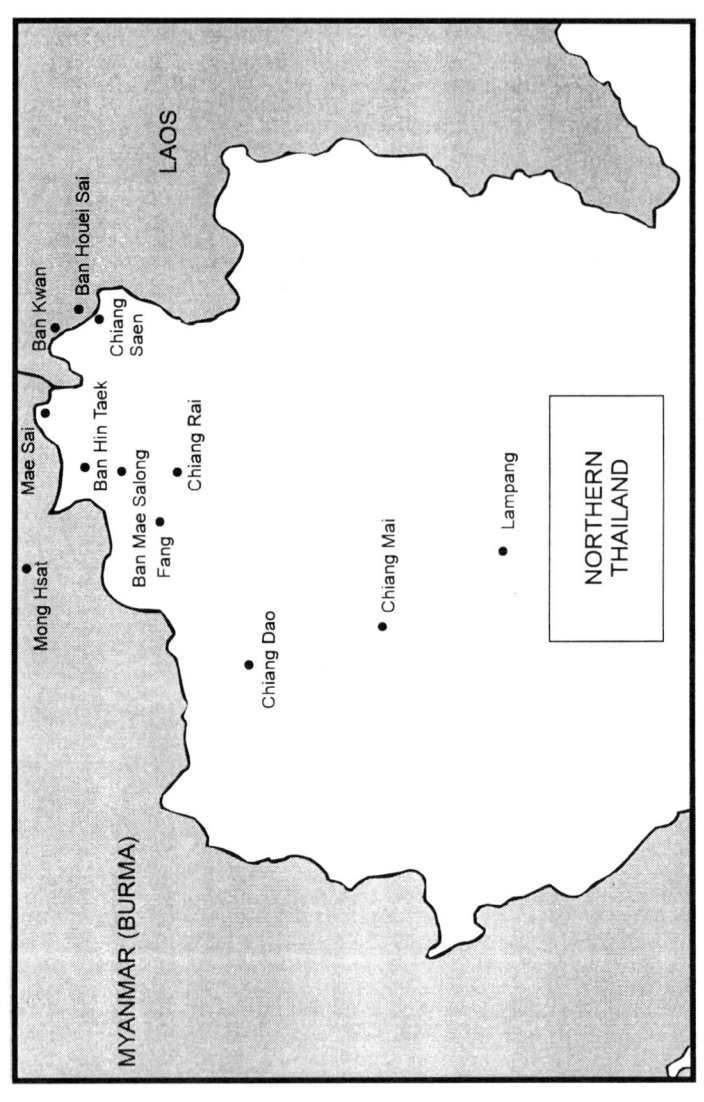

Introduction

Professors of History, would-be Professors of History, Fellows and would-be Fellows write learned histories and historiographies. This book is not intended to be either a history or a historiography: neither is it a text book. It is instead a commentary on a pattern of events beginning with the onset of the Second World War in South-East Asia and ending with the bloody days of May 1992. It primarily concerns political events in Thailand itself whilst also introducing relevant elements of activities in adjoining states. It also considers the entangling features of local drug production.

During my work in a commercial field in Thailand from the mid-1970s until the early 1990s I was an observer of events which form the latter part of this book. It was also my good fortune to work with or talk to many who were closely involved with the earlier part. I have been able to discuss the content of a research programme with Thais and others who have been able to confirm or to discount much.

Why this particular period and why the particular choice of events? In my view, modern Thailand owes much to the traumatic effect on it of the Second World War and its disturbance of previous international relationships. The infiltration of young Thai officers into their enemy-occupied homeland, by both America and Britain, to join ranks with the Pridi-led home-based Seri Thai had a far-reaching effect on the immediate post-war period. So too did some of the more dubious manoeuvres of the American OSS, although the long-term tragic effects of those manoeuvres on American youth could not have been foreseen at that time.

Errors of judgement made by Britain — and in particular the rice fiasco — also played their part. Britain, economically impoverished by the war and historically in a period of substantial political change, still assumed itself to be a major power and allowed the emotion of revenge to displace logical thought. To the north, the American-backed Chinese regime of Chiang Kai-shek was collapsing and sections of its Army were to find their way south from Yunnan into the foothills of the Himalayas which tumble down through the Shan States into northern Thailand. This allowed the displaced army elements access to, and the development of, poppy-growing areas which were to become known as 'The Golden Triangle'.

With the loss of China to communism, Thailand became a keystone of American policy in eastern Asia. Thailand was used, or its dominant military element was used, to implement American policy, not only in relation to Thailand itself but also throughout South-East Asia, to such an extent that the appearance was given of Thailand becoming a puppet state. But many Thai citizens profited from that policy.

A Thai response developed through student revolt and then through new political leaders, supported by a strong monarchy, all of whom endeavoured to give Thailand freedom from American dominance. Commerce and trade were expanded. Political endeavours achieved a degree of success but there were a number of hiccups along the way.

Thailand's attempt at political progress was made difficult not only by its internal attitudes to a form of democracy but also by the ravages of war and internal strife in the volatile states which border it. This strife was aggravated both internally and externally by the expanding activities in the poppy-growing areas, first through opium and later through heroin. Beyond the immediate area of South-East Asia, Thailand was affected by the interplay of the major powers — China, America, and the USSR. A search continues for democracy in Thailand — but not by everyone.

Being unable to read original Thai text has been an obvious disadvantage. I am indebted to numerous Thai students unknown to me personally, who, usually in search of a PhD at an American university, have translated large slices of Thai text into English. Necessarily, I have assumed the translations to be correct but I have sometimes disagreed with the conclusions drawn from the extract in relation to other events.

When extending the field of research I became more and more aware of how selective were some authors in their interpretation of facts. Personal background and prejudice appeared to play a substantial role in many interpretations. Without question I shall be found equally guilty of selectivity and prejudice although, no doubt like others, I have tried to avoid it. I have tried to work to the principle that while comment is free, facts are sacred. Unfortunately the recording of political so-called fact appears to be a far from perfect science and accounts frequently appear to reflect biased pre-held views of the recorder.

I shall be seen to have a different approach to some events from the young PhD seeker and the younger element of academia. I am of a vintage which fought its way through the desperate days of the 1939-45 war and my views and interpretations are coloured, or perhaps clouded, by that experience. That is probably so, particularly, in relation to the events of the earlier part of the period about which I have endeavoured to write. I hope that I reflect in my interpretation of wartime and early post-war events, the logical and not merely the emotional attitudes of those days.

It is easy to criticise Thailand for its ways of government but those of other nations, if closely examined, also leave much to be desired. The political scene has a degree of similarity the world over: power-seeking and frequently greedy, with little more than crocodile tears for the less fortunate in society. Corruption of different scales and styles abound in societies from the crude pay-off to a sophisticated pin-striped variation. Give a country the opportunity to add to the mix, the access to a major source of raw material for drugs and the opportunities become legion.

I am indebted to the School of Oriental and African Studies in London, the Siam Society in Bangkok, the Special Services Club of London, and the University of Kent at Canterbury — each of which has permitted me access to its library in my search for information or corroboration. I am also indebted to the Public Records Office, the Imperial War Museum, The United Nations Library and the Liddell Hart Centre for Military Archives at King's College (all of which are located in London), and to the Narcotics Suppression Bureau in Bangkok, for access to their records.

I am also indebted to numerous people in Thailand who have given of their time and personal knowledge in helping me to differentiate between fact and fiction. I have respected the wishes expressed to me by many Thais not to have their names included in the text or notes. Those whose names have already reached the public domain have been documented. Additionally, where material has been drawn even in general terms from published works, a record of that work has been included, either by a general reference to the book or by reference to specific pages.

No one is to blame for any mistakes, other than me. My many friends in Thailand (who will, I hope, remain my friends after reading this book) will understand that this has a strong *farang* slant to it. That

ix

is inevitable. My views on many issues will not necessarily be the same as theirs and I shall rely on two of the virtues of Buddhism — tolerance and forgiveness — for which I have often been grateful during the past almost twenty years. May I commend to them two lines from Scotland's most famous poet, Robert Burns:

> *"O wad some Pow'r the giftie gie us*
> *To see oursels as others see us!"*

Finally, my thanks go particularly to my wife, Bobbie, who tolerated not only our quiet English cottage being inundated with books and documents of Thai history and quasi-history but also the hundreds of hours spent poring over them. Further afield, my thanks go to many friends in Thailand with whom I have worked, eaten, drunk, and conversed — and especially to a veteran of the Seri Thai who still, sometimes, only signs his letters as 'Pete'.

Well End
June 1994

NOTE

In the footnotes shown on various pages the abbreviation 'JSS' indicates that the work was published in the Journal of the Siam Society, Bangkok. Details of these and other published works to which reference is made are contained in the Bibliography.

CHAPTER ONE
The Fall and Rise of Phibun

All great men make mistakes and Field Marshal Phibun Songkhram, prime minister of Thailand, was no exception. As the shadows of the Second World War gathered over the Pacific he had no option other than to decide with which of the belligerents he was to ally his country. It was not an easy decision, and, like others throughout history, Phibun made the mistake of picking the wrong side. It was an understandable mistake in the circumstances in which he found himself.

Phibun's objective in life was to preserve neither the British nor the French colonial empire, and most certainly not the French. Neither was it to help develop an expanding American economic empire. Nor was it to subscribe to the Japanese theory of the 'Greater East Asia Co-Prosperity Sphere' or 'Asia for the Asians', which he might well have believed to mean 'Asia for the Japanese'. He would not have been alone in so believing; Japan's attempts to expand its colonial domain in the 1940s were seen by many to be entirely the same as those of the earlier European colonisations.[1] Phibun's very proper objective was to continue the independence of, and protect from foreign interference, the kingdom formerly known as Siam but whose governing National Assembly he had persuaded to rename 'Thailand'.

At the time of the outbreak of hostilities in Europe, Thailand's boy-king, Ananda Mahidol, was absent at his studies in Switzerland. Phibun was still developing a form of government under a recently created constitutional monarchy. A coup d'état of June 1932, conceived in student discussions in Paris, had precariously bluffed its way into reality, led by a part-military, part-civilian group. The coup had left uneasy trails behind it. Pridi Banomyong, its intellectual leader and the foremost of its civilian participants, had come under early suspicion from the pro-royalist military of having communist leanings. He had been exiled temporarily during 1933 because of the consternation caused by his land reform proposals but had been brought back to hold high government office. He was still looked upon

---

[1] *Far East Economic Review*, 8 September 1949

as the leading civilian member of the 1932 coup group. The military element, having first turned to respected seniors for leadership, had discarded them and accepted in their stead the politically-minded soldier, Phibun Songkhram, who by 1938 had become prime minister. Pridi was his minister of finance.

Following the outbreak of war in 1939, France, concerned for the safety of its Indochinese possessions, proposed a non-aggression pact with Thailand. This suited Phibun but he asked that the French should in turn accept that the boundary between Indochina and Thailand was established in accordance with international law. This was 'Thai-speak' for the Mekong River boundary, which Phibun saw as his natural defence barrier. He also wanted the return of the river islands earlier annexed by the French. Agreement was reached in principle and Phibun then sought to widen the pact to include Britain and Japan. In April 1940 Britain was prepared to accept the principle; Japan wanted a share of the spoils. America, Germany and Italy were informed of the proposals and all saw it as an earnest attempt by the government of Thailand to remain neutral in any future Asian conflict while not missing a golden opportunity. The pacts with Britain and France were signed in Bangkok on twelfth of June 1940, only a few days after the British Army and a remnant of the French Army had been evacuated from France via the beaches of Dunkirk and La Panne. The pact with Japan was delayed but Phibun was prepared to bide his time. He had already formed a view that the Japanese intended to annexe Indochina and when they did, he planned to take back the provinces that Thailand had ceded under threat to France at the end of the previous century.[2] In Indochina itself there was a belief that Phibun would grant bases in northern Thailand to the Japanese to assist them in an attack on the Burma Road, a major supply route to the Chinese armies of Chiang Kai-shek, with whom Japan was at war.[3]

On eleventh of September 1940, following the fall of France, the Thai government formally requested a resolution founded on the Mekong boundary, a request which soured relationships between Thailand and both Britain and America. These two countries were not only concerned about Thailand but were also keeping a watchful eye

[2]   *US-Thailand Diplomatic Relations during World War II*; Sethachuay Vivat, pp77–84

[3]   *The First Vietnam War*; Peter Dunn, p36

on Japanese activities in South-East Asia. The Roosevelt/Churchill axis was already in discussion with the Japanese government on the subject of the neutralisation of both Indochina and Thailand under joint guarantees by America, Britain, Japan, and China. In exchange there would be a renewal of American/Japanese trade.[4] During September, the newly-formed Vichy France government formally drew back from earlier agreements and refused to ratify any change. This decision split the Thai Cabinet. Pridi and his civilian supporters called for peaceful negotiation, but the military element espied glory.

Thailand invaded the Vichy-controlled territories of Laos and Cambodia. In Thai eyes, it was a just act of revenge for French blackmail and annexation in 1893 followed by the breaking of verbal agreements in mid-1940. To others it merely appeared as opportunism. To Phibun's wife, the Lady La-iad, Phibun's aim was to counter *"outright territorial aggrandisement by the French".*[5]

If Indochina was to change hands, then the Thais were anxious that some of it should revert to Thailand, thus making practical a defence line against possible Japanese aggression along the natural barrier of the Mekong.

The Thais had some early land successes, whilst on fifteenth of December the French bombed the town of Nakon Phanom. With the ratification of the treaty with Thailand in December, Japan handed over a number of bombers and tanks, subsequently shipping back-up supplies which included anti-aircraft guns and field artillery. Fighting along the Mekong front was at first sporadic but by fifth of January 1941, full-scale fighting erupted with the battle for Samrong. It lasted for twenty-two days and, as a result, Thai troops were able to occupy all of its lost territory on the banks of the Mekong. At sea, it was the French who prevailed and they sank a number of small Thai naval craft. On twenty-fourth of January 1941, under Japanese pressure, a cease-fire was agreed.

The deputy commander of the Thai force in Cambodia was General Phin Choonhavan. The Thai forward unit was the horse-mounted 1st Cavalry Regiment, and commanding one of its companies following the early death of its initially appointed commander was Phin's son, the newly commissioned Chatichai Choonhavan.

---

[4] *Second World War; Winston S. Churchill, Vol. III*; pp389–390
[5] *Porrtraits of Thai Politics*; Jenton K. Ray; p200

Phibun approached Britain with a view to drawing up a joint military defence plan. Under it, he was prepared to cede the right of Britain to build military defences for the defence of Malaya and Singapore as far north as Petchaburi, one hundred and fifty kilometres south-west of Bangkok. The British prime minister, Winston Churchill, despatched a cable to Phibun through the embassy in Bangkok, to express regrets that Britain was not in a position militarily to come to Thailand's aid. Such a response was not surprising. In the autumn of 1940, Britain had beaten off the first threat of German invasion of its land through the skilful but desperate use of its limited air-power. It was only to be expected that the spring of 1941 would see that threat arising again. America, unsure of where Phibun's ultimate loyalty lay, would not supply him with arms for an entirely different reason. It was concerned that such arms would fall into Japanese hands and be used against China, America's ally.

A treaty of ninth of May 1941 between Thailand and France, brought about under the almost dictatorial influence of the Japanese, the Tokyo Treaty, made the River Mekong the boundary between Indochina and Thailand, thus transferring two small areas of Laos on the west bank to Phibun's rule. Thailand also acquired a large area of northern and western Cambodia consisting of the provinces of Siamreap and Battambang. To its annoyance, Thailand was required to make a payment in compensation for the territory.[6]

At the end of its incursions into Indochina, Phibun gave the Army a heroes' parade through Bangkok. He built the Victory Monument and in July promoted himself to the rank of field marshal. He had previously been a major-general but had no problem in dispensing with the intervening ranks of lieutenant-general and general. Despite Thai self-glorification the whole episode was nothing more than a skirmish. In April 1941, a French officer wrote: *"... it was soon over... but no one seemed to know what it was all about. ... the Japanese, who had been pulling the strings since the start of the incident, had found the moment favourable to appear in the light of mediators, and were seizing the opportunity to establish themselves in strength in Cochin-China"*. The French Army force appeared to have

---

[6] *Fall of the Phibun Government, 1944*; B. A. Batson/JSS; p92 and *The Balancing Act*; Joseph J. Wright, Jnr; p110

had more of its time taken up in shooting game and deer than Thai soldiers.[7]

For the Thais, and particularly for Phibun, the campaign served to boost morale. It also acted as a first stepping-stone to the concept of a greater Thai nation. At the formal transfer of the Cambodian provinces, Thailand was represented by Khuang Aphaiwong, the son of a one-time Thai governor of those territories. The province of Siamreap, meaning 'the defeat of the Thai' and named from an earlier battle, was quickly renamed in Phibun's honour.

Japan strengthened its hold on Indochina. Throughout 1941 it increased the number of its bases and piled up men and weapons. In June it demanded, and obtained from Vichy France, further bases in southern Indochina. On twenty-fourth of July, American President Roosevelt called for a Japanese withdrawal from Indochina and for the neutralisation of that territory. To reinforce his demands, America, Britain, and Holland froze all Japanese assets.

With the latest Japanese moves, Thailand was feeling distinctly vulnerable. To curry favour with the West, Phibun made a number of ministerial appointments which he believed would be considered favourable by the Allies, including that of General Adun Dejcharas, head of the police, who became deputy prime minister. Phibun took other steps. On twelfth of August a formal statement was issued that Thailand would resist with force any invasion of its territory, from whatever direction. This was incorporated into an Act of eleventh of September, providing for a scorched-earth and fight-to-the-last-man policy.[8] Thailand at this point appeared to the outside world to be preparing itself for all-out war. Phibun thought otherwise. With America concentrating its effort on the defence of the Philippines and Britain only able to offer a few field-guns, he saw the future of Thailand as either total domination by Japan or some form of alliance with it.

Despite Phibun's moves to foster relations with the Allies, both American and British observers, as far back as June 1933, had held a growing belief that Phibun was pro-Japanese. There were good grounds for such suspicions. It was discovered later that in 1933,

---

[7]   *Source of the River Kwai*; Pierre Boule; p36

[8]   *Thailand and the fall of Singapore*; Nigel J. Brailey; p96; and *The Balancing Act*; Joseph J. Wright, Jnr; p113; and *US-Thailand Diplomatic Relations during World War II*; Sethachuay Vivat, pp145–6

Phibun had made promises to Japanese minister Yatabe of rights of passage, if necessary, against the British, in exchange for support against any Anglo-French reaction to the 1932 coup.[9]

In the autumn of 1941, American intelligence services correctly assessed that Japanese plans for aggression were well advanced. On sixth of September, the Japanese Imperial Conference set out its principles. War against America, Britain, and the Netherlands was to have the aim of removing the influence of those nations from all of South-East Asia, thus improving the defence of Japan itself and creating between Japan and that area an inseparable relationship in military, political, and economic affairs. More specifically, with Japanese stocks of important raw materials and fuel being reduced by blockade, South-East Asia must be conquered within a few months to obtain oil, bauxite, nickel, rubber, and tin.[10] It was no longer a question of whether or not Japan would invade South-East Asia, only of when and where. On twenty-sixth of November, President Roosevelt informed the American High Commissioner of the Philippines that *"advance against Thailand seems the most probable"*. Later, British intelligence indicated that the Kra Isthmus was the most likely area of attack and by sixth of December a fleet of thirty-five transports, eight cruisers, and twenty destroyers were known to be in the Gulf of Thailand.[11]

On seventh of December 1941, Japan delivered an ultimatum requiring rights for troops to pass through Thailand to attack the British in Burma, and early on the morning of eighth of December Japanese troops invaded Thailand at nine points. Thai resistance was not merely token but was *"fierce, albeit short-lived, ... with much bloodshed"*. It could not be sustained because of lack of ammunition.[12] After a few hours, Phibun ordered his troops to cease fighting and he permitted the passage of Japanese troops. In exchange Japan agreed to respect Thailand's independence and sovereignty.

When, in 1945, information was sought by the Allied War Crimes Commission, an eyewitness account of events was given by Direk Jayanama who was foreign minister at the time.[13] On the night of

---

[9]   *Thailand and the Fall of Singapore*; Nigel J. Brailey; pp86–7
[10] *The First Vietnam War*; Peter Dunn, citing Japanese author Nobutaka Ike
[11] *Second World War, Vol. III*; Winston S. Churchill; p532–5
[12] *Portraits of Thai Politics*; Jenton K. Ray; p201
[13] *Into Siam, Underground Kingdom*; Nicol Smith and Blake Clark; pp261–6

seventh of December General Adun, the deputy prime minister, was dining with Direk when he was called to a meeting in the residence of the absent prime minister. Direk was summoned later, to find that the Japanese ambassador and his staff were waiting in the reception area. With the prime minister away on the Indochina border and at that time incommunicado, General Adun was anxious to avoid a meeting which would place him, personally, in a situation from which he could not extricate himself. Direk was therefore requested to meet the Japanese party.

The Japanese ambassador, Tsubokami, was angry not only at being kept waiting and at the absence of the prime minister but also at the refusal of be deputy prime minister to see him. He informed Direk that Japan had that day declared war on both America and Britain and that it sought authority for free passage of Japanese troops by land, sea, and air through Thailand as it was, he asserted, a matter of life and death for Japan. Refusal would result in bloodshed. The Japanese military attaché then announced that Japanese troops were at that moment landing at various places in Thailand. Direk told Tsubokami of a decision to call a Cabinet meeting in the morning and that a plane had already been sent to the border to bring back Phibun. The Japanese ambassador returned at six o'clock but again had to kick his heels as Phibun himself did not arrive until seven, at which time the Cabinet assembled. To those present, it was obvious that Phibun had already made up his mind on the decision that the Cabinet should reach. He asked his questions only of members whom he knew would give him the answers he wanted. He brushed aside the objections raised by Pridi who argued for consideration of world opinion and of national honour. The high principles of 'scorched earth' and 'fight-to-the-death' were set aside. At seven-forty-five, Phibun left the Cabinet meeting and told the Japanese ambassador that his request for the free passage of troops would be granted.

There were two matters of which other members of the Cabinet were not aware. Firstly, Phibun had already considered with Tsubokami that a further development of a joint alliance would be justified as being in the defence of Thailand. Secondly, Phibun, in October 1940, had told the Japanese that if they would support his border requirements with Indochina, he would allow them passage through Thailand in the event of war.[14] Before Bangkok's own sacred guardian spirit, the Emerald Buddha, Phibun personally signed the agreement. Direk as foreign minister was not required to sign. He offered his resignation but it was refused. He was demoted to deputy foreign minister and early in January 1942, by some strange prime ministerial sense of humour, he was appointed ambassador to Japan. Defending her husband, Lady La-iad denies that there was any deal of support in exchange for territory, and she has also said that the 'guarantee of independence, sovereignty, and honour' was signed by Direk and Tsubokami, and not by Phibun.[15] Argument over who signed the document is academic: the decision that it should be signed was Phibun's.

Pridi was worried. He believed sincerely that the action which had been taken betrayed the national honour. Beyond that, as finance minister, he saw only too well the effect of an armed occupying power on the economy of Thailand. Until this time Phibun, despite his differences with Pridi, had allowed him to develop many of his concepts of government. Now, Pridi was to have little further say in that government as, at the request of Tsubokami, he was removed from his appointment as finance minister. Phibun, still needing Pridi's support, arranged for him to become one of the absent King Ananda's regents.

Thus parted the careers of two of the most distinguished men in Thailand's modern history. Both were deeply involved in the 1932 coup d'état against the absolute monarchy. Each held the other in high regard and this regard was to continue for some years. Pridi's career was to lead on through the Regency, to being the recognised head of the freedom-seeking Seri Thai, to fame, to immense popularity as the Elder Statesman of the land and to international acceptance. It would then move on to disillusion and exile. Phibun's career was to take him on through absolute power, downfall, and trial for his life. He would return to power as the first of the Thai dictators and then he in his turn would suffer humiliation and exile.

Born Plaek Kittasangkha on fourteenth of July 1897, Phibun, the son of a prosperous fruit farmer, spent his life from the age of twelve in the Thai Army. After attendance at the Military Academy he

14 *Thailand and the Fall of Singapore*; Nigel J. Brailey; p86; and *F. M. Phibun Songkhram*; B. J. Terweil; p17
15 *Portraits of Thai Politics*; Jemton K. Ray; pp202-3

specialised in artillery. As a romantic young officer he met a thirteen-year-old girl, La-iad, to whom he wrote love poems and two years later they were married. Phibun moved to the Army Staff College and from there, by scholarship, to France to the artillery schools at Poitiers and Fontainebleau. In Paris he became a member of the Association of Siamese Students in France and there he met Pridi, then president and secretary of that potentially revolutionary gathering. Phibun himself became a president of the Association and on his return to Thailand in 1927 he helped in the organisation of Army officers sympathetic to the cause of the overthrow of the absolute monarchy. He was only a junior member of the 1932 coup d'état but in 1933, as a lieutenant-colonel of artillery, he played a major part in crushing the counter-revolution of the princes, the Boworadej rebellion, using his artillery with great effect in the battle for Dong Muang airfield. Serving with him at that time was an aspiring infantry officer, Phin Choonhavan. That same year, with the help of an armoured corps, Phibun was a key figure in ousting Manopakon from the premiership and in reconvening the National Assembly. As a result, he was invited by the incoming prime minister, Phahon Yothin, to join his Cabinet as deputy-commander-in-chief of the Army. 1936 saw Phibun as Rector of Chulalongkorn University and by 1938 he was a major-general and his country's prime minister. 1938 also saw the third attempt at his assassination. In 1934 and already minister of defence at the age of thirty-six, he had been shot in the neck and shoulders while attending a soccer match. Only the prompt intervention of a then-unknown aide, Phao Sriyanon, who had thrown himself at the gunman saved Phibun's life. In November 1938, on the night of the festival of *Loy Krathong*, Phibun had been shot in the arm at close range by his valet, alleged to be in the pay of royalists. In December 1938 he, his family, and guests survived an attempted poisoning of their food. It was an event which was not helpful to his social life and an invitation to dine in Phibun's company became an occasion to avoid.

The first Phibun government, dating from fifteenth of December 1938, was ruthless and one of extreme nationalism in the German/Japanese style. Phibun purged the ruling military of all opposition, particularly of royalist supporters, and he summarily executed eighteen of them. The trappings of fascism, if not the substance, appeared, with school children put into uniform in parallel with the *Hitlerjugend*. Phibun had an intense dislike of the ethnic Chinese minority within the country and also of the French in Indochina. His government relied on the military for power and had its political and social base in the bureaucracy. Between them they formed a state within a state. They did not provide the economic thrust. This was principally in the hands of the ethnic Chinese bourgeoisie. As the members of the new ruling élite were salaried officers and officials, they had to build their personal capital through co-operation, a situation which allowed powerful cliques to combine their interests with the higher ranks of entrepreneurial Chinese to form important business empires. For the Chinese, marginalised by the regime, these business empires became a substitute for any opportunity to become a political force.[16]

Phibun developed a theory of 'Greater Thailand'. He saw it incorporating the numerous Thais who lived in surrounding regions, not just in old Siam, and arising out of it, in 1939, he persuaded the National Assembly to change the name of the country from Siam to Thailand. Although there were connections with an old civilisation of 'Syam', the name 'Siam' could readily be discarded as that imposed by the British in the unequal treaties of the previous century. Phibun's apparent aim was ultimately to incorporate into an empire the whole of Laos, Cambodia, the Thai-speaking Shan States, and those of the Malay states which had been under Thai suzerainty before the British took possession of Malaya. Many of his contemporaries disagreed with the incorporation of any part of Cambodia, fearing that the Kampucheans would merely produce another ethnic minority problem. The disagreement was not extended to Laos where the population were essentially of the same ethnic background as in 'Isan', the north-east of Thailand. Phibun's friendship with the Japanese also became a source of disagreement and among the protestors at the increasing dependence upon Japan was the ex-King. King Prajadhipok, who had abdicated in March 1935 and was living in England. He telegraphed Phibun at the end of February 1941, *"Siam"* he said, *"does not want to be under the direction of any nation... It has been the traditional policy of all the kings of Siam to be friendly with Great Britain... To*

---

[16] *State Building and Ethnic Society*; Dr Chai-anan Samudavanija; research paper published by Bangkok Post, 16–18 August 1989

me it would seem that Siam would be behaving almost suicidally if she were to make herself Britain's enemy".[17]

The war in Asia was only a few months old when Phibun moved Thailand closer to the Berlin/Rome/Tokyo axis powers. According to the Cabinet secretary-general, Thawee Bunyakatu, the eventual decision to declare war on Britain and America was made in Bangkok at noon on twenty-fifth of January 1942. The event which had more than anything else convinced Phibun to side with the Japanese had been the sinking of the two British battleships *Prince of Wales* and *Repulse* within days of the outbreak of hostilities.[18] Phibun's political strategy in the early days of 1942 came as a surprise to America, to Britain, and even to the Japanese. The mouse had roared. There is no doubt that Phibun, even before the loss of these two great capital ships, was under severe pressure from the Japanese to increase his contribution to the axis partnership but the alacrity with which he rushed into his declaration was a clear indication of where he felt his opportunism would best reward him.

Neither America nor Britain formally declared war upon Thailand. Britain, who considered Phibun the prime culprit, merely noted in the *London Gazette* that a state of war existed. In Washington the minister of the Thai Legation, Momrajawong (M. R.) Seni, decided for himself not to hand over the declaration. But it was not all opportunism on Phibun's part. The Thai forces possessed only fifty tanks, limited stocks of ammunition, and an Air Force which had already been proved inferior even to that of French Indochina. It was a fighting force of no significance in relation to the Japanese war machine.

For over a year and a half, Japan went from victory to victory and Phibun's decision appeared to have been well-judged. In May 1942, at the request of the Japanese, his Army conducted a small-scale, successful campaign in the Shan States of Burma. In this campaign Major-General Phin Choonhavan commanded the 3rd Division while his son, Chatichai, continued to serve with the 1st Cavalry Regiment as part of the 4th Division. Sarit Thanarat was an infantry battalion commander and also in the 4th Division. The 3rd Division captured Kengtung, and Phin raised the Thai flag over the city. The 4th Division moved into the eastern parts of the Shan States and served there for the next three years.

---

[17] *King Prajadhipok and the Apple Cart*; Nicholas Tarling/JSS; p38
[18] *Pridi Banomyong*: Vichitvong na Pombhejara

In July 1943, Japanese prime minister Tojo visited Bangkok. During his visit he announced that two of the Shan States around Kengtung and four of the northern Malay states — Perlis, Kedah, Kelantan and Tregganu — would be transferred to Thai administration. This was subsequently confirmed in a treaty between Japan and Thailand on twentieth of August of that year.[19] Phibun had now, by acts of war, recovered for his country the lands which King Chulalongkhorn, for purposes of peace, had diplomatically ceded in the previous century.

Britain's wartime consideration of post-war policy for the Far East was reviewed in a study by G. F. Hudson, a Balliol College academic serving with the Foreign Office Research Unit. Hudson recommended that measures of retribution should be limited to the removal of Phibun, the return of British territories, and commercial compensation. He attached importance to the avoidance of Thailand falling under Chinese control and to its remaining a strong and friendly buffer state. Thailand was to be left with an army sufficient to avoid dependence on foreign protection and capable of dealing with large-scale disorders which might be fomented from abroad, particularly by China. He also recommended an insistence on Thai sovereignty and the avoidance of tutelage, which would probably open the way to Nationalist China intrigue. America should, however, provide the economic and foreign affairs advisers in order to demonstrate its interests. Hudson advised against trying to solve France's problems, an act which he considered would alienate Thai national feelings without any compensating gratitude from the French. Interestingly, he foresaw long-term ethnographic development resulting in a voluntary union between Thailand, Laos, and the Shan States.[20] He also wanted to re-establish assurances given by the Thai government in the annex to a treaty of tenth of March 1909 that it would not permit any danger to arise to British interests anywhere in Thailand.[21]

It was unfortunate that Hudson's review did not command greater respect at the British Foreign Office. Opinions of dyed-in-the-wool

---

[19] *Thailand: A Short History*; David K. Wyatt; p258 and *Atonement before Absolution*; Nicholas Tarling/JSS; p31
[20] *Atonement before Absolution*; Nicholas Tarling/JSS; pp27–9, citing FO371/35979 of 2 February 1943
[21] *Atonement before Absolution*; Nicholas Tarling/JSS; p48 note 99

South-East Asia colonialists had a greater and adverse influence, to the detriment of British prestige. There were also a number of complicating factors from outside Britain. In 1942, American Chiefs-of-Staff had unilaterally declared both Thailand and Indochina to be within the sphere of influence of America and thus of her ally, Chiang Kai-shek. Chiang was unlikely to surrender that position if there might be any loss of face on his part, although later in the war Lord Louis Mountbatten, Supreme Allied Commander, South-East Asia, was able to agree a pragmatic modification with Chiang, fundamentally resulting in the spheres of influence being those territories over which the respective armies advanced. The American Command in China was also involved, making claims to have the absolute right to operate in South-East Asia. The claims had no validity whatsoever as it was hopelessly placed to put such a policy into action. In Europe there was further intrigue where the anti-British American ambassador to Vichy France, Admiral Leahy, was endeavouring to have the whole of Indochina taken out of Mountbatten's command.[22]

Despite the early successes of the Japanese, history was to prove Phibun's judgement wrong. Although he was prepared to close his eyes to the surreptitious activities of the Regent and many of his senior colleagues in their establishment of a resistance force of free Thais (the Seri Thai), there was to be no forgiveness for him personally. In July 1944 he was ousted from power. When he saw the possibility of Japanese defeat, Phibun conceived a plan that would remove both the national capital and the Army base from Bangkok to Petchabun. The move was calculated to assist him in any struggle which might ensue with the Japanese forces of occupation. Phibun's attempt to force the plan upon the National Assembly failed and on twenty-fourth of July 1944 he offered his resignation. The Lady La-iad claimed, years later, that Phibun chose resignation rather than disclose details of the plan to the National Assembly, as it would provide information for the Japanese. Others believed that he was confident that his resignation would not be accepted by one of the two regents, his friend Lieut-General Prince Aditya.

His confidence was misplaced. By mid-1944 there was growing public dissatisfaction with the regime both within and without the Assembly. The military, the Air Force, and most intellectuals

---

[22] *The First Vietnam War*; Peter Dunn; pp79—80, 89—91

intensely disliked the Japanese. Only the Chinese-Thai element appeared to tolerate them, possibly because there were big profits to be made. The Japanese in their turn became disenchanted with the prime minister and doubted his loyalty to them.[23] Phibun surrendered the office of prime minister on twenty-sixth of July 1944. The Japanese reacted by grounding the Thai Air Force. Phibun was unwilling to give up the post of supreme commander of the Armed Forces and retired to the Army base at Lopburi. Thus he endeavoured to retain not only an element of personal pride but also the pride of the Army, an Army which had dominated Thai politics, if not since the revolution of 1932 itself, certainly since the defeat of the Boworadej counter-coup of 1933.

Phibun was replaced as prime minister by Khuang Aphaiwong, the Deputy Speaker of the National Assembly. Khuang dealt with Phibun's retained military position and his refusal to resign by simply abolishing the post of supreme commander. General Phahon was appointed commander-in-chief. He bestowed upon his predecessor the nominal title of 'Adviser of the State'. In the shake-up of the military that followed Phibun's fall from power, the former prime minister's supporters were removed from key positions. Among those who particularly suffered were the Indochina and Shan State veteran soldier Phin Choonhavan and his son-in-law, Phao Sriyanon, who had been Phibun's aide since the 1933 rebellion.

In January 1945, the British Foreign Office formally studied the strategic importance of Thailand in the post-war world and possible United Nations requirements in the area. It examined particularly the likely need for a United Nations base at Patani, Songkhla, or in the general area of the Kra isthmus. It also considered Britain's relationships with Indochina and Singapore. Thailand was seen to be of secondary importance to Indochina although its potential as a base for bombers in defence of Indochina was noted.[24] Much of the thinking was pie-in-the-sky. A Britain with diminished power and finances would not be spending its money on such propositions. Unfortunately, the principal effect of the study was to increase American suspicions of Britain's intentions.

On sixth and ninth of August, atomic bombs fell on Hiroshima and Nagasaki. A few days later, the Japanese stationed in Thailand

---

[23] *Fall of the Phibun Government, 1944*; B. A. Batson/JSS; p105
[24] *Atonement before Absolution*; Nicholas Tarling/JSS; p50–51

informally surrendered. Two days after this, Pridi, as Regent and in the name of King Ananda, issued a peace proclamation. It declared null and void and contrary to the will of the Thai people Phibun's declaration of war of twenty-fifth of January 1942 against America and Britain. It offered the return of the British territories, the repeal of any prejudicial laws, and full co-operation with the United Nations.

Khuang, during his short, first stay as prime minister laid the groundwork for civilian rule. He then resigned and gave way to supporters of the Seri Thai, first to a seventeen-day premiership of Thawee Bunyaketu, and then to M. R. Seni Pramoj, who had been recalled from his post as minister of the Thai delegation in Washington.

Khuang resented the second of these appointments, believing that Seni had been out of Thailand for too long. Others felt, justifiably it proved, that Seni's experience was essential in dealing with a possible peace treaty with Britain, on which his influence in Washington might be brought to bear. Unfortunately for both parties to the treaty, he brought with him not only that influence but also a strong anti-British attitude which he had acquired principally at an air conference in Chicago in 1944 when, as a diplomat of limited experience, he appeared to have mistaken the language and tactics of commercial negotiation for British government policy.

Britain's immediate post-war reaction to Thailand was to put pressure on the newly-formed government to accede to a long list of demands. Among these was Britain's right to station troops in Thailand in order to disarm the Japanese, full restitution for all losses of British property, the immediate return of the usurped territories, preferential economic advantages, and the provision of one and a half million tons of rice, free of charge. These demands reflected the anger which Britain felt over the Phibun's declaration of war and his personal, willing co-operation with the Japanese. Little credit was given for the quiet resistance of the Seri Thai. The British position was summarised by the newly appointed socialist foreign secretary, Ernest Bevin, on nineteenth of August 1945. Whilst Britain acknowledged the assistance of the Seri Thai, it had yet to consider the Thai peace declaration carefully to see *"if there were grounds for reconsidering the wrongful position which Thailand would normally be deemed to have placed herself in"*. The attitude of the British government would *"depend on the extent to which the Thais co-operated with the British forces in Thailand, on how far the Thais were willing to correct the faults of the previous regime and pay compensation for damage, destruction, and hindrance caused in the interests of the British and the Allies, and on how far they helped and co-operated in restoring peace and economic well-being in South-East Asia."* [25] Unfortunately, by allowing its anger to develop into political myopia, Britain had started a downhill trend of its interests and influence in South-East Asia.

The first British troops, principally from the 7th Indian Division which were the most readily available from any of the Allies, arrived on third of September 1945. The military co-operation requirements, in the circumstances of war, were in no way as unreasonable as many writers lacking a practical knowledge of the Second World War conditions have attempted to infer. The British 20th Indian Division used Bangkok airport for staging on the way to preserve law and order in Saigon, pending the arrival of French forces. The British force in Thailand was small by any standards and bore no relation to that of an occupying power as M. R. Seni has alleged. At its peak it was merely one infantry brigade, the 114th Indian, and some ancillary troops to establish an inter-services mission. Its administrative papers make it clear that the parameters of its operations were within the 1939 frontiers of Siam. The responsibilities were closely defined as the recovery of allied prisoners of war; for surrendered Japanese, whose numbers had mounted to one hundred and fourteen thousand; for civilian labour brought in by the Japanese; and for displaced Asiatics. It was responsible for the civilian population *"so far as it is necessary to prevent disease and unrest"*. In meeting its commitments it was charged *"... to make maximum use of local resources in so far as this causes no embarrassment to the Siamese Government"*. A logistics order stressed that local supplies *"... will not be issued unless they are surplus to the requirements of the normal population"*.

Throughout the detailed instructions it was obvious that the force was of a temporary nature with an overriding priority to recover and rehabilitate allied prisoners of war. The recovery programme was stepped up when stories began circulating not only of Japanese ill-treatment but also of a belief that instructions existed for foreign

---

[25] *Pridi Banomyong*: Vichitvong na Pombhejara

prisoners to be killed in the event of a Japanese defeat. By April 1946, instructions had been published covering the phased withdrawal of 114 Brigade: *inter alia* they forbade the removal of either local goods or currency. At the end of July the British force handed over its fuel supply depot to the Shell Oil Company and in August issued its orders for final withdrawal by the end of October. After that date, all that was left were two railway companies, brought in especially to assist with rice exports, and a company of Sikhs, brought in to guard the 'wanted' Japanese in Bangkwang gaol.[26]

Some of Britain's demands were not reasonable and, if accepted, would have crippled the already sick Thai economy. The approach was coloured by the fact that Britain itself had suffered massive war damage and had been fighting desperately for five years for its very survival. In the opinion of the British government, Thailand had not. It should, therefore, now make a contribution to the peace. However, a proposal for one and a half million tons of rice to be supplied free of charge in a world market crying out for supplies, and from a country with open borders, was not only unreasonable but also was a reflection of insular thinking. It was impractical and unenforceable.

Initially the demand for rice had been played low key but as American interference in the British political settlement with a country which had declared war upon it increased, rice became a major issue not only in Thailand but also in Washington, where it provoked an ill-informed outburst of self-righteousness. In considering its post-war policy with Thailand, the British Foreign Office had, as early as 1944, come to a proper conclusion that any reversal to pre-war imperialism which might appear to infringe on that or any other country's independence was unacceptable. Indeed, any other policy would have been in breach of the Joint Declaration by America's President Roosevelt and Britain's Prime Minister Churchill of August 1941, which later became known as "The Atlantic Charter". The first two operative clauses of that charter dismiss any search for territorial aggrandisement or change. While in practice that historic document remained unsigned, it nevertheless morally committed both countries to its enforcement. Documents of that period related to Thailand in the

---

26 Papers of Major-General R. M. Somerville, Bangkok Troops Order No. 1; Imperial War Museum, London, and letter from British Ambassador, Derek Tonkin to *The Nation* published 27 July 1989

Public Record Office in London give no indication of any British intention of transgressing that charter's constraints.

Not all of the members of the British government saw the road ahead in the same way, and particularly, on occasions, its former ultra-imperialist prime minister. Britain's enormous psychological problem, aggravated by being on the winning side of the Second World War, stemmed from its failure to perceive the true extent of the diminution of its power in the world. At the height of its emotions after a long and devastating war, it did not take kindly to what it saw as Phibun's treachery. It had been inclined throughout the war to see countries as either for it, or, if not for it, unquestionably against it. It viewed the scene very differently from America, where for four generations its citizens had no experience of the deprivations and sacrifices that war on or against its territory could bring. Close to the scene the British government was fortunate to have a man of wisdom. The political adviser to the Supreme Allied Commander, South-East Asia, was M. E. Dening, a highly skilled and experienced diplomat and a British specialist on Far East affairs. Dening wrote to his Foreign Office superiors of the primary British need being that of markets, and stressed that the goodwill of countries such as Thailand was in Britain's long-term interests.[27]

Britain, at that time, had to be concerned with its responsibilities to such countries as Malaya, Burma, and the Dutch East Indies, as those countries were then called. Famine presented a grave danger to stability and it saw the surplus rice stored in Thailand as a solution to its problems. The aim was to get the maximum amount of rice out of Thailand and for much of it to be supplied free of charge, not as reparations but as a belated contribution by Thailand to the overall war effort.[28] Whilst taking into account the internal needs of the Thai population, the British demanded one and a half million tons of rice or paddy, free of cost at Bangkok, at as early a date as was practical. The rice cultivator himself was to be paid by the Thai government at a price determined by a British-dominated Allied Rice Unit, an assumption which at ten thousand kilometres distance might have seemed practical, but overlooked the important role of the miller, middleman, and financier, usually a self-interested ethnic Chinese trader.

---

[27] Dening to FO 3 August 1945, FO 371/46546
[28] *Rice and Reconciliation*; Nicholas Tarling/JSS; p69

The toughest line of approach towards Thailand came not from London but from Australia and New Zealand, both of whom saw Phibun's behaviour as a threat to the whole of the Pacific area. Early in August 1945 both were consulted by Britain. The Australian reply on seventh of August was that treatment of Thailand must be 'stern'. Pro-Japanese Thais must be arrested and brought to trial as war criminals and there was to be no haste in admitting Thailand to the United Nations. Australia expected to see the occupation and Allied military control of Thailand through the Seri Thai, with arrangements being made for elections and the development of a truly democratic government. New Zealand replied along similar lines.[29] Thailand was to be treated as an enemy state until she gave proof of goodwill over a reasonable period.

London partially rejected these views. They were not in keeping with the relations which Mountbatten had developed with Pridi, and overlooked the fact that the Thais were specifically requested by Mountbatten not to rise against the Japanese. London was looking for a form of democratic government but realised that its effective control would depend largely on limiting the power of the Thai military. It wanted to ensure that there would be no repetition of the Phibun regime, with its xenophobia and totalitarian methods.[30] Sir Josiah Crosby, formerly British minister in Bangkok, had pressed upon the British government in October 1943 that the Allies must reduce the power of the Thai military, just as the Allies were planning to do in Germany. A dominant Army was seen as a menace to the civil liberty of the Thai people, and its taming was a matter of crucial importance.[31]

Britain aimed at a quick deal with Pridi, free of interference, which would secure rice for other countries in South-East Asia and compensation for damage to British commercial interests. The demand that the rice to be supplied should be free of charge arose from the simple fact that at the end of the war Britain was desperately short of funds. The free rice was the equivalent of between twenty and thirty million pounds sterling that it could ill afford. If payment was made, such expenditure would also provide the Thai government with funds

---

[29] Australian Government telgram of 17 August 1945, No. 217 – FO371/46545 and NZ telegram of 11 August 1945, No. 222 – same FO ref.
[30] Edited from FO telgrams and minute 9 August 1945
[31] *British and American Influence on Post-War Thailand*; Frank C. Darling/JSS

and thus unwelcome purchasing power within the sterling area at an inopportune time. A quick deal was also a requirement before Chiang Kai-shek tried to claim that Thailand was within his sphere of influence and thus requiring his endorsement of any settlement.[32]

America, whose pre-war interests in South-East Asia were seen by Britain as negligible, viewed the position in Thailand somewhat differently. James Byrnes, its Secretary of State, announced, on twenty-first of August 1945 that America had always believed the declaration of war to be against the wishes of the Thai people. He referred to the continuous contact through the OSS with the Seri Thai and acknowledged the contribution which that organisation had made to the war effort. America viewed Thailand as a country to be liberated from the enemy, not the enemy itself, an approach which Britain found distinctly curious.

At the end of the Second World War, America had a philosophical problem. It had not yet moved to the rabid anti-communism obsession which, following the arrival of Eisenhower and Dulles, was to dominate its thinking for decades. Its current crusade was anti-colonialism and it saw colonialists under every bed, before they were replaced by reds. It was highly suspicious of Britain's intentions and its suspicions were fanned by a combination of its own OSS staff in Bangkok and M. R. Seni, who suffered similarly from a colonialist-under-every-bed complex. Because of this, telegrams between the American State Department and Britain's Foreign Office became acrimonious, and some American officers openly encouraged the Thai government not to sign parts of the British peace proposals. The Thais at first were willing, if reluctantly, to consider the one and a half million tons of free rice. M. R. Seni in London on third of September 1945 did not question the quantity and said that such an amount was already under consideration for the alleviation of famine in South-East Asia.[33] According to Thawee, he, Seni, telegraphed Pridi to notify his commitment. In subsequent discussions with Pridi, M. R. Seni referred to 1.2 to 1.5 million tons. Later they both maintained the principle but left the actual amount to be determined. In deference to Pridi, Britain amended its proposition so that the rice

---

[32] Minutes 18/24 August 1945, FO 371/46546 and 20 August 1945, FO 371/46545; Minute of meeting of Cabinet 78/33 of 4 September 1945

[33] Portraits of Thai Politics; Jenton K. Ray; pp162 and 169

should be offered by the Thais, rather than be included as an imposition in the final draft of a peace treaty.[34]

At this point America, technically not at war and therefore not a party to Britain's peace treaty with Thailand, started serious interference. The ludicrous situation was reached where the two powers involved with the proposed treaty, Britain and Thailand, were willing to sign, yet a third power, America, which had no reason to be a party to the agreement and purely on the grounds of its own dogmatic obsession, objected. The Thais, ever capable of deviously taking advantage, played one off against the other. Washington behaved more and more as though it was the protector of the Thais against attempted colonial domination. It was aided in its behaviour, to some extent, by Mountbatten, who stepped in ahead of the British Foreign Office with an announcement that he proposed to sign two agreements, a six point military and a fifteen point all-embracing agreement with Thai representatives. One of the fifteen points referred to rice, but made no mention of the free rice. Washington's suspicions of the British increased and Mountbatten was instructed by London not to sign. He demanded that he be allowed to sign at least the military element of the treaty, and gave twenty-four hours notice that he proposed so to do. It was signed on eighth of September 1945.[35]

At the same time, American OSS officers in Bangkok were manipulating the American State Department to bring about delay, while encouraging M. R. Seni that he need give nothing away within a British peace treaty. Dening, ever more able to detect the tides of fortune than others, and with an eye on future British interests in the East as a whole, warned his Foreign Office, *"I think we should avoid at all costs laying ourselves open to the accusation that we are assisting the West to suppress the East. Such an accusation will rise readily to the lips of the Americans and Chinese and would create an unfavourable impression throughout Asia"*.[36] The major agreement was put back for months, principally on the question of free rice but also because of other matters which Washington saw as a restoration of colonialism.

By the end of November, Dening, preoccupied with the onset of famine and concerned about numerous other British interests in the

34 *Rice and Reconciliation*; Nicholas Tarling/JSS; pp77–8
35 *Rice and Reconciliation*; Nicholas Tarling/JSS; pp80
36 Minute FO 371/46308 of 9 September 1945

Far East, as well as anxious to back Pridi, saw the free rice as a grave disadvantage to negotiations. He was, however, frustrated in his attempts to resolve matters by official Foreign Office policy which in turn reflected the attitudes of other British government departments, each of which sought its pound of flesh. Dening's task was made impossible. As late as December 1945, the American government was actively trying to prevent signature of an agreement. The United Press representative in Bangkok, aided by Seni, who gave him full access to the confidential files on treaty negotiation, provoked editorial allegations in Washington of an attempted British colonial take-over.[37] High level government discussions failed to remove American suspicions. Fortunately by then, it somewhat belatedly, wiser heads in Britain were beginning to take a longer term view. The prevention of famine and a firm friendship with Thailand came to be seen as more important than short term costs, despite the desperate position of the British economy.

An agreement was signed on the first of January 1946, the Thai government accepting it with apparent reluctance as the minimum to which Britain would agree. However, signing an agreement in Thailand and enforcing it frequently turn out to be two different things. This agreement was so to prove.

The Chinese middlemen, no lovers of any government, were reluctant to sell rice to the Thai government at the low price being offered, not only because of the price itself but because they were to be paid in Thai currency. The future value of Thai currency at that time was decidedly uncertain. The middlemen could get substantially more by smuggling the rice out of the country, a not too difficult matter given the geographical position of Thailand and the impracticable task of border control.

During January 1946, the British government decided to defer the delivery of free rice until 1947, reduce the target to one and a quarter million tons, and to pass on to the receiving country the costs of any purchases necessary to assist in the initial flow of Thai rice. By March, the target was 1.2 million tons at a price not exceeding fifteen pounds sterling per ton for best quality and the obligation to supply free rice was dropped. Washington, for the benefit of its own producers, had a vested interest in raising the level of the world price of rice. In its turn, the British government saw any sum paid as a

---

[37] *Alone on the Sharp Edge*; David Van Praagh; pp70–1

measure of its own sacrifice. Pridi considered the price of fifteen pounds sterling per ton to be about right, but suggested lower quantities. Telegrams shuffled for a further period between London, Washington, and Bangkok until on sixth of May 1946 a tripartite agreement was signed. The Thais generally, and M. R. Seni in particular, saw it as a substantial victory over Britain.

The agreement of payment for the rice made no difference: the rice did not flow. The Chinese merchants continued with the more lucrative practice of smuggling. A new agreement was accepted on twenty-fourth of December 1946 with lower volumes and with the price raised to twenty pounds sterling per ton. In September 1947 the price rose to thirty-five pounds per ton, on a par with the price in Burma. This was still so far below the Malaya black-market price of one hundred and ninety that smuggling remained a main attraction.

The rice agreements had led to a political disaster for all concerned. Britain, piqued by Phibun's declaration of war gained neither rice in any quantity nor the goodwill which it eventually tried to promote. Instead, by clinging to its old view of its own importance in the world, by its stubbornness, by its pedantic and over-cautious approach, and by its failure to understand the Thai way of life, it aroused suspicions of empire-building at the very time that its policy was that of empire-dismantling. Washington, while agreeing with Britain that stability in South-East Asia depended much on stability in Thailand, failed to rid itself of its suspicions of colonialism. It had not appreciated the significance of the arrival in Britain in July 1945 of a left-of-centre government which for years had advocated the dismantling of the British Empire. Advised by missionaries rather than professional diplomats, and despite its then limited commercial interests in the area, it dabbled in politics in a naïve manner, effectively led by the nose by shrewd Thais. It gave the appearance of expending more effort in undermining agreements than in helping with their completion. It confused idealism and sentimentality with the need for pragmatism. Its very interference in an area where it was neither knowledgeable nor skilled, helped to destroy the fragile Thai democracy which might otherwise have blossomed. The eventual outcome of that interference was the return to power of the military elements which Britain had endeavoured to neutralise. A University of Arizona professor has succinctly summarised the effect, saying that America *"overlooked the fact that the preservation of Thai national independence by itself was no guarantee that the Thai people would live in freedom and enjoy the benefits of political and social justice".*[38] Thailand may have seen itself as gaining substantially by backing off from its earlier acknowledgement that it should make a deferred contribution to the war effort by way of much needed rice. In practice, it lost its way politically and, through weakness, smuggling, and corruption, saddled itself once again with a politically motivated soldiery from which, even in the 1990s, it has yet to escape. As a result of the Seni leak of confidential information, any remaining trust was destroyed and, just as at the end of the nineteenth century, the fate of Thailand's freedom had been settled in Paris and London, so in the middle of the twentieth century it was settled in Washington and London. The commercial relationships of Thailand with Europe were severely damaged and it began its drift to come under the gradually increasing economic and political influence of Japan and America.

As if American interference was not enough, an irritating complication for the British ran like a thread throughout the whole negotiating period: the French. In 1945, France was anxious to return to Indochina. International opinion on the desirability of its coming was mixed. Britain, with one eye on the strategic importance of Indochina in its geographical relationship to China and the other on European relationships, supported France. Nevertheless, at the time, the British and French philosophies were basically at odds over the future of colonies, not only in South-East Asia, but also in other parts of the world. Dening referred specifically to the French as the evil influence in South-East Asia.

Britain was not prepared to damage its own position by insisting that agreements with France had to be linked with those of Britain. America, although even more distrustful of French colonialism than of British, had no policy to oppose its return. The Thais, hoping to retain the Laotian and Cambodian provinces ceded to them in 1941, looked upon France as a defeated nation which was fortunate to have successful allies. This was a common view in South-East Asia. A member of Dening's Foreign Office staff operating in Indochina wrote on the subject. *"They do not realise that in the eyes of the natives* (sic)

---

[38] *British and American Influence on Post-War Thailand*; Frank C. Darling/JSS

the French are no longer the superior beings that their domination and their force of arms made them appear in the past. " [39] The Indochinese were not in any way enthusiastic for the return of the French. The British, meanwhile, had placed the disputed territories along the Mekong under its Thai force commander, General Evans, and not under its Indochina troops commander, General Gracey, an arrangement which did not commend itself to the French.[40] Despite its reservations, America eventually declared for a return to the pre-1941 Indochina boundaries without prejudice to any subsequent adjustment.

France, not surprisingly with General de Gaulle in power, took an autocratic line. It declared a responsibility for the people of Indochina and that it did not intend to reach any compromise just to humour America. While technically not in a state of war with Thailand, France would consider itself at war until full restoration of its territories had been made, at which time it would then consider what reparations were required from Thailand and what degree of control should be imposed upon that country. There would be no negotiation on the status of the territories.[41]

Britain became alarmed. It feared that France would attempt to give the impression that Britain supported French imperialism. Because of its European interests and of its wartime alliance, Britain was still prepared to include, temporarily at least, a clause within its draft agreement concerning the French position in Indochina. When the first draft of the French terms reached London the level of alarm increased. The draft included a demand for the return to Vientiane of Thailand's most revered religious image, the Emerald Buddha. The Emerald Buddha, not in fact carved from emerald but from a green jasper quartz, had been discovered near Chiang Mai in northern Thailand in the fifteenth century. After moving its seat around a number of temples in northern Thailand, it had found its way to Laos, through Luang Prabang and on to Vientiane. Thailand's King Rama I had retrieved it by force of arms in the latter part of the eighteenth century, since when it had occupied its lofty seat in a temple of incomparable splendour adjoining the old Royal Palace in Bangkok. Reputed to be two thousand years old, its power was seen to be such that oaths made before it were the most binding. To this day, only the

---

[39] *The First Vietnam War*; Peter Dunn; pp145 and 279, note 8
[40] *The First Vietnam War*; Peter Dunn; p316
[41] *Rice and Reconciliation*; Nicholas Tarling/JSS; p73

King of Thailand, himself, is allowed to change its seasonal jewelled robes. The demand for its removal to Vientiane was an attempt at the utter humiliation of Thailand. The British Foreign Office at this stage saw the French proposals as an embarrassing liability and French policy more akin to that prevailing in the nineteenth century. It was determined not to back France on this particular issue. Eventually, foreign secretary Bevin raised the issue with his French counterpart, Bidault, but despite this high-level intervention a clause covering the return of the Emerald Buddha was included in the French draft.

Early in October 1945, France requested Britain not to sign any agreement with Thailand until Franco/Thai negotiations began, and again the British Foreign Office suggested dropping the Emerald Buddha clause. It was then removed but its inclusion in the first draft had created a bitterness which was reflected in Franco/Thai discussions. The bitterness spilled over on to British discussions as the Thai government suspected that Britain had supported France over the Emerald Buddha claim, the contrary of the truth. That same month Dening put to the Thais that if they failed to reach an agreement over the more reasonable elements of the French proposals, France might prevent the entry of Thailand into the United Nations. Eventually Britain decided to exclude from its own draft agreement any reference to the French territories. Instead, it notified by letter that it did not recognise the 1941 territorial transfers.[42]

The formal end to hostilities with France took much longer than with Britain. The Thai government did its best to hold on to the Laotian and Cambodian territories which, with Japanese help, Phibun had acquired in 1941. Eventually, in the face of a French threat to veto Thai admission to the United Nations, an agreement was signed in January 1947.

———

Britain in general, and Mountbatten in particular, came under attack from both American and Thai writers as treating Thailand as a diversion from the mainstream of events. To Britain, in its own desperate struggle for survival and the attainment of its principal objectives in Europe, it may well have been the case. In Churchill's

---

[42] *Rice and Reconciliation*; Nicholas Tarling/JSS; p110; FO telegrams Nos 928 and reply No. 1262 (FO 371/46556) and Nos 933 and 1330 (also FO371/46556)

massive history of the Second World War, Thailand is mentioned fleetingly once only in its more than four thousand pages.

Pridi accepted no responsibility for the war and in so doing he was able to divert all blame on to Phibun and a small group of his close associates. A call from the victorious Allies for the trial of war criminals was aimed principally at Phibun, but despite the immediate passage of M. R. Seni's War Criminals Act of 1945, Phibun was released from trial. The Supreme Court, the San Dikka, ruled that because *ex-post-facto* legislation was constitutionally invalid, the law could not be implemented.[43]

The Lady La-iad has commented with some bitterness on her husband's arrest and partial trial and also on his being given no credit for his attempt to assist the Allies against the Japanese. It was left to the Japanese commander in Thailand, General Nakamura, to testify at Phibun's trial in his support and to Pridi to assist in his release.[44] In Phibun's favour it must be said that he could have moved, if not to destroy, certainly seriously to limit the Seri Thai activities in Thailand. That he chose not to do so might be interpreted either as a sign of his deviousness or perhaps of his wisdom, in keeping in touch with both sides of a war which was neither of his choosing nor of his making, and so protecting the long-term interests of his country. In the intense emotions of a wartime Britain, such behaviour was not seen as wisdom, but later a British ambassador was to take a more charitable view. *"Who could blame her for bowing to the inevitable,"* he wrote. *"She was clever enough to give the minimum co-operation to her occupiers; she retained her own government and where possible, gave succour and comfort to British prisoners of war... With the greatest respect and admiration I was apt to compare her political stance to that of an agile oriental fish, which could swim very fast in any direction, emitting an ink cloud to conceal its movements. As a result she retained her independence and, unlike her colonial neighbours in French Indo-China and British Malaya, her national self-respect".*[45]

With the Japanese troops repatriated and its task completed, the small British force was withdrawn. During the period it had been in Thailand, there had been constant pressure to get the troops out again

---

[43] Ruling of the Dika Court on war Criminals, Case No 1/2488 of 23 March 1946

[44] *Portraits of Thai Politics*; Jenton K. Ray

[45] *A Marvellous Party*; Sir Berkeley Gage, Ambassador to Thailand, 1954–7; (privately printed) p176

as soon as possible, both from the British government for the purpose of the general release of soldiers from long and weary war-service and also from Indian politicians, reluctant to have Indian troops serving under a British flag in an Asian theatre of war. Both Thai fears and American suspicions of an attempt by Britain to maintain a military presence were shown to be without foundation. Left behind was a country with many problems. Shortly before the end of the war, Allied bombers had knocked out numerous major bridges, freight yards, rolling stock, and telephone communications. There was little water and only a glimmer of electricity in the capital. Allied Forces had already experienced difficulties of this nature when attempting to recommission damaged plant, but military engineers had improvised numerous solutions. With the withdrawal of adaptable Allied troops the problems of reconstruction were left to the home government. To its problems were added those of half-hearted measures for the demobilisation of its own military and widespread food shortages.

Political events and Thailand were on the move. On sixteenth of January 1946, M. R. Seni, who was frequently at odds with his Cabinet, resigned, clearing the path for elections. The result allowed for the recall of Khuang as prime minister, the first elected prime minister in the history of Thailand. Not for long. The Khuang government collapsed following the rejection of a relatively unimportant bill and on twenty-fourth of March, Pridi himself was forced to take over as prime minister. He was no longer aloof from politics and his rivals lost no time in attacking him for all of the post-war misdeeds of his followers.

In the midst of this unsettled politico-economic scene came royal tragedy. Ananda Mahidol had first come back as King from his home in Switzerland to Thailand on fifteenth of November 1938 and remained only until thirteenth of January 1939. His visit was one of pageantry and public acclamation, the return of the 'Lord of Life'. It was only pageantry, not substance. Real political power had already passed firmly into the hands of Phibun. The Army had been purged of royalist elements. For many it meant life sentences in gaol; for others, execution. Phibun had achieved complete control of the Army and with it the country.

A call from Pridi, his Regent, for King Ananda to return to Thailand on his twentieth birthday, the twentieth of September 1945, was countered by a request from the King to stay in Switzerland to finish his studies. In the end a compromise was reached. The King would return temporarily to Thailand at the beginning of December 1945. The Regency was set aside and Pridi was formally recognised by the National Assembly as Elder Statesman with advisory powers. The British Royal Air Force flew the King home in a wartime Dakota. The King was to return to Switzerland to complete his studies in the first week of January 1946. Delay occurred and eventually a return date was set for June. On the morning of ninth of June 1946, some four days only before his return and in circumstances which later became shrouded in doubt, the young King Ananda was discovered shot in the head while still in his bed.

As month followed month there was an ever-increasing outcry over mismanagement of the country and of failure to solve the mystery of the King's death. M. R. Seni later described the situation as Gestapo-like and one that would intimidate rival politicians and regiment the people. There were accusations of communism, harping back to the 1930s. Pridi was suspected of wanting a republic to replace the monarchy. Claims were made that although Pridi had formally disbanded the Seri Thai, its arms were still held for future use.[46] On twenty-third of August, Pridi resigned as prime minister on grounds of alleged ill-health and was replaced by his close associate, Rear Admiral Thamrong Nawasawat, previously a minister of justice under Phibun. Thamrong had a rough ride as prime minister. In May 1947 the opposition, led by Khuang and M. R. Seni, grilled him in the National Assembly for a whole week over a variety of matters which included economic policy, currency weakness, law and order, foreign policy, corruption, and the failure of the government to solve the mystery of the death of King Ananda. Thamrong survived the parliamentary attack but premiership was not to his liking.

Pridi meanwhile was concerning himself with the wider issues of South-East Asia. A meeting in Delhi in April 1947 of the first Conference of Asiatic Nations led in September to the founding of the South-East Asia League, an association of free, self-governing national states made up of Thailand and the three component states of French Indochina. The cornerstone was anti-colonial solidarity. It was

---

[46] *Portraits of Thai Politics*; Jenton K. Ray; pp172

anti-French and anti-Japanese in Laos, Vietnam, and Cambodia where nationalism was on the increase. Into it were linked hilltribe separatist movements. The headquarters of the League was in Bangkok and Seri Thai associates of Pridi, Tiang Sirikhan and Thawi Udon, fronted it. Both were also political leaders in the Isan area, and it was questioned whether or not Isan might try to secede and be incorporated within the League as an independent state, or possibly combine with a Lao state. Also involved in the League were Thong-in Phuriphat and Chamlong Daoruang, both one-time Seri Thai men.[47] With his strong Chinese ancestry and with a history of his pre-war approach to economic development, Pridi was suspected by the royalists and military of communist inclinations. A second suspicion was that Pridi might set up a Thai republic as a part of the South-East Asia League. It became academic, for at the end of 1947 the French were back on the Thai-Lao border, preventing, temporarily at least, both any Lao independence or any Lao interest in Isan.

The disposal of Seri Thai arms increased hostility towards Pridi and was to dog what was left of his political career. Despite the formal disbandment of the Seri Thai, Pridi, much to the irritation of the Army, kept control of the OSS supplied arms. The stockpile amounted virtually to a private arsenal. When he was in Paris in the late 1920s, Pridi had formed a close friendship with a student, Nguyen Ai Quoc, later known as Ho Chi Minh. In Ho Chi Minh's hour of need, Pridi transferred some of the surplus Seri Thai weapons to him. They were more modern than those held by the Thai Army. Such a transfer of arms was interpreted as the promotion of communism in South-East Asia. The post-war South-East Asia League and then the arrival in mid-1947 of an embassy staff of two hundred Russians made it easy for those who so wished to label Pridi a communist or a republican, or sometimes both. Although the perception of communism was less intense in post-war Thailand than in America, the label 'communist' had a damning ring about it and it was a convenient label, particularly when a cover-up was necessary, to tie to an unwanted rival.

Pressure built up against the prime minister, Thamrong, and through him against Pridi, not only from political opponents but from a far more dangerous quarter — the Army. The Army was discontented with the position in which it found itself in 1947. Until

---

47 *Thailand and the Fall of Singapore*; Nigel J. Brailey; p151

the outbreak of war, the Army had been the strongest political element in Thailand. Its hero, Phibun, had taken up the office of prime minister in 1938. The arrest of Phibun as a war criminal had been a grave insult to the Army. At the end of the Second World War the Army was being blamed for not fighting a war, despite having been ordered to cease its early resistance to the Japanese and despite the role of its Northern Army which, in 1941, had advanced into the Shan States to prevent Chinese infiltration. It had suffered heavy losses in the Shan States, although most were from sickness rather than battle casualties. As minister of the interior in the Seni government, Thawee ordered the Northern Army back home but there was insufficient transport for it. As a result, the Army, rather than making a triumphant return, was dispersed far away from its home bases. Officers were relieved of their duties and they and their demoralised troops were left to stagger south as best they could. Kat Katsongkhram was a rough and tough no-nonsense soldier. He had been a participant in the coup of 1932, he had given distinguished service in helping to counter the Boworadej rising, and he had been a deputy finance minister to Phibun in 1942/3. Later, having rejected Phibun's handling of wartime affairs, he had become a Seri Thai sympathiser and a liaison officer in Kunming. Of the return home of the Army, he wrote: *"The whole army withdrew in sad disorder. People looked at Thai soldiers as if they were Japanese prisoners of war... the troops were worn out in body and soul. People believed that there was no use in having an army any more"*.[48] Officers were then compulsorily retired, causing further resentment and under the new 1946 constitution serving officers were not permitted a political role.

The Seri Thai leaders in power gave strong indications of the lesser role that they planned for the Army with the appointment in July 1946 of Police-General Adun as Army commander-in-chief and of Rear Admiral Sangwon Yutthakit as both police chief and adjutant general of the armed forces. Both were friends of Pridi. To some citizens, Seri Thai who had become ministers gave the impression that they preferred no army at all to an army which might fall under control of another military dictator. Thawee formulated proposals for a much smaller, better paid, professional army as being more in keeping with post-war needs, but this was not what the Army sought.

---

[48] *The Country's Force and Power*; Kat Katsongkhram; p27

There is little promotion in a small army and no room for a bevy of well-paid generals, dear to the heart of the Thai military.

Naturally there were exceptions to the returning ragged Army. Where in this world the many stumble, there the few prosper. Colonel Sarit prospered: after success in battle in the Shan States he had been made military commander of Lampang province. Now he was appointed to command the 1st Regiment of Infantry in Bangkok. Captain Chatichai prospered: the 1st Cavalry Regiment survived and was moved to the south. As a horse-cavalry company commander, Chatichai led his small, mounted detachment from the Shan States down through the length of Thailand to take up occupation duties in the Malaysian state of Perlis, which the Japanese had given to Thailand some two years earlier.[49] His father, Lieut-General Phin, did not prosper militarily: he was forced into retirement from 1945 until 1947. He attempted farming in the north-east but was harassed to such an extent that he fled to Bangkok. He was a witness to its disorder and to its queues for clothing and for food, even rice, of which Thailand was such a great provider. He met with other retired commanders and with active commanders, discreetly discussing the prospects for a military coup. The response was good but Phin needed to find the right leader.

Problems arose for Pridi both from within the Bangkok élite and from lesser people throughout the country over his policy which gave preference to Seri Thai supporters over the military. Although in line with his wartime undertakings Pridi had disarmed the Seri Thai, the Army was conscious only of its own humiliation. Isan leaders were strongly represented in the elected Lower House and in the appointed Senate of the National Assembly, principally because of their strong Seri Thai connections. They were highly unpopular with the Thai élite who looked upon the Isan people as peasants. Pridi had made very little attempt to incorporate any members of opposing interests in his government, a fact which alienated many civilians as well as the Army.[50]

The eventual cause of the downfall of the Pridi/Thamrong regime was the chaotic economic and social state of the nation. While from time to time Britain modified both its demand for and the pricing of

---

[49] Discussion with Major-General Chatichai Choonhaven, London, 1 July 1991
[50] *Thailand and the Fall of Singapore*; Nigel J. Brailey; p125/6 and discussions with Pisoot Sudasna na Ayutthaya in January 1987

rice and for the export of raw materials to its direction, its overall pressure on the Thai economy contributed to the chaos. American pressure and ill-chosen interference with its ally's legitimate aim to feed the starving in South-East Asia also contributed. In September 1947, the price of rice had risen to the Burma market rate and by early November, Britain had withdrawn all of its excessive demands. Its policy to feed starving South-East Asian nations from cheap Thailand rice had failed.

Post-war conditions in Thailand took their toll on the standard of morality. It had been an accepted and even applauded practice to steal from the Japanese but now, with the developing shortages and massive inflation, black-market activities and corruption became widespread. Government salaries lagged woefully behind prices and corrupt practices spread to the top of the civil service. 'Squeeze' or 'lubrication' became the recognised order of the day. Government shops set up to sell goods at controlled prices had to be closed after only six months because of the scandals which became associated with them and which spilled over into the government sale of pigs and cattle. A newspaper's editor's view was of *"a merry, swindling collection of characters, a crew of playboy politicians"*, shipping in Buick cars for the ministers while most of the country lived in abject poverty.[51]

It was not surprising that the Pridi-controlled government created Army resistance, but to be effective, the resistance needed leadership. It came in the form of retired officers supportive of Phibun and was encouraged to some extent by Phibun himself when, on nineteenth of March 1947, he announced his return to politics for the purpose of self-vindication. An old adviser who became first a wartime foreign minister and then an ambassador to Tokyo, Witchit Watthakan, helped to form for him the 'Supreme Justice' party, from which position Phibun offered occasional advice although he himself did not appear to be politically active.[52] This was the vehicle and leadership that retired Lieut-General Phin required for his own plans.

There were by now established in Thai politics, three principal elements. The left-of-centre Seri Thai, led by Pridi, held sway. The

51 Alexander McDonald, Editor of the *Bangkok Post*
52 *Thailand and the Fall of Singapore*; Nigel J. Brailey; p147

right-of-centre cum royalist/democratic element, led by Khuang and the Pramoj brothers, Seni and Kukrit, was in formal opposition. Thirdly, waiting in the wings, was a resentful military.

Phibun's wife, the Lady La-iad, explained the developing position: *"Soon, however, there emerged a small nucleus of military men who helped crystallize the feelings of many of their fellow soldiers. They strongly felt that the military was being deliberately misrepresented, the soldiers' loyalty unwarrantably questioned, their sufferings through the war unrecognised, and their importance drastically downgraded, and that they should do something to retrieve the prestige and power of the military."* She named Lieut-General Phin, Colonel Phao, and Colonel Sarit as the core of the coup. She believed that Phibun was unwilling to join in the coup itself even although his two sons were implicated and had requested his help. *"Finally, however, with deep conflicts in his mind, Phibun announced his backing for the coup, and a bloody coup was narrowly averted".*[53]

Phin Choonhavan had been a successful soldier. He had enlisted in the infantry as a private soldier and through his outstanding ability had been selected for the officers' school. He was a staff officer in 1932 at the time of the coup d'état. At the time of Boworadej rebellion he had fought with the infantry at the side of Phibun's artillery and was then appointed infantry regimental commander at Khorat. In the Indochina war he had fought as deputy commander of the North-Eastern Army. In the Northern Army campaign in the Shan States he had commanded the 3rd Division and had captured Kengtung, albeit in both theatres of war against slim opposition. At the end of that war he had commanded the Northern Army. Whilst it was Phin who was generally credited in recruiting Army commanders to support the coup, doubts have been expressed about his personal enthusiasm. It was held to be more likely that his support was principally directed at the enhancement of his commercial interests. It was his son Chatichai, who by this time had become a major at the Cavalry School and commanded the 1st Cavalry Battalion, who was the more active of the two.[54] Out of retirement came Phibun's former aide, Colonel Phao Sriyanon, to act as liaison officer between his father-in-law, Phin, and his fellow conspirators on one side and Phibun on the other. Another of Phin's

---

[53] *Portraits of Thai Politics*; Jenton K. Ray; p172
[54] Discussions with Pisoot Sudasna na Ayutthaya in January 1987 and discussion with Major-General Chatichai Choonhaven, London, 1 July 1991

sons-in-law, Major Pramarn Adireksan, joined from the Army Transport Corps. Support from the list of retired officers was strong and it was enhanced by the arrival on the scene of Senator Kat Katsongkhram.

As subsequent history has proved, critical to any coup in Thailand is the support of troops stationed in Bangkok, and only when such support was forthcoming from the commander of its 1st Regiment, Colonel Sarit Thanarat, was success virtually assured. Sarit had served alongside, but was junior to, Phin Choonhavan in the Northern Army and, having been won over, was instrumental in providing the bulk of the force necessary for success. Supporting Sarit then, as they would in future political adventures, came Lieut-Colonel Thanom Kittikachon from the Royal Military Academy with a number of fully armed cadets and Lieut-Colonel Praphas Charusathien, commander of the 1st Battalion of the 1st Infantry Regiment. Further down the military hierarchy came Captain Krit Srivara who, some twenty-five years later, was to stand so firmly against both Thanom and Praphas.

Thus the Coup Group was assembled and, after some delay for careful thought on his part and after cautiously warning the prime minister that trouble was brewing, Phibun became its accepted head. Who could then have foreseen not only the ruthless, personal ambition the group contained within its numbers, but also the effect that such ambition would have upon the kingdom? Wealth and power in abundance would accrue to some of its members. The tigers were to be unleashed and their expectations were high.

Army commander-in-chief, General Adun, faced a predicament. From the prime minister, Thamrong, he knew of the possibility of trouble but also knew that most of his Army officers were more likely to be loyal to the plotting generals than to him. That loyalty would be enhanced when it became known that Phibun was at their head. At one stage, Phin had thought of offering the leadership to Adun, but once Phibun took the bait, Phin no longer needed Adun. But neither did he want Adun's wholehearted opposition. Fortunately for Phin, Adun had no respect for Thamrong's corrupt government and had already agreed with Pridi that he, Adun, would be willing to take it over later that month. Had that act been played out, it might well have pacified the military. Phin had timed the coup for twelfth of November but, when it was realised that word had reached Adun, the timing was advanced first to tenth of November and then, almost in desperation, to one o'clock on the morning of eighth of November. Adun had waited too long.

As all coup participants seek to justify their actions, so did the November 8 group. A statement of principles issued sought to show that action had been taken and would continue to be taken for the good of the nation as a whole, not for the individuals themselves. Efficient government administration would be restored from which the people would benefit, a claim which might be described as universal in Thai military coups, being a mixture of pious hope and hypocrisy. Under the group's supervision, the honour of the Army would be upheld. A new government would be formed which would respect both a new constitution and the principles of 'Nation, Religion and King' — a trinal concept of loyalty formulated by King Rama VI, Vajiravudh. The country would be saved from communism. Furthermore, the plot against King Ananda would be resolved and those responsible would be brought to justice. Among the military, the resolving of the suspected plot was an emotional issue and was of a high priority. Whatever else happened, this had to be achieved. While many outside direct involvement in the coup would see this latter objective as an attempt at justification, even more than forty years later Chatichai believed sincerely that it was the one issue more than any other which had united the plotters and sparked the coup.[55]

The coup succeeded but plans to capture the government leaders, Pridi, Thamrong, and Sangwon, failed totally. The arresting party was headed off by Adun who ordered it back to barracks, thereby protecting his Seri Thai friends. By the time Sarit had countermanded the order and the arresting party was sent back, it was too late. With the help of the Navy all of the Seri Thai leaders escaped and were provided with an escort to the Satahip naval base. Realising that his presence at Satahip would create problems for his Navy friends, Pridi set out for Bangkok with a view to fleeing the country. Disguised as a naval petty officer, he arrived in the early morning of twentieth of November at the residence of his acquaintance, Captain Stratford Hercules Dennis, a much decorated, heroic Second World War naval officer and at that time the British Naval attaché. Whilst the British and American ambassadors did not favour the coup, they were not in a position to intervene. Stratford Hercules Dennis, one-time destroyer commander, one-time Grand National jockey, had no such qualms.

---

[55] Discussion with Major-General Chatichai Choonhaven, London, 1 July 1991

There were urgent consultations at the British Embassy and later discussions with the American ambassador, Edwin Stanton. The ambassadors turned for practical assistance to a former Burma railway prisoner-of-war, the general manager of the Shell Company of Thailand, William Adam. Shell had a tanker leaving for Singapore. As a result, Pridi was taken downstream by the US naval attaché, Captain Gardes, in the American picnic boat, a former submarine hunter. Coup group forces set out after the departing picnic boat but were defeated by bad weather The Shell tanker had already left the mouth of the Chao Phraya river and so the picnic boat chased out into the Gulf of Thailand, eventually allowing Pridi to board the tanker some twelve hours after he had knocked at Captain Dennis's door.[56]

Early on the morning of ninth of November, Phibun broadcast to the nation. He called for a cease-fire, which Adun brought into effect. Adun to all appearances had failed to attract the loyalty of his troops and to defeat the plotters, no doubt the price of his absence from the Army as chief of police for a long period and also of his earlier support of the Seri Thai. The Lady La-iad has said that Adun, out of loyalty to his old boss, Phibun, instructed the troops not to fight.[57] It is more likely that Adun, loyal throughout to Phibun, first wanted to ensure Phibun's involvement before committing himself to either side. While he took sufficient steps to protect Pridi himself, his loyalty to Phibun pre-dated that to the Seri Thai generally. When the chips were down, it was the old Army loyalty which came first.

It was left to General Phin to tell the press of the details of the coup and of the justifications as the group saw them. To the group's assessment of the need to protect the interests of the people, government inefficiency, the rice shortage, and the problems of the Army he also added the charge of corruption. This allegation was confirmed by formal proclamation, a document which was to become a virtual model for succeeding enterprises.

The military, civilian officials, police, and the Thai people have unanimously agreed that the present situation in Thailand could not be solved by the government, resulting in misery for our brothers and sisters. The present government is also aware that it could not solve these problems — worsening conditions

---

[56] *Pridi Banomyong*: Vichitvong na Pombhejara; pp260/1; and *The Devil's Discus*; Rayne Kruger; pp116/7

[57] *Portraits of Thai Politics*; Jenton K. Ray; p211

of living and the rice shortage. In addition, it has allowed widespread corruption, although the government has the power to stop it. Furthermore, some politicians have used politics as a cover for graft and corruption amidst the people's hardships and have without shame accumulated riches in self-interest. At a time when people are starving, the government and other opportunists live in wealth and extravagance and ignore the cries of the people. The corruption and inefficiency within official circles gave grief to all.

Because of our concern for the people and hatred for corruption, we were forced to take over power to force the resignation of the government and create a new one according to the constitution to help ease graft and corruption and rid the people of their woes.

Therefore for peace and quiet we urge the public, both Thai and foreigners, to remain peaceful and not do anything to obstruct our work. Civil servants should carry on with their duties as usual and wait for future directives. On November 9 1947, government officials should work as usual".[58]

Looking back on the events and behavioural pattern which the 1947 coup unleashed, the proclamation must be one of history's outstanding examples of sheer, unadulterated hypocrisy.

Sir Josiah Crosby's 1943 fears had become a reality: Phibun and the military once more held the reins of power. Both America and Britain were to blame. The short-sighted attempt by Britain to impose a penal and unworkable solution to what it saw to be its own problems of food shortage in South-East Asia, based more on wartime emotion than pragmatism, ignored the careful thoughts of Hudson and the advice of the experienced Dening. It was aggravated by the interference of inexperienced American officials, mostly OSS operatives, who dabbled in matters in which they had little, if anything, to contribute. Whilst some in Thailand interpreted their own behaviour as a victory, they were in the end the principal losers as the democratic freedom that the country sought slipped from its grasp.

---

[58] *The Sarit Regime*; Thak Chaloemtiarana; p46

CHAPTER TWO
The Seri Thai

The Act of September 1941 had been quite specific. It was the duty of all people in Thailand, whatever the cost, to resist entry into the country by an invading force of any nation whatsoever. The Act reflected the pride of the Thai people in their continued escape from colonial rule despite the pressures brought to bear on them for many decades by Western powers. When, therefore, in December of that same year, its prime minister, Phibun, chose abject surrender to the Japanese, others turned to resistance. Among the Thais of December 1941 there were many who linked resistance with national honour Some of them lived in Thailand, some in America, and some in Britain. Not only were there numbers, there were also natural leaders.

When, in the Spring of 1940, M. R. Seni Pramoj, a highly successful graduate from Oxford University and the English Bar, was appointed minister of the Thai legation in Washington, he asked Phibun to explain to him Thailand's foreign policy. Was it pro-Japanese, pro-English, pro-American or pro-anything? Phibun replied that Thailand's policy was not pro any other country in particular. It was pro-Thailand. Thus it came as a shock to M. R. Seni in far away Washington DC to learn in December 1941 that Thailand had agreed to the passage of Japanese troops through its territory to facilitate the invasion of Burma and Malaya. It was, perhaps, less of a shock than the instruction which was to follow on twenty-fifth of January 1942, formally to declare war in the name of Thailand on the United States of America.

At the time of the surrender, M. R. Seni had come to the conclusion that the government could not be entirely responsible for its actions and that it would be necessary for him to establish a movement of opposition. On twelfth of December he called a press conference to declare himself free of the Phibun government and to announce the creation of the Free Thai movement, the Seri Thai. That same day, a short wave broadcast took the news to Thailand.

According to Seni's version of events, his action in January was even more dramatic. He put the telegram of instruction to declare war on America in his pocket and went to see Cordell Hull, the American secretary of state. He told Hull of his instructions and that he had no intention of obeying them. Cordell Hull pointed out to him that if he did not declare war on America, then America could not very well declare war on Thailand. The telegram remained in M. R. Seni's pocket.[59] Whilst he was to make three post war contributions as prime minister and as an outstanding democrat within a military scenario, at the age of thirty-six he had perhaps made his greatest contribution to the long-term freedom of his country. But was it of significance? Splendid as Seni's gesture may appear, it seems unlikely that Phibun would have entrusted such an important declaration solely to a man who had already broadcast to the Thai people announcing his opposition to Phibun himself. It is equally unlikely that America, through its Bangkok embassy and routine intelligence channels, was unaware of the true state of affairs in a country which for some time had been under close observation. The Swiss had been asked to represent Thai interests in America, and were by January the natural channel of communication. The legend of Seni and the declaration of war bears the hallmark of an interesting historical aside rather than of substance. Nevertheless, Seni's general stance had been sufficient to persuade Cordell Hull that any notice from Bangkok should be viewed with suspicion. The declaration of war was ignored by America, as well it might be with its limited pre-1941 territorial and commercial interests in that geographic area.

There were in December 1941 about one hundred and ten Thai students in America. A letter from M. R. Seni to each of them produced support from about a hundred. The Seri Thai group was thus formed and taken under the wing of the American Office of Strategic Service, the OSS. Forty of the hundred became active service officers, professionally trained for guerilla warfare. The others became support staff, engaged on radio, information, and intelligence work. Some gave assistance to the American Office of War Information in its broadcasts. Despite Seni's fears that the January 1942 declaration of war by Phibun might destroy the group, it did not. The withdrawal by the Bangkok government of the rights of Thai citizenship from M. R. Seni and his supporters was ignored — these rights would be formally restored after the end of the war.[60]

[59] *The Thai Resisitance Movement during the Second World War*; John B. Haseman; p29; and *Alone on the Sharp Edge*; David van Praagh; pp33/4

[60] *Alone on the Sharp Edge*; David van Praagh; pp23/39

M. R. Seni set out his objectives for his Seri Thai, the principal of which was to restore freedom to Thailand. There was to be no formation of a political party and while the Phibun government was to be looked upon as a Japanese puppet, the true enemy was Japan. There would be no interference with the position of the crown or with the succession. Constitutional government would be restored to Thailand at the end of hostilities. Political prisoners would be released and war criminals brought to justice. The Seri Thai would represent all free Thais anywhere in the world.[61]

Important to the development of the Seri Thai was Colonel Kharb Kunjara, a British-trained artilleryman who was the Washington military attaché. Kharb was a faithful supporter of Phibun, both before and after his prime minister's temporary fall from power. One of his tasks in Washington was to ensure the entry of Phibun's elder son into West Point Military Academy. He was on the point of accomplishing that when Thailand surrendered to the Japanese. The application was withdrawn.[62] Kharb was seen by Seni, however, as having been appointed by Phibun to keep an eye on Seni himself, but, despite that, a good working relationship was developed, to the benefit of the Seri Thai. Pro-Phibun historians have claimed Kharb to be a deliberate Phibun 'plant' and, from that, concluded that the whole of the OSS operation that followed was evidence that it was essentially Phibun who made the running to support the Allied cause.[63] It is an interesting *ex post facto* theory, but it neither falls into place with the recollections of some of those who took part in the operations, nor was it reflected in the treatment of other OSS members during Phibun's second premiership.

America, through Cordell Hull, decided to support the Seri Thai movement, and its support was made tangible by the release of ten million dollars of Thai funds for use by the Thai Legation. This release was an act of good faith and an expression of apparent confidence not only in M. R. Seni but also in the calibre of the volunteers.

---

[61] *The Thai Resisitance Movement during the Second World War*; John B. Haseman; p31

[62] Discussions with Pisoot Sudasna na Ayutthaya over a number of years but specifically in January 1987, January 1991, and November 1993

[63] *Thailand and the Fall of Singapore*; Nigel J. Brailey; p100

In Britain, the formation of a Seri Thai group took longer, and at no time received the same whole-hearted government support. However, the circumstances were different in that the Thai Ambassador to Britain had chosen to deliver the declaration of war as he had been instructed by his government. A self-established group of Thai students, centred on Cambridge University and opposed both to Japan and to Phibun, had developed sufficiently by April 1942 to make contact with M. R. Seni in Washington. Unable to travel himself, M. R. Seni sent his representative Mani Sanasen. Mani was not the man the British authorities wanted and its Special Operations Executive, the SOE, were more interested in Mom Chao (M. C.) Suphasawatdiwongsanit, more easily remembered as M. C. Supha, as the leader of a Thai section. M. C. Supha had left Thailand after being involved in the Boworadej attempted counter-coup in 1933, and because of his very strong royalist views he was not popular among the young Seri Thai. He was however assigned to lead the military section of the British arm of the Seri Thai and acquitted himself both bravely and competently in the years that followed. Post-war pro-American elements in Thailand, of which Seni himself was a prominent member, sought to interpret M. C. Supha's appointment as an attempt by the British government to re-establish the Thai royalty in absolute power with the British pulling the strings.[64] Whilst this interpretation was based on suspicion rather than fact, M. C. Supha's role was eventually important for Anglo-Thai future relations. He was trusted by the British government, and because he backed Pridi he became the catalyst for the overdue change in post-war British attitudes in eventually seeking a friendly rather than punitive relationship.

Fortunately for the SOE, within the student ranks, studying at the London School of Economics but temporarily at Cambridge, was Dr Puey Ungphakorn, who was to become one of Thailand's outstanding post-war citizens. He had graduated in 1936 at Thammasat University, Bangkok, the university which Pridi himself had founded. Puey was to record later the principles by which the SOE-controlled group was governed. Students would enlist in the British Army, not to help the British but to serve Thailand through the help of Britain. To this end they would enlist as soldiers in uniform and not be used as

---

[64] *The United States and the coming of the Coup of 1947 in Siam*; Thanet Aphornsuvan/JSS; p194

spies or secret agents. They would not seek to become involved in Thai politics nor use the movement for personal gain or recognition. They would be prepared to join with any effective free Thai movement opposed to the Japanese.[65]

Meanwhile, back in Thailand itself and quite independent of the happenings in Washington and London, an internal resistance movement was being established in the very heart of the political scene. Following the Cabinet discussions of the night of seventh/eighth of December 1941 and his anti-Japanese protestations, Pridi had been discreetly kicked upstairs to fill a vacant post as one of the three members of the Council of Regents appointed for the absent King Ananda Mahidol. Only four days after the Japanese had invaded Thailand, a group of natural dissidents met in Bangkok to consider steps which might be taken to oppose them. Some were members of the original 1932 Coup Group and it was inevitable that they would look once more to Pridi for leadership.

Without question, Pridi Banomyong was one of Thailand's foremost political leaders. Born on eleventh May 1900 in Ayutthaya province, he was the son of a farmer of substance. As a boy of only twelve in a Bangkok school he was recognised as being 'politically aware' and intrigued by ideas aimed at the regime of the day. He won a very difficult lawsuit at the age of nineteen (his first and last case) and entered the civil service. In 1920 he won a government scholarship to study law at the University of Paris, and there he and his friends formed a student club, the Association of Siamese Students in France. Many of its members later became stalwarts of the 1932 coup, aimed at ending centuries of absolute monarchy and introducing constitutional monarchy.

Returning to Thailand from France in 1929 he became the secretary of the department for drafting legislation, later to become the Juridical Council. He was also a teacher at the Royal Law School. He was an early participant in the planning activity which led to the twenty-fourth of June 1932 coup and was looked upon as its intellectual leader. He was the author of the 1932 provisional constitution and later the author of a radical economic plan which was intended to change dramatically the Thai economic system. It was a plan which frightened a number of the more conservative members of the first government, and in 1933 Pridi left the country for France,

---

branded as a communist. Returning later that same year, he became a member of frequently changing governments, either as minister of the interior, foreign minister, or finance minister. At the time of the Japanese invasion he was the finance minister. In 1934 he had detached the Law Faculty from Chulalongkorn University to create the separate Thammasat University, specialising Paris-style in law and politics. He was its first Rector.[66]

In December 1941, the newly-formed resistance group, known initially as the XO group, met either at Pridi's house or occasionally at his Regency residence. The more prominent members of the XO group were Direk Jayanama, previously foreign minister, and Admiral Sangwon Yuthakit, deputy commander of the Royal Thai Navy. Among others were members of the National Assembly or successful businessmen. They first considered the establishment of a government-in-exile, knowing that European governments had adopted this mode of resistance. However, circumstances were not the same. The Thailand government had not fled the invading enemy; it had stayed and accepted it. A proposal of establishing a resistance army in the north of the country, close to the Chinese armies, was discarded as impracticable at that time. The decision was for a passive resistance movement which, as circumstances would allow, would become an active movement. The Seri Thai movement was born in Thailand only twenty-one days after the first Japanese troops had landed on its shores.

Chamkat Balankura, an Oxford University graduate, formed his own freedom group. It included a number of members of the National Assembly, among whom was the forceful Thammasat graduate, Tiang Sirikhand, from the Isan area. Having learned of Pridi's involvement, Chamkat brought his people into the XO group. Other groups that spontaneously formed did likewise. Many dissenters came from the civil service and the police, all concerned with upholding the honour and freedom of Thailand. From its early days, the Bangkok Seri Thai group could count on a geographical and political mix which would form the basis of its information network. The early objectives of the XO group were aimed at spreading disinformation. Phibun's influence was to be undermined, contact made with the allies, and later, when practical, the Japanese war effort was to be sabotaged.

---

[66] *Pridi Banomyong*: Vichitvong na Pombhejara

Thus the three elements of the Seri Thai were established; that from America and that from Britain knew of each other but were working for different and sometimes competing masters. Early contact between the external elements was negligible. The principal element, the internal XO group, knew little of the existence of the other two, and they in turn knew nothing of it. Eventually, radio broadcasts from America alerted the XO group to the existence of activity in Southern China. Further progress then depended on improved communication.

In 1942 the OSS realised that Thailand was the blind spot in its intelligence network in South-East Asia. General Stillwell lacked information on Japanese troops approaching his Burma battlefields and whether or not Thai forces were set to join them. The American Army Airforce wanted to know what to bomb. The State Department wanted to know the political realities of Thailand. Lieutenant Nicol Smith was invited by the OSS to act as quartermaster and finance officer to a group described to him as *"some of the most intelligent men that OSS has ever recruited — a group of handpicked Siamese PhDs and MAs from Harvard, MIT, and other leading American universities".*[67] Nicol Smith had travelled extensively in the Far East in pre-war days. He had quartermastered an expedition to the Yunnan in 1939 and earlier had been in Burma. He had studied and written about the Burma Road. He had been an intelligence officer in Europe. The Seri Thai were fortunate in being given such experienced support.

Colonel Kharb Kunjara gave up his post as the Thai military attaché in Washington and took command of the group. It was briefed on the intricacies of intelligence on the southern China border by a representative of General Tai Li, the all-powerful Chinese secret service commander. By the summer of 1943 the group had reached Chungking via Bombay and a training camp in northern India. At this time, Chungking was the base for the Sino-American Co-operative Organisation, where American intelligence officers endeavoured to function within the spider's web of General Tai Li's control. By a directive of the Allied Joint Chiefs of Staff, Tai Li had to approve all possible attempts to penetrate South-East Asian territories from

---

[67] *Into Siam, Underground Kingdom*; Nicol Smith and Blake Clark; p17

southern China,[68] an unfortunate directive which was fated to hamper OSS effort. General Tai Li was first and foremost a Chinese nationalist and the servant of Chiang Kai-shek. It later materialised that the reason that the Allies had an intelligence blindspot across Thailand was simply that Tai Li, in his quest for personal power or on the assumption that he alone knew what was best, did not pass much of the information within his knowledge on to his Allied colleagues. He had his intelligence tentacles in Thailand long before the OSS arrived on the scene. A Thai working with Tai Li during that period described him as a man consumed with vanity and self-importance.[69] Tai Li was not alone in the failure of Chinese sources to communicate. Later, Mountbatten, requested by Chiang Kai-shek to keep him informed of clandestine activities in South-East Asia, replied that he would *"do the same as you do"*. From that day onwards he received no information whatsoever from China.[70]

A milestone in communication was reached with the safe arrival in Chungking of a senior member of Pridi's underground movement. A first attempt to break out had been made at the end of 1942 but the seven-man party disappeared without trace. A second four-man party was also lost. The third attempt, by XO Group member Chamkat Balankura, involved his travelling from Bangkok on twenty-eighth of February 1943 via Laos, Hanoi and Lieuchow, reaching Chungking on twenty-first of April. But for three months Tai Li put a wall of silence around him, and although Chamkat met Generalissimo Chiang Kai-shek, American intelligence in Chungking was not aware of his arrival until early August. Seni knew of the presence in China of Chamkat as early as April but appeared to have known neither by whom he had been sent nor the objective of his mission. Chamkat's message was essentially political, not military. He particularly stressed that the declaration of war was unconstitutional and therefore no state of war existed between Thailand and America and Britain, thus leaving intact the treaties of friendship. He proposed that a 'Free Thai' government should be set up in India, a proposal which, if implemented, would involve bringing out Pridi and other senior

---

[68] Allied Joint Chiefs of Staff Directive, No. 245, cited in *The Thai Resistance Movement during the Second World war*; John B. Haseman
[69] Discussions with Pisoot Sudasna na Ayutthaya over a number of years but specifically in January 1987, January 1991, and November 1993
[70] United Kingdom, PRO, Doc. Ref. Prem 3/178-3

resistance leaders. Once established, the 'Free Thai' government would seek access to funds presently frozen in British and American banks.[71]

M. C. Supha, now representing the British Seri Thai, was also in Chungking and in the first week of August 1943 he was able to arrange meetings with Chamkat. From these, British intelligence learned of the establishment of the XO group and endeavoured to communicate with it, the objective being to be able to take members of the group out of Thailand by submarine for consultation. The endeavour failed and, in any event, much of Chamkat's message was of little interest to the British who were looking for proposals for military action against the Japanese, not for post-war political solutions.

The Head of Far Eastern Department, British Foreign Office, at the time was Sir Maurice Peterson. He was totally opposed to recognising any free Thai government in India or elsewhere, seeing a European parallel with Denmark. SOE was keen on at least a Free Thai Committee, involving Mani Sanasen and Seni, with an indication to Pridi that a government in exile might be developed later. Peterson opposed it, pointing out that Thailand had opened its gates to the enemy. He later argued that any statement made should go no further than the Atlantic Charter with a disavowal by Britain of any territorial ambitions. Such a disavowal would not, in his view, exclude the possible setting up of a military base if later judged to be desirable. Later, in response to statements made by China and America, it appeared necessary to make a British statement on the territorial integrity of Thailand. Unfortunately, internal differences within the British Government could not be resolved. The statement, dismissed by the foreign secretary, Anthony Eden, as 'a bore', was eventually lost, at the behest of Peterson, in a tangle over the future of Burma, Indochina, and Malaya. While it is a matter of fact that the future of Thailand was in no way paramount in British thinking, the absence of any formal statement at that time aroused America's suspicions of Britain's intentions.[72]

Kharb needed to discuss mutual problems with Chamkat, but the intelligence confusion in Chungking was such that Tai Li was able to prevent direct contact between these two leading representatives of the

---

[71] *Bangkok Top Secret*; Sir Andrew Gilchrist; p23
[72] *Atonement before Absolution*; Nicholas Tarling/JSS; pp35/40

Thai resistance. Two more Seri Thai XO group supporters, Sanguan Tularak of the Ministry of Finance and Daeng Khunadilok of the Ministry of Foreign Affairs, arrived from Bangkok in August 1943. They also encountered Tai Li's 'protection' with the result that they met neither Chamkat nor American intelligence staff for some weeks. Eventually, Kharb met up with Chamkat, Sanguan, and Daeng, and with that meeting learned for certain that a resistance movement was already established in Thailand. Furthermore, he was at last able to appreciate that it was operating at a top government level, even although the personal involvement of the Regent was not at that time disclosed to him. By this time Chamkat had prepared a full report on the XO group, its organisation, intentions, and leadership. It found its way via Sanguan to an appreciative OSS and State Department in Washington. Nicol Smith was able to come to the assistance of Sanguan and Daeng by financing their journey to Washington from where, after de-briefing, they travelled to Britain for further discussions. It was too late to help Chamkat. He had become seriously ill and died of a stomach cancer in Chungking on seventh of October 1943.[73]

In the midst of this intelligence mish-mash, Nicol Smith was trying to infiltrate his chosen men into Thailand. Eventually, there were signs of progress. There was news that Tai Li had sent out men to buy horses for the journey south. He then brought in General Tso, his commander from Cheli, a town on the banks of the Mekong near the Laos border. Tso was to escort the Thais to Kunming and thence to Cheli. Christmas Eve was spent in Kunming and it was here that the Thai party first met General Lu Wi Eng, the commander of the Chinese 93rd Division. The Seri Thai, despite their personal battle inexperience, recognised in the 93rd Division a poor quality formation with more support troops than active soldiers, ill-kempt, lacking in fire power, ammunition, and supplies, and whose discipline was maintained by the simple method of shooting anyone attempting to desert.[74] The horses provided for the OSS Thai officers in Kunming turned out to be skinny creatures and the pack-horses were little better. To move the heavy OSS base signalling gear would have presented a monumental task. A fortunate meeting between Nicol Smith and one of General Chennault's staff, and then with the General

---

[73] Discussions with Pisoot Sudasna na Ayutthaya, 1987–1993
[74] Discussions with Pisoot Sudasna na Ayutthaya, 1987–1993

himself, a friend from days on the Burma Road, resulted in the base being moved from Cheli to Szemao where there was an airfield. On fifteenth of January the party's heavy equipment and most of the party moved by air to Szemao where it paid for its ride by guarding Chennault's gasoline stocks. Szemao had, over time, suffered from a combination of earthquakes, malaria and bubonic plague. Formerly a great Chinese trading centre, it had become a seedy, thinly-populated market town on a caravan route to Tibet from the south and in the heart of tiger and bandit country. It became a Seri Thai base and by twenty-ninth of February 1944 the first group of five agents selected by Colonel Kharb was ready to start its journey to Cheli and thence back to Thailand.

Working within the area controlled by the Chinese Kuomintang (KMT) 93rd Division, Nicol Smith realised that the Thailand intelligence blindspot which he had first been sent to remedy was not so blind as the OSS had thought. It was obvious that General Tai Li had extensive knowledge of happenings in Thailand through agents travelling north and south along the old trading trails, knowledge which he was not passing to America. A second source of information was available to the 93rd divisional commander, General Lu Wi Eng. Although Lu was theoretically at war with Thailand he had made friendly contact with the Thai Northern Army stationed in Kengtung. A new, if tenuous, line of communication between Thailand and the OSS officers opened up through the 93rd Division when it was discovered that a senior officer of the Thai Army in the Shan States was a personal friend of Kharb.[75] Supporters of Phibun, and the Lady La-iad in particular, were to claim later that the Northern Army was stationed there for the prime purpose of establishing friendly contact with Generalissimo Chiang Kai-shek's Army,[76] while others maintain that this contact was essentially a direct link from Kharb to Phibun who had 'planted' him in the Washington embassy.[77] Both were unlikely. Once Kharb's OSS section was settled in China, he became deeply involved with the Chinese and particularly so within the web woven by Tai Li, who ensured that a beautiful young Chinese girl kept a close watch on his movements.

[75] *Into Siam, Underground Kingdom*; Nicol Smith and Blake Clark; pp144/6
[76] *Pridi Banomyong*: Vichitvong na Pombhejara; p183
[77] *Thailand and the Fall of Singapore*; Nigel J. Brailey; p100

It was at General Lu Wi Eng's headquarters at Meng Hai, near to Cheli, that Smith met Father Jean Tong. Tong at the time was the political adviser to the KMT 93rd Division, a strange role for a Chinese catholic priest. At one time an amateur boxing champion in Shanghai, he had learned some of his nine languages in that city and others in Switzerland. He had travelled the wild border mountain country, accompanied by his dedicated servant who went under the title of 'the Catechist'. To add to his master's fund of languages, the Catechist could add every dialect from Yunnan south to the Thailand mountains. Tong had earlier escaped a strafing of Kengtung market by Thai aircraft and had moved to the mountains where he now served the KMT 93rd.[78]

General Tso brought promises but no results. Infiltration became haphazard. Two of the leading group, travelling together, were allegedly captured by Japanese/Thai forces and killed. Other Seri Thai believe that they were killed by Tai Li's men for the gold they were carrying. Phone Indarathat, whose first attempt at infiltration had been utterly frustrated by local Chinese, and although aware of the murder of two of his group, made a second but this time solo attempt. He crossed the Laotian plains and reached Phitsanulok in Thailand by May. He then gave himself into protective police custody to avoid capture by the Japanese. Ian Khamphanan and Karun Kangradomying made their way in late April through Chiang Sae to Chiang Rai where they were taken into custody by Adun's secret police, the *santiban*, and moved to police quarters in Bangkok. Months passed before their fate was known in Szemao.

Despite the approach of the rainy season Nicol Smith considered the possible use of his second string of agents. Divine intervention must have seemed to be his only hope of success but while God did not come in person to his assistance, he sent his appointed representative. Back to Szemao from a visit to Kunming came Father Tong. It was he who now suggested a new trail from Cheli to Meng Long and then south across the narrow strip of Burma which cuts like a panhandle into Laos. He disclosed that he personally had made the

---

[78] Discussions with Pisoot Sudasna na Ayutthaya, 1987–1993; and *Into Siam, Underground Kingdom*; Nicol Smith and Blake Clark; pp144/146; and *The Shan of Burma*; Chao Tzang Yawnghwe; p85

journey during the monsoon season and in the end, following the suggestion that medicines and funds which he badly needed to build a church would be made available to him in exchange, he undertook to guide the Thai volunteers. Tong limited the party to four, and Kharb chose volunteers coded Bunny, Pow, Pete, and Sam — otherwise Boonyen Sasirat, Pao Khamurai, Pisoot Sudasna, and Sawat Chieusakun. They left on twenty-seventh of April 1944 and took a week to reach Cheli from where they would head south.[79]

They were no longer a second team. They were now the chosen few who were required, as far as they knew, to be the vanguard of the OSS volunteers making the long and dangerous journey back into their native land. Neither they, nor Father Tong, nor Nicol Smith, let alone the OSS in Washington, were to have any idea of how arduous the journey was to be and, in the long term, of the political implications of the mission on which they were embarking. Kharb reminded his young warriors of their excellent training, their unique good fortune in having Father Tong as their guide and, as he saw it, their heroic mission. As they made their way along the trail to Cheli they came more and more to realise the responsibility which was now theirs. They were trail-blazers and, come what may, they had to get through the mountains into Thailand and south to Bangkok. But how exactly?

They were disguised as wandering lowly medical pedlars. Medical pedlars in the mountains were usually seen in parties and with a mix of skills. They did not barter their skills and medicines for goods. They offered such treatment as they were able. They gave such medicine as was available and needed. In return it was customary for medical pedlars to be accepted by a village which they visited, to be fed and to be offered sufficient food to take them on to the next village. When the OSS party set off, each member fitted himself out with three pairs of shoes of straw. These lasted only a short time over the rough paths and soon they were all barefooted, driving their pack animals before them. Weeks of practising to walk barefooted paid off; proper shoes were out of the question as no one in that remote area south of Meng Long would be wearing shoes. Radio sets were wrapped in waterproofed blankets at the bottom of the panniers and covered with leaves and straw. The panniers also contained their pedlar's wares, needles and thread, mirrors, and their medicines,

---

[79] Discussions with Pisoot Sudasna na Ayutthaya, 1987–1993; and *Into Siam, Underground Kingdom*; Nicol Smith and Blake Clark; p155

mixed with bolts of cloth and coloured ribbons to sell to the tribes' girls. Quinine pills were there not only for the agents but also for friendly gestures to local headsmen.

A gentle mist covered the hills and softened the earth beneath their feet. The packhorses were sliding as they walked, but they were adequate for the journey as far as Meng Long. There, Father Tong planned to change the packhorses for mules. There also he planned to find provisions for the journey south, taking rice, strings of Chinese sausages, and dried local vegetables. Army rations of any sort were excluded, apart from some broken chocolate. There was to be no canned food unless it could be acquired with markings indicating a Japanese origin.

Reaching Meng Long they surveyed the route ahead from the top of the jungle-covered Meng Long mountain. Before them lay the beautiful green countryside of the Burma panhandle which they must cross. Beyond it they could see the final ridge which would take them down to the Mekong and the ferry. They were able to observe nearby positions of the Thai soldiers of the Northern Army. There was no sign of warlike action. In this theatre of war there was a happy understanding that unless a Japanese officer was in sight, the Chinese and Thai armies left each other in peace. The pedlars were ordered not to make any contact with the Thai Army as the most likely result would have been to be handed over to the Japanese. From now on, if they came across an inquisitive Japanese, it was a question of kill or be killed. Early on an April morning, these young men from the élite families of Thailand, their degree and PhD studies thousands of miles behind them, left the foot of Meng Long mountain and made their way south.

The first casualty was their machine gun. Its loss was noticed at the end of the first day and despite back-tracking, it was never discovered. The four were not over-surprised. It had been apparent to them that Lu Wi Eng had coveted the gun which was much superior to anything he himself possessed. Later they were to come to the conclusion that the Catechist had sold it to the Chinese general. Mosquito nets were also lost early on.

Father Tong had decided that risk of capture could best be reduced by keeping away from the lowland Lao, where gossip would outstrip their progress, and move from village to village in mountain country among the upland Hmong. This meant that each inter-village journey was down a mountainside and up the next to where the Hmong villages were sited, well above the thousand metre line. The objective was to spend each night in a village to avoid the danger of attack by tigers and leopards which hunted the mountain jungle. Not only were the wild animals dangerous to the party itself, but also the mules were terrified by even the scent of them. They were nearly demented when it became essential to spend two of the nights in the forest. Wandering from village to village, the party would sometimes be moving in its general south-westerly direction, but just as frequently heading north-east.

The monsoon rains dogged their journey, resulting in fast flowing rivers and mountain streams, slippery paths, and mud. Most of their time was spent in and between Hmong villages in Laos. Three times they crossed the Mekong. When the mules were desperately tired, their feed was spiked with opium. When food ran out, the pedlars risked trading gold for food, a hazardous operation because it not only made them stand out from ordinary medical pedlars but also exposed them to potential robbery and the fate of the earlier volunteers. With the guidance of Father Tong they avoided the Thai Army, the Chinese Army, and the French Army. They were left more dead than alive by Tong on the Thai border in that part of Laos ceded to Thailand under the Tokyo Treaty of 1941. They had walked for eighty-seven days and some three hundred and fifty miles through Yunnan, Laos and Thailand. Once in Thai territory they posed as police on a secret mission, a pose supported by forged (*santiban*) documents given to them by Kharb. They eventually met up with members of the *santiban* searching for them, and were escorted south to Bangkok. There they lived under the protection of General Adun, the head of police. At no time was their infiltration known to the Japanese and thus there was no request to interrogate them.[80]

The British approach to the Seri Thai was through SOE-controlled Force 136, based at Kandy in Sri Lanka (Ceylon, as it then was). The sub-unit was the Siam Country Section. SOE was originally established to operate in Europe for the task of harrying the enemy until such time as full-scale operations could be conducted. Because of

[80] Discussions with Pisoot Sudasna na Ayutthaya, 1987–1993; and *Into Siam, Underground Kingdom*; Nicol Smith and Blake Clark

this objective, very suited to affairs in Europe, the British took a more 'gung-ho' approach to operations and looked firstly for a Seri Thai force which would blow up bridges, railways, and Japanese installations, rather than one which merely produced amateurish intelligence. Post-war political philosophy was certainly a non-runner. In August 1942, indirectly under the guidance of M. C. Supha, Thai students in Britain were first collected into the Pioneer Corps, a British Army dumping ground for enemy alien volunteers, and sometimes, soldiers of limited ability. They underwent basic training until late April 1943. Of them, thirty-six reached India, and of these thirty-six, twenty-two eventually arrived at Force 136's specialised training ground in Poona in May of that year. There they underwent a further period of training before being commissioned in the following October. They became known as the 'White Elephants', or just 'Whites'. To command them, Force 136 searched for rare birds, Britons who were suitable for SOE work, spoke the Thai language, and would volunteer to join. In June 1943 Major Peter Pointon was appointed to command the Siam Country Section, with Captain N. F. Nicholson as his second-in-command. Pointon not only spoke Thai but was familiar with the teak forest areas of Thailand. Nicholson, also a Thai speaker, had escaped from Bangkok in December 1941 and led a party in a nightmarish journey across the River Kwai and the Three Pagodas Pass into Burma. He had joined British Army intelligence, was in the retreat from Burma, and also had the unenviable yet useful experience of working with Tai Li's intelligence network. Eventually to join them was Andrew Gilchrist who, as a member of the British Embassy staff in Bangkok on seventh of December 1941, had been interned by the Japanese but later exchanged for Japanese diplomatic staff. It was not until November 1943 that he was able to escape the clutches of the British Foreign Office and the second half of 1944 before Force 136 was to see him.[81]

The Siam Section saw four possibilities of infiltrating its Whites into Thailand: by land from Kunming, by submarine, by parachute, or by Catalina flying boat. A first attempt saw M. C. Supha safely in Kunming, in discussion with Chamkat and endeavouring to get a message through to the Seri Thai in Bangkok. The request was for them to meet a submarine landing attempt off the west coast which was to be made in November 1943. While the submarine, carrying

---

[81] *Bangkok Top Secret*; Sir Andrew Gilchrist; pp31/32

three Whites led by Dr Puey, stayed near the rendezvous off Phang Na for nearly a week, no contact was made. Time was to provide a simple explanation for the failure of the mission — the message-carrying party did not reach Bangkok until June the following year, 1944.[82]

The second attempt was by a precarious route, that of a blind drop by parachute. Parachuting with only limited knowledge of a terrain and without a supporting reception party, even into one's own enemy-occupied country, is full of hazards. Nevertheless, in March 1944, three young volunteer Whites, led again by Puey, were dropped into the teak forest country in the Sukhothai-Sawankhalok area some four hundred and fifty kilometres north-north-west of Bangkok. The first attempt was aborted as the pilot could not find the dropping zone. From the air, the second attempt appeared to be successful but over the next six weeks there was neither a signal from the team nor reports over monitored radio about the team. A second team, led by Samran Varn Briksha, was also blind-dropped in the teak forest area of the first; again, there was no report. In June 1944, Bangkok radio reported that Puey and the five other Whites were in prison. It was also announced that they had already been interrogated by the Japanese, a statement which could have meant anything.

Puey and his pathfinder team had missed the dropping zone by about thirty kilometres, and Puey himself had the misfortune to sprain his ankle in an awkward landing, both happenings being normal hazards of a parachute drop. They had been dropped close to a village and one of their supply parachutes had landed in the middle of the village, right in front of the temple. Puey, unable to move at any speed, was soon discovered by the villagers. The other two escaped but were captured in a nearby village. Chained at the ankles, Puey was interviewed by series of officials of ever higher status but in a not too unfriendly manner. The police, in particular, treated him with consideration, even collecting money to help him buy food on his journey south. On his arrival in Bangkok he was lodged within police custody. The second parachute group arrived in police custody within the month. A submarine group and then a flying boat group followed. A number of OSS Seri Thai joined them. The gaol itself was not large enough for all of them and so they were accommodated more

---

[82] *Bangkok Top Secret*; Sir Andrew Gilchrist; p45; and *Siam and World War II*; Direk Jayanama; p31

comfortably in police living quarters. Others, of whom the Japanese were aware, were kept in a formal prisoner-of-war camp but were guarded by the Thais themselves. On the occasions that the Japanese sought to interrogate them, they were at all times carefully protected by Thai police.[83]

Behaving as prisoners by day, the OSS and SOE groups were permitted to make their radio contacts at night, using the houses of some Seri Thai as radio stations. They received considerable help from a wide range of people, from local officials to those holding high posts in government. Puey told of having *"The support of the police, and later of the army, navy, and airforce. Military officials from generals to privates, and civilians from Ministers to common citizens enthusiastically gave us a hand".*[84] Assisted by his own Thammasat University background and with a highly supportive Police Captain, Phayom Cantharakkha, himself a Thammasat graduate, and Professor Wichit Lulitanond, the secretary-general of Thammasat, Puey was able eventually to relay to the Regent, Pridi, a message from the Supreme Allied Commander, South-East Asia, in which Pridi was formally recognised as leader of the Seri Thai.

Ordinary chains of command and subordination appear not to have applied. Police Captain Phayom was working for Regent Pridi while still in the service of Police-General Adun. Adun himself was working both for Pridi and at the same time for his prime minister, Phibun. Reviewing this complex of loyalties some years later, one of his 'prisoners' came to the conclusion that Adun, notably a cautious man, saw himself as the true co-ordinator of the Seri Thai. As such, he could protect his Army comrade and great friend, Phibun, while helping Pridi whom he saw as playing a more active role in the national interest.

August 1944 brought changes. Firstly in Bangkok itself there was the replacement of Phibun by Khuang, and as a result the Seri Thai were reinforced by the support of the newly-appointed assistant prime minister, Thawee. For the Siam Section there was news of the position of six Whites. The Section learned that they were well and had not as yet been physically handed over to the Japanese. It learned, with some puzzlement, that all were in the custody of an apparently friendly Thai police and, even more strange, that they were in close

---

[83] *Portraits of Thai Politics*; Jenton K. Ray
[84] *Siam and World War II*; Direk Jayanama; p139

touch with the Seri Thai movement in the capital. The Whites were asking for radio contact to be established on the originally agreed frequencies. Soon messages came in regularly from which it was learned that any Japanese interviews of prisoners had been conducted in the presence of Thai police. Puey had managed to discuss the position of the Whites with Adun, only then to discover that the police-general himself was deeply involved with the internal Seri Thai. This is the stuff of fiction rather than military operation and it was therefore not surprising that when a further parachute operation was planned in circumstances which were somewhat risky, questions were asked in London as to whether or not a trap was being hatched by the Japanese. On instruction from Force 136 Headquarters in Kandy the operation was cancelled. British intelligence, because of its experience of betrayals and losses in Europe smelled a very large rat. Fortunately there existed the opportunity to make an independent check through Puey and Direk Jayanama to Pridi himself, and when the response was routed back correctly through the suspect channels, the suspicion of a trap was removed. Force 136 now knew for sure that, however strange the circumstances, it had a reliable line into the Seri Thai in Bangkok.[85]

British foreign secretary Eden admitted not understanding the Far East and he was unhappy about the whole business. Dealing with a country which he saw as merely a bunch of collaborators, and through channels so clandestine, was not calculated to bring forward his support or even interest.[86] That lack of interest allowed attention to be drawn to the views of others, and particularly to Sir Josiah Crosby, previously the British minister in Bangkok. Crosby, having diagnosed precisely in 1943 the problems which would arise as a result of any emergence of a Phibun-styled military, developed further his personal theory to the extent that, following the end of the war, there should be imposed upon Siam a period of tutelage.[87] The importance and authority of the statement was greatly exaggerated and it caused dismay in Thai circles. But ex-ambassadors do not make government policy. Britain had already accepted the wording of the Atlantic Charter which, *inter alia*, protected the borders and rights of sovereign powers.

---

[85] *Bangkok Top Secret*; Sir Andrew Gilchrist; pp69/82
[86] *Atonement before Absolution*; Nicholas Tarling/JSS; p42
[87] An article published in UK magazine *International Affairs*, July 1944

With suspicions allayed, a new parachute operation was given the green light by Force 136. Krit Tosayanonda and Prasert Padumananda dropped into a well-organised reception party under the control of one of Pridi's most important operational leaders, Chan Bunnako. Chan was soon to be in charge of all underground security. He worked only with close friends and relatives, thus exploiting the strong, closely-knit Thai family relationships. Others were to copy his example, each developing the 'need to know only' cell which had quite separately been developed in Europe for agent protection. Within twenty-four hours, Puey's Whites had signalled the safe arrival of the newcomers. Before another twenty-four hours had elapsed the Krit/Prasert team were signalling back themselves. The Siam Section now had a team in Thailand, apparently totally independent of police goodwill.[88] Krit Tosayanonda made early contact with former foreign minister Direk, and before long was in contact with Puey. He in turn was by then in daily touch with police-general Adun. Bodies were followed by supplies. South of Hua Hin came the first Sten and Bren guns and ammunition.

The Siam Country Section's objectives in September 1944 now included the procurement of military intelligence; assistance in the development of the Bangkok Seri Thai; and securing radio links with agents inside the country. It had a further and extremely important task. The Supreme Allied Commander, South-East Asia, was most anxious to ensure that the Siam Section prevented premature action which might well prejudice the Command's future operations and involve unnecessary loss of Thai life.[89] The problem with these objectives was that they did not fit the picture seen by Pridi. He was more anxious to resolve post-war politics than just dabble in limited fields of local intelligence. An attempt to bring out a number of senior Seri Thai for discussion was frustrated by the blinkered attitude adopted by the British Foreign Office when it was learned that the leader was to be the former foreign minister, Direk. Britain wanted intelligence and sabotage of the enemy's war effort, not politics.

Headquarters, OSS, which had been briefed on British suspicions of enemy-controlled signals, was itself dubious of the validity of the signals emanating from within police quarters. Without reference to OSS in Szemao or the SOE in Kandy, it sent in two independent Seri

---

[88] *Bagkok Top Secret*, Sir Andrew Gilchrist; p82
[89] *Bangkok Top Secret*, Sir Andrew Gilchrist; p84

Thai from its base in India. The two had made a first attempt by submarine and small boat but the operation was called off, partly owing to a faulty submarine and partly because of intelligence confusion between OSS and SOE. Given only twenty-four hours to 'volunteer', Boonmark Thesabut and Wimon Wiriyawit, who, only a few months before had been students at the Massachusetts Institute of Technology, were parachuted on ninth of September into Phrae province — but only at the third attempt. On the first, the B24 bomber lost its way and strayed over Laos and Vietnam. On the second, the visibility was poor and again their aircraft took them home. On the third, they dropped in full American uniform at about two thousand feet. It was far too high for accuracy. They missed the dropping zone and Wimon finished high up in a teak tree. He turned himself into a bare-footed peasant and buried his equipment. To prevent robbery he also buried his gold. He passed through the hands of the local headman, the provincial governor, and eventually the provincial police headquarters. From here communication with Adun resulted in his being moved secretly to Bangkok under police protection. Wimon has recorded that he was taken at his own request by Adun to meet Pridi, enabling him to ask them both to work closely together in order to qualify for American support.[90] It was through Wimon and Boonmark that the Regent first learned of American sympathy with his political objectives. The meeting was of significance in the developing scenario in which British and American policy had already shown signs of being at odds.

On fifth of December 1944 Siam Section sent in another team. Dropping beyond Sukhothai, it established a second wireless link well away from the Bangkok police area. At that distance from the Thai capital the link would be less vulnerable to Japanese capture. Large areas of Thailand were free of Japanese as, according to Japanese Army statistics, there were only a mere ten thousand soldiers in the country for much of 1944.[91] Most of these were in and around the capital. The time had come for the Siam Section to expand its activities within Thailand and introduce internal training both for the wireless network and for sabotage. That in itself brought in its train the question of stockpiling arms and equipment for future operations.

---

90 *When I Parachuted into Thailand*; Wimon Wiriyawit pp1/17
91 *The Balancing Act*, Joseph J. Wright, Jnr; p127, citing *Underground Escapes* by Masanobu Tsuji,

Force 136 decided to put a British liaison officer into Bangkok and to bring out volunteers for specialised training.

January 1945 brought the news that Victor Jacques, a thrice-decorated First World War soldier, later a lawyer in Bangkok and now again serving as a Brigadier in the British Army, would be available to be infiltrated into Bangkok. It was not before May that he made his drop, thus leaving the way open for an American liaison officer to arrive first.

By now, intelligence of military movements, air raid results, prisoner-of-war camp locations and other matters much sought by OSS and by SOE had improved in quality and was flowing freely. Much however was still amateurish, lacking in geographical and numerical detail. A sea-change in quality occurred with the recruitment to Seri Thai ranks of the principal liaison officer between the Thai Supreme Command and the Japanese Army Headquarters. Military and police officers increased the support of the movement and a number of senior ranks joined the XO group. Small-scale guerilla activity commenced, particularly against railroads and rolling stock. From the Bangkok signals network, Wimon made his first contact with the OSS through Pao Khamurai, his own equipment having been lost with the misdirected parachute drop.[92] Important contact was made with another close ally of Pridi, Tiang Sirikhand, who was operating much further to the north-east than any previous contact. The district of Sakhon Nakhon was reported to be free of any serious Japanese occupation and could provide a suitable dropping zone for supplies. It had a strong Seri Thai representation led by Tiang, and supplies of arms and wireless equipment were dropped within the course of a few days.

By January 1945 the OSS were tired of operating within the Tai Li web and, being sure of its infiltration, closed down its operations in Szemao. Smith and its remaining agents were moved to Sri Lanka to train people brought out from Thailand. Nicol Smith himself became a personal representative of the Supreme Allied Commander, Mountbatten. He was sent first to Washington to brief the State Department and then to Bangkok as Mountbatten's representative to

---

[92] *When I parachuted into Thailand*; Wimon Wiriyawit; pp15/16

the underground Seri Thai. He brought authority to bear on the Thai resistance fighters to stop any premature rising. In May, the American Chiefs of Staff placed all OSS activities in Thailand under the British Force 136 because of its greater experience.[93] An outside observer might have suspected that the order was somewhat diluted by the time it reached the operating level.

The priority now changed to getting people out rather than in. A first hazardous effort by flying boat brought out eight volunteer policemen. The following operation, involving two flying boats, brought a further batch of volunteers but also much bigger fish. Out for discussions at Supreme Allied Headquarters, South-East Asia Command, came Direk Jayanama, General Chatr Nakrob, a future commander of the Thai Army, and Thanat Khoman, a future foreign minister, with Dr Puey in attendance. Militarily, the discussions were very helpful but the Command was still on a tight rein from the British Foreign Office and thus political discussion, which was the very reason for the high level Thai mission, was limited. The Seri Thai forces were formally acknowledged as a resistance movement and the negotiating party was put safely back into Bangkok within a week.[94]

By the end of March there were matters of great import in the air. One of the options for a major counter-attack upon the Japanese was the recapture of Singapore and Malaya. To support this, peninsular Thailand was to be invaded at Phuket to prevent, or at least seriously delay, Japanese troops being brought into battle. The island of Phuket itself was to be captured and troops fanned out to keep its airfields free from shellfire. Another option considered was the push of troops from Rangoon through to central Thailand. The Seri Thai intelligence network became of great importance. It would have been even greater had it been in the peninsula and not just in Bangkok and the North-East. To avoid moving teams internally and thus risking a breach of security, Seri Thai Whites and British officers went in directly to the Phuket area to prepare for the main thrust at Phuket Island. The preparatory operation in the first days of April, 1945 was a success and throughout be summer of 1945, OSS and SOE staff entered and left almost at will under the watchful protection of the Seri Thai. Then, to the chagrin of all of the free forces operating in the Thailand theatre of war, the main thrust was cancelled and an

---

[93] *The First Vietman War*; Peter M. Dunn; p109
[94] *Bangkok Top Secret*; Sir Andrew Gilchrist; pp110/130

alternative plan for a direct attack on Singapore took its place. The Potsdam Conference had decreed that all priority must be given to the Pacific thrust and South-East Asia took a backseat.[95] Cancellation followed cancellation. The Singapore thrust was itself made superfluous by the atomic bombing of Hiroshima and Nagasaki.

The relations between British and American intelligence organisations were characterised by intrigue, suspicion, and an absurd duplication of activities in all fields, excepting that deep in wartime Bangkok, Brigadier Jacques and his American opposite number, John D. Wester, worked in close harmony. But while, in intelligence, confusion may have reigned, in politics America was a giant's step ahead of Britain. It had been abundantly clear for some time to both American and British authorities that Pridi wanted to talk post-war politics and not just short-term intelligence. America was sufficiently far-seeing to realise that its future influence in South-East Asia could be built around a stable Thailand. It was also helped in its approach by its exaggerated anti-colonial attitude which, in South-East Asia, meant principally anti-British and anti-French. It had readily accepted that the declaration of war by Phibun did not represent the wishes of the people of Thailand and that politics were always on Pridi's agenda. It had accepted the role of M. R. Seni and the supporting OSS Seri Thai who had made the tremendously difficult journeys across the mountain trails. American officials had expressly questioned OSS Thai officers on matters political, and treated as significant the reports of Seri Thai activity within Thailand which had been brought out by Sanguan. The British Foreign Office did not. It discounted the SOE Thais, and was itself discounted by the Thais in favour of a constructive relationship with America. The difference in attitude might in part, but only in part, be attributed to the fact that the declaration of war was formally delivered in Britain and not in America. The British saw this as a betrayal which had to be redeemed by the Thais 'working their passage home' despite protests from America. Why so? Britain did not suffer from ideological purity. It was quite prepared to work with communist regimes in Yugoslavia and Greece which it disliked intensely, and even with Russia itself. It also accepted both Italy and

---

[95] *The Second World War, Vol. VI*; Winston S. Churchill; pp545/559

the Thakin nationalists of Burma as its allies, although each in its respective theatre had pursued a bitter war against it. It was not as though its own theatre commander was unaware of the importance of the role of Pridi. Speaking at a luncheon on seventeenth of December 1946 on the banks of the Thames in London, some six thousand miles away from the activities of the Seri Thai, Lord Mountbatten acknowledged the great part that Pridi had played in the overthrow of the Japanese Army of occupation in Thailand. He described the peculiar situation of a supreme commander exchanging vital military plans with the head of a state technically at war with him. He told of how Pridi had organised sabotage and guerilla forces, how he had been an inspiration to his followers, and how he had never failed the Allied cause.[96] Such was the man whom, despite the wise advice of Dening, the Eden/Peterson partnership failed to appreciate. It was a failure which was principally responsible for limiting British influence in South-East Asia for decades to follow. America's prompt acceptance of the Thai position of a rescued ally rather than a defeated enemy was a major stepping-stone in its post-war economic and political progress in South-East Asia.

The intentions of the Seri Thai have been questioned. Post-war controversies imply that the resistance movement failed to carry out systematic attacks on the Japanese and that it was simply a part of the façade designed to pull the wool over Western eyes to obtain the best possible deal from the side winning the war.[97] If that were true, it would have been a most elaborate, expensive, and cynical hoax. It would also have meant that both the whole of South-East Asia Command and the OSS controllers were utterly fooled. It can be discarded as a post-war armchair theory. The lack of guerilla fighting has a different answer. The OSS Seri Thai were trained, if somewhat hurriedly, for the special role of intelligence gathering and, as junior officers of the American Army, were under military orders. They had been directed by the OSS not to get involved with cloak-and-dagger activities.[98]

Another and more sceptical theory was that Pridi's interest was not in the Allied victory but in displacing Phibun whom he saw as having

---

[96] *The Times*, London; 18 December 1946

[97] Statement by Thawee, *Portraits of Thai Politics*; Jenton K. Ray; p110; and *Thailand and the Fall of Singapore*; Nigel J. Brailey; p113

[98] Discussions with Pisoot Sudasna na Ayutthaya, 1987 to 1993

stolen his 1932 revolution. His Seri Thai base, complete with the American arms, was to be used to counter the military and police in a post-war struggle for power. The roots of this theory were in the pre-war disputes between Phibun and a number of Isan leaders who were politically left-of-centre and who became prominent in the Seri Thai movement. This theory was denied by Thawee, but the rumour was strong enough to call for his denial.[99]

On the day that the war ended, Allied officers popped up all over Thailand to represent the victorious powers until formal representatives arrived. The Seri Thai held a victory parade in Bangkok and, to the dismay of the poorly-equipped Thai military, ten thousand of them appeared with shining new weapons provided by the Allies. Thawee led the parade; Pridi took the salute. He addressed them, not as Regent, but as a comrade in arms. He spoke of the high-principled intentions of those who had founded the movement in America, Britain, and in Thailand itself. No claims were made for the benefit of any person, for official appointment or for reward. The Seri Thai had been founded for the good of the Thai people as a whole. Then, as had been promised, they were disarmed. The arms were stored and the Seri Thai movement was formally disbanded.[100]

Forty years later, when those who had survived not only the perils of war but also post-war brutality were to be seen at reunion gatherings, many had risen to the top of professions or had made an indelible mark in post-war Thai development. Among them, M. R. Seni became the first post-war prime minister, the first of three occasions on which he held that post. Colonel Kharb Kunjara returned to Washington and later reached the rank of Lieut-General. Wimon Wiriyawit, decorated by America with the Medal of Freedom, bronze palm, for his heroism went to the Royal Thai Air Force and after his retirement as Group-Captain, became chairman of the government committee responsible for the development of Thailand's petroleum reserves. Dr Puey Ungphakorn became the country's most prominent economist of his day, a bank governor and later Rector of Thammasat University, as Pridi had been before him. After the Thammasat student massacre of 1976, he left the country to spend the rest of his life in England. One of the 'medicine pedlars' who had walked for eighty-seven days across Yunnan and Laos, and most of it barefooted,

---

[99] *Thailand and the Fall of Singapore*; Nigel J. Brailey; p114
[100] *US-Thailand Diplomatic Relations during World War II*; Sethachuay Vivat; pp293/4

became Director-General of Mineral Resources and a director of a number of Thailand's premier companies. Many who became political activists, including Thawin, Thongplaew, Chamlong, Thongin, Phone, and Tiang, particularly in the cause of the neglected north-east, Isan, were to suffer death at the hands of a cruel police regime.[101] Others survived the early harsh regimes to become political leaders in their turn.

When histories and, more so, biographies came to be written, fading and selective memories of those involved tended to claim exaggerated credits for any successful operation. Failures were quietly left to moulder. In a 1972 portrayal of views, Thawee Bunyaketu spoke highly of Pridi's leadership, of his own whole-hearted support for the Seri Thai, of the closest consultation with both the British and American Allies and of constant contact with South-East Asia Command in Kandy. As a short-term prime minister, he welcomed the arrival of the British Indian troops for the purpose of disarming the Japanese.[102] He was in and out of governments for a number of years.

M. R. Seni's views, dated in that same year, contain frequent expressions of self-importance and throughout the expression of views there is a thread of bitterness entwined with jealousy of others' attainments. This is unfortunate, because as a young and inexperienced diplomat he had achieved much. A 1972 interview plays down the alliance between his own Seri Thai and those of Pridi. He saw his own appointment in Washington as owing to Pridi's personal jealousy of his own popularity at Thammasat University. A staunch royalist himself, he viewed Pridi as essentially anti-royalist and an active communist, but in that view he was not alone. He made virtually no mention of the operational leadership of Colonel Kharb. There was only passing reference to the latter's appointment in Washington as that of a military man sent by Phibun to spy upon him. He gave no credit to the British Force 136 Thais but protests inaccurately and with almost boring monotony against British intentions on the independence of Thailand, finally claiming bitterly that British troops were sent to engrave defeat on an enemy country. He was still playing his story like a broken gramophone record as late as a 1992 Seri Thai reunion and also to a biographer who, in turn, played it all over again.

---

[101] Discussions with Pisoot Sudasna na Ayutthaya 1987 to 1993; and *The Sarit Regime*; Thak Chaloemtiarana
[102] *Portaits of Thia Politics*; Jenton K. Ray

Pridi's own courageous contribution was generously acknowledged by the Supreme Allied Commander, South-East Asia Command, Lord Louis Mountbatten, himself a man whose own courage as a fighting officer had been tested in battle. Pridi's stand for freedom was an example of great moral courage, both in the face of a cruel enemy and in the teeth of political opposition within his own country. His example and leadership legitimised the brave efforts made by the young men of the Seri Thai to work with foreign powers for the freedom of their nation. It was with sadness that the Allies saw the downfall of Pridi, a sadness well reflected in the dedication of a book by amateur soldier and professional diplomat, Sir Andrew Gilchrist, when he referred to the ex-Regent as *"long a sick and embittered exile in China"* and hoping that he would *"remember the days when (we) trusted him with the lives of our friends"*.[103] Not all great men make good politicians. Perhaps it is because they are too honest. Pridi became an admirer of the highly effective British socialist prime minister, Clement Attlee, and even more so of his brilliant party secretary, Harold Laski. Laski never became a successful politician and Attlee was later to say about Laski, *"He never quite got the hang of it"*. Perhaps that is what should be said, with regret, about Pridi's political leadership.

What of Phibun and the Seri Thai? At his trial as an alleged war criminal, Phibun argued that his move of the Army into the Shan States was designed to give him the opportunity to make contact with the Allies through the Chinese and late in the conflict such contact was indeed attempted.[104] On fifth of February 1944 Lieut-General Netr Khemayothin, at Phibun's behest, made contact with the Chinese 93rd Division. On second of April, Netr and Phibun's Thai delegation had crossed the River Lum into China for a meeting with the 93rd Division commander, General Lu Wi Eng. The meeting led to a concept that the Chinese would work with British troops to meet up with elements of the Thai Army in north-west Thailand. In the meantime, the Thais had taken the opportunity to explain to the Chinese what they considered to be the necessity of their co-operating with the Japanese and their intention to support the Allied cause at a later date. They had asked that the British and American governments

---

[103] *Bangkok Top Secret*; Sir Andrew Gilchrist
[104] *US-Thailand Diplomatic Relations during World War II*; Sethachuay Vivat; p237 and US archives OSS file XL 24260

be informed. A meeting scheduled for the first of August, to which the British were to be invited, was cancelled. It was too late for Phibun who had by then been ousted. Was there a likelihood of success? The answer must be in the negative as, in 1944, Kuomintang China saw this part of the world as being its own sphere of influence. It would not at that time have welcomed a British incursion that would have separated it from possible southwards expansion.[105]

The Lady La-iad asserts that Phibun and the Army were putting into effect Thailand's first underground movement of the war years. *"It included sending the Thais to establish contact with the Chinese and Indians, and through them to the Americans and English. It was unfortunate, however, that the existence of the whole gigantic movement was not later reported in detail to the public. The existence of this movement, preceding the Free Thai Movement, launched under Pridi's leadership towards the end of the war, was known to the Allies. The fact that they chose not to acknowledge it remains a small mystery. ...it constitutes indisputable evidence that the Phibun government had no intention whatsoever of aligning itself with Japan — militarily or politically"*.[106] That seems to be taking wifely devotion a little too far. Phibun, if only out of opportunism, had certainly thrown in his lot with Japan, had declared war upon the Allies, had given the Japanese economic and financial support, and had done nothing to hinder the Japanese war effort. It was only when the pendulum started its backward swing that he saw the error of his earlier judgement. He clearly backed a wrong horse at the beginning of a two-horse race and hastily tried to cover himself by backing the other, but too late. Yet against this view, it has to be said that he could have broken the Seri Thai movement if he had set his heart on so doing.

It is not unreasonable to deduce that a key figure in the whole of the Seri Thai story was Lieut-General Adun Dejcharas. Insufficient credit seems to have accrued to him. As a deputy prime minister and head of the Thai police, he also had the power to make or break the Seri Thai. He gave the impression to some of the young Seri Thai in his daytime custody that his preference was to lead the Seri Thai

---

[105] Discussions with Major-General Chatichai Choonhavan, London, 1 July 1991
[106] *Portraits of Thai Politics*; Jenton K. Ray; p203

himself, not to be responsible either to Phibun or to Pridi. He was
seen by his own junior officers as a very correct soldier of high
integrity, but cautious. He was seen by his contemporary and
colleague, Thawee, as *"something of a Gestapo chief"*.[107] It is true
that he controlled the country's secret police, the *santiban*, but its
activities were not of the Nazi kind. He had been with the military
element of the 1932 coup d'état group, working closely with Phibun.
He was Phibun's military classmate and a firm friend. Phibun had
appointed him to head the police force and in August 1941 had made
him a deputy prime minister. While he protected the young men of the
Seri Thai from the Japanese and fed them with information from his
police network, he also ensured that nothing was done to harm the
nation in general and Phibun in particular. He was not always in
agreement with Phibun. When, in April 1944, Phibun had suggested
to Adun that he, Phibun, should go to Chungking to meet Chiang
Kai-shek and offer the services of Thai forces to the Allied cause,
Adun not only pointed out to him that it was already too late for such
a mission but also refused to go in his place. He advised his prime
minister that in view of his past actions, he would not be trusted by
any of the Allies and that such a visit might have the most unfortunate
effect of disturbing 'the sleeping giant', and bring it down upon
Thailand.[108] Within the Seri Thai movement itself, Adun was the
natural focus for the military element, while Pridi held that role for
the civilian element and especially for those with left-wing tendencies.
Adun was a man who, with little thought for publicity or
self-glorification, played the major role in war-time in the practical
protection of Thailand's liberty.

   While essentially a man of caution, Lieut-General Adun was also a
man of sanity, a man who later, unfortunately, at a critical moment in
his life in November 1947, hesitated out of loyalty to his long-time
Army friend, Phibun. For some days in late 1947 he was of a mind to
strike out for the premiership. Had he done so, he would have had
Pridi's backing. He had then felt tempted to join the coup group but,
in the end, he backed away from both, constrained by his sense of
duty to the Army as a whole. As commander-in-chief of the Army he
did not take adequate steps to prevent the coup when it was within his
power so to do. He chose not to shed blood but in so choosing he

---

[107] *Portraits of Thai Politics*; Jenton K. Ray
[108] *Pridi Banomyong*; Vichtvong na Pombhejara; pp211/2

unwittingly allowed a fragile democracy to be stamped out for decades. At this moment of truth, his loyalty was to the Army and his fellow 1932 coup colleague, Phibun.

After the 1947 coup, Adun retired as commander-in-chief of the Army and was appointed by Khuang to the Regency Council. In this appointment he played no further active role in Thai politics. He withdrew to his house at police headquarters and until his death he shunned any form of public comment. He had played out his important role with moderation and with humanity.

CHAPTER THREE
The Unsettled Years

Government in Thailand in the years immediately following the Second World War was a not a matter of competing political parties but of competing political cliques. Each clique, usually with some element of military support, scrambled for power and when in power set about enriching itself and its friends. The parameters of its enrichment were set principally by the power of other cliques. In parallel with this scramble the Chinese element of society, essentially the trading arm and the wealth providers for the country, lived in tolerance with changing governments. Each element guarded and endeavoured to enlarge its own slice of the national cake. Each would look after the other, at a price. It was a pattern which, apart from an occasional oasis of effort by meritorious citizens, would continue for decades.

There was in Thailand, as frequently elsewhere in the post-war world, a lust for power and with it the fulfilment of greed. Its continuation was well demonstrated as late as the end of 1990 when concern was being expressed over the need for the government to ensure the fostering of the economic boom. Doubt was expressed over the appointment of a specific government minister, who was described as *"generally viewed as a Thai politician in the traditional mould, putting personal, political, and party concerns first".*[109] In the period 1947 to 1957 two powerful politico-economic cliques emerged. One, the Soi Rajakru clique (possibly 'clan' is a better description) was based on the police and headed by Phao Sriyanon, his father-in-law, Phin Choonhavan, and the latter's other sons-in-law and family friends. The other, the Sisao Deves clique, was Army-based and led by Sarit Thanarat. The names of the clans had no special significance, merely indicating residential connections in Bangkok. The clans lived mostly in harmony when there were enough goodies to go around, but quarrels arose from time to time over the most sought-after of all commodities — opium.

Once the dust of the 1947 coup had settled there arose the question of a new constitution and particularly one which would give maximum

---

[109] *Far Eastern Economic Review*; 27 December 1990

advantage to the organising group. Plans for this had already been laid and a rough draft prepared which, because of its hiding place in the days before the coup took place, came to be known as the 'water jar' constitution. *Inter alia*, the new provisional draft allowed the absent King to dismiss any specific member of the Cabinet or the Cabinet as a whole. It also gave to the King the right to appoint senators. With these rights also went a new constraint upon the King himself, with the introduction of an Army appointed advisory body or King's Council. Whilst the plotters assumed that Phibun would naturally become the new prime minister, there were reservations on how the Allied powers, and America in particular, would react. It was determined that the time was not yet ripe for his return to ultimate power and he was re-appointed commander-in-chief of the Army. Khuang was brought back temporarily as prime minister. Before accepting the appointment, Khuang extracted a personal assurance from Phibun that he, Khuang, would be supported by the military and it was on the express understanding of non-interference that he agreed to take up the post.

Outside Thailand, the legality of a government so formed was questioned but, despite this, Khuang was able to persuade sufficient men of prominence to join him. From Phibun he received a letter handing over powers to him from the 1947 group.[110] From the point of view of the western powers, it was expedient that the known anti-communism of the powerful military backing group was sufficient to legitimise it. A blind eye was turned to the method of achievement of power. Britain's feelings towards Thailand and the almost immediate acceptance of the controlling military regime by America, were mixed. It saw in American pressure an anxiety to secure Japan as an independent state and with it, establish a bulwark in South-East Asia against the spread of Soviet influence, in which Thailand might play a role. It was a bitter-sweet attitude of an acceptance of wartime events, tainted with the disdain in which it held Phibun whom it saw as an opportunist running with any power in the ascendant. Britain had a very definite preference for Khuang, seeing in him the possibility of a truly democratic leader.

An early concern of the 1947 group was to set out in some detail for American consumption why the coup itself had been necessary. An

---

[110] *US Foreign Policy and Thai Military Rule 1947–1977*; Surachart Bamrungsuk; pp38/9

explanation to the American ambassador alone was thought not to be sufficient, and so a delegation was despatched to Washington, led by a pre-war Thai diplomat. In a supporting role was Major Chatichai Choonhavan. Chatichai was in fact on his way to spend the following year at the US Armored School,[111] but his presence in the delegation was significant when taking into account his active behind-the-scenes role in the coup itself.

Seeking to strengthen its position at home, the 1947 group had Sarit Thanarat appointed to command the 1st Infantry Regiment and given overall responsibility for law and order in the Bangkok and Central Plains area. It also proposed to have Phao appointed as deputy director-general of police and head of the Crime Suppression Squad. The proposal brought from the minister of the interior, Lieut-General Sinat, a prominent Seri Thai, the celebrated comment that a person of Phao's qualifications was not even suitable to be a patrolman, let alone a deputy police chief.[112] It was not a remark that Phao would either forget or forgive. He was appointed and he set about establishing his police power base. He made early arrests including Thamrong's finance minister and some of the minister's colleagues. Another in his sights was his own superior, Sinat.

On twenty-ninth of January 1948, elections were held for the lower house of the National Assembly and, despite intimidatory tactics on the part of the Phin-Phao clan, the Democratic party won a majority of seats. Khuang was again called upon to form a government. There were few Cabinet changes and to improve relationships with the 1947 group, Khuang invited Phin to join his Cabinet. There was a notable omission, Sinat. Phin declined to join as he was more concerned with the affairs of the 1947 group than day-to-day politics. He was also concerned with the military activities of a rival, Kat Katsongkhram. Khuang was again successful in attracting men of substance and integrity to his Cabinet, and the American ambassador, Edward Stanton, referred to its containing *"some of the most intelligent, capable, and honest men to be found in the Kingdom".*[113]

Khuang's third government lasted only a few weeks. The military demanded large sums of money for its support and Khuang had no

---

[111] Discussions with Major-General Chatichai Choonhavan, 1 July 1991

[112] *The Sarit Regime*; Thak Chaloemitiarana; pp48/518 and *Thailand and the Fall of Singapore* Nigel J. Brailey; p149

[113] *Thailand and the fall of Singapore*; Nigel J. Brailey; p148

honest way of providing it. On sixth of April 1948, at the instigation of Phin, Phao, and Sarit, four Army colonels called upon Khuang and demanded the resignation of his government.[114] Police-Colonel Bangchongsak, a Seri Thai, strongly advised Khuang to resist the demand and offered the services of eight hundred loyal police officers.[115] Later in the day Phin himself, with Kat Katsongkhram, called to reinforce the demand. Khuang resigned. On eighth of April, Phibun once more became prime minister. The Lady La-iad wrote *".... having sworn off politics with justifiable bitterness ....* (Phibun was) ... *borne into the mêlée by the surging tide of circumstances .... It was the artistry of these men (Phin, Phao, and Sarit) that whirled him back into the prime minister's office".*[116] Phin became commander-in-chief of the Thai Army and Kat Katsongkhram became his deputy-commander.

Khuang left office, and with him went any immediate hope of a democratic government. His departure was Thailand's loss. A survivor of a long and perilous four-month withdrawal from Cambodian territories under his father's command early in the century, Khuang had grown up to become a discontented civil servant under the absolute monarchy. Despite being of royal blood he was, at the testing time, loyal to his friends of the Association of Siamese Students in France rather than the crown. Not entirely trusted by other members of be Association as it developed its early strategy, he later became accepted and was given a key role in the 1932 coup. In the early days of confrontation in the newly formed National Assembly, he was instrumental in nursing the fragile democracy. It was Khuang who opposed the government of the day, accusing the prime minister of attempting to take dictatorial powers while he himself claimed supreme powers for the Assembly. In the writings of Thai history there are frequent references to him being nicknamed 'the joker'. They arise from his habit of quick-witted responses to questions, often giving a false impression of flippancy. The 'joker' references derogate a highly competent man who, in practice, made a substantial contribution to democratic political development in Thailand, both in government and in opposition. His draft constitution which would come into force in 1949 was a major step towards a hoped-for

---

[114] Announcement of the House of the Prime Minister, 6 April 1948
[115] Cremation memorial book of Khuang Aphaiwon
[116] *Portraits of Thai Politics*; Jenton K. Ray; pp211/3

democracy. In less brutal circumstances he might well have become a long-serving prime minister, indeed he might still be properly considered as the outstanding democrat of his day.

The Lady La-iad has insisted that Phibun was merely a titular head of the group for a considerable time after the November coup.[117] Phibun certainly appears initially in a modest role, more interested in deliberately fostering the careers of both Phao and Sarit. He regarded both as firm supporters of his regime while at the same time, in order to preserve his own position, he maintained competition between them. As he once more took over the prime ministerial role he received early recognition by Western powers, but encountered a growing fear of the spread of communism. With the success of Mao Zedong spreading throughout China, careful consideration had to be given to the Chinese element within Thailand. Many Chinese had been there for generations. Many had integrated within the Thai civilisation to the extent that it was difficult to say who exactly was Chinese and who was pure Thai. Even today it is not necessary to scratch a Thai too deeply before reaching a Chinese. Phibun's principal supporter, Phin, was closely involved with the Chinese society, and his family roots were deeply embedded in their native land. The Thais feared for their own national identity. In a population of about 18.1 million there were between 3.5 and 5 million Chinese, most of whom had come from the Hainan and Swatow areas. Many had arrived as recently as 1946 and 1947, fleeing from the communist armies, and altogether they dominated the Thai commercial world. It was not a problem that Phibun could ignore, founded as his regime was on greed and jealousy. In a statute deliberately aimed at both curbing the power of the Chinese and encouraging them to take up Thai nationality, he introduced the limitation of land ownership to Thai nationals.[118] He had to play his hand carefully as an allied problem was the need for foreign investment and the modernisation of the Thai economy. The attitude he adopted towards the Chinese and the attitude of the Chinese themselves was critical if other nationals were to be persuaded to invest.

Within his April 1948 Cabinet, Phibun was able to attract a number of notable figures from the outgoing Khuang government together with earlier ministers who were essentially pro-royalist. But

[117] *Portraits of Thai Politics*; Jenton K. Ray
[118] *Far Eastern Economic Review*; February 16 1949

many of the more distinguished citizens resigned their appointments after only a short period in office and gradually it was the original supporters of the 1947 coup who became the centre of power in the government.

In 1948, the Thai government was seen externally to be politically unstable through uncertainty, indecision, and an inability to control cross-border smuggling. It also lacked efficient administration; even published figures for the production of its principal crop, rice, bore no relation whatsoever to actual output.[119] This did not deter America, which had its eye not only on South-East Asian politics but also on possible commercial gain. There was a considerable increase in trade between America and Thailand. Within a month of the coup, America had not only recognised Phibun but also received from its embassy in Bangkok a request for permission to enter immediately into arms deals with the Thai military before British firms arrived.[120]

The path of the 1947 group was not straightforward. In October 1948, there was an attempted counter-coup, this time principally by members of the Army general staff. It was timed to coincide with the wedding reception of the commander of the 1st Infantry Division, the recently promoted Lieut-General Sarit. The organisers could safely anticipate that most senior officers as well as a number of members of the Cabinet would be present. The plot was badly handled and failed. Nineteen plotters were initially indicted and later there was to be added the redoubtable Major-General Netr Khemayothin, an old friend of Phibun. He had been his representative in wartime discussions with the 93rd Chinese Division and was also associated with the Seri Thai. Thawee had also been asked to join and was promised that he would be made prime minister. Thawee, a man of both caution and integrity, wisely held back saying that he would only accept such a post at the specific invitation of the National Assembly. Phao arrested some twenty military officers including his former minister, Sinat, and rival senior police officer, CID chief Banchongsak Chippensuk. There was a suspicion that a number of old scores were being settled. Thawee himself was arrested but released after questioning by Phao. As further information came to light Thawee was re-arrested and imprisoned for a month, an act which he believed to be in revenge for

---

[119] *Far Eastern Economic Review*; 31 March 1948
[120] *The US and the Coming of the Coup of 1947 in Siam*; Thanet Aphornsuvan/JSS; p208, citing NADD telegram of 11 December 1947

the fact that he, Thawee, had personally put Phibun under arrest for war crimes. Thawee also stated later that he believed that Phao had given Phibun an undertaking to deal with him. Three police officers had been detailed to find him and shoot him. In fear, he fled to Penang where he stayed until 1957, after Phibun and Phao had been ousted. During his time in Penang, Thawee was visited by Phao with blandishments of forgiveness if he were to return to Bangkok. Thawee has asserted that Phao, in a drunken moment, admitted that he had come on behalf of Phibun to ensure Thawee's return,[121] a return which would not have been for Thawee's benefit.

As deputy-director of police, Phao ran the prosecution of the counter-coup group. He had already become recognised not only as one of the more powerful members of the 1947 group but also as a ruthless pursuer of personal interest. In addition to the prosecution itself, he was given the right of review over the case, a prospect which few of the defendants could have relished. Nevertheless, the prison sentences imposed by the court were not excessive and many defendants were released. Thawee remained in Penang; ex-Seri Thai Banchongsak was dismissed from police service.[122]

Trouble from a different source appeared on the 1947 group's horizon. One time Seri Thai activists, who were now National Assembly members and had strong connections with North-East Thailand, 'Isan', were suspected of attempting the creation of an independent state. In February 1948 one of its more prominent members, Tim Phuriphat, was arrested and was gaoled until 1950. Later four other Isan leaders, Thong-in Phuriphat, Thawin Udon, Tiang Sirikhan (all three of whom were senior Seri Thai), and Fong Sittitham were accused of attempting to organise an autonomous state of Isan which was to become part of the 'Federated States of the Golden Peninsula.' All were arrested but later released.[123] Whilst some saw these attempts as isolated and spontaneous, the government suspected a connection with the activities of the exiled Pridi.

In February 1949, Pridi himself appeared again on the scene when, with a number of members of the Seri Thai and the Navy, he staged a counter-coup — the 'Palace Rebellion'. The choice of timing appears either to have been odd or perhaps just unfortunate as from

---

[121] *Portraits of Thai Politics*; Jenton K. Ray; p131
[122] *Thailand and the Fall of Singapore*; Nigel J. Brailey; p151
[123] *The Sarit Regime*; Thak Chaloemtiarana; p61

twenty-third of February the military was indulging in a live ammunition exercise. On twenty-sixth of February, Pridi and friends, using wartime Seri Thai arms, took over Thammasat University as a headquarters and captured a radio station. A first announcement, made just before midnight on twenty-sixth of February, was that the leaders of the 1947 group, Phin, Kat and Phao, were sacked and that Phibun had been replaced as prime minister by Direk Jayanama. Senior naval officers were appointed by Pridi to the Ministry of Defence and the Supreme Military Command. The announcement was premature. It alerted the government and the military, in particular Sarit, to what was afoot, thus allowing action to be taken to forestall it. A force led by Pridi's close associate, Captain Wacharachai, captured the empty Grand Palace, a sound psychological move. Simultaneous uprisings in Isan however came to naught and a force of marines which was to reinforce the attack found itself stranded downstream by a miscalculated low tide.[124]

Sarit moved fast. He forced the Palace entrance with an armoured vehicle mounted with a 40 mm gun. His élite troops of the 1st Regiment stormed in to overcome the rebels. The remnants of Pridi's force were routed. Phao's police made numerous arrests, aimed at dealing once and for all with Seri Thai dissidents. The rebellion was crushed and both Sarit and Phao had moved into even stronger positions within the government. Phao was promoted to director-general of police.

On third of March, four Seri Thai leaders were murdered by elements of Phao's police force while being transferred from one prison to another. His one-time rival, ex-CID chief Banchongsak, was murdered in his own home. Phone Indarathat, the courageous pioneer from Celi, was another victim.[125] Pridi wandered around Bangkok for some five months before returning to China. He had been responsible for the bloodiest of all of the coups and attempted coups up to that time and he had reached the end of the political road. His 1932 aspirations, together with his Seri Thai rejuvenation, had come to nothing. Until his death on second of May 1983 he would live in exile. His first chosen destination of China served only to convince the

---

[124] *The Sarit Regime*; Thak Chaloemtiarana; p63
[125] Discussions with Pisoot Sudasna na Ayutthaya, 1987 to 1993

military of its earlier belief that, at heart, he was a communist. Some still maintain that belief to this day.[126]
Viewed from the British Embassy he was not a communist. A social democrat might have been a better description. He was respected by foreign governments and for a time early after the Second World War there was great hope that he, with Khuang, would be the saviours of democracy in Thailand. In their so becoming, it was hoped that they would displace or at least constrain the military. Pridi was certainly held in high esteem by the British government but at its Bangkok embassy there were grave doubts that there had been adequate backing for him from London. Perhaps the best judgement of his position was his own. *"All my knowledge was book knowledge. I did not take into account human elements as much as I should have. ....When I had power, I had no experience, and when I had experience, I had no power".*[127]

On nineteenth of July 1949, neighbouring Laos was in the news with the signature in Paris of the Franco-Lao Convention under which Laos became a political entity and autonomous within French Indochina. It was not the wish of all the population of that land-locked state and there was resistance in the north. The 'Red Prince', Prince Souphannouvong, fought the settlement and was wounded in a rebellious action against the French. He was taken to Bangkok, and after recovery he returned to the northern provinces of Laos where he later formed and led a left-wing guerilla force which came to be known as the Pathet Lao ('the Lao people').

Trouble from one of its own members, Kat Katsongkhram, was the next item on the 1947 group agenda. Having had himself promoted Lieut-General and deputy commander-in-chief of the Army, he was not content to follow meekly the patterns set by the group. He set out to build his own sphere of influence among the military. Threats of resignations from offended ministers did not deter him but matters were brought to a head when he was the cause of the resignation of a

---

[126] Discussions with Major-General Chatichai Choonhavan, 1 July 1991
[127] *The Balancing Act*; Joseph H. Wright jnr; p186 citing Anthony Paul, *Pridi through a Looking-glass*

minister of finance after Kat had used a large sum of foreign currency for improper entertainment of Army personnel. On twenty-seventh of January 1950, Kat was arrested by Phao in the office of the prime minister, threatened with a charge of treason, and removed quickly to Hong Kong. In his absence he was formally indicted for rebellion. After a year's absence he decided to return to face the charge, but discretion on the part of all concerned prevailed. He was allowed to retire from the political and military scene.[128]

The Phin/Phao clan was now the principal power behind a nominal head, the prime minister, Phibun. Chatichai was appointed assistant military attaché in Washington. In November 1944 he had married the dynamic and influential Boonruen, a niece of the Princess Mother, who had spent many years with the Royal Family in Switzerland. Boonruen was held in high favour by the Royal Family and Chatichai was moving into a position of potential leadership. But waiting in the wings was Lieut-General Sarit.

Rivalry between the Army and the Navy was of long standing. The Thai Navy was essentially the 'Royal' Navy in all senses of the word and among its commanders over the years, it could count one king and many princes of the blood. It was the service of the aristocracy and the élite. The Navy had given some support during the 1932 coup d'état and in wartime it had thrown in its lot with Pridi and the Seri Thai. Its half-hearted support of Pridi in the 1949 'Palace Rebellion' had lost it some of its senior officers. As a result, a radical element had moved into middle ranks, made up of men who were intent on restoring the Navy's lost prestige.

This was the position in mid-1951 when on twenty-sixth of June the prime minister attended the formal transfer of the dredger *Manhattan*, a gift to Thailand from America. Under the very noses of the corps of international diplomats a naval officer, Lieut-Commander Manas Charupha, with a group of armed Navy men, arrested Phibun. Accounts of the incident vary, but that of a reliable and neutral American journalist is of a prime minister who looked death in the face with both courage and dignity. The religious ceremony completed, Phibun was met by the naval party with automatic weapons trained on him. Told of his arrest, he ordered others aside and sauntered down the gangway to another armed naval squad, waving

---

[128] *The Sarit Regime*; Thak Chaloemitiarana; p36, and discussions with Pisoot Sudasna na Ayutthaya 1987 to 1993

goodbye to shocked diplomatic corps dignitaries, many of whom were flat on their faces on the dredger. He walked slowly along the length of the ceremonial compound to where he was escorted aboard a Navy-owned infantry landing craft and taken to the Royal Thai Navy's flagship the *Sri Ayutthaya*.[129] Meanwhile the Navy coup leader, Captain Anon Puntarikapha, issued orders for naval units to converge on Bangkok and stand by for orders from the Navy's commander-in-chief.

The Navy rebels had miscalculated badly. They had assumed that with the capture of Phibun the government would crumble within a few days, an assumption which proved to be entirely false. They had put a value on the life of Phibun at a level much higher than that perceived by the military and police commanders, Sarit and Phao. They had failed to realise that if in any fighting Phibun was inadvertently killed, either Sarit or, more likely, one of the Phin/Phao clan would be only too happy to succeed. In the eyes of the clan, Phibun was clearly expendable, a conclusion which both he himself and the Lady La-iad subsequently reached. Naval establishments were quickly routed by the two hatchet-men, Sarit and Phao, and while Phibun was still held prisoner aboard the *Sri Ayutthaya* the Air Force, under Air Chief Marshal Fuen Ronnaphakat bombed and sank it. According to the Lady La-iad, Phibun was in the washroom when a bomb tore through his sleeping quarters but *"miraculously failed to burst until it had fallen all the way through to the engine room below"*. The bomb also damaged the magazine in the process, and the *Sri Ayutthaya* sank immediately.[130] At six o'clock on the night of thirtieth of June, Thailand's prime minister was obliged to dive overboard and swim to the riverbank to save himself. He was met by loyal Navy men and escorted to Government House. All resistance was mopped up and the casualty list was given as at least sixty-eight killed with eleven hundred wounded.

When asked who could have had the authority to give an order which resulted in the bombing by the Air Force of a warship with the prime minister on board, Chatichai said that he always believed it was something the Air Force did of its own volition. *"It was a most extraordinary incident. The artillery and armoured units played very*

---

[129] *From Siam to Thailand*; Jorges Orgibet; pp62/3
[130] *Portraits of Thai Politics*; Jenton R. Ray; pp213/4

little part in the affair. In an incident of this nature it is the infantry and the police which are the effective arms".[131]

Indeed it was a most extraordinary incident. The *Sri Ayutthaya*, pride of the Thai Navy, was a 2,200-ton gunboat, built in Japan during 1936/8. It did not provide any advantage to the plotters as at that particular time it was out of service and undergoing repair.[132] It seems highly improbable that a senior air force or army commander would not have been in possession of intelligence reports which covered the state of readiness of such an important unit of national defence. Thus both commanders should have known that it posed no threat to either of them and through them, to the government. So why bomb it? To say the least, it would be strange if an air force commander of any nation took it solely upon himself to bomb and sink the nation's flagship — and with the nation's prime minister on board. An air force commander does not adopt such tactics unless of course he is commanded to do so by someone with the necessary authority. Then who authorised it? With its dictatorial prime minister on board the target ship itself, no one in the Thai government formally had such authority. It was unlikely that Sarit called for the bombing. For such an act, as an army commander, he would have turned for authority to his commander-in-chief. This leaves only the commander-in-chief himself, Phin, or in these particular circumstances the effective commander of the civil paramilitary arm, the police, Phin's son-in-law, Phao. Some of an age to remember the incident clearly and responsibly, and without the family connections such as Chatichai's, believe that it must have been Phao, who was much more ruthless and ambitious than Sarit at that stage of the development of the coup and who had sufficient backing to grab succession.

The *Manhattan* incident was looked upon in retrospect not only as a naval revenge for earlier slightings and for the hostility it encountered from Phibun and Phao, but also partly in support of the ex-members of the Scri Thai in general and Pridi in particular. It was also seen as a protest against the extra-military activities of the Phin-Phao clan which Phibun was unwilling or unable to restrain.

Phibun immediately took command of his government and the 1947 group savaged the Navy. It was cut back to bare essentials and banned from any jurisdiction over shore territory. All officers

---

[131] Discussions with Major-General Chatical Choonhavan, 1 July 1991

[132] *Portraits of Thai Politics*; Jenton K. Ray; p213

suspected of implication in the *Manhattan* affair were dismissed and the naval headquarters was moved from Thonburi out to Samutprakan. Its battleship station was moved out of the Chao Phraya river at Bangkok to the Sattahip base. The naval air wing was transferred to the Air Force. The Army, as well as taking over all dismantled naval armament, even added a final insult by taking over its band. The marines were re-organised almost out of sight, and surplus naval manpower was distributed among the police, Army, and Air Force. In the process, the Army virtually destroyed its traditional competitor for power — the Navy. But in so doing it had created a new rival for that power. The police had become much stronger under Phao.

The next institution to be dealt with by the 1947 group was the National Assembly. The 1949 constitution, drafted principally by Khuang, prevented Army officers from becoming members of the National Assembly and, even more important, from being members of the Cabinet. However the existence of the National Assembly was an asset when dealing with America and with European powers, and one which could not lightly be shed. There were, nominally, political parties although they carried little power and by nature were loose associations used on a temporary basis for self-interest, both financial and political. Reshuffles of support and the splintering of parties were not infrequent. In July 1949 the Democrat Party had called for an Assembly vote of no-confidence in Phibun's coalition government, seeking to attract as much opposition as possible, and particularly so from wayward members of its own party who were from time to time inclined to back the prime minister, rather than their own party. With the vote in the balance and the Democrats wavering, Phao appeared in the Assembly. Nine Democrats immediately decided to vote with the government and against their own party, thus leaving the government to carry the day. The turncoat members might have recalled that it was less than four months since the police murder of the four Isan MPs.[133]

Army commander-in-chief Phin, director-general of the police Phao, commander of the 1st Army Sarit, and the Air Force commander-in-chief Fuen Ronnaphakat were not directly involved in the proceedings of the National Assembly, but despite this they had strong influence on the pattern of government. In time they became irked by the growing pressure from Isan Assembly members

---

[133] *The Sarit Regime*; Thak Chaloemtiarana

demanding funds and special consideration for the north-east of the country. The irritation was increased by a parliamentary enquiry into the *Manhattan* affair and allegations of harshness and over-reaction. Phibun declared that harshness had been necessary because of an alleged communist plot to take over the government of the country, always a useful ploy.

The 1947 group's frustration over its lack of control of the National Assembly came to a head on twenty-ninth of November 1951, when Phao broadcast to the nation. He suspended the National Assembly, banned political parties, and replaced Khuang's 1949 Constitution by that of the 1932. So-called reasons given by proclamation for the new coup, which others would see merely as excuses, included international threats of communism, infiltration of the National Assembly and the Cabinet by communists, and the need to reintroduce the 1932 Constitution to enable firmer government.[134] The claim was made, as it had been four years earlier, in the name of *"patriots who wanted to preserve the ideals of Nation, Religion, the House of Chakri, and Constitutionalism"*.[135]

Quasi-justification was thus made for other acts which would follow, and the coup was carefully timed for the 1932 Constitution to be in place before the return of King Bhumibol from Switzerland. It is inconceivable that it was sheer coincidence that the proclamation was made only a few days before the King's return. The King was not only on his way by sea, but at the time of the announcement, en route between Singapore and Bangkok. Thus he arrived, bound by the dictatorial 1932 Constitution with its greater freedom of powers for the military. Political meetings were banned. There had been a fear that the old royalist-inclined Senate might urge the King to use the prerogative of dismissal stipulated in the 1949 Constitution. The change to the 1932 Constitution prevented this.

Sarit and Phao issued a joint statement, claiming to have planned this 'silent' or 'radio' coup without Phibun's knowledge to avoid delay and that this joint effort would be followed by their standing together in the future. Phin also claimed to be in charge of this coup.[136] A temporary executive committee was established of three members

---

[134] Announcement in the *Royal Thai Government Gazette*, Special Edition vol. LXVIII (part 71 of 30 Nov, 1951)
[135] *Thailand and the Fall of Singapore*; Nigel J. Brailey; p161
[136] *Thailand and the Fall of Singapore*; Nigel J. Brailey; pp161/2

from each of the Army, Air Force and Navy. Its principal power came from the Army representation by Phin, as its chairman, and Sarit. Fuen was one of the representatives of the Air Force. Its principal enforcing officer was Phao who, as director-general of police, was made responsible for internal law and order. He was to be *"sole guardian of the peace, strictly to preserve peace throughout the entire Kingdom"*,[137] a responsibility which led to a McCarthy-like witch-hunt throughout the land.

With the greater freedom of political appointment permitted by the re-introduction of the 1932 Constitution, the 1947 group leaders were brought into the Cabinet. Phin became a deputy prime minister. Sarit became deputy minister of defence, but none of his principal supporters gained office. Phao became deputy minister of the interior and Fuen became minister of communications. Phin's other sons-in-law also became deputy ministers of communications, commerce, and agriculture. All of the new ministers retained their military ranks and appointments. The 1947 group appointed a new Senate and permitted elections for the lower house. As parties *per se* were banned, the election was of individual members, allowing the group to finance numerous candidates to win support. Phin and Phao became the effective leaders and the power brokers with Phibun as their nominal head of government. Sarit had also moved into the forefront of Thai political affairs.

In parallel with these developments over the period 1947 to 1951, America was evolving a policy for South-East Asia in general and for Thailand in particular. With the fall of the Kuomintang government in China, America had dropped its neutralism and moved steadily to obsessive anti-communism. Its concern was expressed in a national security paper. *"It is important to United States security interests that all practicable measures be taken to prevent further communist expansion in Southeast Asia. Indochina is a key area of Southeast Asia and is under immediate threat. The neighbouring countries of Thailand and Burma could be expected to fall under communist-dominated governments. The balance of Southeast Asia would then be in grave*

---

[137] Announcement in the *Royal Thai Government Gazette*, Special Edition vol. LXVIII (part 71 of 30 Nov, 1951)

hazard." [138] In January 1950 both the Chinese and then the USSR governments recognised the communist Ho Chi Minh regime in Vietnam. In February 1950, America and Britain reacted by recognising the Bao Dai regime. In December of that same year America signed a Mutual Defence Assistance Agreement with France, Vietnam, Cambodia, and Laos for aid to the three South-East Asian countries and particularly for equipping a Vietnamese national army under French command. It was quite an extraordinary move in view of American strident anti-colonialism. All American ambassadors to eastern Asian nations were called to confer and in February 1950 they met in Bangkok under the chairmanship of the President's ambassador-at-large, Phillip C. Jessup. The Washington attitude towards communism at that time was highly acceptable to Phibun. To the Thai prime minister, any dissident or radical movement opposed to the thinking of his government must be communist inspired. Thus the Thai regime fitted neatly into American concepts and became significant in its strategy for South-East Asia. Earlier decisions not to send arms to Thailand following requests in 1947/48 were now reversed as Thailand fell naturally into an area described as the 'General Area of China'. [139] The Bangkok meeting did not go unnoticed in Beijing, from where it provoked a hostile radio attack on the Phibun regime.

Phibun found no difficulty in quickly validating the new trust. In July, only weeks after the outbreak of the Korean war, he sent four thousand combat troops to support the mainly American forces in South Korea. Thai troops were to be found fighting beside British Commonwealth forces and with them, first as a cavalry commander, went Major Chatichai. Later he became the Thai liaison officer to General Douglas MacArthur, both in the field and in Tokyo. In October 1950, Phibun followed up the provision of troops with two corvettes, the 'Prasae' and the 'Bangpakong' and the troop transport 'Sichang'. [140] Subsequently he provided forty thousand tons of rice for Korean refugee relief. The American response to his initial commitment was immediate. At the end of July it announced that it

---

[138] National Security Paper No. 64, subsequently published in the 1971 Pentagon Papers, Vol. 1, pp361/2, cited in US *Foreign Policy and Thai Military Rule 1947-1977*; Surachart Bamrungsuk; p43

[139] *US Foreign Policy and Thai Military Rule 1947-1977*; Surachart Bamrungsuk; pp42/46

[140] *The Korean War*; Max Hastings; pp445/6

would enter into a military agreement with Thailand and was prepared to provide equipment for the Thai armed forces. The Agreement Respecting Military Assistance was signed in October that year.[141]

The development of the 1947 coup d'état was now complete. Dissenting interests had been removed and Phibun's position as prime minister was consolidated with power resting in a carefully selected and controlled National Assembly. Law and order was secure in the hands of the competing interests of Phao's heavily armed police and Sarit's Army. But another factor had entered indirectly into the political scales. H.M. King Bhumibol had quietly returned to his Kingdom.

By 1951, America had replaced Britain as the influential power in South-East Asia in general and in Thailand in particular. The short-sightedness of Britain's immediate post-war policy, the inability of the politicians to recognise the national pride in freedom which had been the characteristic of the Seri Thai movement, and most of all the attempted imposition of a burdensome rice agreement had diminished its position of influence. Thailand was an independent sovereign state, to be courted by America in its ideological battle against communism and in pursuit of trade and raw materials.

---

[141] *US Foreign Policy and Thai Military Rule 1947-1977*; Surachart Bamrungsuk; pp46/47

CHAPTER FOUR
Earlier Times

Seen from twenty-five thousand miles out into space, on a day which might be free of clouds, the great land mass of Eurasia would show its mountainous ribs in the form of a long-stemmed flower. The bending stem stretches back from the Hindu Kush to Anatolia and beyond to the Alps. The outline of a budding lotus flower takes its southern shape from the great Himalaya range, swinging round to form a barrier to the north of South-East Asia. Its northern edge is formed from the ranges circling the Gobi, joined to the stem at the Karakoram of Kashmir, beyond Tibet to the mountains of Nan Shan. Perhaps the sacred lotus is not the closest resemblance because the form is more bulbous and more square at the top of its stem. Is it perhaps more like the seed pod of *papaver somniferum*, the opium poppy?

Outside the southern barrier are the populous lands of India, Bangladesh, Burma, and mainland South-East Asia. Down from the Himalaya range above South-East Asia run the jungle-covered foothills, still some three thousand to nine thousand feet above sea level, broken north to south by the deep valleys of powerful rivers. Here flow the Irrawady, the beautiful Salween, and the king of rivers, the Mae-kong, corrupted by western foreigners to Mekong. From Yunnan in southern China and from the Shan mountains, more north to south rivers break through the Shan States and northern Thailand, the Ping, the Wang, the Yom and the Nan, flowing near their sources in gorges thousands of feet deep. In Yunnan it was said of the river system that there were 'six roads to the south'. Now, hydro-electric dams, with their attendant lakes and controlled irrigation, hinder their passage to Thailand's mother river, the Chao Phraya, and onwards to the Gulf of Thailand.

Amid the jungle of the foothills an occasional limestone knife-edge or cone stands clear of the green sea of vegetation. Towers of limestone rise sheer from river beds. In the early morning each mountain seems to be protected by its own cloud with streamers of fog climbing up from the valleys to above the three-thousand-foot contour, where grows the *papaver somniferum*. Here too sprang the legend that the Hmong, the mountain people, tell of a time long ago when they still lived in China. A Hmong leader had a most beautiful daughter but for some reason, although many yearned for her, no one would marry her. As a result, she died of a broken heart. Out of her grave there grew poppy plants and the flowers were like the girl, beautiful and delicate, and people took the seeds to grow them. The seeds were delicious and when the sap was extracted for smoking it eased pain and produced a yearning to smoke again. Men yearned for the sap, the opium, as they yearned for the girl, and since then they have grown the poppy plant wherever they have lived.[142]

For hundreds of years Western adventurers have sought to make their fortunes through the Asian narcotics trade, led by the Portuguese and closely followed by the British East India Company and the French. In the third century AD, Arab traders introduced both Islam and the opium poppy into India and south west China, but poppy cultivation and the resulting opium were almost exclusively for medicinal use. For centuries afterwards, poppy cultivation followed the movement of populations.

Within Asian population movements, the 'Tai' or 'Dai' emerge in Chinese history as the inhabitants of the Southern Kingdom of Nan Chao. They were not of Chinese origin and local legend has the race originating in the valley of the Indus. By 50 AD, the kingdom of Nan Chao occupied the western part of Yunnan around Tali Lake, and eventually expanded to roughly the size of modern Yunnan. It was recorded as being a place of happiness, of good harvests, of prosperity, and of peace but at its gate, in 1253, were the generals of Kublai Khan. With their capture of the city of Tali and conquest of the old independent kingdom of Nan Chao, pressure arose over the next two-hundred years for the southwards movement of the Tai.[143]

The Portuguese arrived in Asia in the sixteenth century and with them came opium smoking. By the seventeenth century the Dutch were pushing opium into Taiwan and parts of mainland China. In the eighteenth century the British East India Company became the first large-scale opium smuggler, forcing its product on an unwilling China and by the nineteenth, all European colonies in South-East Asia had introduced opium dens. European empire-builders sacrificed local

---

[142] *Poppies, Pipes & People;* J. Westermeyer; at p360 there is a similar story
[143] According to Professor Coedes, (described by G. H. Luce in JSS 1958 p214 as 'the greatest living authority on the older history of S.E. Asia'); references are also in JSS 1958 pp123 et seq.

inhabitants to the curse of opium addiction to generate profits upon which such empires were financed. While objections to the traffic were raised by individual officials, morality was outweighed by profit.

The new European military and industrial power allowed small armies to carve out vast territories in South-East Asia for the mother-countries. As the leader in the European industrial revolution, Britain became both the greatest colonial power and the greatest opium merchant. With its conquest at the end of the eighteenth century of large parts of northern India, Britain established a monopoly over poppy cultivation. In China, its purchase of silk had resulted in a drain on the silver it acquired in India and it became essential to find a substitute product sale. Portugal, in a similar predicament, found a suitable answer in tobacco from its Brazilian colony. Britain's answer was Indian opium. By 1767 it was forcing this solution on a reluctant Chinese government. In 1800 the emperor of China for a second time banned opium imports, fearful of the effect upon his subjects. The ban was ignored by the British merchants and from 1839 to 1842, after Chinese officials in Canton had dumped British imports in the harbour, British warships were used to blast the trade into China during the first of the 'Opium Wars'. Opium imports continued, but the emperor refused to legalise the traffic. A second 'Opium War' from 1856 to 1858 forced the Chinese government to legalise its importation, by which time it was estimated that British merchants alone were supplying more than fifteen million addicts.

During the second half of the nineteenth century, Britain and France continued their respective infiltrations of the South-East Asia landmass, resulting in the creation of British Burma and French Indochina. While never colonised, the kingdom of Siam fell within Britain's sphere of influence. The period saw the birth of some of the major Asian cities and with it a huge demand for labour. By the early part of the twentieth century, immigrant labour flooded in from China and by 1910 there were over two hundred thousand Chinese in Bangkok. With the Chinese immigrant came the Chinese addictive habit of opium smoking. Opium dens, provided by colonial powers to meet the addiction of immigrant Chinese, soon involved the indigenous population. State-regulated opium monopolies followed. A consumer market for opium was thus established throughout

South-East Asia and the revenues contributed substantially both to colonial income and to new infrastructure.[144]

Mass opium addiction growth throughout the nineteenth century prompted a rapid expansion of Chinese indigenous production. Poppy fields spread out from their original base in Yunnan and Szechwan throughout the south and into central China. By 1880, Szechwan alone was harvesting annually about ten thousand tons of raw opium. The rapid increase in production in China provided for more than the home market and, by 1883, surpluses were exported to French Tonkin (North Vietnam), Burma, and Siam. The mule caravans, protected by armed guards, were able to make there way along trails through the mountains, crossing the virtually non-existent borders.

It was at this time that the Hmong first began to grow poppies for a cash crop. The Hmong and Yao are both tribes of Chinese origin. Some three thousand years ago, the ancestors of the Hmong lived on the banks of the Yellow River and the tribe has been driven south over the centuries by the pressure from the Chinese races. They were first oppressed by Manchu conquerors and then harassed in the historical process of demographic expansion by the Han Chinese. Eventually the Hmong avoided attempts at genocide by becoming a mountain people.[145] They developed as primary forest swiddeners, first to grow rice, but being forced into high altitude refuge they eventually cultivated the principal crop which could be grown readily at such altitudes, the opium poppy. The Hmong have been identified as an overall ethnic and linguistic stock, and known as such both in anthropological and in Sinological circles. They speak a language of Sino-Tibetan origin. Referred to derogatively as Miao or Meo — savages — there are some six million Hmong spread over south-west China and the south-east Asian mountains. The Yao, or Iu Mien, are traceable back some two thousand five hundred years to central China. Both Hmong and Yao still occupy parts of southern Yunnan as well as being scattered throughout the mountains of South-East Asia. The Lisu, Lahu (or Mussur), and Akha tribes are of Tibetan origin and are more prolific in Yunnan and Burma although some have moved into the north of Thailand and Laos. In the years ahead, the Hmong were

---

[144] *The Politics of Heroin*; Alfred W. McCoy; pp58/63 and p358
[145] For the general anthropological background see a paper *The Mong (Green Miao) and their Language*, by Professor Emeritus at Chulalongkorn University, Thomas. A. Lyman; published by the Siam Society in 1990

to become the cannon-fodder of first the French and then the Americans. They were accepted by those who worked with them as a hard-working, brave, intelligent people and within their natural mountain environment they would have lived contented lives, but history and geography were to condemn them to near extermination in South-East Asia.

Migration of Chinese hill-tribes into the mountains of Indochina and Burma moved the cultivation of opium to the Shan hills of Burma, the ridges of northern Thailand, and the north-east highlands of Laos. The Yunnanese merchants still controlled the distribution back to the Chinese coastal cities but with the expansion of opium production in the latter part of the nineteenth century and with the natural trade movement of the Chinese Haw — the Yunnanese muslims — down the six roads, opium found its way to the Chinese in Siam.[146] For the mountain tribes, opium became the principal cash crop and following massacres of the mid-nineteenth century, the Hmong, Yao, and Akha moved further into the mountains of South-East Asia while others settled along the Burma-Chinese border. Acre upon acre of mountain slope were to be seen covered with poppy, grown by the diverse tribes and marketed by Yunnanese traders.

By Thai standards, hill-tribe peoples are not necessarily poor. Opium-producing villages had and still have greater prosperity than the average Thai rural family village. The principal area of occupation in Thailand is the southern extension of the Shan highlands. Others live in the higher regions of the Khorat plateau and to the west in the rugged mountains along the Burmese border above the river Salween. These mountain areas abound with wild life. The climate varies from humid sub-tropical to tropical monsoon. The Hmong and Yao are skilful and industrious peoples, with an acute understanding of the land and soil which will most suit their needs. They exploit the area, exhaust the soil, and move on. Their villages are to be found principally between three thousand and five thousand feet above sea level, near to sources of streams and sheltered from the strong winds that blow up from the valleys in the hot season. At this level there is freedom from the malaria, cholera, dengue fever, and the other ills of the plains. The Hmong, particularly when they moved into Thailand,

---

[146] *Hmong, Opium and Haw*; Terry C. Grandstaff/JSS; pp63/75

brought with them the poppy growing culture and looked for land to satisfy their needs.[147]

The configuration of the land and the soil for swiddening for poppy growing had to be carefully selected. Too much water run-off washes away plants and so the slope needed to be carefully assessed. Southerly or westerly exposures were preferred to take maximum advantages of the sun. The land must not be too open, and should preferably be from virgin forest or long-standing second growth. The burning of the trees produced the wood ash for fertiliser and the remaining standing growth provided the shelter from north and east winds. The fields had to be within a productive walking distance from the village, so that the nearby areas were usually the first planted. When the daily journey became too great, or the fields could not be protected from predators — both animal and human — the villagers moved on. The Hmong are noted for being particularly skilled at site and seed selection, on which yield depends. The poppy may be white, red, purple, or variegated. When the poppy plant is about thirty centimetres high, the field is thinned and the leaves used for salad. As with any other crop, the poppy is subject to natural hazards. Too much cloud or excessive cold brings stunted growth whilst late rainfall will wash away whole fields. Hailstorms damage delicate buds. A poor crop will produce only one or two heads of poppy per plant instead of an anticipated six or more. Elephants, tigers, wild cats, elks, and a whole miscellany of small beasts may make use of the field or the crop either as food or as a mating-time battle ground.

At harvest time the villagers camp out in the fields under rough shelters so that the day can be given to the delicate task of incising the bulbs, a task which takes place in the latter part of the afternoon and the cool of the evening. The collection of the drained, moist resin takes place before the sun has risen, when it can readily be scraped from the pod. Left too long, the resin will dry in the sun and be blown away as dust. Incised too soon, the milky opium will run down the stem of the plant and be lost. An unexpected shower of rain after incision could wipe out a season's hard labour. A few days after the first harvest, a second incision, angled from the original incisions, will increase the fruitfulness of the crop. If the· bulbs are large and the resin plentiful, a third and possibly fourth incision might be made.

---

[147] UN Survey Team; *Report on Economic and Social Needs of Opium Producing Areas*; United Nations report; pp35/6

While a Hmong poppy farmer is as reluctant to disclose details of a harvest as an Irish farmer is to declare the size of his herd, both with an official in mind, estimates are that a family of four adults produces an annual average of between ten and fifteen kilogrammes. In favourable circumstances it might treble this amount. Quantity varies greatly with the time interval between collecting and weighing, and whether or not it has been cooked into smoking opium. Variation depends to a greater extent on what the farmer wants an official to know. The crop will be heavily dependent on the climatic conditions but productivity of land tends to fall by the fifth year. Once used for intensive growing, the land is of no further use and reverts to natural forest or wild grassland.[148]

The Hmong were not themselves addicted smokers and only small amounts were consumed within the tribe. They grew the poppy principally for the goods it would purchase. Labour availability did not permit both the growing of dry farmed rice and opium, and seasonal timing of cropping is all-important. Mountain rice is sown into ash fertilised clearings as the first rains fall in May and is finally cleared from the site in November or December. The poppy crop must be sown in August and harvested over January and February and because of this, rice interferes with the opium cycle. Maize, which can be planted in April, before the rains, and harvested in August is a preferred alternative. Poppy crops can be sown directly on to the maize land without further clearing and this programme also works in reverse, the maize being sown directly on to poppy crop land. In some circumstances Hmong prefer to sow the poppies among the maize to give the young plants protection from the heavy August rains before the maize is hand-cut. The maize is used both for pig and chicken feeding as well as for distilling a potent spirit for times of celebration. The poppy itself is part of an eco-system involving livestock raising as well as cash-cropping and thus when a substitution of opium was planned to take place, the whole food and production cycle had to be considered. The villagers themselves were not traders. Opium was sold from the tribal village to traders and the travelling traders from the beginning were the Haw of Yunnan, moving south through the

---

[148] *Poppies, Pipes & People;* J. Westermeyer; pp36/42 and UN Survey Team; *Report on Economic & Social Needs of Opium Producing Areas;* United Nations report

mountains along their routes which had Chiang Mai as the principal terminal.[149]

The pace of opium development in the Thailand, Burma, and Laos area was not equal to that of southern China, and the South-East Asian area remained about fifty years behind that of Yunnan and Szechwan. The Golden Triangle area, as it became known, did not develop large-scale opium growing until the 1940s. Each of the British and French colonial powers did its best to discourage opium growing in the territories under its immediate control but continued to allow imported and refined opium to be sold through official monopolies. Opium from Yunnan was smuggled in to meet black market demands, bringing a need to establish border patrols in a not very successful attempt to keep the traffic in check. The pattern of the market up to the 1940s was thus created by Chinese officials in southern China encouraging poppy growth, while at the same time the colonial powers discouraged it.[150]

King Rama II first banned the smoking of opium throughout Bangkok, and in 1839 the death penalty was introduced for opium trafficking. Britain broke the ban and finally, in 1852, King Mongkut bowed to British pressure and established a royal opium monopoly which Britain supplied. The 1855 Bowring Treaty between Britain and Siam included an express statement in Article 8 that Britain was permitted to import opium into Siam, free of duty. To compensate for lost import revenues on other commodities, King Mongkut enlarged four Chinese-managed franchises: opium, brothels, gambling and alcohol. The revenues from these four constituted about forty to fifty percent of government income in the latter half of the nineteenth century.

In 1907 the Siamese government eliminated the Chinese middlemen and took direct control of the opium trade. Fourteen years later, the number of opium addicts in Siam reached two hundred thousand and opium profits contributed between fifteen and twenty percent of government revenues. By 1930, opium dens were receiving nearly ninety thousand customers per day. A gradual decline followed

---

[149] *Discussions with Khun Kraisri Nimmanahaeminda*, 26 January 1987 and *The Politics of Heroin;* Alfred W. McCoy

[150] *The Politics of Heroin;* Alfred W. McCoy; pp65/6

and by 1938, opium contributed only eight per cent of revenues. Cultivation did not increase until quite late in the 1940s when large numbers of opium farmers moved into northern Thailand from Laos and the defeated Kuomintang soldiery moved into the Shan States. It was a time when the political climate in Thailand was ripe for opium exploitation.

Although at war, the Japanese and Chiang Kai-shek's Army permitted the trading of opium and throughout the Second World War years there was no local shortage. It was no problem for the Haw traders from Yunnan to find their way from the producer to the market. They had for centuries been familiar with the wild mountains between Yunnan and the Chiang Mai area of Siam, usually entering through Mae Sai, Fang, or Chieng Saen. Over these routes they drove their pack-horses and mules, laden with silks and other saleable goods. If they arrived in the cool season they added walnuts to their loads and in the following months, opium.[151]

Soon after its arrival in Lower Burma in 1852, Britain imported opium from India through its government monopoly but after the passage of its 1878 Opium Act, steps were taken to reduce consumption. In northern Burma matters were different. In its 1886 annexation, Britain acquired the Shan States to the far north-east bordering the Yunnan province of China and with them, a significant hilltribe opium production. The Shan States, with a population then of about 1.2 million, were ruled as thirty-four independent states each with its own *chaofa*, or leader. Seeking to minimise military expenditure, Britain made deals with the individual states, giving each of them control over its own day-to-day affairs. These deals carefully overlooked the fact that much of each State's income sprang from opium exports to Siam, as well as to conquered lower Burma. In 1923 there was passed the Shan States Opium Act. Growers were registered and an attempt was made to buy up all of the opium crop. It proved to be a fruitless task and while opium production and trade was severely reduced it was never eradicated. After the post-war departure of the British, an independent Burmese government passed the 1950 Opium Den Suppression Act. This had little or no effect on the Shan States, which, following the earlier acceptance of their independence by Britain, wanted nothing to do with the lowland government of the

---

[151] Discussions with Khun Kraisri Nimmanahaeminda, 26 January 1987

Burmans. The source of supply remained and opium continued to be moved into Thailand whenever the circumstances suited.

Across Siam's eastern border matters were also different. In 1820 the Vietnamese court had outlawed opium smoking, both on moral and economic grounds. It also tried to prevent smuggling from China. Its efforts were destined to fail as by 1858, South-East Asia suffered the political misfortune of the arrival of the conquering French and, with them, the influence of the powerful and expansionist *Groupe Coloniale* in the French Chamber of Deputies. The Vietnamese emperor was soon forced into long-term debt. With no other available source of revenue, the emperor established an opium franchise in the north of the country and leased it to Chinese merchants. His share of the proceeds were calculated to be sufficient to repay his debts to France within twelve years. Soon the French annexed Saigon and set up an opium franchise to pay for colonial development. Further conquests took them to Cambodia in 1863, central Vietnam in 1883, northern Vietnam (Tonkin) in 1884, and Laos in 1893. In each of these protectorates they established an opium monopoly to finance colonial rule. To improve both efficiency and profitability the separate monopolies were then merged and a new government refinery was built in Saigon, with both Indian and the cheaper Yunnan product being purchased under monopoly control.[152]

<hr>

As each of the two major colonial powers sought to improve the position of its empire in the last two decades of be nineteenth century, Siam became a political football, kicked around in Paris and London with little or no consultation with Bangkok. Initially the French government was prepared to accept the Mekong as the line of demarcation between the two spheres of influence but strong objections to this were voiced by the government of India. It was not because Britain would be installed on the west bank but that France had no rights and should not be allowed as far west as the east bank of the river. The French badly wanted control of the east bank, owing to the belief of the *Groupe Coloniale* that the Mekong would serve as a major waterway for trade with Yunnan and other parts of southern China.

[152] *The Politics of Heroin*; Alfred W. McCoy; pp69/76

The court of Siam made the next move when in 1892 it proposed that Britain should have a form of protectorate over the country. Within the proposal Siam would not cede any part of its territory to any power without British approval, and Britain in return would protect Siam against any attempted annexation.[153] Britain wanted none of it. It wanted Siam as a neutral buffer state between its own and the French territorial interests.[154] Given what it took to be a friendly signal from Britain's Foreign Office, the French sent gunboats up the Mekong and took control of a number of Siamese islands. Siam was too weak to stop them and to avoid a world-wide rupture with France, Britain decided to steer clear of the incident.

Encouraged by this inaction, France, on fourteenth of July 1893, sent two gunboats up the Chao Phraya river to Bangkok and presented an ultimatum to King Chulalongkorn that it proposed to take over the whole of the eastern bank of the Mekong. At the same time it threatened Britain that it would enforce this unless the King agreed to give it at least the two Siamese provinces of Siamreap and Battambang, which today constitute western Cambodia. Such an occupation would have threatened British interests in Bangkok as it would have brought the French to within one hundred miles of the city. It would also have strengthened France's control over the southern reaches of the Mekong. Britain threatened war and by thirtieth of July 1893, Britain and France were on the brink. For its part Britain did not want a major power on the eastern frontier of its Indian empire, which included Burma, nor any threat to its substantial interests in Siam and the Malaya peninsula. It sought a guaranteed neutral Siam. Britain foresaw problems, however, when the mistrusted Hanotaux was appointed as foreign minister. He was viewed in Britain *"as indifferent to the truth as are all Frenchmen, and very tricky"*.[155]

Britain, being neither prepared to provide protectorate status for Siam nor to sign an Anglo-Siamese defensive treaty, considered abandoning Siam. It rejected this stance as the result would have been French occupation which, in turn, would have put pressure on British interests in Malaya. Above all, Britain did not want any power to be

[153] *The Anglo-French Declaration of January 1896 and the Independence of Siam*; Chandran Jeshurun/JSS; pp108/9
[154] *British and American influence in Post-War Thailand*; Frank C. Darling; p1
[155] Lord Dufferin, British ambassador to Paris to his prime minister, Lord Salisbury (Salisbury papers Vol. 114, 1891)

in a position to cut a canal across the Kra Isthmus, which would have shortened the sea route to the Far East and diminished the importance of Singapore. It decided to toughen up its stance, and in March 1895, Gurkha soldiers were despatched across the upper Mekong to occupy part of what is now northern Laos. In May of that year Britain told France what it had done and invited a frank exchange of views. Agreement was eventually reached by way of a Declaration of January 1896 that neither power would penetrate the Chao Phraya valley. What was to happen to the outer territories was left unclear. This Britain interpreted as leaving Siamese territory intact but with perhaps a little scope for itself on the border with Malaya. Hanotaux seized on it as a license for the French to encroach on the eastern provinces.[156]

King Chulalongkorn was also interested in the Malaya border and in April 1897, anxious to sustain a somewhat dubious suzerainty over the northern states of Kelantan, Trengganu, and Kedah, he entered into a secret convention with Britain. The convention recognised his rights over the territories and guaranteed British support against any attempt by a third power to acquire dominion. The sting in the tail was a third clause which restricted the right of the King to grant any special privileges of trade or lands without the written consent of the British government. Ten years later it was described as *"the most deplorable document had ever signed"*.[157] Agreement between the two parties to rescind it was reached in March 1909. To avoid any embarrassment of the King it was also agreed that both the original agreement and the document of abrogation were to remain secret. The Malay states came under British rule and in exchange Britain agreed to a partial surrender of its extra-territorial jurisdiction in Siam. The intention of secrecy was soon frustrated when the Indian government published the text of both agreements that same year.[158]

It was not until the major 1904 Anglo-French Entente Cordiale agreements that the badly-drafted 1896 Declaration ceased to have effect and a new declaration made that neither Britain nor France wished to annex any Siamese territory. Subsequent changes to the eastern frontiers of Siam in 1907 were made by negotiation, not

---

[156] *The Anglo-French Declaration of January 1896 and the Independence of Siam*; Chandran Jeshurun/JSS; pp110/12 and Foreign Office papers; 17/1221 of 18 May 1894

[157] Foreign Office papers; 422/62, Paget-Grey, 3 April 1908

[158] *Anglo-Siamese Secret Convention of 1897*; Mrs. Thamsook   Numnonda/JSS; pp45/60

annexation. The attitude of both Britain and France towards Siam at that time destroys the often quoted claim of Siamese independence being preserved by its own efforts. The reality was that neither France nor Britain wanted to be saddled with the problems of having Siam under its control. Britain specifically refused to have it and France made no great effort to acquire it. It was more useful to each as a buffer state.

By the early twentieth century, opium revenues financed over thirty per cent of French colonial costs in South-East Asia. While a vigorous international crusade against the evils of opium forced other colonial powers to reduce opium activity, French officials remained immune to any question of morality.[159] The outbreak of the Second World War, and the loss of sea-borne opium from Iran and Turkey for its monopoly, was for French Indochina a financial disaster. Smuggled opium did not provide revenue for the government and the task in 1940 was to increase home production by the Hmong. To achieve it the French worked through prestigious local leaders for greater production, the prevention of smuggling, and the routing of the product to its monopoly. Gradually thousands of Hmong migrated to Laos and northern Vietnam, areas which suited their slash-and-burn agriculture. With them went the poppy.

A massive increase in opium production helped the French Indochinese to survive the war. Later, those of the Hmong tribe who resented the French tactics joined up with communist guerillas and in Laos were early members of the Pathet Lao revolutionary movement. Following well-documented Sun Tzu art of war principles, it was the disaffected Hmong with their detailed knowledge of the land who were able to lead the brilliant Vietnamese strategist, General Vo Nguyen Giap and his Viet Minh guns to the ridges from which he brought about the defeat at Dien Bien Phu of the formidable General Christian Marie Ferdinand de la Croix de Castries and his French garrison. The battle, which started on thirteenth of March 1954, resulted in a fifty-five-day siege and eventual surrender. It was a battle which in retrospect was one of the most important in world post-1945 history.

---

[159] *The Politics of Heroin;* Alfred W. McCoy; pp72/6

It was also a warning to all foreign powers of the dangers inherent in a 'people's war'.

After the defeat of the French at Dien Bien Phu, other Hmong, previously loyal to the French cause, found new masters in the American Central Intelligence Agency (the CIA). Decades later they were still to be found fighting in the mountains on the CIA's behalf.[160] American advisers condoned the trade in opium and even assisted it by the use of Air America planes as late as 1970. Opium became the cash-crop to finance anti-communism in Indochina. In Thailand, the situation at that time was similar. Following the ending of legal importation of foreign production the Phibun regime authorised local poppy cultivation in the northern provinces in 1947. It was not made illegal until 1958.[161] During these twelve years, opium production became an integral part of the Hmong economy and a source of great wealth to a number of Thai citizens.

Immediately after the Second World War the production of opium was only about eighty tonnes in the whole of the Golden Triangle area. With the end of the war, smuggling increased from the Yunnan whilst the French and Thai opium monopolies imported legally from Iran. In 1953, the United Nations protocol was signed which banned the sale of opium for both legalised smoking and eating. This had little practical immediate effect as smugglers took up the quantity previously officially supplied by the Iranian government. In 1955 Iran banned the production of opium. Of greater significance to Thailand was the victory of Mao Zedung and his People's Liberation Army of China over Chiang Kai-shek. The new communist government started the phase-out of opium production and the introduction of crop-substitution in Yunnan. The smuggling of opium from China into South-East Asia virtually ceased.[162]

Before the 1950s, three critical factors affected the south-east Asian opium market. The French Indochina government expanded production. The Chinese communist government phased out the Yunnan opium and sealed the border. Thirdly, the Iranian government prevented Iran from being South-East Asia's major supplier.

The Golden Triangle area production was relatively insignificant. For a new expansion, a new motive and new men were necessary. But

[160] *The Politics of Heroin;* Alfred W. McCoy; pp76/79
[161] *The Hmong of Thailand;* Nicholas Tapp; pp20 and 29
[162] *The Politics of Heroin;* Alfred W. McCoy; pp76/79

that was in happier days, before elements of the Kuomintang Army were driven out of China and into the Shan and northern Thailand mountains.

CHAPTER FIVE
Enter the Kuomintang

Over the centuries, Thailand has been unable to shake off the pernicious influence of its western and northern neighbour, Burma. From centuries of wars, when the old kingdom of Ayutthaya was crushed by Burman invaders, to the instability and immorality of the Ne Win regime of the 1980s, Burma has been a source of great concern both to old Siam and to modern Thailand. Hopes of neighbourly relations with an emerging independent state were shattered in July 1947 with the massacre of Burma's leaders. Prospects of a cohesive, stable, prosperous, and independent Burma were destroyed over the years by a corrupt military, and a search for cohesion with the many dissenting minorities disappeared.

A popular movement for independence and freedom from colonial rule in the multi-ethnic state of Burma falls back on religious origins in 1921 in the person of U Ottama, a Buddhist monk and a fiery agitator. In the mid-1930s came the students of Rangoon University, the more prominent of whom were Aung Sang and U Nu. In 1938, the Year of Communist Revolution, came the young radical, Soe. The freedom process was interrupted by the Second World War. Aung Sang found his way to Tokyo and returned to Burma with the Japanese invasion of December 1941. In Bangkok on twenty-sixth of December 1941 Aung Sang, with others who had also found their way to and back from Japan, founded the Burma Independence Army. An early adherent to this Army was the man who was to become known as Ne Win. Serving under command of the Japanese Army, the Independence Army helped capture Rangoon on seventh of March 1942. In August of that year the Independence Army became the Burma Defence Army and one year later, when the Japanese granted Burma its independence, the force was again renamed and became the Burma National Army. It was commanded by Ne Win.

Friction soon developed between the Japanese and the new 'independent' Burma and increased to such an extent that on twenty-seventh of March 1945, the Burma National Army, in an opportunist move, declared war on Japan. A broad-based popular front, the Anti-Fascist People's Freedom League, was established to provide overall political guidance. On thirtieth of May, Admiral Lord

Louis Mountbatten, Supreme Allied Commander, South-East Asia, accepted the Burma National Army, which now called itself the Patriotic Burmese Force, within his command, and its flag was soon to fly over a recaptured Rangoon. With the end of the war it became a regular army force, other than for about three thousand five hundred resistance fighters, to whom such a role was not acceptable. The People's Volunteer Organisation, a paramilitary force controlled by Aung Sang, was formed as a next step.

As with most post-Second World War emerging nations, communism reared its head in the form of the Communist Party of Burma, but alternative approaches to left-wing political theory soon saw its break-up. The more moderate communists (the Stalinists or White Flags) stayed temporarily within the Freedom League while the more radical (the Trotskyists or Red Flags), led by the fanatical Soe and breathing revolution as the only way forward, went underground. The White Flag communists were soon at odds with the League, and in October 1946 they were expelled. Gradually the communist groups of varying hues and allegiances removed themselves to the mountains in the north and west of Burma where the White Flags became the dominant element. They became recognised as the Communist Party of Burma, and in the mountains they established themselves in strongholds which would last them for the next four decades.

On twenty-seventh of January 1947, Aung Sang, in his capacity as leader of the Freedom League, signed an enabling agreement with British prime minister, Clement Attlee, which would give Burma its independence within one year. The following month Aung Sang signed an agreement with the minority groups, the Shan, Kachin, and Chin, to establish the Union of Burma. The Karen did not sign. The agreement gave to the ethnic minorities the right to secede from the Union ten years after the date of signature. This right of secession was particularly important to the Shan in view of the freedoms originally negotiated with Britain. Burma seemed set fair for independence and for long-term acceptance within world society.

Then tragedy overtook it. On nineteenth of July, the Union of Burma virtually disintegrated with the murder of Aung Sang and eight of his most senior colleagues. Aung Sang was then thirty-two. The second-in-command of the Freedom league, U Nu, took over and in October 1947 he signed a second agreement with Attlee which gave independence to Burma on fourth of January 1948. U Nu was its prime minister. Sao Shwe Thaike, the *chaofa* of a group of Shan States and an ethnic Tai, was President. Within weeks all was in disarray. The communists went underground against the government, whilst the Karen established their own defence unit, the Karen National Defence Organisation, and commenced their long battle for 'Karenistan'. Communist forces waged a campaign in the west of Burma and sundry other small factions broke away from U Nu's new independent government. The jungle mountains of Burma were full of factions in revolt. On the first of February, Ne Win took up the posts of chief of the general staff and supreme commander of the armed forces including the civil and paramilitary police. At the same time he became deputy prime minister in charge of defence and the home ministries. With Second World War-hardened field commanders at the government's disposal, order was established out of chaos, but the stability was fragile.[163]

The last thing that Burma needed was an incursion from Yunnan of a remnant of hostile Chinese forces but that, to its lasting disadvantage, was its fate. The quality of troops which were to form the remnant had been observed in February 1944 by Nicol Smith and his OSS Thai volunteers. Smith's men were moving from Kunming to Cheli. In spectacular countryside of mountains and grasslands, Smith caught up with three hundred soldiers who were joining the 93rd Kuomintang (KMT) Division under the command of General Lu. *"They were the sorriest-looking soldiers I had ever come upon. Dressed in padded, bluish cotton jackets and pants, tattered cloth leggings and straw sandals, with faces pockmarked, bodies spindling and frequently burning with an angry rash, virtually all were undernourished or tubercular... An attempted deserter was shot and left; the road was littered with dead bodies of troops who had fallen out, many partially eaten by tigers.... The troops had no canteens for boiling water but drank out of polluted streams; there were no mosquito nets."* [164] In contrast to his pitiful soldiery, the commanding general lived at his headquarters at Meng Hai, a cluster of attractive white plaster-coated bamboo houses. The walls of his Operations Room were covered in maps, most of which had no relevance

----

[163] *Outrage*; Bertil Lintner; pp28/44
[164] *Into Siam, Underground Kingdom*; Nicol Smith and Blake Clark; pp129/145

whatsoever to the theatre of operations. All was *"modernity and comfort and correctness"*. It may not have been an all-conquering army but to Burma, the later arrival of even a poorly equipped, bedraggled remnant was most unwelcome.

The precipitous collapse of the Chinese Nationalist government in 1949 came as a shock not only to countries in South-East Asia but also to America. The shock was greatest for its China lobby which, fed on optimistic reports from the Chiang Kai-shek household, had underestimated the Long March Maoists.[165] The government in Washington was compelled to recognise the character of the Chinese revolution as one of emancipation from feudalism and to accept that its new problem was to assess the likely flow of communism into South-East Asia. As Mao's People's Liberation Army drove south, Chiang Kai-shek planned to make the mountains of Yunnan his last bastion. When the communist armies entered Yunnan in December 1949 the local warlord sided with them. The KMT troops were driven out of all the cities but the liberating armies did not at that time reach the border with Burma. An area of mountains and jungle, it was populated only sparsely by a miscellany of tribal groups. The boundary had no clear definition or marking, and neither government, Chinese nor Burmese had any control over the movements of the hill-tribes.

Late in 1949, the KMT started to cross over into Burma. Despite the earlier OSS opinion of its soldiery, this KMT force was disciplined and stronger than anything else in the mountains. It had been driven out of Burma once before by the Japanese without any particular distinction in its fighting record. Now it was returning in different circumstances and free of pressure from the People's Liberation Army, and it had time to organise itself in this jungle wilderness. As the Maoist armies pressed south through Yunnan, so more and more wandering remnants of defeated soldiery moved into Burma. Some were merely roaming bands of deserters. Five thousand who crossed into Indochina instead of Burma were disarmed by the French and sent to islands in the Gulf of Thailand. They were later used by the French colonists as labourers in the coal mines near Hanoi and on rubber

---

[165] The 'Long Marchers' were Mao Zedung's close associates who formed the foundation of his communist revolution, fought the KMT to a standstill, and, by 1 October 1949, triumphantly proclaimed the state of Communist China. They were the die-hards who, long into their old age, controlled the fate of the new China

estates in the south of Indochina.[166] Some were sent to Taiwan in June 1953.

The Burmese Army was less successful than the French. A force of about two hundred KMT entered Kengtung State early in January 1950 and established itself at Mong Yang. In March of that year, some one thousand five hundred men of KMT 8th Army, 26th Army and 93rd Division invaded Kengtung State. General Li Mi commanded the 8th Army and became the Force Commander. His most senior general, Liu Kuo Chwan, commanded the 26th Army, and Major-General Ma Chaw Yi the 93rd Division. Liu Kuo Chwan had commanded the 93rd Division in the early 1940s.[167] The troops were principally Haws from the Yunnan and many were familiar with the trails south. They made their way first to the south-east of the Shan States around Tachilek, across the Thai border from Mae Sai. Five hundred wives and children went with them. The Burmese government demanded that the KMT invaders accept internment or leave the territory, but Li Mi rejected the proposal, threatening battle if necessary to resist it. In the second week of June the Burmese Army launched an offensive and by twenty-first of July had re-occupied the town of Tachilek. The KMT troops moved to Mong Hsat, about forty miles from Tachilek and fifteen miles from the Thai border. The Burmese Army, which was having problems of its own with both the Karen and the communists, pulled back from the commitment.[168]

With American assistance the Chiang Kai-shek government in Taiwan proceeded to reinforce and build up the KMT stragglers into a fighting force. In the Shan States, Li Mi used the Kokang ruling house as his local recruiting agent and soon his divisions were strengthened by recruits from both sides of the Mekong as well as by Wa and Lahu tribesmen. The Nationalist China-American strategy had become clear to the government of Burma. The Shan States were to be used as a base for the establishment of redoubts in Yunnan. Thailand was to be used as the logistics base and supply route to the Shan States staging area, and from there the KMT would invade China through Yunnan in

---

[166] *Foreign & Domestic Consequencs of KMT intervention in Burma* (Cornell University paper No.93; Robert H. Taylor; pp11/32
[167] *Golden Triangle: Frontier and Wilderness*; Kuo Yi-tung; p108
[168] *Nationalist China Troops in Burma; Obstacles to Burma Foreign Relations, 1949 to 1961*; K.R. Young; pp49/52 and *KMT Aggression against Burma*; Burma Ministry of Information; p3

preparation for, or in support of, a full-scale sea-borne assault from Taiwan.[169]

Mong Hsat became an important centre for Nationalist China. In size it was no more than a large village but it suited the KMT troop remnant. Eighty miles south-west of the town of Kengtung, it was centrally located in a fertile valley with a large area of rice cultivation for subsistence. It was surrounded by hilly terrain on all sides which formed natural defence barriers. Areas in the vicinity provided parachute dropping zones and could be used as training grounds. It had access to the Thailand border and hence the supplies that could be obtained through that country. During the Second World War, Allied forces had constructed an emergency landing strip at Mong Hsat. The KMT improved and later lengthened it. The Burmese Army, in February, March, November, and December 1951 and again in late 1952, unsuccessfully attempted to oust the KMT force from its base. Mong Hsat was a good defensive position and remained the headquarters for the KMT troops in Burma for over four years.[170] It also came to be considered by Chiang Kai-shek, away in Taiwan, as the provisional seat of the Nationalist Yunnan government under Li Mi.

General Li Mi was a Nationalist Chinese Second World War hero. He was born in Yunnan in 1899 and appointed in 1949 by Generalissimo Chiang Kai-shek to be commander-in-chief of all forces in Yunnan. Nationalist sources identified him: *"Li Mi was a Nationalist officer leading a regular Nationalist force and not a mere dissident guerilla. Li Mi's troops were under the direct command of the military headquarters in Formosa".*[171] A Thai opinion of him was that *"he was a regular soldier and a genuine commander of his army. He was not an opium grower".*[172] In accordance with American cold-war strategy and anti-Mao stance in the 1950s, coinciding with the French Indochina war, the Korean war, and the shelling by Mao of

---

[169] *Shan of Burma*; Chao Tzang Yawngwe; pp102, 145 and 201
[170] *KMT Aggression against Burma; Burma Ministry of Information*; p33 and *Nationalist China Troops in Burma; Obstacles to Burma Foreign Relations 1949 to 1961*; K. R. Young; pp52/3
[171] *Nationalist China Troops in Burma; Obstacles to Burma Foreign Relations, 1949 to 1961*; K.R. Young; pp100/104, quoting Formosan newspaper, *Kung Lun Pao* in April 1953 and Patrick Soong, Chinese Nationalist chargé d'affaires in Bangkok, taken from *The Times* of London 30 March, 1953
[172] Discussions with Major-General Chatical Coonhavan, 1 July 1991

insubordinate offshore islands, Li Mi received American support and the whole-hearted backing of the Chinese government in Taiwan. In a letter dated fifth of January 1951, Chiang Kai-shek wrote to Li Mi: *"Before long our forces (intend) to counter-attack the mainland* (and) *shall join hands with you. It is hoped that you will increase and preserve to the utmost your fighting power in order to prepare for assistance in the counter attack. Lastly, may I inform all the brave fighters of all the rank and file that... all the armed forces of the Anti-communist organisation shall enjoy the same privileges as those enjoyed by the regular army".*[173]

On thirtieth of December 1949, President Truman approved a study by the National Security Council designed to create a policy which would: *"...block further Communist expansion in Asia".*[174] The Joint Chiefs of Staff recommended in April 1950 that steps be taken to *"... reduce the pressure from Communist China. In this connection the J.Cs of S have noted the evidence of renewed vitality and apparent increased effectiveness of the Chinese Nationalist forces".*[175] The Joint Chiefs were grasping at straws. The statements were vague enough to give rise to a number of interpretations both on the ground at the time and also by later examiners of the effect of the declared policy. There was a suspicion that over the period 1951 to 1953 the American 'China Lobby', and General MacArthur in particular, wanted to stir up trouble in Yunnan and other parts of southern China to ease pressure on Korea. Indeed, on twenty-fourth of March 1951, only eighteen days before he was relieved of his command by President Truman, MacArthur issued a statement from Tokyo calling for a *"decision by the United Nations to depart from its tolerant effort to contain the war to the area of Korea, through an expansion of our military operations to its coastal areas and interior bases to doom Red China to the risk of imminent military collapse".*[176] Later, in 1958, General Chennault testified that MacArthur had a plan to put KMT

---

[173] *Nationalist China Troops in Burma: Obstacles to Burma Foreign Relations, 1949 to 1961;* K. R. Young; p104 quoting UNGA Official Records A/2423

[174] *Foreign & Domestic Consequences of KMT intervention in Burma* (Cornell University paper No. 93); Robert H.Taylor; p41 citing Pentagon Papers

[175] *United States Joint Chiefs of Staff memorandum to the Secretary of Defence,* 10 April 1950

[176] *Foreign & Domestic Consequences of KMT intervention in Burma* (Cornell University paper No. 93); Robert H. Taylor; p42 citing Carl Berger — *The Korea Knot*

divisions from Taiwan into Southern China. President Truman, however, restricted the China Lobby to defensive measures. When General Dwight D. Eisenhower became President in 1952 his appraisal of the KMT adventure in Burma was forthright. He saw no strategic virtue in the KMT element in the Yunnan and Burma, and requested Chiang Kai-shek to remove it.[177]

Li Mi's use of the Kokang ruling house to try to persuade the Shan to join the American Nationalist China venture proved to be only partially successful. The Shan princes and leaders generally thought it too risky and instead they supported the Anti-Fascist People's Freedom League. Because of their attitude, Li Mi was unable politically to consolidate the KMT presence in the Shan States and consequently was unsuccessful in establishing forward bases in the Yunnan.[178] He sent agents to the northern borders of Burma where he recruited Yunnanese refugees and brought them back to the Kengtung State for training and arming. His force grew steadily, and to it he conscripted muleteers, with their mules, to form a transportation unit. Early supplies of arms and ammunition were received via Thailand.[179]

The CIA entered the battle area to side with the KMT force. The American Joint Chiefs of Staff called for a programme of *"special covert operations designed to interfere with communist activities in South-East Asia"*.[180] No details were specified and the American ambassador to Burma was not informed, a matter which later brought about his resignation in protest. The intention was to turn the China-Burma borderlands into an area that Mao Zedung and his Liberation Army could not penetrate. Early in 1951, unmarked C-46 and C-47 transport planes were observed making parachute supply drops into the Mong Hsat area. Instructors were also flown in from Chiang Kai-shek's command in Taiwan. The CIA helped search the Shan States for surviving KMT and supported a rigorous training programme.

During the latter part of April 1951, some three to four thousand KMT troops from Mong Hsat, under the direct command of General Li Mi, advanced along the Salween basin and established a base at

---

[177] *Foreign & Domestic Consequences of KMT intervention in Burma* (Cornell University paper No. 93); Robert H. Taylor; pp41/4
[178] *Shan of Burma;* Chao Tzang Yawnghwe; pp102, 145 & 201/202
[179] *KMT Aggression against Burma;* Burma Ministry of Information; p12
[180] *The Politics of Heroin;* Alfred W. McCoy; pp128/9 citing US Joint Chiefs of Staff memorandum to the Secretary of Defence, 10 April 1950

Mong Mao in northern Wa state. A smaller force established its headquarters at Mong Yang and both forces were reinforced by local recruitment. Arms were air-dropped in support. A first attempt was made at the re-conquest of the Yunnan. The Mong Mao force, now known as 'The Yunnan Province Anti-Communist Salvation Army', crossed the border into Yunnan. They were accompanied by CIA advisers and supplied by regular airdrops. With Keng-ma captured, the KMT troops advanced northward only to find themselves heavily counter-attacked by the People's Liberation Army. The KMT suffered heavy casualties and some of its CIA advisers were killed. Li Mi and his Salvation Army fled back to Burma. It had been in Yunnan for less than one week. In July, a two-thousand-strong contingent from Mong Yang entered Yunnan, again backed by air-dropped supplies. It took only a few days for the highly motivated Liberation Army to chase it back into Burma.[181]

On twenty-fifth of October 1946, CNRRA Air Transport had come into being as a partnership between General Chennault and Whiting Willaver. Even by 1946, Chennault was a famous name in Asia. He had led the American Volunteer Group, the renowned 'Flying Tigers', in their support of Chiang Kai-shek's forces and from the Tigers came CNRRA Air Transport. Its first contract was solely with CNRRA, the Chinese equivalent of UNRRA, for airlifting rehabilitation products from Shanghai and Canton to the interior cities of China which could not be reached in any other way. The products themselves were supplied by UNRRA. In 1947, evolution resulted in the formation of the Civil Air Transport (CAT) and widened its activities to carry commercial cargo. By late 1947 it was working to a time-racing schedule, supplying cities under siege by the communists and taking out essential personnel whose capture had to be avoided. Its operational base was gradually forced south in front of Mao Zedung's forces from Shanghai to Canton, to Kunming, and then out to Hainan Island. Its last resort was Taiwan. As Phibun had done before, so had Chennault's CAT. It had backed the wrong side and by 1950 it was in liquidation. The CIA bought it. Over the period 1950 to 1952 it gradually developed from legitimate transportation of commercial

---

[181] *KMT Aggression against Burma;* Burma Ministry of Information; pp9/14

cargo to passenger transportation from Taiwan to non-communist destinations, and wrapped into these were the CIA requirements.[182] Later to be known as 'Air America', it operated out of Taiwan in conformity with CIA demands.

In Bangkok, Sea Service Supply had been established by the CIA to handle the import of equipment both for Thailand and for the Burma KMT, using the route through the Thai military to forward supplies to Mong Hsat. Burmese intelligence noted the appearance of brand-new American machine guns, bazookas, and anti-aircraft artillery. In December 1951, the London *Observer* reported *"indisputable evidence that Americans were helping the KMT 93rd Division. Two Americans accompanied it in its ignominious offensive last Autumn, and when retreat followed, a Thai police helicopter was sent in to evacuate them"*.[183]

The KMT force under Li Mi, having retreated in disorder from Yunnan, was now unable to withstand pressure from the Burmese Army in the west and the north. It returned to its defensive position at Mong Hsat. In a further battle it again suffered heavy casualties but these were more than offset by local recruitment. Li Mi and seven hundred of his men left for KMT Headquarters in Taiwan via Thailand on fifth of November. His passage through Hong Kong on Christmas Eve and the fact that he was on his way to Taiwan for discussions with Generalissimo Chiang Kai-shek was reported in a Hong Kong Chinese language news magazine *Sinwen Tienti Weekly*. General Liu Kuo Chwan, his immediate deputy, took over command and to strengthen Liu's position, supplies of arms, ammunition, and medical stores were air-dropped by Air America C-46s and C-47s over Mong Hsat.[184]

In February 1952 General Li Mi, was formally appointed by Chiang Kai-shek to be President of Yunnan as well as commander-in-chief of the KMT troops in Burma and Yunnan. It was a totally unrealistic appointment but gave prestige and status to his

---

[182] *Far Eastern Economic Review* of 19 February 1949 and *Drugs, the US, and Khun Sa;* Francis W. Bellinger; pp12/14

[183] *Foreign & Domestic Consequences of KMT intervention in Burma* (Cornell University paper No. 93); Robert H. Taylor; pp33/37

[184] *KMT Aggression against Burma;* Burma Ministry of Information; pp3/15, p37

local commander. The Generalissimo's son sent a cablegram to General Li Mi, which was to be looked upon as incriminating at United Nations hearings in 1953. In it, Chiang Ching-kuo praised the KMT forces in Burma for their accomplishments, which, he wrote, were made possible through the guidance of the President, his father. Li Mi flew back from Taiwan directly into Mong Hsat airfield, which by then had become a terminus of regular air traffic. His journey from Taiwan with seven hundred returning instructors was reported openly by the press.[185]

By August 1952, Li Mi was ready for another attack on Yunnan. About two thousand troops from Mong Yang penetrated sixty miles into China, hoping to obtain support from a *"rising of the enslaved masses"*. The masses did not seem terribly keen to rise and instead the KMT force was met by the People's Liberation Army, which promptly despatched it back into Burma. Here it resumed the occupation of Mong Hsat and attempts to invade China were abandoned. A firm grip was taken on the Shan territory between the river Salween and Indochina and along the Sino-Burmese poppy-growing border strip.[186] From the Thai military point of view *"the concept of Yunnan as a springboard for the invasion of China by KMT forces was totally unrealistic — a pipedream. From a practical consideration, the attempts were pathetic, even though Li Mi himself was a fine soldier"*. Most of the KMT and the press-ganged armies were *"much happier growing opium than fighting the People's Liberation Army"*.[187]

Situated in a long narrow strip along the Yunnan frontier, KMT troops constituted the only military force of any strength in that part of Burma and thus were in a good position to control the southern import of any illicitly grown Yunnan opium. Even during the attempts at invasion the KMT troops had found time to attack petty traders plying their old profession across the borderlands. Once the abortive invasions were put behind them, the troops were able to settle into a more permanent spread not only across the Yunnan traders' routes but also in the heart of the Burmese poppy growing areas. This gave them

[185] United Press on February 3 1952 quoted in *KMT Aggression against Burma;* Burma Ministry of Information; pp11 & 38
[186] *The Politics of Heroin;* Alfred W. McCoy; pp129/130
[187] Discussions with Major-General Chaticai Choonhavan, July 01 1991

control of local opium production as well as its transportation.[188] KMT forces took over the management of whole districts, set up revenue collecting centres, and subjected local people to ferry and gate fees for entering the areas it controlled. Customs duties were levied on all commodities brought into the area for trade. By both threat and coercion the KMT forced the local inhabitants to accept its rule. It created hardships for a people dependent on each other for foodstuffs and other necessities.[189] Hill farmers were charged an opium tax. Traders were used to comb the hills for supplies. Opium production was increased by the hill-tribes to help to pay the new tax, and failure to comply with local KMT regulation could involve death or torture. Intermarriage with Lahu tribeswomen gave the KMT further access to opium sources. Thus when Mao Zedung stamped out opium production in Yunnan and when eventually the illicit supplies disappeared, the KMT soldiery was in an ideal position to force the expansion of opium production in the Shan mountains.

In September 1952, KMT stragglers in the Wa States regrouped, crossed to the west of the Salween, and began a veritable reign of terror. Atrocities gained momentum and bands linked up with the Karen National Defence Organisation, initially to obtain provisions and minerals for sale, but the collaboration eventually turned into a military alliance. KMT tactics gave rise to the perception that the intent was to dominate the whole of the Kachin and Shan States and force a way through to the sea, eventually taking complete control of Burma, with all the implications that would have for South-East Asia.

It was not until March 1953 that better trained Burmese Army brigades could be brought in to counter this attempt. The KMT troops were driven back across the Salween. In one of the skirmishes the dead bodies of three unidentifiable white men were found with letters in their pockets with Washington and New York addresses, not unnaturally giving rise to Burmese suspicions that the attack was CIA inspired and supported. The American embassy in Bangkok denied this and offered the theory that two of the three were Germans who had escaped from the French Foreign Legion and the third was an unknown bandit. It is interesting to contemplate the decision for a soldier of fortune, whether or not to exchange the discipline of the Legion and the company of his fellows, of whose language he would

---

[188] *The Politics of Heroin;* Alfred W. McCoy; pp130/1
[189] *KMT Aggression against Burma;* Burma Ministry of Information; p15

have had a working knowledge, for the banditry of the Chinese-speaking KMT and link it with the receipt of letters in the English language from America. The embassy theory appears to have incorporated a fair degree of creative thinking.

The government of Burma, while not branding Washington directly responsible for the activities of the KMT remnant, saw it as indirectly responsible by association. It estimated that some twelve thousand KMT soldiers and supporters occupied various parts of Burma and feared that the newly-elected Eisenhower government was encouraging the unleashing of Chiang Kai-shek on mainland China. Worried by such possible development, Burma abrogated the American Aid to Burma programme. On second of March 1953 it announced that it was going to the United Nations to charge the Chinese Nationalist government and by implication America, with unprovoked aggression.[190] Within seven days of this announcement, the United Press reported General Li Mi's arrival in Taipeh to brief the Chinese Nationalist government on the position.

The Burmese government was not only affronted by KMT troops stationing themselves in the country but saw wider implications. It envisaged, with some justification from the attitude of General MacArthur and the American 'China lobby', the possible use by America to develop a second front to take the pressure off Korea. This in turn would have jeopardised any good Sino-Burmese relationships and possibly have resulted in China sending its People's Liberation Army into Burma to deal with the KMT who had settled there. There were by February 1952 some two hundred thousand Maoist Army troops in Yunnan, and the Chinese government had begun a new road programme with a number of the roads leading towards Burma. A lesser but more likely problem was in the risk of increased Chinese support for the Burmese communists. China had already been providing training area facilities since late 1949. An additional worry to both Burma and to Thailand was the suggestion by Mao of an autonomous Tai ethnic state which would incorporate all Shans and citizens of Thailand. To Burma, this was an encouragement of Shan separatism. To Thailand, it was the road to domination.[191]

---

[190] *Nationalist China Troops in Burma: Obstacles to Burma Foreign Relations, 1949 to 1961;* K.R. Young; pp83/89 and *The Politics of Heroin;* Alfred W. McCoy; p133
[191] *Nationalist China Troops in Burma; Obstacles to Burma Foreign Relations, 1949 to 1961;* K.R. Young; pp59/68

Apart from a Chinese threat, Burma felt itself at risk internally because of the increase in the availability of arms in the mountains, to the general benefit of all insurgents. The early KMT forces had been armed with a mixture of weapons from China, Italy, and Czechoslovakia with a sprinkling of American arms, but by 1953 they were armed almost exclusively with American carbines Mark II and III, supplemented with light and heavy calibre machine-guns, mortars, and grenades of American manufacture. How was an original force of fifteen hundred armed men transformed into one of twelve thousand well-armed men, supported by occidental advisers? Burma could only deduce that it must be via Taiwan and therefore indirectly from America.[192] An alternative open route to the local KMT soldiery was that of supplies supposedly destined for Thai forces, but which became available as a bargaining counter for Shan opium. Later captures were to give a clear indication that American arms factories were the points of supply. The burden upon the Burmese government was the same, irrespective of the route. The more effort required by its Army to deal with the KMT, the more it drew fire power away from internal control of other insurgents.

Most of the opium produced in Burma in 1950 was shipped south from Mong Hsat through Thailand, the KMT having established mule train caravans from among local drivers. On their return journey they brought equipment, arms, and supplies from CIA sources in Thailand. A liaison officer was placed in Chiang Mai, attached to the Chinese Nationalist consulate. It was his task to deal with the movement of caravans into Thailand. The sale of the opium was usually handled through General Phao's police establishments which activity in turn provided cash for supplies of equipment, clothing, and food to be sent north. Phao handled the movement of the bulk of the opium within Thailand, whether for domestic use or ultimately for export. Apart from the mule caravans, Burmese military sources claimed that Air America planes were used to ferry opium to Bangkok and Taiwan.[193]

Thailand's stance in relation to the KMT in Burma was inconsistent over the years, but this was a reflection of both the power struggle within Thailand itself and the vested interests of some of its

---

[192] *KMT Aggression against Burma;* Burma Ministry of Information; p41
[193] *The Politics of Heroin;* Alfred W. McCoy; pp131/2

commercially-minded citizens. To many within Thailand the 'lost' army, which had originated as the 93rd KMT Division but had since substantially changed in character, was an apparent bulwark in the mountains against any incursions of the new Chinese government and its powerful Army. This attitude was encouraged by Mao's declaration of a Tai State. Thai politicians, and Phibun in particular, could still retain the hope of Thailand's own expansionism into the eastern Shan States which it had acquired temporarily during the Second World War, courtesy of the Japanese, and which the victorious allies had insisted on the Thai government returning. Perhaps best of all was the prospect of substantial American aid, arising out of an American interest in using a possible Thailand–Burma route back to China. This aid in turn led to personal profit, and for some of its traders there was also a prospect of obtaining supplies of wolfram and rubber in exchange for arms. Above all, for a select few and particularly the police, there was the promise of opium and the personal wealth that opium and its derivatives would bring. On the negative side was the inherent problem for the Thai government of a wandering army, acting without respect for territorial boundaries, even where such boundaries were known.

There was no doubt at the time of Chiang Kai-shek's ambitions and intentions to launch a full-scale attack on mainland China from Taiwan, supported by an attack on Yunnan province through the Shan States. It also seems that an element of logistical support would have been provided by America, and Thailand would have been the supply conduit. The long-term consequences for Thailand would have been disastrous, given the strength, ideology, and dedication of the Maoist regime and its People's Liberation Army. Even with massive American support, Thailand, not Vietnam, would have become the battleground of South-East Asia, with all the devastation that such savagery would have entailed.

CHAPTER SIX
The Phibun-Phao Era

By 1947 the opium monopoly in Thailand had thrived for almost one hundred years, but its increasing product price made it a much more attractive source of graft than prior to the Second World War. Foreign imports, chiefly from Iran and China, fell. Later, with the arrival on the Sino-Burmese border of the communist People's Liberation Army, the smuggling from Yunnan went into rapid decline. Countering this, indigenous production was thriving and the Thai government formally authorised poppy growing in the northern mountains. Substantial though the national production became, it was dwarfed by the immense quantities available from the Shan States, which were boosted by the increasing activities of the KMT troops installed there. Over the next decade, Bangkok developed into the hub of the narcotics trade in South-East Asia. With the KMT in Burma receiving much of its arms, equipment, and other supplies from America via Taiwan and Thailand, the forwarding of such material to the north took place under the watchful eye of the CIA's most favoured man in Thailand, Police-General Phao. Similarly when the opium moved south, either in payment or on request, it was controlled principally by Phao, to the considerable frustration of the Army and its commander, Sarit.[194] The opium traffic became so profitable to a number of the Thai élite that an anti-opium campaign, announced in 1948 with a termination date of opium smoking in 1953, was abandoned.

Phao Sriyanon was the son of a civil servant. Born in Bangkok in 1909 he was educated at the Royal Military Academy and graduated in 1930. At the time of the suppression of the Boworadej rebellion in October 1933 he became an aide to Phibun and a close relationship between them developed over two decades. It remained essentially a master-and-servant relationship, not a personal friendship, throughout the whole of that time. After Phibun became prime minister in 1938 Phao served him in a number of important but not first-rank positions. His position in Thai society was greatly enhanced when he married

---

[194] *Leadership and Power in the Chinese Community of Thailand*; G. Wm Skinner; p137

Khunying Udomlak, the strong-willed eldest daughter of General Phin. February 1941 saw Major Phao in Tokyo as a member of a delegation under the leadership of Prince Wan Waithayakorn, there to negotiate with the French and Japanese for an adjustment of the Thailand border with Indochina. Phao had by then become very much a member of Phibun's inner circle and when Phibun was ousted from the office of prime minister and supreme commander of the armed forces, Phao was also put out to grass on the inactive service list.

Phao's rapid rise to power began with the November 1947 coup. He was well placed for the task of liaison officer owing to his earlier contacts with Phibun and to his family relationship to Phin. As a reward for his efforts he was installed, at first unofficially, as head of political police activity and then, to the disgust of the minister of the interior, he was appointed deputy police chief. Phao, who was still not yet forty, was ambitious for both power and the wealth which would accrue from it. He was described as a man of imposing appearance, tall, broad, and commanding in behaviour. His reputation, even by 1947, was that of a fierce and ruthless man with his support founded in both fear and favour.[195] His ability to organise and administer were expressed not only in his police duties but also in his many business enterprises. His views of national and international politics were limited. Everything which could be deemed communist he detested; everything he detested, he labelled communist. His methods offer the conclusion that he would use any means available to him to achieve his personal ends. He achieved prominence despite a peculiar quirk of his military career, that up to his elevation within the police he had virtually no command experience within the Army proper. He was principally a political operator.

By 1948 the Thai economy was beginning to recover from its parlous wartime state. A report published internationally stated that *'minor political disturbances recurred but the depressing effects were short lived.'* The report also noted the establishment, with government support, of The War Veteran's Association and its control over the distribution and sales of cigarettes, of State services including stevedoring at government installations and of ferry services. It also noted the restriction to Thai citizens of the sole right to operate certain industries such as lacquerware, the production of Buddha images, the cultivation of rice, salt farming, Siamese typesetting, and even the

---

[195] *Politics in Thailand; David A. Wilson; pp129/32*

driving of tricycles.[196] Bangkok editor and friend of Pridi, Alexander
McDonald, declared that directly after the 1947 coup and the 1948
removal of Khuang, *"the military moved in precise formation into
government agencies, taking over the juiciest billets for graft. They
even invaded private businesses, young colonels becoming directors of
banks and managers of semi-government industries."* He quoted as
examples the Soi Rajakru clan of General Phin, his soldier son,
Chatichai and his sons-in-law, Colonel Phao and Major Pramarn
Adireksan together with close friends of the family, Police-Colonel
Lamai Utthayananon and Major Siri Siriyothin.[197] Phin, although back
into full-time military service, was noted for not losing sight of his
commercial interests. In this he was strongly influenced within the Soi
Rajakru clan by his father-in-law, an eminent Chinese businessman. It
was the latter more than anyone who kept Phin's mind concentrated on
the profitability of military interests rather than on the mere technical.

As head of the Thahan Samakkhi, a part of the War Veterans
Organisation, Phin's initial interest was in the soft drinks trade but he
soon turned his attention to newly-formed Chinese interests which had
control of the North-East Rice Millers Association. He observed that it
was an Association which lacked clout. Because of the soaring rate of
bribery or 'squeeze' which was necessary to get hold of railway
freight cars, it found transportation to its market both difficult and
expensive. Thahan Samakkhi and the Millers' Association merged
their interests to the considerable benefit of each. By 1949, seventy
rice mills in the north-east had become shareholders of the Thahan
Samakkhi. The Thahan Samakkhi gained full control of the freight
cars and the northeast railway line: squeeze was regularised and
allocated amongst the rice millers. They in return sold a minimum of
fifty per cent of their production to the Thahan Samakkhi which in
turn arranged export sales through government officers.[198]

A policy of 'Thailand for the Thais' resulted in a number of
politically-organised, Chinese-managed monopolies. To keep everyone
happy a suitable military and police representation was incorporated in
the Board of each. In 1950 the military persuaded, if that is the

---

[196] *Far Eastern Economic Review*; 13 October 1949
[197] Bangkok Editor: Alexander MacDonald; pp217/8 and *Thailand and the Fall of
Singapore;* Nigel J Brailey; p158 and *The Sarit Regime,* Thak Chaloemtiarana;
p123/note 88
[198] *Leadership and Power in the Chinese Community of Thailand*; G. Wm Skinner;
pp194/5

correct word, the sawmillers of the north-east to be organised into the North-East Sawmillers Association. It was a natural step for the Association to become a shareholder of the Thahan Samakkhi and for its products then to flow more freely to the market. Under successful Chinese management, the Bank of Ayutthaya saw its deposits increase fortyfold. Such a prosperous bank was an obvious target for government interference and support. Phao became an adviser and so did the president of the National Assembly, who was the head of the overall War Veterans Organisation. Subsidiary companies of the Bank were also obliged to require support. Phao became an advisory director to both the Sri-Ayutthaya Insurance Company, specialising in accident insurance, and to the Sri-Ayutthaya Life Assurance Company.

From 1948 onwards the control of pig butchery in Bangkok was fought out between Chinese interests and the increasingly powerful War Veterans Organisation. In 1952 came pressure to replace all Chinese interests in the pork cycle by interests under the direction of Thai nationals. A solution was eventually reached incorporating all pork interests in a Chinese/Thahan Samakkhi partnerships.[199] The next in line of reorganisation was gold. Phao, together with deputy minister of finance Prayun, took the initiative to rearrange the gold interests and create the Thai Gold Syndicate from the twelve major Chinese gold companies. Competition and gold smuggling were reduced. Gold was to be imported only through a newly-formed Thai financial syndicate and sold within seven days of arrival, at the official rate, to the Bank of Thailand. It naturally followed that, with gold itself under control, there had to be a Gold and Jewelry Merchants Association, representing the hundreds of small firms. Phao, with colleagues, acted as mediator and the Association was then merged with the Thai Gold Syndicate. The government, through a financial syndicate, set the price of gold and with it the profits to be reaped. The Chinese had learned that it was not so much a question of whether or not to co-operate with Phao but of how to get the best terms.[200]

With Phao as the driving force, the commercial empire of the Soi Rajakru clan was expanded until eventually it covered banking,

[199] *Leadership and Power in the Chinese Community of Thailand*; G. Wm Skinner; pp195/7

[200] *Far Eastern Economic Review*; 16 March 1950 and *Leadership and Power in the Chinese Community of Thailand*; G. Wm Skinner; pp198/9

insurance, gold, jute, sugar, maritime and fishing, marble, timber, and livestock.[201]

In parallel, Phao was rapidly improving his police-backed political power but his rise to eminence brought with it a number of grisly incidents. The crushing of the October 1948 Army rebellion led to the harassment of spouses of defendants and to mysterious deaths in prison. The 'palace' rebellion led to the murder of Phao's police rival, Banchongsak. During the confusion of that rebellion in February 1949, Police Colonel Banchongsak, a highly respected police officer, was indirectly implicated with Pridi's supporters. Without his prior consent, the name of Colonel Banchongsak had been suggested by Pridi for the post of head of the Bangkok police. After the suppression of the rebellion, orders were issued by Phao for Banchongsak to be arrested. He was shot and killed, allegedly for resisting arrest. Subsequent investigations revealed that while Banchongsak was in police service in Lampang, he had involved himself in an investigation of Phao's opium shipments. Court proceedings in 1958 disclosed that Phao sent one of his hatchet-men to Lampang to supervise the opium operations and it was also he who, in 1949, had been instructed to arrest Banchongsak.[202]

On third of March 1949 came the infamous "Kilo 11" incident. Four prominent supporters of Pridi — Thawin Udon, Dr Thongplaew Cholaphum, Chamlong Dowruan, and Thongin Phuripat — were shot while in the custody of the police, a piece of brutality which was to plague Phao until his overthrow in 1957. It was alleged by Phao that the prisoners had been killed by Seri Thai who were trying to free them. The allegation was discounted at the time and later a Seri Thai survivor confirmed this not to be the case. Two of the prisoners, Thawin Udon and Thongin Phuripat, were to have been among counsel for the defence at the regicide trial. There had been a long standing enmity between Thongin Phuripat and Phibun's supporters. With other Isan leaders, Thongin had crossed swords with the military clique before the 1941-45 war, first by attacking the 1937 defence budget and then going on to expose a scandal over the disposal of former royal properties to senior officials and senior members of the government.

---

[201] *The Thai Young Turks*; Chai-Anan Samudavajia; p16 citing Thammasat M.A. thesis by Sungsidh Piriyarangsan October 1980; pp226/93

[202] *The Sarit Regime*; Thak Chaloemtiarana; pp109/113

Phone Indarathat, the courageous Seri Thai who had made the solo journey south from Szemao in April 1944, also came into conflict with the police. He was found, handcuffed and shot. Lieut-General Kat Katsongkhram was more fortunate. He was arrested by Phao at gun-point in the office of the prime minister, and under a threat of being charged with treason and rebellion was forced into temporary exile in Hong Kong.[203]

The military was in no position to keep Phao's police force in check as the CIA had fed it with arms, armoured vehicles, naval vessels and aircraft to the extent that, by 1951, the police arm was unchallengeable. The American aid programme then and onwards was so directed in favour of the Thai police that it gave the impression of an American policy of deliberately and systematically distorting the Thai political base. In time the police held ascendancy over the Army, and as a result Phao gradually gained the upper hand in the opium grab. His strength was reflected politically, and for some years Phao was, without question, the most powerful man in Thailand. He used this power to enrich himself and his friends, not only through the handling of opium but also by running vice and protection rackets. He increased his corporate representation. He became the most anti-communist of all the front-rank Thais and his policy was to put pressure on the large Chinese community to remain pro-KMT. In contrast, Phibun's personal policy was to encourage the Chinese to be politically neutral.[204] Phao's support of a pro-KMT merchant policy in Bangkok was allied to his commercial connections which in turn were linked to his CIA support. Another link was to the Chiang Kai-shek-influenced American China lobby and the KMT lost army. This in turn sustained the opium trafficking from the Shan States for its onwards transmission under police management.

Why did America so systematically involve itself with Phao's supremacy? An answer can be found from an evaluation of the general scene of disarray of Asian politics over the late 1940s and early 1950s. Chiang Kai-shek and his Nationalists had fled China for Taiwan, and Mao Zedung's communists had taken over the government of China in

---

[203] *The Sarit Regime*; Thak Chaloemtiarana; pp58/60 and *Thailand and the Fall of Singapore*; Nigel J Brailey; p152 and discussions with Pisoot Sudasna na Ayutthaya 1987 to 1993

[204] *Leadership and Power in the Chinese Community of Thailand*; G. Wm Skinner; p139

October 1949. Further south on Thailand's eastern border, the French were rapidly losing control of Indochina. War had broken out in Korea. The American ambassador in Bangkok, Harold Stanton, advised President Truman that Thailand was threatened and that the possibility existed of a Chinese invasion of South-East Asia. In Washington, the return to power of Phibun in 1947 had been seen as a lesser evil than communist supremacy and invasion. Out of this there grew a convergence of interest. Phibun's recognition of the America-backed Bao Dai regime in Indochina; the establishment in Thailand in 1950 of an anti-communist committee and the despatch by Phibun of troops to support the United Nations forces in Korea, all helped Washington's thinking. In America, McCarthyism had reared its evil head.

In 1951, Washington saw in police-general Phao the essence of a national strongman with a flexible attitude to problems and with the qualities of leadership to implement American policy. It also knew that he could be bought. Phao in his turn saw the opportunity of adding another source of riches to those which he had been accumulating through both legal and illegal means. His legitimate interests were in banking and corporate directorships, which fell to him because of his position of power. His less savoury acquisitions of wealth arose through the control of opium smuggling, the protection of prostitution, and gambling.[205]

A bank director well-placed to know of the transfer through banking channels of gold destined to finance opium operations has spoken of the opium trade and of police involvement. Opium was bought from the poppy growing hill-tribes, collected and transported south to the opium dens in Bangkok which, until the time of Sarit, remained accepted establishments. On the way, there were many people involved in practices of cut and dilution, and eventually government inspectors verified an amount of opium and its percentage of purity. During the Second World War, Phibun's government gave the opium franchise to two people, the more important of whom was eventually to found a highly respected Thai bank. He had numerous contacts among the 1932 group and one of the objectives of the principal franchise deal was the enrichment of the 1932 coup group members and their friends. This principal franchise covered the purchase and sale of all opium for the legalised dens. Sub-franchises

---

[205] *US National Security Policy and Aid to the Thai Police*; Thos. Lobe; pp19/20

were given to people in northern Thailand. Their task was to collect the opium from hill-tribes and to deliver it to a government-owned warehouse in Chiang Mai. By the time it reached there, the sub-franchisees had already diluted the product in order to increase their profit. Before the opium eventually reached the dens, a number of other people had, in various ways, taken their cut. The Phao method was for gold to be transferred north through banking channels and used for purchases in the Shan States. The opium was purchased, brought south of the border, and seized by his police. The opium would then be exchanged for the reward which the government made to informers and to the police, a reward which was usually several times the market value of the opium. This relative valuation was enhanced when Phao himself, in addition to his policing and interior ministry roles, became the deputy minister of finance. He was then in a position to capture the product, determine the level of the reward, and still have the opium for disposal. Captured opium was diluted and sold to the dens. As the diluted opium was not as satisfying as the more concentrated form, the craving of the addicts would be stimulated, increasing the opium demand.[206]

Not all captures were an unqualified success. There were running battles behind the scenes between Phao and Sarit for the control of opium trafficking. While it was kept mainly a private affair, it came splendidly to light in 1950 in Lampang when an Army opium convoy was captured by the police. There was almost a public machine-gun fight but after two days of stand-off, Phao and Sarit arrived to take charge of the disputed product and remove it to Bangkok. Its subsequent fate was not disclosed but there was a general presumption that a deal was cut which profited both.

Phao was not alone in exercising police powers for private profit. A deputy police chief of Chiang Rai told of one of his superior officers near to the end of his career needing money to take care of his own future. He adopted Phao's methods. He gave notice to Phao that if he was not permitted so to do, he would make public Phao's own activities. His route north for the gold bullion was via Chiang Rai. Scouts were sent across the border to obtain the opium, which was then brought south through Mae Sai to Chiang Rai. Arriving there, it was formally seized by controlled police and conveyed by lorry to Lampang, where it was put on rail cars. After its conveyance south to

---

[206] Discussions with Dr Kraisri Nimmanahaeminda; 26 January 1987

Bangkok the reward and disposal process took place. Not all consignments had an easy ride. One lorry was badly shaken and a snake was discovered in the consignment. With the ensuing delay the contents became known to nearby villagers and the whole of the load disappeared. The furious senior police officer launched a replacement operation, sending more bullion across the border and this time bringing the opium out through the Fang route which would have led to Chiang Mai. Lest another load should vanish, he took no chances: he had the consignment seized north of Chiang Dao. It was not surprising, therefore, to find him, in 1952 and still a serving officer, as chairman of a commercial bank.[207]

Phao used his policeman to assist in his business interests, both legal and illegal. His politicised police provided him with economic information used for his personal benefit and at the same time brought fear to his opponents. His use of police powers for personal gain penetrated all areas of Thai society. He was more strongly anti-communist than either Phibun or Sarit, and he worked in secret with the CIA through the Anti-Communist Committee. He became the man America most expected to succeed Phibun, a belief which must have been enhanced by the action taken against the 'Sri Ayutthaya' during the Manhattan incident. That incident had allowed Phao full scope to unleash his hounds and it was the police force which took the lead in responding to the insurrection. Before it was over Phao's police had sacked a number of naval establishments, with heavy loss of life among the rebels. Sarit had brought in lighter elements of the Army, but not his armour. As Chatichai has explained, there is little use for armour in domestic differences of this nature.[208]

Washington needed a paramilitary force that could defend the Thai borders and be uninhibited when it came to trespassing into neighbouring Shan States, Laos, Vietnam, or Cambodia. Sarit's Army command was not as malleable as Phao's new police force, or more strictly, the CIA's police force, which was created as an élite force outside the normal channels of command. Phao agreed to this arrangement because of the increase in power that this new paramilitary force gave him personally against Sarit. The US National Security Council having agreed to build the paramilitary police force,

[207] *Leadership and Power in the Chinese Community of Thailand*; G. Wm Skinner; p167; and discussions with Dr. Kraisri Nimmanahaeminda; 26 January 1987
[208] Discussions with Major-General Chaticai Choonhavan; 1 July 1991

it was left to the CIA to create the front organisation. In Miami, the Overseas Southeast Asia Supply Company, or 'Sea Supply' was established. Sea Supply was the instrument to provide the Thai government, through Phao, with the equipment and the training for use by the new police units. Much of the Sea Supply activity in Thailand was overt. Retired American military men were provided by the CIA to act through Sea Supply as instructors. Their expertise was in intelligence, parachuting, communication, vehicle maintenance, and small-unit warfare. They were not there to tell Phao how to run a police force. Covert work within Sea Supply was provided only by CIA officers. Overt training was run in parallel with the covert delivery of armaments destined purely for the new paramilitary police units, the deliveries being made up of firearms, mortars, anti-tank weapons, grenades, parachutes, and medical equipment. What necessary equipment the paramilitary units did not receive directly, the CIA redirected from other American agencies. With Sea Supply help, Phao founded the first parachute training school in Thailand for the benefit of his police.[209]

In the calmer period which followed the 'Manhattan' incident and the November 1951 'silent' coup, Phao was able to enhance his political power and prestige, thanks particularly to the enriching flow of aid from America. To Chatichai, there was no question of rivalry between the police and the Army. These American supplies were essentially for the border areas and beyond. Therefore it was quite natural for an élite police force to benefit. Sarit, meantime, was concentrating on gathering supporters in the Army, which he would inherit on Phin's retirement. Friendly generals were placed in positions controlling fire-power. Commercial influence through appointments to boards of numerous corporations became the source of funds from which a power base could be strengthened and the loyalty of followers influenced. Phibun concentrated his personal attention on balancing the power of Sarit against Phao, thus preserving his own position.[210]

Not unpopular with the Thai nationals as a method of raising state revenue was the practice of increasing the annual alien registration

---

[209] *US National Security Policy and Aid to the Thai Police*; Thos Lobe; pp20/3

[210] *The Sarit Regime*;Thak Chaloemtiarana; pp96, 104 and 394 together with *From Armed Suppression to Political Offensive*; Chai-anan Samudavanija and others; p40; and discussions with Major-General Chaticai Choonhavan; 1 July 1991

fee. First set in 1939 at four baht, it was increased to eight baht in 1946 and twenty baht in 1949. After November 1951 there was a proposal to set it at two hundred baht, but on sixteenth of January 1952 the Cabinet increased the fee to three hundred baht. The charge was to be levied on all Chinese of eighteen to sixty years. Other aliens were similarly affected, but the dominant Chinese element was the target. Once in the hands of the National Assembly the fee became a maximum of four hundred baht, the actual figure to be decided each year with the Police Department by the Ministries of Interior and Finance. On twenty-fourth of January 1952 Phao submitted an Aliens Registration Bill to the National Assembly. The Chinese community brought all the pressure it could to bear on its friends in government but on twenty-third of February Phao, in his position as deputy minister of the interior, signed the decree. A visit to Phao early in March brought no help to the leaders of the Chinese community. At the end of March they appealed over his head to deputy prime minister Phin. Whilst some leading politicians hinted that they thought the figure of four hundred baht (then about twenty US dollars) was too high, Phao was adamant that the charge could be collected by his police. It turned out to be not as easy as Phao had thought. The Chinese community was up in arms, and disturbances broke out in the streets. Police bren-carriers moved into the Chinese community area, and whilst face-saving modifications were eventually made to the Bill, the nominal maximum remained. The result was that to counter pressure from the police the leaders of the Chinese community were increasingly thrown back on the bestowal of personal or business favours.

In 1951 the American ambassador to Thailand, Edward Stanton, was replaced by William J. 'Wild Bill' Donovan. Stanton, a diplomatic ambassador, was known to be unhappy at some of the activities of Sea Supply and of Phao. Not so his larger-than-life successor. There soon developed greater support for Sea Supply and for Phao personally. For his outstanding bravery in the first world war, Wild Bill Donovan had earned the Congressional Medal of Honour. In the Second World War he had been an American general and had founded the OSS, the forerunner of the CIA. He had no scruples about CIA activities, and thus none concerning Sea Supply.

His Second World War exploits in South-East Asia had involved him in outright confrontation with Tai Li whom he suspected of doing everything possible to hinder OSS and Seri Thai collaboration. He had on one occasion told Tai Li that if he, Tai Li, continued to obstruct American intelligence gathering, then America would act outside the Sino-American Co-operation Organisation. Tai Li threatened that if OSS so operated, he would have the OSS agents killed, to which Donovan retorted that for every agent the OSS lost he would kill a Chinese general. No one doubted that he meant it. Donovan had made a memorable visit to the OSS training school in the Naga Hills of India, jumping into a rickety Tiger Moth to fly to a tenuously held landing-strip behind Japanese lines to see for himself the work the OSS were undertaking and the equipment necessary to help them. Without any identity papers and at the mercy of any passing Japanese fighter plane, he demonstrated to the ordinary American serviceman and to many others the meaning of courage. In so doing, he earned from them their absolute loyalty.[211] Donovan was a great friend of Dr T. V. Soong, the one-time prime minister of Nationalist China and the brother of May-ling Soong, Madame Chiang Kai-shek. He was a forceful member of the American China lobby. He is remembered in embassy circles as a man not only of great physical and moral courage but also a man of great charm.

Donovan was convinced that Thailand was crucial to American interests in South-East Asia and that the CIA was the best instrument for fostering close relations. He firmly supported the arming of an élite Thai police force, the Border Patrol Police, and of increasing Phao's power. His attitude was summed up in his own words: *In the cold war struggle for South East Asia, the independent Kingdom of Thailand occupies a position of unique importance — both to the communist and to the free world, with which Thailand is presently allied. To Red China it is a tempting prize, for China needs rice, and Thailand's rice fields are among the most fertile in Asia. Moreover the conquest of Thailand, whether by invasion or subversion, would so expose neutralist Burma as to make its capitulation to communism almost inevitable. It would enable the communists to give direct support to their guerilla forces in British Malaya. If Thailand should fall, in short, South-East Asia might be lost... Thailand.. has*

---

[211] *Into Siam, Underground Kingdom*; Nicol Smith and Blake Clark; pp56/7 and *The Soong Dynasty*; Sterling Seagrave; pp365 and 397

wholeheartedly aligned itself with the West, and it welcomes US support. And that support can be given without committing ourselves, as we did in Indochina, to the support of a colonial regime doomed by the rising tide of Asian Nationalism.[212]

Donovan's predecessor Edward J. Stanton had earlier run similar arguments in support of Thailand. *"Thailand... is the heart and citadel of the region. ...a defensive system for South-East Asia can best function if it is based on Thailand, which is wholly free from the taint of colonialism. If Thailand's freedom and independence can be preserved, the heart and much of the body of South-East Asia will have been saved."* [213]

Donovan, with his dynamic approach to problem solving, was the man who made the outstanding contribution in developing close US-Thai relationships. He not only 'made' Phao but also became his close personal friend. Diplomacy frequently creates unusual friendships. Among Phao's other friends, say the Thais, was General Sir Gerald Templer, British commander-in-chief in Malaya. The British ambassador was not so sure; if friendship there was, he saw it as arising from knife-edged diplomacy. When the commander-in-chief, Malaya, was visiting Bangkok, Phao invited both him and the British ambassador to dinner at Police Headquarters: wives were not invited. They were greeted by a smart young, Sandhurst-trained ADC and asked to wait as General Phao was busy. Shortly after, the ADC returned and announced, *"The girl is now ready for General Templer. Please follow me"*. How the face of General Phao and the virtue of General Templer, as well as the assumed virtue of a rather beautiful sixteen-year-old Thai girl, were saved, the ambassador has not explained, but puts it down to his superlative diplomatic skills.[214] It might also have been due to the fact that the British ambassador thought that he would be called upon to bat second-wicket-down.

General Sir Gerald Templer had become High Commissioner of Malaya and its Director of Military Operations in 1951. He was a brilliant military strategist. Within two years he had put an end to the insurrection, led by the Chinese communist Chin Peng, which had

---

[212] From US Magazine *Fortune*, published July 1955, quoted in *The US and Thailand*; R. Sean Randolph; p27

[213] From US publication *Foreign Affairs* issued in October 1954

[214] *A Marvellous Party*; Sir Berkeley Gage; p181 and discussions with the author

been on the go for twelve years. A major problem for him was his inability to pin down Sarit and Phao as to who was actually responsible for preventing the leakage of terrorists from Malaya across the Thai border into apparent sanctuary. Templer, the only general in Asia to have won an all-out war with a communist force rather than to settle for a draw, needed the border sealing, but that would have entailed a battle which the Thais preferred not to have. They were more concerned with the north-east and north. It also was apparent that the infiltration of Malayan communists was of less interest to Phao and Sarit than which of them would control the lucrative concessions for soft drinks businesses such as Pepsi-Cola, Coca-Cola, and Green Spot. These were the big names in Thailand, not Ho Chi Minh and Chin Peng. Despite the lack of support given, Thailand owes much to the success of the Templer campaign, without which the insurgency problem in Thailand would have been far worse.[215]

At the beginning of 1952, the 1947 group controlled the government and the legislature. The Senate had been appointed by the group. The Lower House was elected in February 1952 but as political parties were banned the members ran as individuals. The group fielded and financed many of the candidates with Phao as the campaign organiser and fund raiser. Khuang and his Democrats boycotted the elections, claiming them to be immoral. After the elections a new constitution was promulgated, designed to serve the interests of the 1947 group. Within the Cabinet of Phibun's seventh government were Phin and his sons-in-law, led by Phao.[216] Sarit also remained a member of the Cabinet and for the first time his supporter, Thanom Kittikachon, was brought in, but without specific portfolio. The power both of the Phin's Soi Rajakru and Sarit's Sisao Deves cliques continued to increase. Phin had control of the Army, with the help of Sarit. Phao, now the country's strong man, had his power base in the police. Phibun had no internal power base to counter these strengths. The Lady La-iad has stressed the manipulation of power by both Phao and Sarit and has observed that the support given by

[215] *A Marvellous Party*; Sir Berkeley Gage; pp180/1
[216] *Thailand Modernisation of a Bureaucratic Polity*; Fred W. Riggs; p415

America to Phao in particular was noticeable. *"It was not disagreeable to Phibun ... but ... produced in him an uneasiness".*[217]

To avoid too much interference from the National Assembly, Phao established the "Legislative Study Committee". It was an extra-mural Cabinet sub-committee, free of the National Assembly and out of Phibun's direct control. Its objectives were to map out the political plans and assist the passage of bills. The Committee met at Manangkhasila House and Phao was its secretary-general. Under his direction it progressed into a *de facto* party which tolerated no opposition, a situation which continued until 1955. Each member received special compensation with travel privileges and the free importation of cars. Funds were reputed to come partly from the national budget and partly from Phao's opium profits.[218]

From 1947 onwards, in the various attempts of factions to capture power, force had become the acknowledged key to political success. Phao understood this well and perfected it in the build-up of the police as a personal force. The chain of command was tightened and the ésprit de corps of police officers was strengthened through Phao's personal influence. Eventually forty-three thousand strong, the police force was seen by both Phibun and Sarit to be as powerful as a second army. As police officers and policemen had daily duties to perform for the public and did not have as much available time for exercises and indoctrination as the Army, it was difficult for Phao to create a truly army-style solidarity among his men. To counter this he came up with his own tightly-knit group of officers-cum-bodyguards. Phao's corps of intimate followers were known as the *asawin*, usually translated as *knights*. They were police officers who were singled out by Phao for good work, some might say dirty work, carried out on his behalf. He was generous to his *asawin*, and they could be recognised by the gold or diamond rings which Phao would bestow upon them. He would also give to each a special financial retainer. In later years, Phao tried to transfer to Phibun the blame for their extensive brutality but relatives apart, no one doubted that such brutality was committed with Phao's full knowledge. The recognised translation of *asawin* as knight is unfortunate. There was little virtue, honour, and chivalry, or *'sans peur et sans reproche'* about the *asawin*.

[217] *Portraits of Thai Politics*; Jenton K. Ray: p213
[218] *The Sarit Regime*; Thak Chaloemtiarana; p105; and *Thailand and the Fall of Singapore*; Nigel J. Brailey; p163

The Americans, in their own interests, continued to be good to
Phao, supplying him with an almost unending stream of fire-power
The police had its own parachute division and for some years the only
paratroop training school in the country. Sea Supply provided
instructors for guerilla fighting. The strengthening of the police was
used to enforce not so much the law of the land as the power of its
political masters. M. R. Seni has referred to the state of affairs,
"Phao and Phibun turned the country into a Kingdom of fear".[219]
Phao's publicly stated reason for such an extensive police force was
that it was necessary for communist suppression. It was claimed that
there were ten thousand Chinese communists in the country and when
required by Phibun, another plot was conveniently uncovered. In the
suppressions, a number of left-of-centre politicians, Chinese
businessmen, and other dissident elements, including newspapermen,
were arrested. Government attacks on the Chinese brought a degree of
much-needed internal popularity. Police power was used principally
within the cities and particularly the capital, Bangkok. There was a
lack of contact with the country people but equally there was a lack of
challenge from such people until the Communist Party of Thailand
was able to infiltrate them.[220] While Phibun remained as prime
minister and Sarit, after Phin's retirement in 1954, controlled the
Army, it was essentially the fear created by the police which stabilised
the regime.

Phao's methods of trying to suppress civil crime foreshadowed the
methods he was willing to use against enemies of the regime. Shortly
after the 'silent' coup, Bangkok newspapers carried a news item
stating that seven bandits were killed while planning a hold-up. The
incident occurred at a temple while the bandits were allegedly making
their plans. They were not arrested but summarily shot by the police.
The National Assembly, although composed of carefully selected
members, was shocked at such behaviour. On being questioned over
this new police tactic of killing suspects even before a crime had been
committed, Phao replied that the police discovered (later) that all
seven had police records and were wanted for many previous crimes.
Following a similar pattern, force and violence were used to get rid of
Phao's personal and political enemies. Work of this nature was the

[219] *Portraits of Thai Politics*; Jenton K. Ray; p174
[220] *From Armed Suppression to Political Offensive*; Chai-anan Samudavanija and others; p44

province of the *asawin*. There was no means of redress. The violent tactics of the police were well-known and talked about behind closed doors, but investigation was impossible at the time for the crimes were committed by the police themselves. Prosecutions did not come to court until after Phao's removal.

While Donovan was at the American Bangkok embassy, Phao's progress gave satisfaction, and there was widespread expectation over the next two years that Phao would be Phibun's eventual successor. The American-Thai alliance was strengthened. It was aided massively by the Eisenhower administration, early in 1954, developing the Dulles' domino theory. This theory had its concept in a one-by-one falling of the South-East Asian nations and a policy of the need for a fall-back dyke across South-East Asia around the eastern and northern frontiers of Thailand. The close alliance, however, pre-dated the policy and was enhanced by the Donovan period in Bangkok.[221]

Phao's police showed few scruples when there was access to money to be gained. On ninth of March 1952 a fire had broken out in a thickly populated area of Bangkok, destroying housing and making almost twenty thousand people homeless. Little of the estimated two hundred million baht damage was covered by insurance. Most of the people made homeless were Chinese, and the Chinese community, first through the immediate ethnic group and later collectively, moved in to help with charitable relief. Then squabbles ensued between the various ethnic Chinese groupings and between pro-KMT and communist-led Chinese interests. Other fires occurred in the Chinese areas of Bangkok, bringing a call for further relief. In late June, the police joined the fray with a suggestion that it be given three hundred and twenty thousand baht for a new police fire-engine. In mid-July, a deputy police commander raised the amount to eight hundred thousand baht for three fire engines. By August the owner of the land, Chulalongkorn University, had decided that it would, itself, build on the land. Phao now interceded personally, pointing out to the leaders of the Chinese community that if the University was to build, then there must be surplus collection money and that this should be made available for supporting police fire facilities. Chinese involved in the raising of the charitable funds were called to police headquarters for questioning and in September the Chinese committee decided to

---

[221] *Thailand and the Fall of Singapore*; Nigel J Brailey; pp164 and 169/70

concede to the police request and hand over three hundred and twenty thousand baht, enough for one fire engine.[222]

Phao set about attacking internal peace movements and, continuing customary practice, the Chinese community. Allegations made against the Chinese community included the use of charitable funds for political purposes. Some one hundred and fifty Chinese business firms were raided and over two hundred and fifty Chinese were arrested. Community organisations and schools were raided. Many of those so arrested only obtained their release following substantial payments to the police.[223] There was a revival of pro-KMT interests and greater interchange with Taiwan, bringing pressure on the alleged communist influence. Another wide ranging communist plot to overthrow the government was conveniently discovered involving Thai opponents of the government, local Chinese business activities, and the Chinese government itself. Within three days of the first of the raids, Phao submitted his anti-communist bill to the National Assembly. It took the Assembly only a few hours to pass it in all its stages and to become the Un-Thai Activities Act of 1952. It was subsequently determined that there was no 1952 plot and that much of the information directed against alleged Chinese communists was laid by KMT agents allied to the 'lost army' in the mountains. At the time, the Communist Party of Thailand had a strength of less than two hundred although a Chinese-led rival party numbered about two thousand. An amalgamation of the two still left a party of no significance. Phibun was denounced by Radio Peking as a fascist, cruelly oppressing the local Chinese and slavishly subservient to Washington. Peking was more or less right. Persecution of the Chinese stayed in fashion. Some three years later the Thai newspaper *Satiraphap* commented *"It is the easiest thing in the world to bleed Chinese in our country. Merely preferring a charge of being a communist or having communist tendencies is more than sufficient for members of the police to obtain huge sums of money from them as they please"*.[224]

In 1952 a number of prominent Seri Thai disappeared. Thiang Sirikhan was a stout supporter of Pridi and in 1946 he had formed a

---

[222] Leadership and Power in the Chinese Community of Thailand; G. Wm Skinner; pp157/169

[223] *Leadership and Power in the Chinese Community of Thailand*; G. Wm Skinner; pp285/9

[224] Thai language newspaper, *'Sathiraphap'* published 31 August 1955

political party to support him. In 1948 he, with other Isan Seri Thai, had been involved in attempting to create the 'Federated States of the Golden Peninsula'. He was arrested but later released without trial. In February 1952 he was elected to the National Assembly. Approached by Phao to support the Phibun government he agreed but the co-operation was short lived. In the following December he was arrested and interrogated over an alleged plot for a coup in the previous October, a time when he was closely associated with the Vietnamese links of the Communist Party of Thailand.[225] He was not seen again. Phao at first denied knowledge of Thiang's disappearance but later said that Thiang had fled to Burma to escape arrest. Seri Thai contemporaries believed that Thiang was put to death.

Two brothers well known in theatre circles, Chan and Lek Bunnag, were also casualties. Back in 1942 while both were working at the Chalerm Theatre they incurred the wrath of Phibun over a trivial street offence. They were arrested and later harassed by Phibun's young aide, Phao, who in time forced them out of theatre work. But Chan and his brother took up new interests, first of which was film-making and the second was the activities of the Seri Thai. They became friendly with Pridi and also with Thiang. At Thiang's behest, Chan had taken into his film business a friend, Phong Khiewwichit. Arrested in December 1952, Chan, Lek, Phong, and Thiang's chauffeur all disappeared. In 1958 it was established by criminal prosecution that all had been strangled, removed to Kanchanaburi, burned and buried. Excavation of the grave produced confirmatory evidence. Phao had rewarded each of the police NCOs and constables involved in the murders with thirty thousand baht.[226]

Commercial activities continued to flourish. The rice millers in the north were organised into the Northern Rice Millers Association under Thahan Samakkhi auspices so that by 1952 one hundred and thirty-two rice mills and thirty-eight sawmills, principally Chinese in management, were shareholders of the Thahan Samakkhi. The Wei-hsin Insurance Company had been formed to 1951, prior to the silent coup, with an all-Chinese Board. In 1952, following the arrest of its most prominent citizen and Board Member, it decided that alliance with the Thai police might be helpful. The assistant chief of

---

[225] *The Rise and Fall of the Communist Party of Thailand*; Gawin Chutima (University of Kent, paper No. 12); p8
[226] *The Sarit Regime*; Thak Chaloemtiarana; pp115/9

the Police Department Suppression Force and three police colonels joined its Board. The Asia Trust Company also found a need to re-organise its Board: Phao became Chairman.[227] The Phibun government considered re-organisations of this nature to be a reasonable way of increasing Thai interests in companies which drew their wealth from the country. Basically the Chinese provided the capital, the management, and technical expertise. The Thais provided protection, some of its contracts, and the personal safety of the non-Thai members of the Board. The practice started in embryo in 1949, intensified after the 'silent' coup, and reached its peak over the 1952/3 period.

Whilst in its day the Pridi government had attempted to protect Laotian and Khmer "free" movements, Phibun, on taking over power in 1947, drastically altered Thailand's policy towards its eastern and north-eastern neighbours. Communist victories had frightened Phibun into allying his country with the Western anti-Communist bloc. He even re-established good relations with France, one result of which was a renunciation of his "Greater Thai" concept. This renunciation was helped by China. On seventeenth of January 1953 the New China News Agency announced the establishment at Sibsongpanna in Yunnan of a Tai Nationality Autonomous People's government, the capital of which was to be at Cheli. The newly-formed state was to be under the leadership of Mao Zedong and was to *"lead the Thai people to help other nationalities inhabiting the area to establish their own autonomous governments; strive through a common effort to smash the sabotage activities of American imperialists and Chiang Kai-shek's agents; strengthen national defence; and build a new and better life for the population of the region".*[228] Phibun stressed the artificiality of the new state and offered his opinion that principal posts would be filled by refugees from Thailand. As Cheli had been for a time the headquarters of the Seri Thai resistance movement it was assumed that some of the surviving Seri Thai leaders might re-appear. In practice, the pseudo state gave Phibun and succeeding governments no cause for

---

[227] *Leadership and Power in the Chinese Community of Thailand*; G. Wm Skinner; pp192/5
[228] Report of a speech at the inaugural ceremony speech; *Bangkok Post* 26 February 1953

worry but at the time it strengthened the Stanton-Donovan theory of a possible invasion by China of South-East Asia.

1953 also saw the penetration of Laos by Vietminh forces, albeit in the course of their war with the French. They appeared first in April and moved within striking distance of the Thai border not far from the old Laotian imperial city of Luang Prabang. In December they reappeared in the vicinity of Savannakhet, just across the Mekong. Some three months later, the Viet Minh defeated the French at Dien Bien Phu in northern Vietnam.

The developments in Laos brought important issues for Phibun and his government. For four hundred years the ancient Kingdom of Lan Xang, the Kingdom of a Million Elephants and a White Parasol, had spread across modern Laos, north-eastern Thailand, as far as the Khorat Plateau and Chiang Mai, whilst in the south it reached into Cambodia down to Angkor. In the late seventeenth century the area had disintegrated into a number of small kingdoms, the two most prominent of which were Luang Prabang and Champassak. Thai rulers, seeking their own advantage, had made the occasional military sortie. At the end of the nineteenth century the invading colonial French had arrived and Laos was created as a part of French Indochina. The Japanese came and went. In 1946 the French returned and in 1949, Laos became a semi-independent kingdom within the French Union. In 1954, after Dien Bien Phu, the Geneva Accords ended the colonial empire of French Indochina and Laos became an independent, neutral state.[229]

The neutral state was also a state divided into three factions, each led by a prince of the blood. Some of the blood was more princely than the other. The only true neutralist faction, or perhaps patriotic faction, was led by Prince Souvanna Phouma, son of the principal line of Luang Prabang royalty. Souvanna had been twice prime minister in the early years but rightist elements, pressurised by American ambassador J. Graham Parsons, ousted him from office and he became the Laotian ambassador to Paris. The extreme rightist faction was led by Prince Boun Oum of Champassak royal blood and a protégé of the aggressive extreme right wing general Phoumi Nosavon. The extreme leftist faction, which already controlled the two

---

[229] *In a Little Kingdom*; Perry Stieglitz; pp4/9 and *Scope of the US Involvement in Laos*; Richard S. Nixon; p1 (Perry Stieglitz was a US Cultural Attaché in Laos and married Princess Moune, the daughter of Prime Minister Prince Souvanna Phouma)

148

northern provinces, had become the Pathet Lao and the puppets of Ho Chi Minh's North Vietnamese. It was led by the 'red' Prince Souphannouvang, a son of Luang Prabang royalty but of a lesser wife. He was married to a Vietnamese who was herself a supporter of Ho Chi Minh. Thailand's problems with Laos were mostly in the future but the time to be wary had arrived.

At this same time, the American attitude to South-East Asia was hardening. In 1953 General Dwight D. Eisenhower became President on a policy which had declared the Truman administration to be "soft on communism" and principally responsible for the loss of China. It saw communism as swamping the former colonial areas unless it were stopped by firm American action.[230] America stepped up its military assistance to Thailand as well as accepting up to seventy per cent of the cost of the French Indochinese effort, a remarkable step for anti-colonial America. On twelfth January 1954 John Foster Dulles made his 'massive retaliation' speech on behalf of the Eisenhower administration in which he stressed the need for community deterrent power, able to resist a communist aggressor for a sufficient period of time to allow America to strike at vital industrial and communications centres of that communist aggressor *'with massive retaliatory power'*. This view was not unanimously held. The following sixth of April, the young senator John F. Kennedy attacked the policy as *'dangerously destructive'*, leading to a situation far worse than that encountered in Korea.[231]

While it was prepared to risk a war with communist China, America did not seek to provoke one. Instead it sought an agreement between a number of South-East Asian states, each to come to the aid of any state attacked if so requested by that state. Initially Dulles wanted a military alliance in place before any detailed negotiations, seeing it as supportive of a negotiating position. It was in attempting to enforce his policy that he clashed with Britain. Firstly, Dulles could not accept the ascendance of Chou En-lai and Ho Chi Minh as major Asian statesmen with whom he would have to negotiate. Secondly, with his President's approval but without reference to his allies, he included in a dramatic speech to the Overseas Press Club of America

[230] *The US and Thailand*; R. Sean Randolph; p17
[231] *The Furtive War;* Wilfred G. Burchett; p59

on twenty-ninth of March 1954, the reference to the threat of imposition of the communist political system on South-East Asia, 'by whatever means' as being so grave a threat that it *"should not be passively accepted but should be met by united action"*.

It was not long before Britain sought to know whom America considered to be 'united'.[232] Britain did not like and would not accept diplomacy by *fait accompli*. It denied that there was any agreement with Dulles. France concurred.[233] Australia and New Zealand rejected advances to them to discount Britain and enter into a separate alliance.[234] Criticism was heaped on Dulles by the American Democratic Party and eventually the efforts to form an early military alliance failed. With it, the risk of head-on confrontation between America and China, spilling over into Thailand, diminished. The policy and patience of British foreign secretary Eden had brought its rewards, but success in South-East Asia was to cost him dear. Two years later, Dulles, with his President's backing, led America and its foes against its old friends over the battle for the Suez Canal and in the process he destroyed Eden.

There can be no underestimation of the importance of the role of John Foster Dulles in relation to the countries of South-East Asia. It was accepted that he was a man of great intellect, of courage and of a determination to change the whole emphasis of American foreign policy. To him, the task of America was to intervene directly and positively to roll back communism, particularly in South-East Asia. In so doing, he turned his back on Europe and particularly on Britain, thus reversing the Second World War alliance and the relationships of the Truman presidency.

To President Eisenhower, it was an important issue of morality that to America, all non-communist states must be seen to be equal and with no distinction between its allies and others. To Dulles, the world had to be saved by America from colonialism as well as from communism. So concerned was he of the righteousness of his beliefs that proposals of alternative approaches to political problems could summarily be rejected even although made by politicians of far greater experience, and frequently of greater wisdom derived from that experience, than himself. He frequently clashed with the British

---

[232] *New York Herald Tribune* 4 April 1954
[233] *Full Circle;* Sir Anthony Eden; p116
[234] *The Times* of London; 22 May 1954

foreign secretary, Eden, who refused to bow the knee to him. Eden, backed by his prime minister, Winston Churchill, whom he was soon to succeed, believed that South-East Asia problems could be settled by negotiation with states seeking self-determination and that direct confrontation was neither necessary nor practical. He was also closer to his French counterpart than Dulles realised and an attempt by Dulles to divide them and win his own way failed. Both insisted on negotiation with the communists before establishing a South-East Asian military alliance.

The situation in Indochina however was already grave and, despite American help, France suffered a series of reverses until it was eventually forced to the conference table in Geneva. That conference, which took place from twenty-sixth of April to twenty-first of July 1954, produced two settlements. The first was a bilateral armistice between France and the Vietminh. The second was a multilateral declaration which made provision for a temporary dividing line between North and South Vietnam pending general elections to unify the country in July 1956. America did not endorse the Agreement but indicated that it would respect it. That indication of respect sits oddly with an announcement in September in the Laotian National Assembly by the minister of Defence, Kou Voravong, that he personally had endorsed the cease-fire agreements on the instructions of the prime minister, Souvanna, because the minister of foreign affairs, Phoui Sananikone, had been paid one million US dollars by an American agent not to sign. However patriotic, public statements of such a nature are both imprudent and dangerous. Kou Voravong was murdered while dining with Phoui in Vientiane on eighteenth of September. The assassin was reported to be a Thai hit-man, brought across the Mekong for the job by the CIA.[235] The Souvanna government was forced to resign. It was replaced by that of Katay Don Sasorith, the owner of a bank through which American aid funds were channelled. He presided over a period of crisis, the last three months of which were occupied with futile attacks on the Pathet Lao. In December 1955 Katay in turn was replaced, and once more Souvanna became prime minister.[236]

---

[235] *The Furtive War;* Wilfred G. Burchett pp161/2; and *Vietnam, A Diplomatic Tragedy;* V. Bator
[236] *The Furtive War,* Wilfred G. Burchett; pp163/168

Prime Minister Field Marshall Phibun Songkhram.
(The Nation)

General Phin Choonhavan, Commander 3rd Division, Royal Thai
Army, raising the Thai flag over captured Kengtung, 1942.
(From the private collection of General Chatichai Choonhavan)

Free Thai Forces officers at Szemao, April 1944. In the central group
are Lt. Boonyan Sasi-ratana and Lt.-Col. Kharb Kunjara
(commander) at the rear with Lt. Sawasdi Cheow-saleul and Lt.
Pisoot Sudasna in the front.
(From private collection of Pisoot Sudasna)

Father Tong and the 'medical pedlars' at Szemao prior to their
journey through Burma, Laos and Thailand. April 1944.
(From the private collection of Pisoot Sudasna)

Statue of Police-General Phao Sriyanon at the Central Police
Academy, near Bangkok.
(Photograph by Donald F. Cooper)

Statue of Dr. Pridi Banomyong at Thammasat
University, Bangkok.
(Photograph by Donald F. Cooper)

Prime Minister Field Marshall Thanom Kittikachon.
(The Nation)

Eisenhower and Dulles saw the 1954 Geneva agreement as making North Vietnam a first domino to fall to communism with the elections in 1956 likely to produce the second by way of South Vietnam. To the US National Security Council, the 1954 agreement was a disaster which would lead to the loss of all of South-East Asia to communism. Many on the spot thought otherwise. Dulles was seen by them as a man with an obsession over dominoes falling and the need for them to be propped up. Dulles saw communism as something totally monolithic, but more knowledgeable diplomats, the ambassadors appointed to that area, could clearly see it as nationalistic. To them there were evident antagonisms between the Vietnamese, the Cambodians, the Laotians and the Chinese. If, or when, the communist peoples' republics were formed they were certain to start up the old antagonisms, a behavioural pattern which might well have been turned to the advantage of the West. The British ambassador to Thailand admitted later that the idea never occurred to him that America, after its Chinese lesson, would get itself involved in an Asian civil war. Much less could he even contemplate that it would commit the ultimate folly of sending American troops to fight, in its own natural environment, a war-toughened people's army which had already defeated experienced French forces. To him, Thailand was the natural pivot of Western influence.[237]

Phibun had now changed the direction of his foreign policy. In his period as prime minister from 1938 to 1944 there had been a dedication to the creation of a new but fully sovereign and independent Thailand. The bitter experience of 1941, when flexible independence had brought no support from major powers against the overwhelming power of the Japanese, had provoked new thinking. If Thailand could not live with total independence it needed to choose carefully with which power it would align itself. He could not afford to be wrong for a second time. Neither communist China nor Japan, for totally different reasons, was acceptable. Post-war suspicions of Britain may have faded but had not disappeared. Equally, Britain, intent now on shedding, not building, an empire had little interest in support for Thailand if that support required military backing.

America had both the muscle and the money that appealed to Phibun. It was also clear to him that America was prepared to be generous with both to support its own anti-communist obsession and to

---

[237] *A Marvellous Party*; Sir Berkeley Gage; p177

accept the 'domino theory', which he had himself put forward earlier. Eisenhower himself emphasised his belief in the domino theory at a press conference held on seventh of April 1954. Britain made it clear that it strongly supported the containment of communism but that it had no time for what had become a Dulles' crusade against it.[238] Phibun now followed up some of his ideas for a defence organisation for the area on the lines of the North Atlantic Treaty Organization. He was partly successful. Limited aid was offered initially but that in itself brought domestic problems with people who saw him turning Thailand into an American colonial-type puppet. For Phao and also for Sarit, opportunities existed in plenty and they were to enjoy the fruits of the American/Phibun policy.

The American policy for Thailand became more specific. America was to: *"concentrate efforts on developing Thailand as a support of US objectives in the area and as a focal point of US covert and psychological operations in South-east Asia"*. To this end it prescribed that military assistance was to be provided to be sufficient to increase the strength of indigenous forces, thereby helping to control local subversion and at the same time making it easier to observe overt aggression. The programme was to be backed with economic assistance.[239] As a result, American aid to Thailand was intensified, firstly under pressure from the deteriorating situation in Laos and later, after 1964, in response to the American military needs for the Vietnam war.

Gradually, the concept of a South-East Asia defence grouping emerged and came to fruition in September 1954. America was able to bring about the Manila conference and from that the South-East Asia Collective Defence Treaty. With it came the creation of the South-East Asia Treaty Organisation (SEATO). SEATO was not acceptable to the non-militarist countries of India, Burma, and Sri Lanka, and particularly the former which viewed Ho Chi Minh as a nationalist leader, fighting for independence from colonial rule.

The Washington view prevailed, overriding the European wish not to be embroiled in guarantees in the SEATO region. Britain and France were, however, conscious of the key geographical role of Thailand, and because of this, each put its name to the SEATO accord. Other members consisted of the Philippines, Pakistan (for

---

[238] *Vietnam, A Diplomatic Tragedy*, V. Bator; p105
[239] US National Security Committee document No. 5429/2

what was to become Bangladesh), Australia, New Zealand, and America. Phibun had his regional treaty. SEATO headquarters was established in Bangkok and the ex-Thai Ambassador to America, Phote Sarasin, became its first secretary-general. The regional members numbered three only; the external members, some not too enthusiastic, numbered five. Laos, Cambodia, and non-communist South Vietnam were excluded, but it was intended that they should, discreetly, be covered by the treaty. It was not everything that Phibun would have wished but it did at least stress Thailand's pivotal role. It also continued for him the full co-operation of the American embassy in Bangkok.[240] Despite the wishes of John Foster Dulles, SEATO developed as the European governments had hoped, a low-profile organisation dealing more with political exchanges than acts of war.

The Treaty consolidated the Thai regime and particularly the interests of Phibun, Phao, and Sarit. America, unwittingly, became the instrument of a military-dominated government which was bent on removing the last vestiges of democracy from the country as it used international political aid in the cause of security-oriented self-preservation. It was the price that the West had to pay to align Thailand with its own interests.

With the liaison established with Sea Supply, two specialised paramilitary police units had come into being. The first of these had been the Police Aerial Reconnaissance (Resupply) Unit, specialising in parachuting into isolated areas to conduct long range patrols, collect tactical and political intelligence, and to sabotage enemy facilities. By the end of 1953, its personnel, trained by Sea Supply, numbered over three hundred. The second group, the Border Patrol Police, known at that time as the Territorial Defence Police, was responsible for security along the international frontiers. By the end of 1953, the Border Police had expanded to a force four thousand two hundred and thirty strong, ninety-four platoons of forty-five men each. They were well armed, mobile, counter-insurgency fighters specialising in intelligence-gathering along the borders and in conducting cross-border combat and reconnaissance operations. The forces developed an intense loyalty to the King, a feature encouraged by

---

[240] *The US and Thailand*; R. Sean Randolph; pp19/20

Phao and by his CIA backers. The Aerial Reconnaissance Unit's headquarters was moved to a site adjacent to the King's Hua Hin palace. As the paramilitary units grew in strength, so did the power of Phao Sriyanon.

The CIA numbers in Thailand grew. At the end of 1953 there were known to be at least seventy-six overt advisers and as many as two hundred additional covert Sea Supply advisers. Stocks of armaments, from machine guns to tanks and aircraft, were increased. The CIA maintained control and saw the Aerial Reconnaissance and Border Police as 'its' units. CIA and Thai operatives worked, fought, and drank together; sometimes they died together. At the top, the relationship was that of a close personal friendship between Ambassador Donovan with police-general Phao. America had its Thai man in place to serve American policy. Phao prospered from the ambassadorial and CIA relationships. With the political and paramilitary police under his personal command he was able, and did not hesitate, to use that power to extend his corporate financial interest. So great was the level of wealth he achieved that he was able, personally, to extend the arming of forces he favoured. Border Police operations were conducted to eliminate political and commercial opposition. The CIA condoned the practices because of his willingness to perform operations that served American interests.[241]

Phao had another side to him. Not only was he a capable administrator, he was also sociable, and was generous to those who carried out his tasks whether political or commercial. This, together with the loyalty which élitism enhances, contributed to a high ésprit-de-corps. From time to time the British ambassador invited Phao and some of his *asawin* to dine at the embassy. He took the precaution of requiring them to hand over their arms when they entered British territory, a practice which on occasions he was glad to have enforced. Trouble appeared to be brewing on one visit when Phao arrived in an angry state with two Thai banknotes, printed in Britain, bearing identical numbers. Anger, however, appears to have been mollified without diplomatic incident by the hurried arrival in Bangkok of a director of the company, sufficiently experienced in the ways of pacifying Phao without bothering too much about the rights and wrongs of the particular allegation. The astuteness of the director concerned was perhaps reflected in the facts that this beneficial

---

[241] *US National Security Policy and Aid to the Thai Police*; Thos. Lobe; pp24/27

contract long remained in force and that he himself, some years later, became a Lord Mayor of London.[242]

Alongside political change, commercial reorganisations continued apace. The Huanch'iu Insurance Company invited the chief of the Bangkok Metropolitan Police to join its Board, which he did. The Bangkok Bank, originally an all-Chinese organisation, invited among others, from the Soi Rajakru clan, Pramarn and Siri. That same year the Kuang-hsing-li Lighterage Company, formerly totally Chinese, was reorganised as the Luamliang Shipping Company. The government took a ten-per-cent share and Phao became Chairman of the Board with brother-in-law, Pramarn, the Managing Director. Other companies similarly processed included the Siam Trading Company, the Chaloem Nakhon Insurance Company, the Sahajontara Company, and the Thai Commercial Insurance Company. The Thai Farmers Bank, previously an all-Hakka Chinese Board, accepted Thanom from the Sarit camp. Over the period 1951 to 1953 there emerged a number of new Sino-Thai companies. The Sun Life Assurance had the services of Khuang as its managing director. The Thai Nawa Shipping Company was similarly established with strong Thai government or friends representation. The King's Cinema, formed in 1953 not only had Phao as its chairman but also the chief of Bangkok Metropolitan police as its vice-chairman and Pramarn as a member of its Board. The Thai-dominated companies were careful to protect their financial interests and did not risk their profitability by relying on their own limited skills. Most had Chinese entrepreneurial leadership and even the nationalistic War Veterans Organisation had a strong Chinese managerial element.[243]

To give further encouragement to Thai companies, semi-governmental promotion bodies were developed. In March 1953 a Food Trade Promotion Committee, headed by the minister of economic affairs, was established to promote the taking over by Thai trade associations of alien-controlled bodies. In May, priority was given to Thais renting new shop-homes. In June, the Thai Express Transport Bureau took over all trucking from the Port of Bangkok to the exclusion of foreign companies. In July the same Bureau took over all major internal bus routes in Bangkok. Where practical, Thai

---

[242] *A Marvellous Party*; Sir Berkeley Gage; p188
[243] *Leadership and Power in the Chinese Community of Thailand*; G. Wn Skinner; pp192/194

corporate bus companies were licensed on external routes to the exclusion of foreign operators.[244] In November 1953, the Cabinet established the Economic Co-ordination Council, headed by Phin, to assist the expansion of private trade by Thai nationals. Banks were required to provide low-interest loans and the railways were required to give priority to Thai products.[245]

In the meantime there was no lessening of police brutality. Phon Malithong was an elderly member of the National Assembly. He had been a bitter critic of Phao and publicly attacked him both inside and outside the National Assembly. His surveillance by the police and a proposed attempt to frame him were disclosed to him by an informer, hoping for money. Courageously, but unwisely, Phon spoke openly of the issue. He was summoned for police interrogation and later both he and the informer were discovered, strangled, in the Chao Phraya river.[246]

Power is best fed by money. In building up his political following, Phao used his opium trading to finance his political machine. With political parties banned, no other group could organise itself to rival his extra-mural executive committee. He fought the re-establishment of parties on the twisted logic that they would infringe upon the freedom of speech of the MPs themselves. In 1954 the Soi Rajakru clan strengthened its political grip when Siri Siriyothin became minister of economic affairs and Chatichai, now a Brigadier-General, became head of the prime minister's military staff. Phao took over as deputy minister of finance, still retaining his appointments as deputy minister of the interior and director-general of police.[247]

On the night of sixteenth and seventeenth of February 1955 came the ultimate climax of the regicide trial which followed the death of King Ananda in June 1946. The primary researcher, Kruger, has said, *"What can no longer be argued is that three innocent men were done to death by a corrupt regime illegally brought into being..."* [248]

---

[244] *Leadership and Power in the Chinese Community of Thailand*; G. Wm Skinner; p302

[245] *Bangkok Post*; 9 November 1953

[246] *The Sarit Regime*; Thak Chaloemtiarana

[247] *The Sarit Regime*; Thak Chaloemtiarana; p123/note 88

[248] *The Devil's Discus;* Rayne Kruger; p240

Police-general Phao was present to witness the execution. His head-dress for the occasion was a red beret, hardly appropriate when, elsewhere at that time, it was looked upon as a badge of courage. At four o'clock in the morning the first and most senior of the accused was bound to the cross of execution; joss sticks and flowers were placed in his hands. The executioner, hidden by a screen, fired a pre-targeted machine gun. By five o'clock all three were dead.[249]

Kruger's comprehensive study examines in detail the possibilities surrounding the tragic death of the young King. For perfectly understandable reasons over such an unquestionably sensitive national issue, most of the sources of information remain undisclosed but Kruger claims that all information was corroborated. A senior British Embassy official with whom he discussed many aspects of his work held Kruger in the highest regard as a sound, reliable, and painstaking researcher whose writings should be respected. He, the official, believed that Kruger had become convinced that the answer lay in accidental shooting, either by the young King himself or in some way as the result of a tragic mishap between two young men playing together.

King Bhumibol himself has eliminated one of Kruger's options by his personal statement that his brother was dead when he himself entered the room. Such a declaration has the absolute authority of the word of the King. In making it, he has left the principal options exactly as they were in 1946, either an unfortunate accident or, to the Thai people, the unacceptable possibility of suicide. Some thirty-three years after the event, the specific question was put to the King, *"After so many years, how do you believe that your brother died?"* The King, obviously distressed by the question, replied hesitatingly, *"The investigation provided the fact that he died with a bullet wound in his forehead and this is the — it was proved that it was not an accident or not a suicide. One doesn't know. But what happened is very mysterious because the — admittedly much of the evidence shifted. And then because it was political, so everyone was political, even the police were political. So it is a fact — that is not very clear — I only know what happened."* Asked again about going to the scene he replied, *"When I arrived, he was dead. Many people wanted to advance not theories but facts to clear up the affair. They were*

---

[249] *The Devil's Discus*; Rayne Kruger; pp191/2

suppressed and they were suppressed by influential people in this country or in international politics".[250]

Only a year or so before this statement, Pridi, in exile in Paris, had commented on the death. *"From the day I knew of the death of King Ananada Mahidol until the time I learned of the supreme court's ruling on twelfth of October 1954, I honestly believed that the King had ended his life from an accident committed by himself, and there were many reasons for such honest belief."* He pointed out that the police in Thailand were not afforded the same access as elsewhere, as no commoner could touch the royal personage and an autopsy was not performed. The body was moved from the actual position in which it was believed to have been discovered in order to bandage the wound before any police were allowed in the chamber.[251] In other circumstances, such action might have been interpreted as tampering with evidence. Prime Minister Phibun is known not to have believed in the assassination theory. During a visit to his father in exile in Japan, his son, General Anand Phibunsongkhram, established not only this position but also that his father had sought an amnesty for the accused men.[252] An officer of a foreign embassy, later to become an Ambassador, recalled the discussions of the day. Whilst there could be no certainty as to what actually happened, there was a unanimous agreement around the embassies that the three men executed were innocent pawns in the hands of a brutal, police-dominated regime.

The verdict of the regicide court against the three men had been given on twenty-seventh of September 1951. One of the three was found guilty and the case against the other two was dismissed. Both defence and prosecution appealed against appropriate sections of the verdict. In December 1953 the Appeal Court handed down a fourteen-hour judgement. The sentence of death on the first of the accused was confirmed whilst the innocence of the second was overturned and he was condemned to death. The third remained free. Both defence and prosecution now appealed to the supreme Thai court, the Dikka. On thirteenth of October 1954, the Dikka handed down a brief judgement on the appeal from the Regicide Court. All

---

[250] *The Soul of a Nation*; BBC post-production script, written Leo Aylen, produced by Bridget Winter; pp34/35

[251] *Pridi Banomyong*; Vitchitvong na Pombhejara; pp250/253

[252] *Pridi Banomyong*; Vitchitvong na Pombhejara; pp269/71

three of the accused were sentenced to death. Four months later their appeal to the government for clemency was rejected.[253]

Were the judges of the various levels of courts free from pressure from a regime which had put the solving of the crime high in its priorities of justification for the 1947 coup? To the royalist element within the military, solving the 'crime' of the death of King Ananda could more than justify its actions. Over forty years later it was argued that nothing was more important to the plotters of 1947 than this one matter.[254] An unbiased view might be that it became a convenient cause by which to justify the other illegal actions and that nothing would suffice short of an execution.

The position and the status of a judge in Thailand was then not as generally practised in the west. Judges were paid civil servants and many, after a period in office, would (and still do) retire and take up more lucrative employment in industry and commerce. Judges were known to have had pressure put upon them, as in the case of Phibun's release from the war crimes trial. There was a precedent for dismissal from office for giving a judgement unacceptable politically, as in the case concerning the alleged misappropriation of funds by King Prajathipok when the findings were not to Phibun's liking.[255] Asked if pressure was possible in the regicide trial a civil servant of the time said that he had no doubt that Phao, above all people, would have been satisfied with nothing less than a murder verdict and prompt execution. More than one judge was conscience-stricken over a verdict in which he had been involved. One died in unexplained circumstances in a high-speed crash.

Phao claimed that the three men admitted to their guilt and had told him the true facts on the morning of their execution.[256] No one seems to have believed him.

Phao was not alone in his approach to enforcement within or without the law. In a letter in 1960, Sarit made reference to civil court procedure being unacceptable in its concept of giving the benefit of doubt to the defendant "*whereas in my responsibility for the whole*

---

[253] *The Devil's Discus*; Rayne Kruger; pp188/191
[254] Discussions with Major-General Chatichai Choonhavan; July 01 1991
[255] Field Marshal P. Phibun Songkhram; BJ Terwiel; p13
[256] *The Devil's Discus*; Rayne Kruger; p241

nation we should be more concerned over the welfare of the general public than over a small minority".[257]

The prosecution of the alleged Chinese communist plot over the period 1952-4 was not as successful. A trial in March 1955 saw only three Chinese gaoled and the Court was dismissive of the overall Chinese's influence in the alleged plot. Both the plot and the trial would be of little relevance other than for the consequences for Phao rather than the Chinese community. Phibun now decided to remove the strongly anti-communist Phao from Chinese affairs by re-allocating the responsibilities of his two deputy ministers of the interior.[258] All of a sudden, in September 1955, Phao's star was not shining so brightly.

Anti-communist fears were increasing within Thailand and they were not without foundation. They reflected fears of external events, particularly in Laos. The virtually indistinguishable ethnic relationship between the lowland Lao and the people of north-eastern Thailand, 'Isan', with strong linguistic and cultural ties was always a matter of concern to governments in Bangkok. Little was made of formal divisions, and even France at its strongest did not keep the races apart along its seven-hundred mile border. The problems of Laos itself were greater on its own northern and eastern border where the sinocised Vietnamese had over centuries attempted to dominate the more gentle people beyond the Annamite mountains. In the 1950s, Thailand, under the guidance of Sea Supply, saw its own forward defence as being inside Laotian territory as a prevention or at least as a forewarning of any communist approach, led by Vietnam. Vietnamese incursions in 1953 alarmed the Thai government but the various 1954 agreements gave it a degree of confidence. Not for long.

The 1954 agreements, had they been honoured, could have had a stabilising effect on much of South-East Asia. Article 6 of the Agreement on the Cessation of Hostilities expressly forbade the introduction into Laos of any reinforcements of troops or military personnel from outside territories, the establishment of new military bases and the introduction of all weapons of war except a specified

---

[257] *Thailand. A Political, Social & Economic Analysis*; D. Insor
[258] *Leadership and Power in the Chinese Community of Thailand*; G.Wm Skinner; pp287/90

quantity or arms needed for the defence of Laos. The Laotian Declaration, issued immediately following the signing of the Geneva Agreements, contained an express undertaking by the Laotian government that it would not request foreign aid "...*except for the purpose of its effective territorial defence...*"[259]

It soon became clear, however, that the Pathet Lao and Vietnamese forces had no intention of abiding by the agreements. Instead, they strengthened their hold on northern Laos. Proper inspections by the International Control Commission inspectorate were thwarted by the inclusion of a Polish communist who was known to warn the Pathet Lao of likely visits.[260] When internecine strife in Laos worried Phibun in 1955, he found that neither the American government nor SEATO was prepared to take any action. It was to both of them a civil war, not a regional war. No request for SEATO support was received from the Laotian authorities. Thai support for SEATO cooled, but it did not pursue the course of neutralism which was gripping a number of self-described 'non-aligned' countries. By early 1957 SEATO was more of a political liability than an asset to Phibun but his overt support of that body brought American aid and this was not to be lightly discarded. Loss of a flow of American supplies, especially weaponry and the revenue which might flow from it, would not have been popular with his immediate subordinates.

By 1955, Phao's police force was way ahead as the major opium trafficker in Thailand and the level of corruption was held to be remarkable even by 1950s Thai standards. Police escorted convoys from the Shan and Laotian borders to the towns, or if for export to the ports. Police warehouses in Chiang Mai safeguarded it. Police aircraft and vehicles moved it. Police naval vessels protected the product offshore until it was safely handed over to the foreign buyer Bangkok's own opium dens were supplied from product which had been 'captured' by the police and for which they had been paid a reward, a reward frequently assessed by the deputy minister of finance, Phao. Few traces were left. So-called informers disappeared and smugglers, remarkably, nearly always evaded capture. One remarkable case cited was that of ninth of July 1955 when police

---

[259] From documents appended to Storm over Laos: Prince Sisouk na Champassak
[260] *Storm over Laos*; Prince Sisouk na Champassak

waited at Mae Sai, allowing KMT troops to bring twenty tonnes of opium across the river. As soon as it was all safely over, the police 'captured' the consignment but, in accordance with all-too-common practice, failed to apprehend even one of the smugglers whom they had been observing all night. With maximum publicity the police escorted the opium to Bangkok to receive the congratulations of Phao, who also signed a request for a reward of over one million US dollars. As deputy minister of finance he paid the cheque over personally to an unnamed informer, who then conveniently fled the country.

That the CIA was directly involved has been alleged and generally accepted. No one doubts its knowledge of the continuing police opium scandal and that it was an invaluable asset to Phao in managing the traffic. The CIA was his source of the whole range of modern transportation which endowed him with the capability of moving opium from the mountain poppy fields to the market. His role in protecting military supplies from Sea Supply to the KMT in Burma put him in the ideal position to be the exclusive importer/exporter of KMT opium. Phao must be viewed as the principal creator of Bangkok's world distribution centre and in this he was not only supported by CIA money and a Nelson-like oversight but also by the military discipline of the KMT armed units in Burma. Through the decade of the fifties, opium production expanded in Burma from forty tonnes to between three and four hundred tonnes, whilst that in Thailand went from about seven tonnes to over one hundred.[261]

Phibun appears to have realised that there was nothing that he could do to retain a personal grip on the government and he feared Phao's possible takeover. In 1955 he took himself off on a lengthy tour of America and Britain, with the surprising result that he developed an unusual interest in democracy as practised in the Western world. On his return he announced a new era of full democracy and of the lifting of political oppression. He began to relax the authoritarian control. With the Political Party Act he legalised parties and lowered the voting age to twenty. He then instituted a more democratic approach to local government, removed controls on free speech, and set in train the process for a parliamentary election to be held early in 1957.

To encourage free speech he allowed a form of 'Hyde Park Corner' freedom to enable people to speak publicly on almost any

---

[261] *The Politics of Heroin*; Alfred W. McCoy; pp140/5

subject, provided that they did not speak against the monarchy. The move was seen as an attempt by Phibun to build for himself a power base in the general public, free of Phao and Sarit, making the creation of a western-type democracy the crowning achievement of his long career. In a public address in July 1955 he attempted to reduce the involvement of public servants in business. He stated that *"government officials, whether soldiers, civil servants, or police, whether permanent or political, should not engage in business affecting the general economy of the nation and the lives of the people"*.[262] The policy was soon modified. In October it was stated that government officers could both hold shares in and serve on the boards of public companies but they could not hold executive positions. However, there was unlikely to be much change while Thai protection was desirable and the Chinese held the purse strings. To support Sarit, Phibun appointed Thanom as a deputy minister and Sarit himself began to criticise Phao's activities. The time had come when Sarit could see that his own fortunes would advance, while Phao's would falter.

The Mai Sai opium capture incident was Phao's undoing and he was sent on a tour of Japan and America. While he was out of the country, Phibun relieved him of his appointment as deputy finance minister; he made open, critical comment on the Phao opium trade and cancelled Phao's special police interrogatory powers concerning communism. He also took over personal responsibility for police paramilitary activities.

The Soi Rajakru clan ran into other setbacks during the first half of 1956. Phao no doubt had his sights set on the formal leadership of the country and the Lady La-iad observed: *"Phao on many occasions let it be known that he would still want Phibun around as a senior statesman in case he should some day become the Premier ... as a guardian angel"*.[263] Meanwhile Phao's police remained a formidable military and political force. Sarit, fearful of the power which was accruing to Phao, started to exert the authority of the Army, and the perceived rivalry between Phao and Sarit gave courage to other critics of police methods. Criticism of Phao was at last voiced publicly. The CIA became directly implicated in the charges[264] and Phao's happy relationship with it ran into serious trouble. While this was taking

[262] *Bangkok Post*; 19 July 1955
[263] *Portraits of Thai Politics*; Jenton K. Ray; p214
[264] *US National Security Policy and Aid to the Thai police*; Thos. Lobe; p27

place, Field Marshal Phin's appointment as deputy prime minister was terminated.

Relationships with communist China began to improve. At first, Phibun's attitude was that nothing should be done to offend America and he opposed Sino-Thai trade proposals even after Malaya had begun selling large quantities of produce to that country. In mid-June he had a change of heart and removed the ban on all non-strategic goods for export to China. China itself had warmed somewhat to the Thai government, sensing, perhaps, that its southern neighbour was not as happy about its American alliance as it had been in earlier days.[265] With the Chinese-owned press moving towards the political left, it began to carry more favourable reports of mainland China and a degree of anti-KMT comment. To offset the leftward trend Phao, with Chinese leaders financing and managing, had sponsored the establishment of a paper, 'Shih-chieh Jih-pao'. By October even this, the most right-wing of papers, was beginning to show a more neutral approach and at the end of that month the strongly anti-communist editor was sacked.[266] As a means of improving the Thai economy the long-term traditional Chinese market began to look attractive. China was no longer to be looked upon as the great ogre. Phao, with Phin's ancestral ties to assist him, turned around and with American support for him diminishing, he sought new alliances in China. It was Sarit who now became America's favoured son.

Elections were soon due. M. R. Seni recorded *"...on the eve of the dirty elections of February I had to raise the lone voice in laying bare the conspiracy of General Phao to hand over the country to Red China.... He, Phibun, had no time to restrain Phao from getting dangerously close to Red China."* His newspaper *"... took a pronounced pro-communist line."* Seni claimed that Phao received money from Red China and, *inter alia*, advocated the scrapping of the SEATO Treaty, thus encouraging China to take over Thailand. By going public on this issue, Seni had brought about attempts on his own life.[267] Even allowing for some exaggeration within the statement, it

---

[265] *Thailand and the Fall of Singapore*; Nigel J. Brailey; p197
[266] *Leadership and Power in the Chinese Community of Thailand*; G. Wm Skinner; p292
[267] *Portraits of Thai Politics*; Jenton K. Ray; pp170/9

remains a most amazing turn-about. Phao made his reputation, partly, as an oppressor of the Chinese in general, and the communists in particular. Did his lack of principles take him to the brink of outright treason?

An estranged relationship had developed between the prime minister and his head of police, yet Phibun still relied heavily on Phao, even to the extent of his preparing for the February 1957 elections. With their approach, and after years of experience in the Interior Department, Phao represented to Phibun an incomparable intermediary with the provincial administrators, and thus represented votes for the Phibun camp. In April 1955 Phao had set out for Phibun a memorandum preparing the way for apparently strengthening the powers of local administration, through the provincial councils, the *changwads*. The proposal had been for each province to be recognised as a legally autonomous unit of government with increased powers and allowing the *changwad* governor to be its chief executive. Each of the governors would continue to be responsible to the Ministry of Interior and thus to Phao. Phao himself could have seen in his proposal the likely extension of his personal power, through the *changwad's* provincial councils, augmenting the control he already exercised over the governors themselves. The resulting Changwad Administration Act of 1955 gave the governor the power of veto over the council. More important for Phao was that a possible use might be made of this link in future elections, and in part help in the balance against Sarit.[268] That time had now come. Phibun saw it otherwise and possibly felt that he could create from this, through Phao, his own power base instead of relying on his balancing act which in turn depended on the antagonism between Sarit and Phao. In the period before the election, Phibun also began to look around for more direct personal support and turned to the labour unions as a counter-force to the military. The Thai National Trades Union Congress was the body concerned and a labour law passed into force on the first of January 1957. Trade unions were granted the right of collective bargaining and, at least in theory, the right to strike.

By the end of 1956, Phao had established a government political party for Phibun under the new democratic rules issued following the prime minister's tour. Phao's extra-mural Legislative Study Committee became the foundation of the Seri Manangkhasila party

---

[268] *Thailand: Modernisation of a Bureaucratic Polity*; Fred W. Riggs; pp188/194

and Phao became its secretary-general. The civil service was dragooned into working for it. Phao's task was to ensure that the party won the elections.

The February 1957 elections were to prove to be the last for twelve years. Phao had a central role in the election campaign, both as the organiser of the government's political party and as a target for the opposition. The Seri Manangkhasila party was alleged to have spent ten times as much as any other party on its election campaign and endorsed two hundred and thirty candidates over the whole of the one hundred and sixty seats. Phao was not himself a candidate but played for high stakes in the success of the party. In the end, the party won only a narrow majority which was, in practice, a failure. There were widespread accusations of malpractice and that the result was only achieved *"by blatant fraud, vote rigging, tampering, and coercion"*.[269]

Phibun's reliance on Phao to run his campaign was seen to be a grave misjudgement. Although enough seats were won, there was bitter criticism of the way in which the election was conducted. There was no way back for either Phibun or Phao, both of whom were now committed publicly to the establishment of an open, democratic society. To return to authoritarianism at this stage would have been unacceptable, and without Sarit's help would have been quite impracticable. It had been sixteen years since Phibun had put his personal reputation at risk by backing the Japanese during a time of war. Now, in a time of peace, he had shot himself in the foot in relying on the authoritarian Phao to orchestrate his late conversion to democratic thought.

Phibun's answer to the election result was typically Thai. He strengthened the military aspects of his Cabinet. In the March Cabinet, Phibun's eighth government, Phao became minister of the interior. Sarit became minister of defence, with both of his two principal henchmen in post — Thanom as deputy minister of defence, and Praphas as deputy minister of the interior. Field Marshal Phin was made minister of agriculture with his son-in-law, Pramarn, minister of industry. Lamai was appointed deputy-minister of agriculture and Siri became minister of co-operatives. Despite the apparent setbacks of the

---

[269] *Thailand, A Short History*; David K. Wyatt; p274

year before, the Soi Rajakru clan held the key commercial posts but the powers of defence and, in part, interior were now weighted much more in favour of Sarit.[270]

That year an even worse than usual drought in north-east Thailand, combined with a plague of locusts and the government's failure to give sufficient consideration to either, brought streams of refugees to Bangkok. Agitation for improvements came from both the Isan members of the Assembly and from students. As minister of agriculture, Phin made air surveys and reported the rice harvest as 'fair'. Little provision was made to help the peasants. Finally the government tried to buy its way out of trouble with an allocation of funds of fifty-three million baht to the fifty-three Isan members of the Assembly.

Concurrently came the lumber swindle. With the granting of a World Bank loan to construct the Bhumibol hydroelectricity dam, the best of the forest in the area to be flooded was to be cut and sold. The forced resignation of an official who refused to issue the logging permits requested by Phin disclosed that huge sums were likely to flow to a company associated with the minister, and profits of some fifty million dollars were quoted. Sarit backed the dismissed official and commented adversely in public on the affair. There was also, within a press campaign, a suggestion that Phin should be impeached for improper use of his powers.[271]

On twentieth of August Sarit resigned from his post as minister of defence. In support of him, Thanom and Praphas also quit the government. But Thanom remained as commander of the 1st Army with Praphas as his deputy. One of the reasons given for Sarit's resignation was his poor health and there is no doubt that this was already a serious handicap for him. A second reason offered was Phibun's insistence that Sarit repay a missing sum of twelve million baht from the State Lottery funds. The Press took Sarit's side and Sarit continued to develop his 'clean' image. Forty-six appointed members resigned from the Seri Manangkhasila party.

The lack of success of the government party in the 1957 election had weakened the hold on power of both Phibun and Phao. As a result, the press plucked up courage to criticise them openly. Numerous articles appeared on police opium smuggling, bribery, and

---

[270] *The Sarit Regime*; Thak Chaloemtiarana; p123/ note 88
[271] *The Sarit Regime*; Thak Chaloemtiarana; p151

prevailing institutional corruption. A campaign to undermine both Phibun and Phao, which had been smouldering for two years, now climaxed with a general debate in the National Assembly on twenty-ninth of August. The debate was inconclusive, but it contributed to the tense atmosphere which provided the backdrop for action by Sarit's military supporters. The general debate was led by Sarit's half-brother who had formed the Unionist Party to support Sarit in the Assembly. Within the debate itself, much of the attack centred on Phao. An allegation was made that he supported a newspaper which ran news criticising the monarchy and that he was contemplating the arrest of the King. There was also an allegation that gold and counterfeit money brought in from the Sea Supply Company and amounting to twenty million US dollars was in part used to finance his newspaper. Some of the paper's headlines in criticism of royalty were quoted.[272] The allegations were not proven but enough mud was thrown for some of it to stick.

On tenth of September, a group of senior military men held a meeting at 1st Army's HQ and determined that if Phibun did not meet demands for the government's resignation and force Phao into exile, then the group would have to take steps. Strong opposition to any military action was led by Brigadier-General Chatichai. Interestingly enough, at the same time, Phibun, Phao, and the Manangkhasila party were meeting to decide what to do with Sarit and his friends. On eleventh of September, the prime minister called a meeting of all important Cabinet members and invited Sarit to join them, an offer he wisely refused. On thirteenth of September, Sarit's military group issued an ultimatum: the government must resign and Phao must go into exile. On the evening of fifteenth of September there were further demonstrations in Bangkok which resulted in the gates of Government House being broken down and mass calls for the resignation of the prime minister. On the morning of the sixteenth of September, Sarit's military group had an hour's meeting with the prime minister and his colleagues. It was the final meeting. Sarit suspected rightly that Phibun, Phao, and colleagues were in session to determine how best to arrest him, Sarit, and his military group. Space at Bang Khwan prison and on the fourth floor of the Erawan Hotel had been reserved.[273]

---

[272] *The Sarit Regime*; Thak Chaloemtiarana; pp152/3
[273] *The Sarit Regime*; Thak Chaloemtiarana; pp511/3

Just before midnight on sixteenth of September 1957, Sarit seized control of the government. His Army took over key installations in Bangkok, encircling the Border Patrol Police and the Sea Supply/CIA training camps. Despite his wide powers, Phao made no effort to resist the Army. He accepted an offer to go into exile and within twelve hours he was escorted on to a plane bound for Europe. He lived out his life in Switzerland, handy to his reputedly phenomenal bank account and died there in 1961. Whilst some attribute his death to alcohol and sclerosis of the liver, the British ambassador who knew Phao best was convinced, more charitably, that away from his police empire he died of sheer boredom.[274]

Phibun did not wait for Sarit's permission. He fled by car and by boat to Cambodia and then on to Japan where he lived for a number of years. He repeatedly asked for permission to return to his native country but his requests were refused. Even when Phibun was making a journey to India to spend some time in a Buddhist monastery, Sarit did not allow him to put foot on Thai soil. On eleventh of June 1964, a month before his sixty-seventh birthday, Field Marshal Phibun Songkhram died in Japan of a heart attack. His ashes were returned to Thailand for burial in a Bangkok monastery.[275]

Looking back across the years, Phibun remains an outstanding figure of modern Thai history. He stamped his authority on the changing pattern of Thai culture as the country moved from absolute monarchy through the early years of constitutional monarchy. He was the undisputed leader of the new age.

Phibun was a dictator. The argument that he was not, because he always ruled with a National Assembly, does not hold water. The Assembly was a façade with insufficient practical authority to limit him. His initial European army training left him with admiration of military management and particularly for dictatorial regimes — German, Italian, and Japanese. Suggestions made that in his treatment of the Chinese in Thailand there was a similarity to Hitler's treatment of the Jews and gipsies are not sustainable. There were no Bangkok gas chambers, no genocide, and no intense attack on the culture of a faith. The Lady La-iad was right to say that references to Nazi

[274] *A Marvellous Party*: Sir Berkeley Gage; p190
[275] *Field Marshall P. Phibun Songkhram*: BJ Terwiel; p28

methods were a gross exaggeration. Harsh treatment from time to time there most certainly was, principally at the hands of Phao and his police, and it would be wrong to exonerate Phibun from blame for the activities of his police-general. In the later years there seems to be no doubt that he lost control of both of his immediate subordinates, Phao and Sarit, and, to protect his personal position, he relied more and more on balancing the power between them. His political gamesmanship was astute and his sense of timing, in 1947, was impeccable. The 'Manhattan Affair' in 1951 must have demonstrated to him that his subordinates considered him readily expendable but he took back the reins of office with determination. The incident was also an illustration to the many present of his personal courage in the face of likely death.

It must be deduced that he had sufficient knowledge of the Seri Thai to break the movement had he so chosen, but he had the political foresight to realise that, through them, he had, or at least Thailand had, a chance to back the second horse in a two-horse race. He was, without question, double-dealing the Japanese from early 1944, but was ousted before the ultimate confrontation took place.

He was a highly respected leader He was an opportunist, an absolute nationalist, and devious as well as ruthless: many of his opponents were removed summarily. Despite adverse comment, contemporaries have said that a visitor could not be other than charmed in his presence. A diplomat of that time, reflecting on Phibun some thirty years later, said of him, *"He was a courageous man. He had charming manners, a sophisticated sense of humour, and a wife of distinction, the Lady La-iad. Whatever he may have been, in my time he appeared more civilised than Phao or Sarit, the two tigers he was riding"*.[276] His nationalism was not always royalism. He has been referred to as emerging in 1939 as the uncrowned king of Thailand. Phibun's wife, the Lady La-iad described her husband as *"a man of scholarly disposition, not just a strong man,"* essentially, *"a professor of field artillery"*. She was also to defend him against charges of both fascism and racism. His attacks upon the Chinese she saw as the transference of Thai rights from the skilled, wealthy, non-naturalised Chinese by a policy of reserving for the true Thais certain occupations and trades. She stressed that it was done to encourage Thai

---

[276] *Portraits of Thai Politics*; Jenton K. Ray, pp75/84

naturalisation, and with it, loyalty to the country.[277] One contemporary, Thawee, had mixed views. He said of Phibun that he was a great patriot who tried to promote the interests of his country in his own way: perhaps his efforts were not always well thought out, but that did not negate his deep patriotism. On another occasion he was not so generous, referring to Phibun as surrounding himself with yes-men and of suffering from Napoleonic delusions.[278]

Phibun's late attempts at Hyde Park Corner democracy in 1956 were ill-advised and they were impractical within a Thai approach to democracy. Phibun was, by then, running out of options. He overestimated his personal popularity and underestimated the stigma which attached to him through his lack of control of Phao. Despite this, in a society where personal profit and the craving for power to attain that end appeared to be uppermost, he remained a man for whom the interests of his country, as he saw them, remained a priority. He remains free of the allegation that he abused power in order to amass a personal fortune.

Sarit made no move against his one-time commander and Army predecessor, Field Marshal Phin, who, by 1957, was deeply involved with business matters and less concerned with the detail of government. Phin lived out the rest of his life in Thailand and died in the early 1970s. There is the allegation that although Phin was commander-in-chief of the Army from the time of the 1947 coup until twenty-fourth of June 1954, he did not concern himself too deeply with its development. Phin saw things differently and attributed to himself a range of reforms of structure, training, and the restoration of morale and discipline.[279] There is no question that in 1947 he took over an army in disarray after its post-northern campaign treatment and as its commander he revitalised it, even although he is not given credit for its modernisation. Despite his military enhancement and his accumulation of great wealth, he remained disappointed that, in his lifetime, neither he nor any member of his family had held the premiership.[280]

---

[277] *A Marvellous Party*; Sir Berkeley Gage; p190
[278] *Portraits of Thai Politics*; Jenton K. Ray; pp190/200
[279] *Thailand and the Fall of Singapore*; Nigel J. Brailey; p212
[280] From a public statement by M. R. Kukrit Pramoj, per Bangkok Post 29 July 1988

Phin's son, Chatichai, who at the time of Sarit's coup had been Commandant of the Armoured School, was virtually banished from the political scene for nearly fourteen years by Sarit and his successors. He was given a series of diplomatic appointments, all distant from Thailand and starting with Argentina. But Chatichai's day was still to come. Some doubts have been cast on Chatichai's actual intentions at the time of the 1957 coup. As the Commandant of the Armoured School he had access to substantial fire-power to bring to support a regime to which he was close by family ties and which had been good to him over the years. One side of the story was that he would have moved to support Phibun and Phao had he been able so to do, but at the critical moment the tanks were found to have been immobilised by an enterprising middle-rank officer under his command who had sent the batteries for a routine overhaul. The story continues that Chatichai never forgave the young officer for his action although, with his early removal from post and virtual exile he had little opportunity to take action against him. In later days he was not in a position to take up the matter. The enterprising officer was Prem Tinasulanonda, later to be his commander-in-chief and prime minister. Chatichai denies this story. At the time he was the regimental commander and Prem was one of his battalion commanders. *"In the end I had no choice but to support the Army against the police, otherwise I was finished. I was always an army man, and even family relationships could not affect my decision. I took no part in the 1957 coup"*.[281]

Chatichai was one of the very few people who had a good word to say about Phao. He obviously has felt that Phao was a very misunderstood person whom it was fashionable to criticise. *"He was rather a nice chap really"* — but Phao was married to Chatichai's eldest sister who, herself, was a domineering character in the Phin household. In retrospect what is there left to say about Phao which his own behaviour has not already illustrated? He made his mark as the strong man of the regime, but such a description does not prevent him being described as ruthless. He had few scruples in his quest for power and wealth, his *volte-face* from anti-communism to courting communist China at the end of his career is almost unbelievable. He used opium trafficking as an important element in his creation of personal wealth, with total disregard for the misery of millions which

---

[281] Discussions with Major-General Chatichai Choonhavan; 1 July 1991

followed. He used opium to finance his political machine in the National Assembly as well as to encourage his personal followers in the police force. It was an open secret that Phao's *asawin* were involved in trafficking, and in some cases rewards were actually offered for the seizure of opium which slipped through Phao's fingers. It was Phao's claim that he never stole one cent from the Thai people. The rejoinder must be that it depends on how you do the calculations.

His penetration of the political arena was the most extensive of any member of the 1947 group. He was its most dynamic worker and organiser, and in the late 1940s and early 1950s his star rose rapidly. He held high government office and a position of trust throughout the Phibun era. He was an official spokesman of the government in the National Assembly. He was a feared personality because of his security and intelligence powers and his special anti-communist interrogation powers. Under Phao's guidance, the Criminal Investigation Division and the Crime Suppression Bureau acted harshly. Political agitators, people suspected of being anti-government and hence pro-communist, were arrested. Many simply disappeared. A number of infamous cases came to light after Sarit's takeover. Only then were many cases of long-suspected police brutality substantiated.

The effect of Phao's years of power lived well beyond him. By the end of the 1950s the output of opium from the Golden Triangle, of which he had been a principal instrument of development, was estimated to be half of the total world illicit output of between one thousand two hundred and one thousand four hundred tonnes. World observation of the situation makes it unbelievable that the CIA did not know what its chosen agents, Phao and the local KMT, were doing. In this quiet, developing country a police-general, little known internationally, satisfied a lust for personal power and greed in a manner which was to make his activity a fertile source of the Western world's greatest social problem, the trafficking of opium and, in the years to come its derivative evil, heroin addiction. Heroin, in Phao's day was not the great world-wide scourge, but all that was needed was to add skill and find the ready market. The skill would be provided by the Hong Kong chemists. The first great expansion of the market came with the arrival in Vietnam of an unhappy GI army.

Perhaps it was right that a judgement of his activities was written in the country most involved in his devastating career. Phao, wrote a correspondent of *The New York Times*, was *"a superlative crook"*.[282] But that is not the whole story. Just as the American government, through its various agencies, used Phao to suit its own ends, so also Phao shrewdly used American provisions of money and material to suit his. He was an incredible opportunist when it came to accumulating wealth and there were many in Thailand who benefited from Phao's considerable acumen. Unfortunately, many more suffered in the process.

---

[282] New York Times (correspondent C. L. Sulzberger); 6 November 1957

CHAPTER SEVEN
Sarit, The Great Dictator

On the first of January 1956, Sarit Thanarat was promoted to Field Marshal, the youngest holder of the appointment in the post-1932 period. He had come a long way.

He was born on sixteenth of June 1908, the son of an army officer and a Lao mother, and at eleven years old he entered the Army Officers' School. At the age of eighteen he was formally registered as a soldier in the regular Army, a member of the class of '70 (BE 2470). On completion of his training, Sarit reported to the commander of the 1st Battalion, 2nd Regiment, King's Body Guard. By October 1933 he was engaged in countering the Boworadej rebellion and helping to push the rebels back from Dong Muang airfield. Promotions over the pre-war years resulted on twenty-fifth of January 1942 in Sarit being assigned to command the 33rd Infantry Battalion of the 12th Infantry Regiment, newly formed as a part of the Northern Army. In mid-1942 that Army was dealing with trouble along the Salween river. Sarit quickly gained a reputation as a good, although stern, commander of his own troops, one who had no hesitation in carrying out the summary execution of captured enemy agents.

The 33rd Battalion, as part of the 2nd Division, moved jointly with the 3rd Division under command of General Phin, to attack Kengtung in the Shan States. Sarit captured the fortified village of Mong Hsat, after which the 33rd Battalion was transferred to Phin's 3rd Division and took part in the capture of Mong La. General Phin was appointed military governor of the area. Sarit then took the 33rd on to the Lam River, where that river forms the border between Burma and China. Later he was given command of a machine gun battalion at Lampang in Japanese-occupied Thailand and then made military commander of Lampang Province.[283]

---

[283] *The Sarit Regime*; Thak Chaloemtiarana; pp491/506. Thak annotated his dissertation extensively and much of his basic material was drawn from Sarit's Cremation Volumes (*Collected Speeches of Field Marshall Sarit Thanarat 1959-61 and 1969-63*) and General Policies of the Revolutionary Council which were based on a compilation of lectures broadcast over 'Radio 20'. Although published after

With the end of the Second World War, Sarit was among the more fortunate of the Army officers. Not only did he remain on the active list but on the first of January 1946 he was appointed to command the 1st Regiment, situated in politically unstable Bangkok. It was to Sarit that the 1947 group had turned for troops. He, in the end, was persuaded to bring his forces to the support of the plotters. This was ironic. Phibun was known to be contemptuous of Sarit whom he, the scholarly Phibun, considered a mere peasant, owing to his mother's Lao background. Ill at ease in his youth Sarit, like Phin before him, had opted for the despised infantry rather than the élite cavalry or the prestigious artillery, which had been Phibun's own choice. Phibun saw no danger to himself in allowing the advancement of foot-soldier Sarit.[284]

Sarit's deployment of the troops under his command was critical to the success of the coup and he was given the responsibility of protecting the coup group itself. On ninth of November he was made commander of the infantry controlling Bangkok. On the first of January 1948 he was promoted to major-general, and on the first of February he was appointed commander of the 1st Division. With that appointment Sarit strengthened his hold on the military situation over the Bangkok and central plains area.

He was called upon to deal with both the 1948 officers' counter-plot and then with Pridi's 'palace' rebellion. His leadership was rewarded by the government with the appointment on the first of January 1950 as commander of the 1st Army and promotion to Lieut-General. Wisely, he retained command of the 1st Division and with it his Bangkok troops power base.

In June 1951, Sarit became deputy Army commander-in-chief, but again he retained the command of the 1st Division and of the 1st Army which stood him in good stead only one month later at the time of the 'Manhattan' incident. He set about 'Americanising' the Thai Army and changed the Chulachomklao Academy syllabus to West Point training. In December of that year Sarit was enticed into politics as deputy minister of defence to Phibun. He had the complimentary titles of Vice Admiral and Air Vice Marshal bestowed on him in 1952

Sarit's death they are known to reflect his attempt to introduce "Thai-style" democracy as opposed to Western democracy

[284] *Thailand and the Fall of Singapore*; Nigel J Brailey; p202 and *The Sarit Regime*; Thak Chaloemtiarana; pp491/506

and those of Admiral and Air Chief Marshal in 1955. Despite his stated dislike of politics, he retained the post of deputy minister of defence until 1956. With Field Marshal Phin's retirement in 1954, Sarit became commander-in-chief and in his acceptance speech on twenty-fifth of June, Sarit promised the Army that he would ensure that it would reach a *"pinnacle of development"*.[285]

He carefully placed into position his supporters, General Thanom, General Praphas, and General Krit Srivara, within the 1st Army and 1st Division. In 1954, Thanom assumed command of both the 1st Army and the 1st Division. When in 1957, Sarit became minister of defence in the last Phibun government, Thanom became his deputy minister and Praphas was given command of the 1st Division and appointed deputy minister of the interior. The first indication of the entry of General Krit into the corridors of power was his appointment as deputy commander of the 1st Division under Praphas. Thus Sarit built his power base on the Army, whilst in parallel, Phao had built his on the militarised police and special forces.

Sarit was also not slow in advancing his material interests. In 1951 he gained control of the Lottery Bureau and in 1952 he secured a seat on the governing body of the War Veterans' Organisation. He soon acquired no less than twenty-two seats on boards — some private and some government controlled.

With the passage of the 1955 Political Party Act and the proliferation of parties, Sarit became deputy chief to Phibun of the Seri Manangkhasila Party, but the reins of the party were held by its secretary-general, Phao. Sarit played no significant part in the party development. He steered himself clear of the troubles and the later allegations of vote rigging and corruption which followed the February 1957 elections.

When public discontent boiled over following the 1957 elections, Sarit sent troops to control the Bangkok streets and then himself set out to investigate. By the time he reached the Makkhawan bridge, troops confronting the demonstrators had already assumed a firing position. Fortunately, the immediate commander of the troops, Arthit Kamlang-ek, then an Army captain in an early stage of his high-profile career, realised that in response to taunts and stone-throwing, his men might open fire. First he ordered them to take their fingers off the trigger and then to shoulder their rifles. Realising

---

[285] *The Sarit Regime*; Thak Chaloemtiarana; pp391, 491/507

the impact of the bloodshed which might follow, Sarit went further and ordered the troops to let the demonstrators through, at the same time urging the crowd not to shed the blood of other Thais. When a mob broke down one of the gates of Government House, it was Sarit who calmed them.[286]

Phibun had declared a national emergency and appointed Sarit to be supreme commander with power over the Army, Navy, Air Force, and police. With increasing student unrest, Sarit spoke frankly to the students of Chulalongkorn University and it was there that he made his particular reference to the cheating which had taken place at the 'dirty' February elections. It reinforced his perceived role as the man to protect the populace against Phao's activities. A few days later the appointment of supreme commander was abolished. Phibun had realised that he was setting up too powerful a rival.

When the September upheaval came, Sarit was able to sweep the government of Phibun out of office in just a few hours, without either loss of life or bloodshed. At eleven o'clock on the evening of sixteenth of September, Sarit's Military Group seized power, and one hour later the following Royal Proclamation was issued in the name of 'Phumiphon Adunyadet, Rex':

"Owing to the fact that the government of Field Marshal Phibun has been unable to govern with the trust of the people, to wit, that it has been unable to maintain peace and order, the military group led by Field Marshal Sarit has assumed the duties of Special Military Administrator for Bangkok. We ask that people remain peaceful and that all government servants follow the instructions of Field Marshal Sarit".[287]

This proclamation was of major importance to Sarit: it legitimized his overthrow of what was, despite the description of dirty elections, an elected government. It was, in practice, the only claim to legitimacy.

Sarit introduced absolute rule to a degree beyond anything previously experienced in modern Thailand. He swiftly emasculated Phao's power base. All heavy armaments were transferred to his own favoured groups within the Army. Police numbers and the police

[286] *The Sarit Regime*; Thak Chaloemtiarana; pp509/10
[287] *The Sarit Regime*; Thak Chaloemtiarana; pp513/4

budget were dramatically cut. The Police Aerial Reconnaissance (Resupply) Unit was merged into the Army, and the Border Patrol Police transferred to the regular police command. Many paramilitary responsibilities were removed. Police promotions were temporarily suspended, other than the appointment of Lieut-Colonel Sanga Kittikachon, General Thanom's younger brother, as deputy commander of the Crime Suppression Squad. Field Marshal Fuen Ronnaphakat, commander-in-chief of the Air Force, was relieved of his post. General Sawai Sawaisaenyakon, commander of the Khorat-based 2nd Army and an old friend of Sarit, became the new police chief. He celebrated his appointment by immediately sacking one of Phao's police brigadier-generals and indicting him for involvement in the smuggling of six tonnes of opium. There was a similar shake-out in the Navy. American interference in Thai affairs was chopped. The CIA/Sea Supply was forced to send most of its operatives home and American financing of the Border Patrol Police and the Police Aerial Reconnaissance (Resupply) Unit ceased. While CIA personal relationships continued within Thailand, it maintained a lower profile and became more circumspect in its political manoeuvrings.[288]

Parliamentary democracy was put into abeyance. The National Assembly was replaced by an appointed but emasculated Constitutional Assembly and of a hundred and twenty-three MPs appointed under the 1932/1952 Constitution, only three were from the police. The Army was not again to be challenged as the supreme force. Whilst the Phibun/Phao regime was totally unacceptable to Sarit he hesitated to strike for immediate personal supremacy himself. He installed a temporary prime minister, Phote Sarasin, who was free of taint of the past regime. Phote had spent some years of diplomatic service in Washington and had then become secretary-general of SEATO. Phote was also rich, and therefore, in Sarit's judgement, less likely to be consumed by a search for personal gain.[289] A telling comment from a Thai source was, *"He was so rich he could afford to be honest"*. The Defence Ministry went to Thanom and the Ministry of the Interior to Praphas. Sarit became supreme military commander of the armed forces. Thawee returned to politics as economic adviser

---

[288] *US National Security Policy and Aid to Thai Police*; Thomas Lobe; p28
[289] *The Sarit Regime*; Thak Chaloemtiarana; pp169/173

and vice-chairman of the Constituent Assembly but refused ministerial appointment.

Phote's previous connection with SEATO improved the relationships with that organisation, and in November Sarit declared his full commitment to it.[290] Relationships with America were not entirely smooth but Washington was reassured by the appointment of Phote although it was not particularly happy to find that the new government took a more relaxed view of trade with Communist China. Sarit intended to keep at a greater distance from America than had Phibun and when approached shortly after the coup by Ambassador Bishop with an offer of help, he informed the ambassador that while willing to receive aid he was not prepared to have strings attached to it. Nevertheless, Sarit knew that he needed American aid, both financial and military.[291]

The elections set up by Phote took place on fifteenth of December 1957 and Sarit's own Sahaphum party won more seats than any other — forty-four, against the Democrat's thirty-nine. But overshadowing these two figures, fifty-nine independent members gained seats. Most of these were the old Seri Manangkhasila party of Phibun and Phao, who still commended themselves to the electorate, either personally or by vote-buying, and did not need party labels. The Sahaphum candidates were routed in the major cities. In Chiang Mai, the party leader Sukich Nimmanheaminda, a member of a distinguished local banking family, was the only one of a strong delegation to be elected. To resolve his electoral problem Sarit sponsored a new party, the National Socialist Party, with himself at its head, Thanom and Sukich as deputies, and Praphas as party secretary to involve both Sahaphum and Seri Manangkhasila MPs. Phote Sarasin at this point decided that his obligations to his country had been fulfilled and resigned. He strongly disapproved of the new military-controlled party and chose not to be tainted by it. On the first of January 1958, General Thanom, Sarit's protégé became prime minister.

Thanom's first period as prime minister was not a success. This was partly due to the dominance, then illness, of Sarit himself and thus of Thanom being looked upon as merely a caretaker prime minister. It was also partly due to his relationship with his own immediate subordinate, Praphas. To Praphas, with his Phao-like

[290] *Thailand and the Fall of Singapore*; Nigel J. Brailey; p204
[291] *The Sarit Regime*; Thak Chaloemtiarana; p175

dictatorial attitude, Thanom's moderate approach to government was a sign of weakness.[292]

Sarit, who had long been suffering severe after-effects of malaria contracted in the Shan States during the Second World War, became seriously ill in January 1958 with cirrhosis of the liver. It was a condition hardly improved by his inclination to drink at least one bottle of brandy at a sitting, and he left the country for major treatment in America. By June 1958 he was well enough to travel from America to England to recuperate. He was persuaded to fly there westwards following a call for help from Thanom who by then was having difficulties, not only with a troublesome National Assembly but also with Praphas over a matter of military expenditure. Sarit landed in Bangkok on twenty-seventh of June 1958. After a brief consultation with Thanom and still far from full recovery, Sarit arrived in London in July.

He used his period of recuperation in England to review his political strategy. He called in Thanat Khoman, the Thai ambassador in America, and Witchit Wathakan, the revered scholar, who was serving as Thai ambassador in Switzerland. They reviewed the constitutions of other countries. It was Witchit who may well have been responsible for Sarit's next moves by setting out the philosophy on which he would base his future government. Thanat later analysed the Thai problem thus: *The fundamental cause of our political instability in the past lies in the sudden transplantation of alien institutions onto our soil without proper regard to the circumstances which prevail in our homeland, the nature and characteristics of our own people, in a word the genius of our race, with the result that their functioning has been haphazard and ever chaotic. If we look at our national history, we can see very well that this country works better and prospers under an authority, not a tyrannical authority, but a unifying authority around which all elements of the nation can rally".*[293]

Sarit himself put it more succinctly in saying that Thai democracy was like a Thai plant. It was supposed to grow mangoes and bananas, not apples and grapes. The problems in Thailand were principally those of immature and inexperienced democracy. There was still a

---

[292] *Thailand and the Fall of Singapore*; Nigel J. Brailey; pp205/6 and Political Conflict in Thailand; David Morell and Chai-Samudavanija; p51
[293] *Thailand: a Short History*; David K. Wyatt; p280 and Bangkok Post 10 March 1959

National Assembly and political parties, and even a free press with a right to criticise the government. But all were constrained in their functioning. There were trade unions which could strike, if they were so to choose. But there was unhealthy squabbling among members of the National Assembly seeking rewards which would accrue to themselves and their friends if they were appointed to ministerial post. Sarit came to the conclusion that there was no way forward without changing the whole of the Thai governmental machine. He believed that a constitution which was designed for Thailand itself was necessary if the country was to be properly administered. Both Thanat and Witchit Wathakan agreed with him that another simple coup d'état would solve nothing. The country needed a revolution which would overthrow the whole political system which had evolved since the coup of 1932.

Witchit Wathakan had been, over the years, a very influential figure in Thai politics. He had entered the priesthood in his teens. He had studied languages at his temple and then left the priesthood for a career in foreign affairs. He was a writer of considerable repute, and apart from his many plays and books he was known to be a frequently-used speech writer. His past service had been in foreign affairs and in party propaganda, but he was also a political thinker in his own right. Phibun had used him as a foreign secretary during the Second World War and also for a short period as his ambassador to Tokyo. In pre-war days he had seen service at the Paris embassy. He was instrumental in guiding Phibun's approach to the historical role of Thailand in relation to its neighbouring countries. He is said to have written over one hundred speeches for Sarit — indeed, there were very few which he did not write. Witchit is given the credit for the survival of Sarit's reputation following the posthumous exposure of his corruption and lechery. Only a master-writer could have so projected him in his lifetime.[294] When Sarit became prime minister, Thanat became his foreign minister, but it was Witchit, in a Richelieu-like role, who became Sarit's principal adviser until he, Witchit, died in 1962.

---

[294] *Thailand and the Fall of Singapore*; Nigel J. Brailey; p216

In early October 1958, Prime Minister Thanom was in dire trouble with Praphas and the right wing. After using Praphas's police to quell a riot, Thanom was facing a possible take-over of his premiership by Praphas himself. He appealed to Sarit to return to Thailand and on the night of eighteenth of October, Sarit landed in secret to forestall any move by Praphas. The next morning Sarit consulted with the prime minister and other important government figures, and there was general agreement that major surgery was essential to solve the nation's problems. On twentieth of October, Thanom and his government resigned, and in the evening of the same day Sarit's 'revolution' began. The causes and the perceived circumstances are included in a number of revolutionary announcements. Proclamation No. 1 was the usual call for everyone to stay calm and go about his daily duties, for the military and police to remain in post and accept the orders of their superiors, and for there to be no movement of troops. But all revolutions and coups d'état need the proclamation which seeks to justify the action of those who have already taken it. This was No. 2, issued on twentieth of October.

"Following up on announcement No. 1 of the Revolutionary Group, to wit, that power has been seized in the name of the Thai people, the Revolutionary Group wishes to announce that this seizure of power was a matter of necessity, it was done with the acquiescence and support of the previous Government, and it was done with the agreement of the majority of the people who were concerned with the state of things in the nation. It was done because both the internal and external situations were increasingly threatening, especially the communist menace which was daily growing in Thailand, and because it was impossible to choose any other course than to seize power and conduct a revolution along suitable lines.

The Revolutionary Group guarantees that it will not alter any institutions to a degree greater than is necessary to insure the safety of the nation. The Revolutionary group intends to govern in accordance with constitutional practices and to respect the person of His Majesty the King as inviolable. This seizure of power was for the purpose of preserving the institutions of his majesty the King as the head of the nation, the Royal Family, and the Privy Council. The Revolutionary Group will respect and safeguard all foreign nationals and property, specifically all foreign embassies, consulates and international organisations located in Bangkok, to the utmost of its ability. The Revolutionary Party will give further details on why it was necessary to act on this occasion in subsequent announcements."

Proclamation No. 3 was a detailed administrative document. Within it Sarit suspended the 1932 constitution and Phao's amendment of 1952, prorogued the National Assembly, and dismissed all Assembly Representatives. He then gave overall power to a Revolutionary Council over which he presided and under which civil servants were given authority to act in the place of ministers. Needless to say, the proclamation made special reservations for the administration of the military, and whilst it did not introduce formal press censorship by the police, it threatened to lock up any editor or journalist who failed to report in a manner which the Revolutionary Council considered 'balanced'.

No. 4 went into further justification for the action. The communists were blamed for infiltration of politics, the economy, and society in general.

"*They use propaganda methods and many clever stratagems. They have expended large amounts of money, both publicly and secretly, to further their plan to cause disruption in the nation. They seek to undermine the monarchy, they have tried to destroy all the institutions that we Thai's have fought so hard to preserve. ... Our negotiations with foreign countries have been hindered by the actions of these people .... Even more seriously, they endeavour, both openly and secretly, to destroy the trust and confidence that other countries have in Thailand. .... Half measures are not enough to effect a cure. None of these problems can be solved by a change of governments, a change of personnel or a change of just some procedures. ... What is required is major surgery and a revolution is the only cure for the serious disease from which the nation now suffers. ... We have to find a way to create new stability in our country, to build a firm foundation for democracy, to organise our economy and society in a manner appropriate for our people and way of life. .... these problems and dangers did not come into being because of any fault on the part of the Assembly or Government. They developed because at the time the Assembly and the Government did not have the tools to deal with them.*

That is why it is necessary to create new tools which will enable us to lift up the nation".[295]
The fine-sounding words were no doubt a product of Witchit Wathakan. Behind the words was the intent to reverse Phibun's westernisation and make law and custom fit into Thai tradition and culture. Whereas Phibun encouraged the development of Thai nationalism along western lines, Sarit sought to maintain Thai conservatism.

The Revolutionary Party then reaffirmed that it would abide by the United Nations General Assembly *Declaration on Human Rights*, only deviating from it *"to protect the nation"*. It would also abide by all international agreements and treaty obligations into which the government had entered. It promised to safeguard the freedom of the courts and hold fast to the principle that the King and the Thai people were indivisible and that it would not tolerate any slander of royalty.

Sarit then wrote to King Bhumibol, reaffirming his total loyalty, the protection from harm or any insult of the Royal Family, and putting the blame firmly on communism. *"If this menace is not dealt with soon, it will engulf the nation, and all the royal institutions which the Thai people have so long cherished will perish".*[296]

The King's reply in the tenth year of his reign is particularly interesting in that it reflects the delicate wisdom for which he was later to become renowned. Acknowledging, through his principal private secretary, the first nine proclamations he went on to say: *"the intention of the Revolutionary Party, as set forth in its announcements, to maintain the safety and interests of the nation and to encourage its progress, is laudable indeed. Having established these goals, it is fitting that the Revolutionary Party should proceed to implement them faithfully and honestly by holding fast to the principle of the common good. Whatever steps must be taken in the future should be thoroughly considered so that objectives are actually achieved. This would accord with the guarantees made in the Revolutionary Party's announcements and would gain His Majesty's gratitude".*[297]

The King had quietly put Sarit on the spot, calling for the fine words of proclamations to be adhered to and for future actions to be

---

[295] *The Sarit Regime*; Thak Chaloemtiarana; pp517/20
[296] *The Sarit Regime*; Thak Chaloemtiarana; p523
[297] *The Sarit Regime*; Thak Chaloemtiarana; pp524/5 citing letter from the principal Private Secretary to H.M. The King to Sarit, dated 21 October 1958

entered into as part of the proclaimed objectives. Thai governments had not been used to such direction. The King also signed an Act giving an amnesty to all who took part in the twentieth of October 1958 affair. It seemed fairly innocuous in the circumstances of the time, but it set an unfortunate precedent which was to be used after the 1992 carnage to prevent the justifiable trial of military officers alleged to be involved.

More proclamations followed. A Constituent Assembly was set up to draft a new constitution and, temporarily only, to act as a legislature. The National Economic Planning Council was instituted to oversee a continuous national plan, and indications were given of changes in public finance and education. Others concentrated on the suppression of communism. No. 12 formally declared martial law to be operative from twenty-second of October 1958 and Phao's 1952 Anti-Communist Act was strengthened by bringing all breaches before military courts, with authority for unlimited detention while investigations took place. No. 24 was more concerned with arson, for which the communists were blamed, and it announced that executions had already been carried out. *"...a final warning is given to communists themselves that if they persist in creating difficulties for the Thai people and the Thai nation, measures more severe than have ever been used throughout the history of Thailand will be employed to suppress them."* [298]

Sarit's limited administrative knowledge was countered by Witchit's wide experience, both political and administrative, and it was he who was to be seen behind not only the paperwork but also behind the oppression which followed. There were numerous arrests including those of newspaper editors and journalists.[299] There was a new wave of repression on anything which might be deemed communist. From October 1958 to June 1962 over a thousand alleged communist suspects were arrested. Some three hundred of Vietnamese origin were deported. Of the Thais, only four hundred received a formal trial and four were executed. The Act giving the right to trade unions to bargain collectively and to strike, granted by Phibun in January 1957, was repealed.

Sarit adopted a Phao-like approach to life — everything that was communist he detested, and everything he detested he labelled

---

[298] *The Sarit Regime*; Thak Chaloemtiarana; p528
[299] *Thailand and the Fall of Singapore*; Nigel J. Brailey; p217/9

communist. Intellectuals with left-wing tendencies were silenced or eliminated.[300] To emphasise his point, Sarit opted for public execution by firing squad. In 1959 he executed the secretary-general of the banned Central Labour Union. In 1961 he executed two ex-members of the National Assembly, said to be involved in a separatist Thai-Lao plot. In 1962 he dealt similarly with a member of the Communist Party of Thailand governing committee. The execution of the latter occurred only a few months after that party, at its third congress in 1961, had adopted a strategy of revolutionary armed struggle, and then began broadcasting from a Yunnan transmitter as the "Voice of the People of Thailand".[301] Prior to this open defiance of authority, the communists had been of only minor practical concern and had been looked upon merely as a residual rump of the early left-wingers, led by Pridi. They were, however, a useful peg on which to hang suppression for whatever true reason it was introduced.

The seeming obsession of Sarit over communism can be better understood by looking east of the Mekong River, an area which the American government was continuing to view with grave concern. America was determined to concentrate its efforts on developing Thailand in support of its own objectives. After the loss of Chiang Kai-shek's China, Thailand was accepted as the focal point of its covert and psychological operations on mainland Asia. The interests of the citizens of Thailand appear to have played little part in this consideration. The emphasis was essentially on use in support of American objectives. After the overthrow of Phibun, and despite reservations about Sarit himself, America gave immediate support and issued a statement that American-Thai relations would not be affected.[302]

Sarit's approach to his premiership was the introduction of a paternalistic style of rule, with the loyalty of the citizen focused on the monarch and the legitimacy of government resting on its acceptance by the monarch. By this means, respectability was added to government. Paternalism that was solicitous for the welfare of the people was also accompanied by severity in the laws against wrongdoers. It was not necessarily Sarit's laws themselves but more

---

[300] *Thailand a Short History*; David K. Wyatt;pp281/3
[301] *Political Repression in Thailand*; Euro Committee for solidarity with the Thai people; London University; p14
[302] *The Sarit Regime*; Thak Chaloemtiarana; p198

so their implementation which gave rise to alarm. Amongst those which provoked most resentment was the decree enacted to deal with persons branded as hooligans. It became an instrument of harassment against opposition of every sort. It was still used as an example of what should not be enacted almost thirty years later, when another bunch of generals seized control and attempted to seek sweeping powers.[303] Sarit was strict in his attack on petty crime, prostitution, and opium smoking. The opium dens were closed and trafficking outlawed. The attack on the opium dens proved to be a two-edged sword as, very soon, cheap, low-grade No. 3 heroin, only about five per cent pure, was being produced both in Bangkok and northern Thailand, while morphine base was produced in the tribal areas for export to Hong Kong and Europe.[304]

Sarit fostered the tripartite mutual acknowledgement of monarchy, Buddhist religion, and paternalistic government — the latter controlled by the military. The role of the King became both more public and more active, and Sarit was fortunate in that, in King Bhumibol Adulyadej, he was supporting a monarch who would become the most hardworking in the history of the kingdom. The government's effectiveness was enforced by a number of foreign, experienced technocrats who in turn encouraged the expansion of overseas-trained Thai specialists. Sarit saw it as a new approach to democracy. It was not. It was dictatorship but it was a policy which commended itself both to the Thai old guard of royalists and to the economic élite.

Sarit has been likened to Field Marshal Phin. They were both essentially professional soldiers who sought in their earlier careers to avoid politics, but both of whom knew how to use the situations offered to each of them not only to become Army commander-in-chief but also to make himself immensely rich. During the 'Manhattan' incident Sarit had acted swiftly and ruthlessly to use the Army, almost matching Phao's ruthlessness with his police. He reinforced his personal support through the follow-up promotions of Thanom, Praphas, and Krit, all of whom were to continue his regime into the 1970s. Thanom became his deputy prime minister, minister of defence, deputy supreme commander of the armed forces, and

---

[303] *Bangkok Post Weekly*; Aug 16 1991

[304] *Thailand a Short History*; David K. Wyatt; pp 281/3 and *The Politics of Heroin*; Alfred W Mc Coy; p245

assistant commander-in-chief of the Army. Without question, he was being put forward as Sarit's successor.[305]

One of Sarit's immediate problems was the risk of a counter-coup by the up-and-coming soldiers at colonel and other field rank levels. The Revolutionary Party decided that the best policy was to buy their loyalty, recruiting them by means of bonus payments and salary supplements. There was an immediate problem as supplements and bonuses required money, and money of that sort was not in plentiful supply. The Party's remedy was to adopt the Phao approach and reorganise the opium trade. Army and Air Force officers were sent to Singapore and Hong Kong to arrange the sales. Police and military were sent north to mountain traders to alert them to the increased market available. When the poppy harvest neared its end, the military manoeuvres for the year were staged in the north, with every available form of transport, aircraft, truck, and car pressed into service to maximise collection. After shipment from Bangkok, the revenue was sufficient to douse any flickerings of a counter-coup. The question then arose as to whether or not the Revolutionary Party would foster this revenue as a matter of policy. Many of the Party were indifferent; Praphas favoured its continuation, but both Thanom and police-general Sawai were concerned about international reaction. Finally, it was decreed that the police and military would no longer function as a link between the Burmese poppy-growers and the ocean-going smugglers. Whilst this was a very proper step for the government to take, it did not in itself reduce the output. It merely left the way clear for Chinese syndicates to take over the trade and for a number of Thai leaders to receive generous retainers. Bangkok remained a major centre of drug trafficking.[306]

Sarit isolated many of the military from decision-making. He brought back into government roles men such as Phibun's foreign minister, Direk, M. R. Kukrit Pramoj, and a former premier, Thawee. He trusted Thanom sufficiently to allow him to take charge of the Defence Ministry, but he removed Praphas from command of the 1st Army to the less influential post of assistant to himself as commander-in-chief. At the same time he took managerial control of the police with a deputy director-general kept on a short lead. If he had little trust in Praphas, the opposite was true of Krit. He promoted

---

[305] *Political Conflict in Thailand*; David Morell and Chai-Samudavanija; p51
[306] *The Politics of Heroin*; Alfred W Mc Coy; pp143/4

him, first to be deputy commander of the 1st Army, then to command the Khorat-based 2nd Army, and eventually to command the 1st Army itself.

Millions of baht now began to flow into the pockets of Sarit and his family. The *modus operandi* was almost Middle Eastern in its simplicity. Non-competitive government contracts were procured for his own companies which, being unskilled themselves, sub-contracted the work to skilled companies.[307] For the community in general there were reductions in the retail prices of numerous commodities, lower railway fares and school fees. Outside the family, his 1957 group was kept together by bribery and intimidation.

Meanwhile, across the Mekong the political situation was deteriorating and, to the Thai government, developing into an international problem of considerable danger. There were reports that Thai hill-tribesmen were being recruited, brainwashed, and trained in communist areas of Laos, after which they were sent back to operate in Thailand. The Thai government had always looked upon Laos as being within the Thai sphere of influence and it sought to avoid any hostile Laotian leadership. In the 1950s the communists had increased their hold on Vietnam. In Laos the communist Pathet Lao, under Prince Souphanouvong, had strong Vietnamese backing. Within an agreement of sixteenth of October 1957 the Pathet Lao were persuaded to join a Lao government coalition under Prince Souvanna Phouma, but the agreement was barely worth the paper on which it was written. Elections in May 1958 increased Pathet Lao influence. Then a right-wing government, styled the Committee for the Defence of National Interest, was established with General Phoumi Nosavan as minister of defence and backed by America through the CIA. At a quoted price of one hundred thousand US dollars per National Assembly vote, all earlier agreements were violated. The Pathet Lao representation was forced out. In July 1958, the moderate Souvanna Phouma resigned and gave way to the right-wing Phoui

---

[307] *Portrait of Thai Politics*; Jenton. K. Ray; p40

Sananikone.[308] This swing to the CIA-backed right suited the Thai government, but Laos was becoming unstable.

In July 1959, Pathet Lao forces with support from North Vietnamese forces attempted to re-occupy the northern province of Sam Neua which they had given up in 1957. There was no popular uprising to support them as they had hoped. Laos's neighbours were quick to appreciate the problems and an offer of help was made from Saigon, where the South Vietnamese government saw all of this activity as a prelude to invasion of its own territory. Thailand, through its deputy prime minister, General Thanom, announced that Thai military forces had been alerted to go to the rescue should the Laotian government call upon SEATO for help. The Thai government knew that Laos could not protect Thailand from the North Vietnamese but interpreted the invasion of that country as an alarm. Not only for the Thais was it a question of a tolling bell. For the Western Powers there were the seeds of international conflict and a third world war. The USSR and Britain, as co-chairmen of the Geneva Conference, were called upon to take action against the repudiation of agreements. The USSR sent notes: the British government kept a diplomatic silence.[309] President Eisenhower's domino theory for South-East Asia had referred to Laos as a domino likely to fall early and to Thailand as the most important of the dominoes. In 1962, America was far more concerned about Laos than it was about Vietnam. So was Thailand.

Thailand had supported the right-wing Laotian movement under Prime Minister Phoui Sananikone and his defence minister, General Phoumi Nosavan, who was related to Sarit. By September 1959, Phoui had put Souphanouvong in gaol and pushed Souvanna off to Paris as ambassador. Phoui, with American support through its meddling ambassador, J. Graham Parsons, was threatening to seize control of the government. In December, Phoui got rid of Phoumi but only for a few days, an occurrence which evoked the classic remark from American under-secretary of state, George Ball, that it *"could have been a significant event or a typographical error".*[310]

[308] *From Armed Possesion to Political Offensive*; Chai-anan Samudavanija and others; p50 and *The Furtive War*; Wilfred G. Burchett pp171/2 and *Storm over Laos*; Sisouk na Champassak

[309] *Storm Over Laos*; Prince Sisouk na Champassak; p110 and *Thailand: Society and Politics*; J. L. S. Girling; p173

[310] *The Ravens*; C. Robbins; p100 citing Walter Isaccson and Evan Thomas *The Wise Men; Six Friends and the World they Made*

In late December, General Phoumi ousted Phoui Sananikone and seized control of the government. A new caretaker Cabinet, dominated by Phoumi and the Committee for the Defence of National Interest, prepared for April elections. These, with considerable help from the CIA,[311] it managed to rig to the extent that Phoumi was able to claim all fifty-nine seats. At this time Souphannouvong was still in gaol and Souvanna still in Paris. The latter hurried back to Laos. At the end of May, the Red Prince, with fifteen of his fellow Pathet Lao prisoners, escaped from captivity to rejoin the Pathet Lao forces in a manner which was remarkable even by comparison with Colditz legends.[312]

Accepting Phoumi's Lao Army as the principal local anti-communist force, America armed it, trained it, and paid it,[313] but European powers found Phoumi unacceptable. They saw that with him, a military-controlled political structure on the lines of Thailand was likely to emerge, and this they opposed. Furthermore, with Russia and Vietnam backing the Pathet Lao, direct worldwide confrontation was on the cards.

On ninth of August 1960 an unknown commander of the 2nd Parachute Battalion, Kong Le, with a mere seven hundred men, seized the Laotian capital and proclaimed a new government. Surprisingly, he did not claim it for himself but invited Souvanna Phoumi to be head of a neutralist government. Kong Le had been specially trained by American forces in Thailand to command a parachute battalion, but he resented attempts to buy his loyalty. He grew to see the Americans as a people with a master-race complex and despised them for it. He opposed the fratricide which he saw as only benefiting America and sought support first from Prince Boun Oum, who turned him down, and then Souvanna who, having first referred to the action as *"a vulgar little mutiny"*, decided to back it.[314] Kong Le called for the new state to end civil war and have friendly relations with all foreign powers. That was not the message sought by Washington as "all foreign powers" would include China. Thus the new government found itself under pressure from America, from the right-wing faction under Phoumi and from the left-wing Pathet Lao together with their

[311] *The Ravens*; c. Robbins
[312] *Storm Over Laos*; Sisouk na Champassak; pp150/3
[313] *In a Little Kingdom*; Perry Stieglitz; pp19/28
[314] *Storm Over Laos*; Sisouk na Champassak; pp155 and *The Furtive war*, Wilfred Birchett pp188/9

masters, the North Vietnamese. Thailand also felt itself threatened by anything other than an American-backed right-wing government and was hostile to Kong Le.

Phoumi reassembled the Lao Army under command of General Ouane Rattikone but within his own control, and America supplied him through Savannakhet, which now looked upon itself as the national capital. In the meantime Sarit blocked supplies to the Vientiane government. The city of Vientiane was at the time being shelled but its citizens were unsure which faction was firing. There was a suspicion that many of the shells were from the Thai Army.[315] Phoumi sent a force to drive back the Pathet Lao and also attacked Vientiane. The Pathet Lao had no trouble seeing off Phoumi's troops and re-established itself throughout Sam Neua province. Phoumi's force, moving on Vientiane, was ambushed and routed by Kong Le at Paksane. America, which was financing the Royal Lao Army to the tune of forty million American dollars per year, was getting very little value for money. Once more, the arrogant ex-ambassador, J. Graham Parsons, entered the scene, this time as under-secretary for Far Eastern Affairs, backing Phoumi's illegal force. Countering this, the USSR was flying in massive supplies to support both Kong Le and the Pathet Lao.[316] European views of world confrontation seemed to be coming true.

Thailand remained important to America in its policy for South-East Asia, and it was at this juncture that the Thai government moved towards important agreement with America for Thai defence. America had become concerned not only by the increase in strength of the Pathet Lao and with it the possible weakness of Souvanna's government, but also by its own inability to dictate to SEATO. The CIA was moved in with some four hundred clandestine American Special Forces, "The White Star Mobile Training Teams",[317] to assist Phoumi Nosavan. Air America flew supply missions from Bangkok to Phoumi's forces. Thai and Filipino 'volunteer' parachute troops were sent as reinforcements.[318] The White Star teams fostered the development of the Hmong fighting units under Vang Pao.

---

[315] *In a Little Kingdom*; Perry Stieglitz, p32
[316] *Storm Over Laos*; Sisouk na Champassak; p165 and *The Tragic Mountains*; Jane Hamilton-Merritt; p93
[317] *Storm Over Laos*; Sisouk na Champassak
[318] *The Sarit Regime*; Thak Chaloemtiarana; p314

The CIA established its forward command headquarters in Laos at the secret city of Long Tien, officially known as Lima Site 20 Alternate to give the impression of an emergency-only landing strip. Lima 20 itself was situated at Sam Thong and the two were connected by the only reasonable dirt road in the area. To some, Alternate was near to Shangri-la, whilst to others, in view of the large numbers of CIA agents there, it was more rudely referred to as "Spook Heaven". Situated some three thousand feet up in mist-shrouded mountains, it was set in a bowl-shaped valley, its city a mixture of primitive village and a corrugated-roofed modern settlement housing high-tech telecommunication equipment.

Here also was the base of General Vang Pao, the dedicated leader of the Hmong mercenaries who were fighting America's war. It was the Hmong who were to bear the brunt of the casualties of the next few years of war in Laos, and then to experience eventual exile or the atrocities of revenge at the hands of the Pathet Lao.[319] Vang Pao first went to war when barely in his teens and later he was trained and commissioned into the French colonial army. He was a member of a force which attempted in vain to relieve Dien Bien Phu. As General Vang Pao, his force was, theoretically, a part of the Royal Laotian Army and like the remainder of that Army, paid by America. Long Tien was a hive of air activity. From here the courageous Ravens and fearless Hmong pilots would fly. To here the CIA's private airline, Air America, ferried supplies and manned helicopters in support of Hmong operations, and acted as an air-rescue service to downed Ravens and other pilots. To here, Thai pilots flew in operational support from a command base back across the Mekong at Udon Thani.

Large numbers of Souvanna's Laotian government troops were deserting to General Phoumi and the Prince gradually found himself crushed between the extreme right and left wing factions. But Souvanna would have nothing to do with Parsons' extremist right-wing views and on eleventh of December he left for Cambodia. Phoumi attacked Vientiane; a joint force of Kong Le's neutral troops and the Pathet Lao defended the capital but to no avail. The city was heavily shelled, American helicopters directing Thai artillery units. On thirteenth December the Pathet Lao retreated to their northern

---

[319] *The Ravens*; C. Robbins; and Articles by Dr Jane Hamilton-Merritt , PhD Pullitzer prizewinner for coverage of the Vietnam War, subsequently extended in *The Tragic Mountains*; Bangkok Post; 15 February 1981 and March, 1982

provinces and Kong Le re-established his force on the Plain of Jars. A Lao revolutionary committee, similar to Sarit's and headed by Boun Oum, took over government on eighteenth of December 1960. America immediately recognised it as the legal government and downgraded Souvanna Phoumi to the status of a rebel. Most of the remainder of the world saw it the other way round. Increasing its own intervention, the USSR set up a re-supply operational base and flew in arms, supplies, food, and Vietnamese technicians.[320] Thailand's fear of events had been assuaged, at least temporarily, but the price in increased tension was still to be paid.

In Phnom Penh, Cambodia, where he was staying with Prince Sihanouk, Souvanna Phouma was interviewed by *The New York Times*. Of the interference of J. Graham Parsons, Souvanna said, *"He understood nothing about Asia and nothing about Laos. .... He is the ignominious architect of disastrous American policy towards Laos. He and others like him are directly responsible for the recent spilling of Lao blood."* [321]

That same month, January 1961, Souvanna returned to Laos and joined Kong Le, his particular objective being to ensure that Kong Le did not transfer his allegiance to the Pathet Lao. In March, Phoumi's right-wing force moved on Luang Prabang but sixty miles out from Vientiane they were routed by Kong Le and fled. Phoumi's American backed and trained army was at that time some twenty thousand strong; Kong Le could only muster a force of a few hundred paratroops, but it was enough.

Much to the dismay of Sarit, American policy towards Laos now changed dramatically. In a press conference of twenty-third of March 1961, the new American President, John Kennedy, rejecting the policy sponsored by J. Graham Parsons, said, *"The security of all South-East Asia will be endangered if Laos loses its neutral independence."* [322] He went on to warn that, although he preferred to see an independent and neutral Laos, America and its SEATO allies could not stand by in the face of present communist activities. At a SEATO meeting later that month, Thailand pressed for military intervention in Laos, but the

---

[320] *Storm Over Laos*; Sisouk na Champassak; p170 and *The Sarit Regime*; Thak Chaloemtiarana; p318

[321] *The New York Times*; January 20 1961, cited in *In a Little Kingdom*, Perry Stieglitz; pp33/8

[322] *The Scope of the US Involvement in Laos*; Richard S. Nixon; p1

move was opposed by Britain which wanted the Geneva Conference reconvened, and also by France. A claim of Vietnamese invasion of Laos proved untrue, and to Thailand's dismay only a weak communiqué of warning was issued. Sarit's strongly held view that defending Laos was the same as preventing war in Thailand did not prevail. Frustrated by SEATO, he maintained his view and provided 'volunteer' Thai troops and artillery.

In May 1961, the fruits of the new American policy were to be seen. On twenty-third of March Britain agreed with the USSR to a recall of the Geneva conference and it was followed in April by a call for a cease-fire throughout Laos. On third of May the cease-fire came into effect and on sixteenth of May the International Conference on the Settlement of the Laotian Question opened in Geneva under the joint chairmanship of the USSR and Britain. Also attending were Burma, Cambodia, Canada, China, France, India, Poland, Thailand, North Vietnam, South Vietnam, and America which was now represented by a man of experience and wisdom, Averell Harriman. From Laos came the three quarrelling factions, the Pathet Lao, Souvanna's neutralists, and the military right-wing, headed by Phoui, who seven years earlier was said to have accepted one million US dollars not to sign the original agreement. Setting up the conference was one thing: producing results was another. The meetings dragged on and gradually the Lao delegations took to meeting separately from the major powers, sometimes in Switzerland, sometimes in Laos on the Plain of Jars.[323]

In September 1961, Sarit's foreign secretary, Thanat, on a visit to the United Nations General Assembly, held important bilateral discussions with American leaders and particularly with the secretary of state for foreign affairs, Dean Rusk. Sarit and Thanat were still anxious about the SEATO arrangements. Thailand sought an unequivocal guarantee from America that it would defend Thailand in the event of communist attack, irrespective of what other SEATO members might decide.

In February 1962 the Thais had reacted to a renewed Pathet Lao build-up by deploying Army units along the Laotian border, without

---

[323] *In a Little Kingdom*; Perry Stieglitz; pp38/42

any prior consultation with SEATO. Thanat's previous September visit now paid off. He was invited to return to Washington for discussions with Dean Rusk and later President Kennedy. Out of these meetings came the Rusk-Thanat communiqué, in which Thailand at last had the assurance it sought, the strongest commitment of defence support ever in the history of the two nations. The communiqué included the following two paragraphs:

"The Secretary of State reaffirmed that the United States regards the preservation of the independence and integrity of Thailand as vital to the national interest of the United States and to world peace. He expressed the firm intention of the United States to aid Thailand, its ally and historic friend, in resisting communist aggression and subversion.

The Secretary of State assured the Foreign Minister that in the event of such aggression, the United States intends to give full effect to its obligations under the Treaty to act to meet the common danger in accordance with its constitutional processes. The Secretary of State reaffirmed that this obligation of the United States does not depend upon the prior agreement of all other parties to the Treaty since this Treaty is individual as well as collective." [324]

Sarit had now obtained what Phibun had sought unsuccessfully in the mid-1950s, and with it Thailand was no longer concerned with the need for the unanimity which it had believed was required under the SEATO Treaty. With this American new Treaty interpretation and commitment Sarit, while not enthusiastic, was prepared to accept the principle of a tripartite coalition government in Laos.

The ink on the agreement was barely dry before it came into use. The military situation in Laos again deteriorated. In March 1962, Phoumi allowed seven thousand of his troops under General Ouane to be bottled up in a valley by Kong Le and the Pathet Lao. It was a situation similar to Dien Bien Phu. Massive air supply kept them going for two months. Forces attempting to relieve them were cut to pieces. After a partial breakout, that part of the Lao Army able to run, fled across the Mekong into Thailand. Sarit feared that the Pathet Lao and possibly supporting Vietnamese units might follow.

---

[324] Published at the Department of State Bulletin of 26 March 1962 and cited in *US and Thailand*; R Sean Randolph; pp41/2

The American response was prompt. On seventeenth of May, a US Marine task force of one thousand eight hundred men landed in Bangkok and moved up to the north-east, twenty-five miles from the Laotian border, supplementing a thousand-man American force which had remained over from a SEATO exercise. Further arrivals of engineers and American Air Force personnel soon brought the total to ten thousand men. Small military units from Australia and New Zealand also joined the force, to which Britain added a squadron of Hunter ground-attack aircraft, stationed at Chiang Mai.[325] Tension in Laos eased and the SEATO force was withdrawn over the July to September period. Arms were left stacked in Thailand for use by SEATO troops if the threat re-emerged. Whether the force was assembled at the request of America or at the invitation of the Thais has been left as an unsolved riddle, there being two opposing versions of events, according to which country is speaking. Whatever the version, the result was essentially American partial occupation of Thailand, and with it the risk of a third world war.

With the Pathet Lao tension eased, the three Lao factions were able to reach an agreement in principle to establish a coalition Cabinet. The Geneva Conference was resumed and on twenty-third of July 1962, representatives of fourteen nations met to sign the Declaration on the Neutrality of Laos. The declaration stated that none of the countries would threaten, or use, force against the Kingdom of Laos, that each would refrain from direct interference with the internal affairs of Laos, would not involve Laos in any military alliance, would not invoke the SEATO Treaty's protection for Laos, would not introduce any foreign troops into Laos, and would not use the Kingdom of Laos for interference with the affairs of other countries. The seventh of October was the deadline for the removal of all troops in the area. America claimed that it removed all six hundred and sixty-six of its personnel, but stated that the North Vietnamese had withdrawn only forty out of over six thousand.[326] Souvanna was once more the prime minister and Kong Le was a general, commanding Lao troops on the Plain of Jars. Both Sarit and his foreign minister, Thanat, had serious doubts that the Pathet Lao would observe its part of the agreement. Sarit was to be proved right.

---

[325] Discussions with Sqn Leader Johnathan Pote, R. Aux A.F., then a UK VSO

[326] *The Scope of the US Involvement in Laos*; Richard S. Nixon

In Laos a new neutralist Cabinet was formed under Souvanna Phouma, with four right-wing, four Pathet Lao, and eleven neutralist members i.e. supporters of Souvanna himself. It left Sarit unimpressed and he saw it as only a prelude to a full communist take-over.[327] One result was an increase in American troops stationed in Thailand together with a substantial increase in military and economic aid. Many Thais began to see their country as virtually an American colony, its "unsinkable aircraft carrier". Others, however, saw the concessions partly as an effort to increase Thailand's own security and partly as a debt it owed to America for the latter's post-war support. Others again, more attuned to the commercial approach, saw the situation as a source of profit.

Whilst military personnel were excluded from Laos by the Geneva Declaration, Air America as a commercial airline was not. Thus, operating out of Bangkok, American aid could flow unofficially to the right-wing forces. Anti-communist Hmong tribesmen were flown out of reach of Pathet Lao forces. American aircraft carried out reconnaissance flights over Lao territory, but American fighter-bombers were flown by Thai and other non-American pilots.[328]

In the late 1950s, Cambodian relationships with the Chinese People's Republic became closer, while Thailand still formally favoured the Chinese Nationalist government in Taiwan. The border with Cambodia was closed. Thailand formally broke off relations in 1958. The final straws were a territorial dispute over a small area of land on which was sited a famous temple, and also Prince Norodom Sihanouk's formal recognition of the People's Republic of China.[329] Looking westward across the Mekong, there was genuine and justifiable concern and distrust in both Laos and Cambodia at Thailand's growing relationship with America. Throughout the Sarit period, American-Thai relationships grew closer despite a grave suspicion on the Thai side that America would one day withdraw its forces from the area, and on the American side a shadowy distrust of Sarit himself. Eventually, Thai national development became essentially a part of the execution of American policy and with it came

---

[327] *The Sarit Regime*; Thak Chaloemtiarana; pp318/20
[328] Discussions with and Sqn. Leader Johnathan Pote, R. Aux AF
[329] *The Sarit Regime*; Thak Chaloemtiarana; pp322/3

heavy infrastructure investment running into tens of millions of US dollars per annum.

By 1963, Sarit was again a very sick man and on eighth of December, less than a month after the assassination in Dallas of President Kennedy, he died. While Sarit's body still rested in its royal golden vessel, awaiting cremation on seventeenth of March, the first massive scandal over his accumulated wealth broke with a lawsuit initiated by his first wife and her son.[330] This family squabble over his estate publicised the fact that it was valued at about one hundred and fifty million dollars, including vast areas of land, property, and immense private interests in banking and construction. He had used his political power to help his friends, mainly outside the system of formal government control. The case also brought to public attention the remarkable collection of mistresses with whose affections Sarit had dallied, estimates of the numbers ranging from fifty to over eighty. All of a sudden, the much respected military idol who had cleaned out Phao and his scurrilous activities was shown to have feet of clay. His personal dubious business connections with a number of companies were disclosed. His Sisao Deves clique — which included the supporting Thanom, Praphas, and Krit — was found to be involved in banking, insurance, shipping and river transport, warehousing, construction, steel, cement, mining, and livestock.[331] Other activities, which eventually led to the resignation in disgust of Thawee, involved government loans to 'brass-plate' companies and government contracts to family and friends.

Sarit's ruthlessness and authoritarian manner were well known but the posthumous disclosure of the extent of his greed shocked many. He had been involved in opium smuggling, even before Phao. He had denied human rights to many people and had hitched Thailand so tightly to the American star *"that he had mortgaged the country's future"*. While *"his self-proclaimed revolutionary goal was to restore a social and political order based on traditional Thai values, inherently monarchical and hierarchical"* he had in practice *"established an enduring political philosophy that exaggerated traditional values and*

---

[330] *Far Eastern Economic Review*; 12 March 1964

[331] *The Thai Young Turks*; Chai-Anan Samudavanija; p17 citing Thammasat MA thesis by Sungsidh Piriyarangsan Oct 1980, pp226/93

institutions, buttressing social and political hierarchy at the expense of egalitarianism and even human rights. "[332] In this, Sarit differed from Phibun, who believed in a western form of democracy and wanted to change the Thai system to conform to it. Sarit thought he could change western democracy to suit Thai values. Both men failed because the two concepts are incompatible.

Thais use the word *nakleng* to define a charismatic, swashbuckling type of leader, a successful taker of risks. Sarit fitted this concept. He towered over early post-war Thai politics and dominated the Thai political scene for five years. His character was a combination of the ruthless gangster, the traditional lavish oriental despot and the shrewd judge of expertise. He was a man who appealed to the man in the street, and, without attempting to exclude the King, he fitted neatly the Thai concept of leadership based on the father-son relationship. His was a dictatorship built from benevolent despotism, if that is not a contradiction in terms, and military strength. Even when prime minister, Sarit made frequent visits to outlying districts, camping out, sleeping rough, and talking to people in market places. His visits to these distant parts were not merely for public relations purposes. Sarit viewed local officials as his eyes and ears. *"The masses,"* he said, *"should be content to remain on the land and go about their daily tasks in an orderly and proper manner. They should have enough to eat, a place to live, and work to do".*[333] That is always an acceptable view, provided the offeror is not one of the masses. It is not too far removed from an attitude of a century earlier when it was written of the rich and the poor: *"God made them high or lowly, and ordered their estate".*

Sarit was himself a contradiction, a paternalistic leader but a greedy despot. He had obsessions with cleanliness, orderliness, and good behaviour from the general public. The streets were cleaner, samlo hand-pushed tricycles were banned, there was less hooliganism, less prostitution, and less arson. There were fewer beggars and the opium dens were closed. Sarit saw himself as the father of the nation, yet his personal morals in relation to greed and womanising were at gutter level.

Sarit's ultimate aim has been seen as *"the establishment of a modernised state which would realise the fundamental values of the*

---

[332] *Thailand: A Short History*; David K Wyatt; pp283/5
[333] *The Sarit Regime*; Thak Chaloemtiarana;pp214/6 and 245

Thai people, values which could be best expressed in the three ideals of king, religion, and nation".[334] The King would remain a revered figure and Buddhism the source of morality and ethical behaviour. Thus would be developed the strength of the nation. The repression of alleged communism or of plots of Isan secession was then justifiable in order to crush any philosophy opposed to his aims. In Sarit's policy, the strength of the nation was also related to the avoidance of foreign entanglements, a policy opposed to that of Phibun. Here the contradiction within Sarit's ideas was obvious. Throughout his rule he became ever more entangled with and in the clutches of America.

Sarit's rule, as well that of his predecessors and successors, came in for severe criticism from the Thai economic historian, Dr Chatthip Nartspha, when he reviewed development over the period 1956 to 1965. Dr Chatthip pointed out that none of the governments set out to aid industry itself to any substantial extent. They were accused of being criminal in their failure so to do. Monopoly power was used to support Bangkok traders, the middlemen, and exporters at the expense of the farmers. The profit was wasted on the import of luxury items. However, the electricity generation expansion, which, before 1973, was a useful broad-brush measure of national product growth in Thailand, was in Sarit's days substantial. It is true, however, that little commercial profit earned actually benefited the individual farmer or worker, and resentment of this would grow over the next decade.

At no time did Sarit forget that the legitimacy of his regime sprang from the dominance of the Army, and he expended substantial energy in expanding its functions, skills, prestige, and control. He operated the management of the Thai Army through a clique of loyal subordinate officers, particularly Thanom, Praphas, and Krit. The Army was his first love and he kept his links with it until his death, maintaining a house in the Headquarters of the 1st Division. The initial legitimacy of his regime by the King's proclamation in September 1957 and by carefully worded support in a statement in October 1958 helped Sarit to use that support to his own advantage. The repressive nature of his regime was partly obscured by the graciousness of the King and his Queen, and royal involvement brought partial respectability to the Sarit dictatorship.

Was Sarit so different from Phao that Sarit should be regarded by writers of history as a hero and Phao a villain? Each was the 'strong'

---

[334] *The Sarit Regime*; Thak Chaloemtiarana; pp221/2

man of his time in the old-fashioned sense, each ruthless in the pursuit of power and of riches. Each was lavish in his hospitality and generous to his friends, even if it were at the country's expense. Each exploited the Chinese commercial element of the community for his own profit. There were differences: Sarit was perceived to be a favourite of the King, an honour not bestowed upon Phao. While Phao was married into the closely-knit Phin dynasty, Sarit's immorality was openly seen. He was a heavy brandy drinker in his early days of power, arriving at a party with his ADC carrying unopened bottles for his personal consumption, to avoid any attempt at poisoning. He was frequently drunk in foreign embassies, but Phao's reputation was similar. Those watching Sarit closely from embassies noted a distinct change in him when he returned in 1958. Despite his private life, he became respected as a first-class national leader. After the Phibun/Phao era, Sarit was probably the leader Thailand needed, at least temporarily. In relation to Phao, the conclusion must be that one must die in power to achieve an heroic reputation. Phao died in exile after defeat.

After Sarit's death and the revelation of his scandalous behaviour, there were suggestions that he should lose his rank of Field Marshal. This was not carried through, but in 1969 he was stripped of his decorations as a mark of condemnation of his corrupt practices. His property was auctioned that same year to reimburse funds misappropriated.[335]

---

[335] *Portrait of Thai Politics*; Jenton. K. Ray; p41

CHAPTER EIGHT
Pressure on the Kuomintang

On second of March 1953 the government of Burma, having already abrogated American aid in protest at the failure of America to call off its puppet government in Taiwan, announced that it was referring to the United Nations the problem of the violation of its territory by the KMT. A telegram requesting inclusion of the matter in the agenda of the seventh session of the General Assembly was sent to the United Nations on twenty-third of March. The paper then submitted traced the history of the KMT troops in Burma and formulated two basic charges. The first was that the Chinese Nationalist government, to which it referred simply as 'Formosa', was guilty of supplying the KMT in Burma with arms and ammunition and the second, that 'Formosa' had direct control over the KMT forces of General Li Mi, and that these constituted an act of aggression against Burma.[336]

The complaint was heard by the Political Committee of the United Nations. On seventeenth of April 1953, the case for Burma was eloquently put by the Chairman of its delegation, the Honourable Justice U Myint Thein. In considerable detail he explained the evidence submitted by the Burmese government, tracing the history of the KMT incursion, the initial aggression, the grouping of the foreign forces, and the incursions into Yunnan from bases in Burma. He gave specific evidence of a relationship between General Li Mi and 'Formosa', training and reorganisation, the strength of the forces, and their increased activity in 1952 which, to the government of Burma, appeared to be an attempt to undermine the autonomy of the government of Burma in the hope of replacing it with a government more amenable to the wishes of the KMT headquarters in 'Formosa'. He drew attention to the grave international complications which might ensue. After summing up a list of activities, Justice U Myint Thein was moved to add, *"If that is not aggression, my Delegation would like to know what is"*.

---

[336] *Nationalist China Troops in Burma; Obstacles to Burma Foreign Relations*; K. R. Young; p96

He went on to list atrocities against the civilian population and he developed further the links with the Chinese Nationalist government in 'Formosa', stressing Li Mi's role as a Nationalist official and admissions of the relationship by the jungle generals themselves as well as by the Chinese Nationalist representative in Bangkok, Mr Patrick Soong. Confirmation from a member of the Soong family, so influential in America from its close links to Chiang Kai-shek, was the quality of evidence that Burma sought and Soong's statement to *The Times* of London's reporter became a much-contested piece of evidence. Such was its importance that *The Times*, on twentieth of April 1953, having received a cable of denial from Patrick Soong, took the trouble to confirm and repeat its reporter's testimony that, according to Soong, Li Mi's troops were part of Chiang Kai-shek's forces.[337] On the evidence presented, it was an overwhelming case of territorial violation.

Chiang Kai-shek's representative, Dr Tingfu F. Tsiang, denied that the Chinese 'foreign forces' in Burma were any part of the Nationalist Army, although it had its origins in KMT soldiers who came from the Yunnan. He expressly referred to the forces as the Yunnan Anti-Communist National Salvation Army, a force beyond the control of his government. He accepted that arms and ammunition were being sent, but by private companies and not by his government. The supplies came from admiring Chinese anti-communists throughout the world. He denied that planes from Taiwan had been used, although the Burmese said that they had absolute proof of such flights. General Li Mi was known to have made a number of visits to Taiwan for discussions and to request financial aid. Much of the Nationalist China defence was based on the argument that the Sino-Burmese border was not agreed and the territory occupied by the KMT soldiers belonged to China. Therefore the KMT forces were not on Burmese soil but were the last remnant of the Nationalist Forces in mainland China. This was a risky defence as, if upheld, it became a virtual invitation to the People's Liberation Army to move into that border area, a situation sought neither by Taiwan nor Burma. It was certainly not a situation sought by Thailand. It was later played down.

Dr Tingfu alleged that the Burmese government had little authority outside a few main towns and he saw General Li Mi's forces as heroes in the eyes of the Chinese people. Nevertheless, he offered his

---

[337] *KMT Aggression against Burma*; Burma Ministry of Information; p79

government's assistance to the United Nations in any attempt to withdraw the force. During the course of the debate, the government of Thailand denied that any arms were being supplied through Thailand. The Burmese government was able to submit evidence to the contrary, claiming that such arms came through American-created companies in Bangkok and that opium was used to buy the arms from Thailand. The Phao connection was beginning to come out into the open. The Nationalist China defence received little sympathy. Almost all of the members of the Political Committee strongly supported the Burmese position, but in the final stages the committee ducked the issue. Led by the British representative, it resorted to the favourite device of reference back to a committee and did not take any direct, positive action on the complaint. It called for the parties directly concerned — Burma, the Chinese Nationalists, Thailand, and America — to seek to deal with the situation.[338]

Embarrassed by these disclosures, Washington convened a four-nation military commission composed of Burma, Taiwan, Thailand, and America in Bangkok on twenty-second and twenty-third of May 1953. Thailand was represented by Lieut-Colonel Chatichai, Phibun's personally appointed representative. On twenty-third of June 1953 the committee issued a joint communiqué setting out the terms under which the complete withdrawal of all KMT troops was agreed. Foreign forces from North-East Burma were to move by air via Lashio to Thailand and thence to Taiwan. Those from the Mong Hsat area were to travel by road to Tachilek, be disarmed, and then cross into Thailand by road, and from there be flown to Taiwan. Foreign forces in the Tenasserim area were to be flown into Thailand, and again on to Taiwan. The Soi Rajakru clan held conflicting roles, with Phao actively supplying arms to the KMT and trading opium with them, while Chatichai was involved in their disarmament.

The KMT jungle generals at first refused to co-operate but on twenty-third of June they joined the four-power Joint Committee in Bangkok. They rejected the United Nations resolution as unreasonable. One of their arguments was simply that the men concerned were native to the area and had no wish to be sent to Taiwan. They called for a neutral zone, a cease-fire arrangement with

---

[338] *KMT Aggression against Burma*; Burma Ministry of Information; pp31/100 and *Nationalist China Troops in Burma: Obstacles to Burma Foreign Relations*; K. R. Young; pp91/112

Burma and an American guarantee of both. Eventually, backed by Nationalist China, the KMT forces offered for evacuation one thousand seven hundred out of the currently estimated twelve thousand 'volunteers'.[339] Burma, without success, pressed for total evacuation. On seventeenth of September Burma withdrew from the Joint Committee and increased its military activity, bombing Mong Hsat on twenty-second of September. The remaining members of the Joint Committee now found it possible, as soon as sixth of October, to formulate an evacuation plan but based on the original number of between one thousand seven hundred and two thousand which had crossed over to Burma. The Nationalist Chinese government in Taiwan then publicly disavowed any responsibility for any of the remaining forces.[340]

Burma again went to the United Nations and eventually, after a great deal of quibbling by Taiwan, it was agreed that two thousand KMT troops would be marched out of the Shan country to Chiang Mai and flown by Air America back to Taiwan. When the Four-Nation Military Commission representatives arrived at the staging area, police-general Phao refused to allow the Burmese to witness the assembly. The first fifty KMT soldiers brought a picture of Chiang Kai-shek and no guns. American ambassador in Bangkok, William Donovan, cabled the American embassy in Taiwan and told it to get to grips with the matter and put it right. At this point he was threatened by Chiang Kai-shek himself that if America did not take off the pressure, he, Chiang, would expose the CIA involvement. He seriously misjudged Donovan who already knew of a Chinese government public statement of December 1951 covering American aid to the KMT in Burma. Donovan cabled back that the Soviets and 'Chi-coms' already knew about the CIA. He kept up the pressure. The KMT withdrawal was resumed. The soldiers now brought out rusting museum pieces as their 'arms'. Burmese observers, now allowed to witness proceedings, protested that many of the so-called KMT were in fact local Lahu tribesmen, but they were unable to force any changes. Taiwan claimed that they were Yunnanese. Of the nearly two thousand KMT evacuated through November and December 1953,

---

[339] *Foreign and Domestic Consequences of KMT Intervention in Burma*; Robert H. Taylor; p47

[340] *Nationalist China Troops in Burma: Obstacles to Burma Foreign Relations*; K. R. Young; pp117/130

many were in fact tribesmen who had recently been press-ganged from their villages, dressed in KMT uniforms, and shipped off to Taiwan. Few were allowed to return.

Simultaneously with the appeal to the United Nations the Burmese government launched an attack on KMT troops in September and October 1953 and made substantial progress. Burma continued to press for total evacuation or disarmament of the forces — five thousand by the end of 1953 and the remaining seven thousand by the end of March 1954. Any interim cease-fire was rejected.[341]

The restraint of the Chinese People's Republic throughout this period was remarkable. Only occasionally did the People's Liberation Army cross into Burma in hot-pursuit of raiding KMT. Burma flirted with the idea of seeking Chinese assistance to destroy the KMT remnant but drew back from such a high-risk tactic. Once the People's Liberation Army established itself by invitation on Burmese territory, there would be no knowing what it might do next. China appeared to accept that a neutral Burma was preferable to a pro-western Burma and left it at that.[342]

Frustrated in its attempt through the United Nations to remove the bulk of KMT troops, the Burmese, in March 1954, again launched heavy attacks on the KMT at Mong Hsat, bombing it for two days and following up with a ground attack. Mong Hsat was captured and its two thousand defenders driven south towards the Thai border. Negotiations in Bangkok over the next two to three months resulted in another four to five thousand KMT troops being flown back to Taiwan by Air America. On thirtieth of May 1954, General Li Mi, now in Taiwan, announced the dissolution of the Yunnan Anti-Communist National Salvation Army. There were still six thousand or more KMT in Burma with a new base camp at Mong Pawng, south-east of Mong Hsat. Fighting continued sporadically. Remnants of KMT forces managed to entrench themselves on Shan soil after the 1954 evacuation. They were later organised into two 'armies' — the 3rd army under General Li Wen-huan, and the 5th under General Tuan

---

[341] *Nationalist China Troops in Burma: Obstacles to Burma Foreign Relations*; K.R. Young; pp114/6

[342] *Foreign and Domestic Consequences of KMT Intervention in Burma*; Robert H. Taylor; pp29/30

Shi-wen.[343] They established themselves in an area embracing the Shan state of Kengtung and as far south as the Chiang Rai province of Thailand. The force was flexible in its movement and could freely cross the border to avoid harassment from troops of either government. It monopolised the contraband business, enriching the Chinese network through family connections in several Asian countries.

Li Wen-huan was only a minor official in pre-Mao Yunnan but proved a shrewd and skilful leader of men. He followed General Li Mi into the Shan States, and in 1956, took command of the 8th Division. After the evacuation of regular KMT troops, Li Wen-huan commanded the small 3rd army, and in the chaos that followed the Shan resistance to Burmese control he became a self-appointed general. By 1959 he was in command of a trade/military fiefdom covering more than a third of the Shan States. Apart from the Burmese Army, his was then the primary military force in the Shan area. He was able to manipulate Shan forces and leaders to further his trading activity, first in opium, then in arms and ammunition, and then in a wide range of contraband, and later in heroin. The Rangoon nationalisation programme of the early 1960s created huge shortages in Burma proper, which enabled him to extend his market. Additionally, when Ne Win's programme for establishing local 'home guard' units, the Ka Kwe Ye, was introduced in 1963, many needed funds. They sought to trade in the same fields as he already was, giving him a further collection of sub-units to exploit. Li Wen-huan had refining and storage facilities for opium available which he was able to offer, subject to taxation on the users. He arranged protection and transportation. Nothing of commercial value — opium, heroin, gems, cattle, hides, elephant tusks, and general merchandise — moving between Burma proper and the Shan States, escaped his controlled involvement and taxation. He reaped several fortunes from the Shan-Burmese government war. In 1971, with a public display of burning some twenty-four tonnes of opium, he attempted to convince the outside world that he had nothing to do with opium and heroin. He portrayed his 3rd army of ex-KMT soldiers and locally raised Lahu, Wa and Shan tribesmen as tough anti-communist fighters who grew

---

[343] *Nationalist China Troops in Burma; Obstacles to Burma Foreign Relations*; K. R. Young; pp136/7

tea and coffee along Thailand's communist-infested northern frontier.[344]

Tuan Shi-wen commanded the 5th army. He was a regular officer of the Chinese Army and he had also accompanied General Li Mi into the Shan States. He took part in America/Taiwan planned raids into Yunnan before the evacuation of alleged regular KMT troops to Taiwan. His troops were supplemented by local recruitment along the Shan-Thailand border, mainly in the eastern Shan States. General Tuan's force was more professionally occupied than that of Li Wen-huan and actively engaged in CIA intelligence gathering. Nevertheless, it found plenty of time for opium, heroin, and other contraband trading. Tuan believed in the theory that the KMT would one day reinvade mainland China.[345] It was General Tuan who is credited with the oft-quoted comment in justification of a drug empire: *"We must continue to fight the evil of communism. To fight, you must have an army. To have an army you must have guns. To buy guns you must have money, and in these mountains the only money is opium".*[346]

Over the period 1954 to 1960, the Burmese Army had made several attempts to drive out the KMT remnants from the Shan States. The attacks of 1956/7 were not successful, but later the KMT were forced to regroup near Mong Pa-liao. In January 1955, a Thai goodwill mission visited Rangoon, and in the following month the Burmese Ambassador met with Thai officials to discuss common border problems. The future of the KMT remnant was among their agenda items. In a joint approach, Burma increased its activities against the KMT, and the Thai border police strengthened the border control. Prime Minister Phibun Songkhram, then in the process of attempting to diminish the influence of Phao and building a new power base of his own, made a follow-up visit to Rangoon and promised aid to Burma against the KMT in the neighbouring Shan States.[347] In practice, little changed.

---

[344] *The Shan of Burma*; Chao Tzang Yawnghwe; p203
[345] *The Shan of Burma*; Chao Tzang Yawnghwe; p241
[346] *London Weekend Telegraph*; 10 March 1967
[347] *Foreign and Domestic Consequences of KMT Intervention in Burma*; Robert H. Taylor; p56

With the struggle no longer commanding attention in Washington, there were reports in June 1955 of KMT troops being flown in from Taiwan and the command structure reinforced with a Headquarters complex established at Mong Pa-liao. Over the period 1956 to 1959, the KMT and the Karen National Defence Organisation joined forces to harass the Burmese government. In 1956 they were sacking towns near Moulmein. In 1959 they were near Kengtung ambushing lorry convoys. The KMT force continued to develop its drugs trade and, by May 1959, had introduced morphine base refineries at an airstrip near Wanton. Later that same year the Burmese Army captured Wanton and uncovered the processing plants. By then, other bases had been established which served not only as listening posts for Chinese Nationalist and American intelligence services but also as jumping-off points from which agents were despatched to China. As a supplementary activity the bases covered opium buying, collection, storage, and refining as well as acting as storage and distribution points for other contraband. They were, in practice, private fiefdoms of local commanders. The Shan launched its futile war for independence from Burma, but even before the first shots were fired in 1959 at the battle of Tangyan, they were seriously hampered by the presence of the KMT troops in the Shan States. The independence of the Shan States was not the KMT's concern and it would not necessarily profit from it. It paid small Shan units to become auxiliary units of the local KMT, and in return they received arms and ammunition to fight Burma's Army while trade profits flowed into the pockets of the KMT and their accomplices in Thailand, Laos, and Hong Kong.[348]

Away from the international press, the governments of Burma and the People's Republic of China resolved to settle the KMT issue. A visit to Rangoon by a Chinese People's Republic delegation, headed personally by Chou En-lai, led to a border co-operation agreement which, *inter alia*, allowed the People's Liberation Army formal hot-pursuit rights inside Burma up to a distance of ten kilometres.[349] A combined attack was made on the KMT Headquarters at Mong Pa-liao. The Headquarters establishment was heavily defended, heavily fortified, and had its own airstrip, capable of handling large

[348] *The Shan Of Burma*; Chao Tzang Yawnghwe; p126
[349] *Foreign and Domestic Consequences of KMT Intervention in Burma*; Robert H. Taylor; p55

transport aircraft. Five thousand Burmese troops and three full People's Liberation Army divisions, a force totalling over twenty thousand strong, eventually overwhelmed the fortress on twenty-sixth of January 1961. Over three hundred KMT were reported killed in the battle and five thousand fled to Northern Burma, to Laos, and particularly to Thailand. Many of the hill-tribe recruits returned to their villages in the mountains. About three thousand joined the CIA-backed troops of General Phoumi Nosavan, the leader of the Laotian political right-wing.

Chiang Kai-shek claimed that much of the fighting against the KMT force in Burma was carried out by the People's Liberation Army, and its involvement was put as high as fifty thousand by Taiwan, whilst the Thai estimate was as low as five thousand. Local reporters of English newspapers *The Sunday Times*, *Guardian*, and *Observer*, all gave information of PLA involvement, but the Burmese government denied it. Among the stores captured by the Burmese Army were American arms of recent manufacture and boxes of ammunition still marked with American labels. Following a further complaint to the United Nations, America disclaimed all knowledge of the arms, implying that they had wrongly been diverted by 'Formosa'. The Burmese Army again attacked the KMT, this time in eastern Kengtung where a pocket of about four thousand were known to have gathered. It resulted in the capture of Kenglap together with large stocks of modern American weapons.[350]

On sixteenth of February 1961 the Burmese airforce intercepted and shot down an unmarked Liberator aircraft, which eventually crashed in Thailand, killing two unidentified pilots. Other crew members seen parachuting from the plane were never apprehended. Taiwan announced that the plane had been sent by one of its charity agencies, that it was unarmed and was dropping food and clothing to Chinese refugees, of which there were one hundred and fifty thousand in the dropping area. Thai and American officials made for the crash; the Burmese were excluded. The Thai report was that the plane itself was unarmed, was not carrying arms, and was a supply-drop plane. Thailand's Air Marshal Thawee expressed some doubt as to its innocence, and later Prime Minister Sarit Thanarat offered a view that

---

[350] *Nationalist China Troops in Burma: Obstacles to Burma Foreign Relations*; K. R. Young; pp144/151 and *Foreign and Domestic Consequences of KMT Intervention in Burma*; Robert H. Taylor; p59

some KMT irregulars may have entered Thailand unnoticed and reached the plane first, dismantled parts of it, and removed any sign of arms supplies.[351]

In practice, Burma was now not so much troubled by the KMT, and estimated that less than one thousand remained on its territory. But it was concerned about the principle involved. On twenty-second of February 1961 Burma cabled the United Nations, complaining of continued violation of its territory by the KMT. On twenty-first of February the American military attaché, with other South-East Asia representatives including Burmese Army officers, had examined the stocks captured at Mong Pa-liao. The report was not published, but shortly afterwards America announced that the KMT remaining in the Burma, China, Laos, and Thailand borderlands would be evacuated. It was not before time. The point had been reached when the presence of local KMT were offending America's principal ally in the region, Thailand. Thailand had no scruples about trading with an armed KMT force in Burma, but took a very different view once that force crossed the border into Thailand. Thai prime minister, Sarit Thanarat, insisted on either chasing the KMT back into Burma or allowing them to remain in Thailand, but disarmed.[352]

There was no doubt, locally, of the culpability of America. Chiang Kai-shek and his Taiwan-based Army were looked upon as American puppets, and as such their improper behaviour as an armed force on Burmese soil could have been terminated had America so wished. The *Rangoon Guardian* referred to the *'parasitic regime in Formosa'* not daring to violate Burmese lands if America put its foot down and the *Washington Post* of third of March 1961 was inclined to agree. On thirteenth of March, Burmese prime minister U Nu called upon America to accept its proper responsibilities and ensure that the Taiwan regime, which could not exist without American protection and assistance, did not misuse the military equipment provided.[353] The new Kennedy administration responded and told Taiwan that it was opposed to the KMT elements staying in Burma and Laos and that

---

[351] *Nationalist China Troops in Burma: Obstacles to Burma Foreign Relations*; K. R. Young; pp152/158

[352] *Nationalist China Troops in Burma: Obstacles to Burma Foreign Relations*; K. R. Young; pp168/170

[353] *Nationalist China Troops in Burma: Obstacles to Burma Foreign Relations*; K. R. Young; pp161/2

it would assist in moving them out through Thailand. In 'Thai-speak', to 'assist' meant paying the bill.

On second of March, Thailand announced that it was taking military action against one thousand KMT who had crossed into Thailand and gave them three day's notice to get back into Burma. The Burmese were not pleased, and the KMT made their way into Laos, thus swelling the numbers which had fled into that country. Not without good cause, China, Russia, and North Vietnam accused America of using the local KMT to aid pro-western elements in the current Laotian civil war against the communist Pathet Lao. The KMT remnant was now becoming an acute embarrassment to America and pressure was put on the Taiwan government to evacuate them. On fifth of March 1961, after some dissent, it announced the withdrawal of 'Chinese escapees' from the Burma, Laos, China, and Thailand borders. The Thailand evacuation committee was headed by Air Marshal Thawee and included representatives of America, the Nationalist Chinese government in Taiwan, and the jungle generals. Evacuation took place in some secrecy to avoid both ambushes by the Burmese Army and any attempt to shoot down the transport planes by communist China's fighter planes. Commencing on seventeenth of March, some two hundred and forty flights were scheduled, and not until twenty-fourth of March were press restrictions lifted.

Independent observers noted numerous American modern weapons among those surrendered at the point of evacuation. On fifth of May 1961, Taiwan announced the conclusion of the evacuation and that four thousand four hundred KMT soldiers and dependants had arrived in Taiwan. The Thai figures were about three thousand KMT, one thousand pro-Nationalist Chinese refugees from China, and five hundred women and children. The Burmese government's number was approximately two thousand. Nationalist China announced that no 'sizeable force' of guerillas was left in the borderlands. Others estimated that there were still five thousand. General Li Mi, by then in retirement in Taiwan, said that there would always be some, *"as long as the Peking government exists"*. Thailand officials claimed that Thailand was clear and Laos officials claimed likewise. At a meeting with the Chinese People's Republic prime minister, Chou En-lai, in April 1961, Burmese officials spoke of the 'serious threat' to both Burma and China of the remaining KMT. The Chinese People's Republic claimed that at least two thousand KMT were left to fight on the right-wing forces' side in Laos and that they were to be found in Houi Sai province, across the Mekong from Chiang Saen, and along Thailand's northern border.[354]

Among the troops returned to Taiwan were the 1st, 2nd, and 4th 'armies'. This left the 3rd army under Gen Li Wen-huan and the 5th under Tuan Shi-wen. That they remained is usually attributed in Chinese Nationalist circles to ties of marriage and local recruitment. There was also opium and the money it brought. Li Mi's so-called retirement to Taiwan had doubts cast upon it when in April 1961, captured documents were alleged to demonstrate that he was still issuing orders to the KMT in his old operational area.[355] In practice, however, both America and the Nationalist China government exiled in Taiwan had washed their hands of whatever remained of the KMT in Burma. They were now a matter for Burma and, indirectly, for Thailand.

At this time Li Wen-huan's 3rd army was made up around a core of about seven hundred and fifty men, and the 5th army, about one thousand five hundred. Each moved its base to Thailand. The 3rd settled at Tam Ngop, but its commander rode on to his luxury home in Chiang Mai. The 5th army endeavoured to settle at Muang An but eventually consolidated around Doi Mae Salong, a wild, tiger-ridden part of Thailand. The army personnel integrated with Lisu tribespeople. General Tuan lived with the troops in the mountains, becoming a leader greatly respected by his army and something of a patriarch. As the two armies settled in and then expanded their local influence on both sides of the border, they restricted the activity of the Burmese communists. Thanks to Chinese Nationalist and American influence, both the 3rd and 5th Armies eventually enjoyed a special status in Thailand as the Chinese Irregular Force, a special anti-communist unit allied to the Royal Thai Army.[356] In relation to the 3rd and 5th formations, the word 'army' has to be seen in local context. The groupings changed frequently in size and character and they bore no resemblance to the term 'army' as it is commonly

[354] *Nationalist China Troops in Burma: Obstacles to Burma Foreign Relations*; K.R. Young; pp175/184 and *Foreign and Domestic Consequences of KMT Intervention in Burma*; Robert H. Taylor; p62 citing Peking Review

[355] *Golden Triangle; Frontier and Wilderness*; Kuo Yi-tung (Bo Yang); p109 and *Bangkok Post*; 25 March 1984; and *Foreign and Domestic Consequences of KMT Intervention in Burma*; Robert H. Taylor; p52

[356] *The Shan of Burma*; Chao Tzang Yawnghwe; p124

understood. They might more aptly be described as roving bands of brigands. Nevertheless, firepower, a measure of discipline, and a motive of greed kept each band as a force with which to be reckoned.

The Shan uprising of 1959, the 1962 Burmese Army coup which brought Ne Win to absolute power, and the subsequent chaos in the Shan States suited the former KMT. There developed in both the Shan State and Burma proper an acute shortage of manufactured and consumer goods, thus boosting the cross-border trade which the KMT controlled. It made rich entrepreneurs of Chinese generals and colonels, together with their trading partners, the network of Chinese merchants and finance houses. Added to this was the newly developing boom in the demand for heroin which arose following an increasing presence in Indochina of American troops.

The disowned KMT armies were not without offers of another sort. Within months the CIA had begun hiring them for operations in North West Laos and later in Vietnam. The Vietnam hiring took place in May 1962 to support the CIA-sponsored 'Operation Sea Swallow', the objective of which was to clear Viet Cong out of an area some three hundred miles north-east of Saigon. The KMT troops were under the surprising leadership of a Catholic priest, Nguyen Lac-hao, and supported by a detachment of American marines. According to one on-the-spot journalist, it became notorious as a unit which *"outdid all others in ferocity and terror"*.[357] It was a natural extension of an old relationship.

In the Spring of 1963, concern in Thailand about armed KMT troops in its northern provinces resulted in a demand for the surrender of such arms. The ceremony of handing over of arms took place in the mountains at Mae Salong, but it was a hollow gesture. After fifteen years of jungle fighting, the middle-aged 'lost' army handed over its arms. Unknown to the Thais, one of Tuan Shi-wen's commanders, Yang Weigang, had hidden weapons to protect the colony against bandits and Shan raiders. Tuan then added to the stock by buying arms within Thailand.[358] By 1965 there was renewal of operations and twice-weekly air-supply drops were observed. In September 1967, a force of some six thousand KMT and its locally raised allies was reported to be back in the borderlands, earning a living by trading opium. Those who settled quietly in northern Thailand were not

---

[357] *The Furtive War*; Wilfred G. Burchett, p31
[358] *Golden Triangle; Frontier and Wilderness*; Kuo Yi-tung (Bo Yang); pp124/8

harassed by the Thanom/Praphas regime and they mostly became involved in the profitable opium business, moving and escorting product to international traders in Bangkok and Saigon. They also continued, at least until 1971, to help the CIA in intelligence gathering.[359]

The chaos which existed in the jungle mountains was caused by a lack of clear political management. When the KMT invaders first moved into Indochina, the French promptly disarmed them and neutralised the force. At the time that the KMT moved into Burma the British had already left; the Burmese government was incapable of taking the necessary steps and the Thailand government was disinclined to move against it. America, obsessed with the containment of communism, was unwilling to bring pressure to bear upon its puppet government in Taiwan to cease its activity, seeing in the KMT element in Burma some forlorn hope of re-entry into Mao Zedung's China. The Chinese government, whilst totally condemning the KMT activities, did not use the KMT as an excuse for further advancement south by the People's Liberation Army into Burma and beyond. It adopted what the Burmese government described as *'an understanding attitude'* and, fortunately, action had been taken to remove a part of the KMT before the end of the Korean War. But for that, China might have taken a tougher line, and Thailand with its massive rice growing areas might have become a target. Thailand itself saw advantages in the KMT presence in Burma, provided that no armed force became too active within its own borders. It saw the KMT troops in the Shan States as a first, if fragile, barrier between Thailand and communist China and many of its citizens found profit in the trade in opium and weapons. Eventually, Washington was forced to intervene and bring its Nationalist China puppet to heel. Although no longer a threat to the security of the State of Burma, the KMT troops in the border mountains had become an international embarrassment. But within Thailand's operational orbit, KMT activity was not yet due for total shutdown.

The United Nations had forsaken Burma in its time of need by failing to brand Chiang Kai-shek's Nationalist China as an aggressor

---

[359] *Foreign and Domestic Consequences of KMT Intervention in Burma*; Robert H. Taylor; p65

nation and by failing to enforce a determined programme which would remove an unwanted foreign army from Burmese soil. Well might Justice U Myint Thein have declared, *"If that is not aggression, my Delegation would like to know what is"*.

CHAPTER NINE
The Communist Threat

While the Thanom decade was essentially an extension of Sarit's regime, it had its own distinguishing features. There was the steadily increasing involvement with America, a forward push towards modernisation and, as a consequence, political changes to which both of these contributed. The major military concern was with events in Laos and Cambodia, and the heavy involvement in America's Vietnam war. Here, it was not only direct action by Thai forces but also indirect action brought about by the use of Thailand as the primary American military base. In its turn, this brought a response from China by way of support for the communist insurgents within Thailand itself.

In his first brief period as prime minister, Thanom was under pressure both from the opposition and from within his own party from the day that Sarit departed. The first major test came in March 1958 when there were partial elections in five provinces. The result was a major setback for Thanom. His supporters obtained only nine out of twenty-six seats, while the Democratic Party obtained thirteen.[360] Sarit rescued him from his problems by his return in October 1958.

Following Sarit's death, Thanom entered his second period as prime minister. He continued to look to the Revolutionary Council to guide the country to a form of rule which had been described by Sarit as *'a Thai way of democracy'*. He worked towards lifting martial law which had been in force since 1958. He reviewed the major infrastructure projects which were outstanding from the previous administration.

There was a fear that an early papermill scandal which brought about Thawee's resignation in disgust from chairmanship of the National Investment Board would bring instability to the government.[361] Even worse, it might bring other scandals out into the open. A likely candidate was that of the pork meat distribution over which a monopoly had been established, resulting in the doubling of its price in the market. There were other such activities in the

---

[360] *The Sarit Regime*; Thak Chaloemtiarana; pp181/3
[361] *Far Eastern Economic Review*; 27 Feb 1964

foodstuffs field although it was Praphas, not the prime minister, who was looked upon as the principal culprit. But scandals were transient matters and they were not allowed to interfere with the strengthening of the regime's control over national affairs, a control which was enhanced by marriage ties when Thanom's son, Narong, a Chulachomklao Class 5 graduate, married Suphaphon Charusathien, Praphas's daughter.

Thanom's position as premier was best protected by the fact that there were three possible contenders in any stakes to overthrow him: Praphas himself; General Chitti Navisathira, the Army commander-in-chief; and General Krit Srivara, the commander of the 1st Army, which controlled Bangkok. Each rival, however, lacked sufficient power to defeat the other two. Thus Thanom, like Phibun before him, positioned himself in a situation of balance between contenders, denying to each the ultimate prize of his own premiership.

An element of particular stability in Thanom's favour was the inclusion in his Cabinet of former prime minister Phote Sarasin who had accepted the important post of minister of national development. His appointment brought about a review of one of Thailand's most contentious capital projects — the construction of the Kra canal. The question of a canal across the narrow Kra area of peninsular Thailand had long been a thought of many countries, not least of all Japan, which was the most likely beneficiary of the shorter shipping route it would provide. Equally, it was opposed by Britain and Singapore because of the trade damage it was likely to inflict on the latter's interest. Phote's 1964 review determined that it would be economically viable only if other activities within Thailand itself, such as freeport areas, were added into the project value. It proposed that the canal should be created not over the shortest route, which would involve numerous locks and consequent shipping delays, but over a longer route across the plains. More contentiously, it proposed that the main channel excavation would be accomplished by the simultaneous firing of a string of ten-kilotonne or hundred-kilotonne atomic bombs, the choice being dependent on the width decided. Whether or not it was from fear of the consequences of this method of construction or because of possible political pressures, Phote abandoned the project. In the early 1990s it remains in that state of limbo.[362]

---

[362] *Far Eastern Economic Review*; 12 March 1964

Sarit's policy of developing infrastructure projects associated with national security arrangements, backed heavily by US financial and technical assistance, continued long after his death. By mid-1964 Thanom saw Thailand's security threatened by external problems, and in its defence he agreed to massive additional facilities for American forces. As America became increasingly involved in Laos and Vietnam, so the investment in back-up military infrastructure projects in Thailand increased. Strongly pro-American in his own political philosophy, Thanom supported the projects and America intensified its interest and influence. Large sums were spent on communication facilities, roads and camps. The expenditure was greatly in excess of any Thai military security requirement and it covered development of American military activities for its own war.

The American government faced a predicament over Laos. It could expose the role of the North Vietnamese in Laos, denounce the 1962 Geneva Accords, and openly fight in Laos. If it did, it risked losing the goodwill and support of the neutralist Souvanna. Alternatively, it could play the North Vietnamese at their own game by operating covertly and attempting to negate the tactics of the communist forces without exposing the world to the risk of super-power confrontation. Souvanna, insisting that Laos was an independent neutral state, was prepared to accept that America might take action by bombing the North Vietnamese invaders in pursuit of its own interests without Laos considering itself at war with North Vietnam.[363] America chose the covert route.

In March 1964, six American planes were stationed at Takhli and a further eighteen were sent to Khorat. Towards the latter part of the year there were seventy-five American aircraft with ground support crews. By the end of the following year the numbers had increased to two hundred. The bombing of North Vietnam and Laos and in particular of the Ho Chi Minh trail now started in earnest from Thai bases. The number of aircraft reached four hundred in 1966 with B52 bombers arriving at the U Tapao airbase in 1967.[364] The bulk of the American forces were in the north-east of Thailand where part of the

---

[363] *The Sarit Regime*; Thak Chaloemtiarana; pp341/344
[364] *In a Little Kingdom*; Perry Stieglitz; p114

military activity was concerned with the conduct of electronic intelligence gathering and radar surveillance.

Soon the bombing extended beyond the Ho Chi Minh trail itself to Pathet Lao bases in northern Laotian provinces. The American clandestine army, run by the CIA, had been increasing in size over the years. By 1961 it had reached about nine thousand men, headed by a few CIA/Green Beret specialists and about one hundred CIA-trained Thais from the Police Aerial Resupply Unit which Phao had established in 1952. Thailand also provided gunners for artillery support although that support was frequently out-ranged by Russian-supplied Vietnamese guns.

Early after his appointment to office in January 1961, President John Kennedy determined his policy to be that all fighting in Laos was to be carried out by local forces. This to the CIA meant principally the Hmong whom they had taken over from the French colonial government and had organised into mobile strike forces. Officially, no American military planes were to be based in Laos and so the CIA's commercial airline, Air America, provided the necessary equipment. The base for the supporting air commandos was in Thailand, near Nakhon Phanom. America did not seek an escalation of hostilities in Laos, deeming it to be the wrong place to risk a confrontation which might lead to a third world war. Its policy, carefully implemented under the direction of its far-seeing ambassador, William H. Sullivan, was to counter communism effectively and with the least possible publicity. Sullivan was an ambassador highly regarded by his peers. He was credited, when only a university student, with coming to the conclusion that the role of America was to live with other peoples and cultures of the world and not merely to dominate them. Following this unusual youthful American wisdom, he went on to live a battle-experienced career in the American Navy before entering diplomatic service. He was a fortunate choice for the task in Laos where clear-headed determination was the need of the day.

Soon, however, the spotlight was off Laos. The interest of the world in general, and America in particular, shifted to Vietnam. *"After 1963,"* said secretary of state, Dean Rusk, *"Laos was only the wart on the hog"*.[365] It was assumed that once North Vietnam had been defeated, the Laotian problem would solve itself. A wart only, Laos may have been, but it tested the courage, dedication, and the old

---

[365] *The Ravens*; C. Robbins; pp108/113 and citing the *End of Nowhere*; CA Stevenson

frontiersman spirit of many young Americans. It was in this unadmitted war that an undisclosed American spotter force, the 'Ravens', flew exhausting schedules of low-level sorties in close support of their Hmong comrades. Attacking targets selected by the Ravens and by Hmong ground troops were the Nakhon Phanom air commandos from the American First Special Operations Squadron, the 'Hobos', flying old but effective Douglas A-1 Skyraiders. In support were Air America helicopter crews, diverted from CIA duties to snatch-rescue downed Ravens and Hobos from time to time. Snatch-rescue was an essential part of the overall operation: there was no mercy for a winged Raven. The skill and heroism of these unacknowledged young Americans puts them in a class of pilot which in other times might have found them in Richthofen's circus or among the Battle of Britain fighter pilots. Some of the earlier pilots flew to battle directly from the Thai airfield at Udon Thani, only forty-five miles from the Laotian border, with gloves covering their hands and dark visors their faces to avoid identification or observation of skin colour before emplaning.[366] To minimise the risk of political embarrassment that America would suffer if any were to be shot down there was a gradual replacement by locally trained Thai, Lao, and Hmong pilots, both in small fighter/spotter planes and then in gunships. But both Ravens and Hobos were still there many years later.

In May 1964, fighting broke out across the Plain of Jars and covert American activity steadily increased. President Johnson's government increased supplies and began flying missions to prevent the progress within Laos of the Pathet Lao and North Vietnamese.[367] As the Pathet Lao Spring offensive got under way and Kong Le called for air support, Udon Thani began its role as a major American strike base. By June, support reconnaissance was flown and by December that support had been extended to bombing. In 1965 Udon was upgraded and became the focal point for the air war in Laos. It was by then home to the American 2nd Air Division/13th Air Force as well as a major training base for Lao and Thai flyers.

---

[366] *The Ravens*; C. Robbins; and *My Secret War*; Richard S. Drury
[367] *Scope of US Involvement in Laos*; Richard S. Nixon; p3

Cambodia, like Laos, sought a path of neutralism, but it was a neutralism which protected Sihanouk and maintained his position. In the opinion of a British ambassador and of a Thai prime minister, both of whom knew him well, this was not as unworthy as it first sounds. Sihanouk, whilst a well-known lover of the *dolce vita*, was not a self-seeking man but a genuine Cambodian patriot.[368] Sihanouk did not trust Thailand, and feared that it had expansionist ideas to recover the territory ceded to it during the Second World War by Japan and which Pridi had handed back to ensure Thailand's election to the United Nations. From the Cambodian standpoint, Thailand was a country which had beset Cambodia for more than six hundred years and had never really given up the wish to absorb it, or much of it.[369] In 1961, Cambodia had broken off relationships with Thailand after Sarit alleged that Cambodia was used as a base for communist attacks on its neighbours, an allegation which Sihanouk interpreted as another excuse for Thailand to move into Cambodian territory. Sihanouk had also for some years adopted an anti-American policy following his intense dislike of a discourteous American ambassador, Robert McLintock. Sihanouk had, at that time, threatened to bring in Chinese advisers and support. In 1961 Sihanouk accused America of anti-Cambodian activities with his neighbours, particularly Thailand — activities which he saw as forcing him into the socialist camp. After further allegations including that of CIA activity in his country, Sihanouk had rejected all further American Aid.

In February 1964, Sihanouk suggested a conference of Cambodia, US, Thailand, and South Vietnam to recognise Cambodia's borders. He proposed that the borders should be monitored by the International Control Commission, for which America, naturally, would be required to pay. America and South Vietnam agreed. Thailand declined, a stance which in itself was enough to arouse Cambodian suspicions. Souvanna became involved but would not put the name of Laos to an agreement involving border integrity. Laos would recognise Cambodian independence but in so doing it would still maintain an old Laotian claim to one of the Cambodian provinces.

---

[368] Discussions with Major General Chatichai Choovhavan; 1 July 1991 and with Embassy Staff

[369] *Far Eastern Economic Review*; 19 March 1964

At the time of the Tonkin incident, Thanom involved Thailand more directly in the Indochinese conflagration by sending pilots of the Thai airforce to Vietnam to fly South Vietnamese planes. He followed this up in 1965 by sending a naval contingent to operate directly with the American Navy off Vietnam. January 1967 saw the first of the Thai ground forces fighting in Vietnam, and by 1969 they were built up to eleven thousand strong. These were all in addition to the constant provision of allegedly 'volunteer' forces to support the American-led and American-paid operations in Laos, forces said to number well over five thousand. During this period, American troops committed to Vietnam reached a peak of over half a million. Its force in Thailand also increased and with the arrival of the American 7th Air Force in Saigon, Udon Thani was expanded to be the Headquarters of the 7/13th US Air Forces. The Thai force included important air navigation system experts whose equipment was installed and maintained by American personnel some seven thousand feet up in the north Laotian mountains at Phou Pha Thi.[370] The post was maintained as a forward operational guidance point for bombing until it was overrun by the Pathet Lao.

Thanom had also to consider his northern flank. In January 1965 the foreign minister of the People's Republic of China, Marshall Chen Yi, announced that there was soon to be a war of national liberation to be launched in Thailand. The Thai communist party became more active and in August of that year it fired its first shots of an insurgency at a village close to the Laotian border. It followed this up on ninth of November by ambushing a military force, again in the north-east of Thailand. The United Thai Patriotic Front was set up later the same year, linking the Communist Party of Thailand to an earlier established Thai Independence Movement.[371]

Despite the publicity which had been given to anti-communist suppression in the past, the movement had been of little importance. Chinese led, Chinese dominated, and with its leading personnel soaked in Chinese dogma from studies at the communist *école polytechnique*, the Marxist-Leninist Institute of Peking, it had attracted little

---

[370] *The Ravens*; C. Robbins; pix
[371] *From Armed Suppression to Political Offensive*; Chai-anan Samudavanija and others; pp186/188

indigenous Thai support. What support it may have had in the urban areas was undermined, first by Phao and then by Sarit. It had become a peasant fraternity among which armed revolution was an unknown concept. It had lacked an intellectual base within Thailand. As a consequence, it had voiced parrot-fashion the thoughts of Chairman Mao and his analysis of class struggle without accepting that the circumstances in Thailand and in China were entirely different. From its original formation and First Congress in December 1942 until its first shots in 1965 it was principally a talking-shop. It was an opposing organisation which suited the style of the Thai military in the mid-twentieth century.

The first clashes with authority came in 1965 and with them came the questioning of the role of the military. An army, if not created for external conquest, is ordinarily seen to exist for the defence of the realm. Its organisation, its natural thinking, and its training are designed to confront an external enemy. The Thai Army's experience in such a normal role was extremely limited. Its Second World War battles were insignificant and it had not, apart from the odd border skirmish, been called upon since to defend its home territory. It had sent contingents to Korea and to Vietnam to fight under the direct control of the American Army, but that did not involve it in strategy or senior command. Now in 1965 it faced an entirely different type of problem — an internal enemy in a people's war, where both sides looked alike, spoke the same language, and had a similar culture but opposing ideologies. It took the Army some years to learn how to handle this new threat. By 1967, insurgency had spread through the northern provinces, and was particularly strong among the Hmong. In the south there were close contacts with remnants of the communist party of Malaysia.

In dealing with the communist threat at home it would be a reasonable assumption that lessons would have been learned by the Thai Army from its forces fighting under American command in Vietnam. They were, but the answers were the wrong ones for Thailand. General Chavalit Yongchaiyudh, later to be commander-in-chief of the Army, was one of the first Thai soldiers to fight in Vietnam. He was taught the American 'search-and-destroy' strategy with airborne support. Years later he was to admit to the total ignorance in which the forces lived and he realised that the Army did not even comprehend the political concepts which underlay the North

Vietnamese operation. Even worse, on its return to Thailand, the Thai military attempted to perpetuate the errors of the Westmoreland strategy in trying to solve the nation's own problems. Gradually in Thailand there came the understanding that there was no straightforward military solution. Communism had to be fought politically. Wise council in America in the form of under-secretary of state, George Ball, had earlier reached the same conclusion but his advice had been ignored. In March 1965, Ball went as far as advising the American President, Lyndon Johnson, whom he thought failed to understand Ho Chi Minh, to do the impossible and walk away from Vietnam. It remained impossible and the sufferings of South-East Asia were to continue for another decade. In the thinking of the Thanom and Praphas government, the Westmoreland, not the Ball, theory prevailed. In 1969, the Thai Army applied maximum force in search-and-destroy operations against the communists, using the whole of its 1st Division plus the marines. The communist management merely grew stronger and countered with the establishment of it own 'people's army'.

If slow to learn, the Army gradually realised that it had to deal with socio-economic and political conditions and not merely military. It had, for so long a period, immersed itself in American training and strategic concepts that it was ill-equipped to solve its own internal problems. It had to determine which was the communists' target — the concept of Nation, Religion and King, or the ruling regime itself. Late in 1965 Thanom had set up the Communist Suppression Operation Command with Praphas in charge, to coordinate all anti-communist effort. The natural reaction of such an appointed body and with such a leader was an assumption that the Communist Party's aim was to suborn the nation itself, not just the regime. It saw communism as an alien dogma with no real roots in Thailand. Thus the new command saw military destruction of all opposition as the only solution, whilst the communist party emphasised the political solution.[372] The Command became noted for its harsh oppression. It did not have the intellectual leadership necessary to win an ideological war and so from 1966 to 1970, communist insurgency increased. Although in a prime minister's order,[373] Thanom called for the emphasis to be placed on political and psychological operations, the approach found little favour

[372] *Forced Back and Forgotten*; Lawyers Commitee on Human Rights 1989; pp57/59
[373] Prime Minister's Order No. 110/2512 of May 1969

with the military as few of Praphas's army officers believed in any solution other than force. Violence and summary execution remained the common practice.

In America, anti-war pressure was mounting on President Lyndon B. Johnson. Resistance increased against being drafted into an army fighting an unpopular war in a part of the world which few knew and with which fewer were concerned. In Washington young protesters on the streets were crying out,

> *"Hey, Hey, L. B. J.,*
> *How many kids have you killed today?"*

It had become Johnson's war and there was a fear of triggering a third world war. Johnson's advisers were aware that he did not understand the youth of his own country, but he and they knew that the American people wanted to be out of Vietnam. James Thomson Jr, a former national security adviser, appraised the situation as from the other end of the telescope. *"They* (the Vietnamese) *knew something we would not acknowledge. They could wait us out; we would go home and they would come back and rebuild what we had destroyed".* Clark Clifford, who in March 1968 took over as Secretary of State from the aggressive Robert MacNamara, recorded that when appointed, he asked what the plan was for victory, only to discover that there was not one. He has claimed that he tried to reverse the policy which had prevailed since 1965, but after over twenty thousand American soldiers had been killed and tens of billions of US tax dollars had been spent, it was beyond human capacity to admit that the policy had been wrong. Johnson did not seek the renewal of his presidency.[374]

Massive American bombing did not prevent North Vietnamese reinforcements arriving in Laos. According to a statement issued on sixth of March 1970 by the new American President, Nixon, the numbers increased to over fifty-five thousand by 1969 and up to sixty-seven thousand by 1970, whilst native Pathet Lao forces were insignificant. The American report states specifically that *"line units of the North Vietnamese Army (were) conducting open aggression".* They were *"in addition to half a million North Vietnamese who have crossed the Ho Chi Minh trail into South Vietnam"* with the object of paving

---

[374] BBC Documentary programme on Vietnam (repeat); September 1991

the way *"for the eventual establishment of a government more amenable to communist control".*[375]

The statement affirmed that there were no American ground combat troops in Laos, there were no plans to introduce them, and that no American person stationed in Laos had ever been killed in ground operations. America confirmed that it had provided equipment and training as well as supplies at the request of the Lao government, increasing these activities as the North Vietnamese activities had increased. The use of units of its Air Force was more generally known but the President's statement claimed that all assistance was limited, supportive, requested, defensive, for the purpose of protecting American lives, and to preserve *"a precarious but important balance in Laos".*[376] The words were carefully chosen and gave no indication of the degree of American interference in Lao affairs and the selectivity of the aid to the corrupt extreme right-wing elements. It was interference which had been kept not only from the American public but also, until 1969, from the Senate. During hearings of its Foreign Relations Committee, information was provided by Ambassador Sullivan of the extent of the operations, bringing from its Chairman, Senator Fulbright, the comment that the operations were *"...most irregular, unusual, and even unconstitutional".*[377]

The communist advance in Laos suffered setbacks from time to time. The Plain of Jars was much fought over but the eventual pressure brought them recaptures and fresh victories. In 1971, despite Souvanna's protests, South Vietnamese forces with American backing crossed into Laos to fight their northern enemy along parts of the Ho Chi Minh trail. Meanwhile the heavy bombardment from Thailand's airfields continued, and Thanom was forced more and more into alliance with America and thus with that country's policy for South-East Asia. Under Thanom, Thailand had become inextricably involved and was virtually a puppet state.

On twenty-second of January 1973, ex-President Lyndon B. Johnson died. Ironically, on twenty-eighth of January, the war which had become so closely associated with his name ended and the peace agreement for Vietnam, signed in Paris, became effective. The last American troops formally left at the end of March.

---

[375] *Scope of US Involvement in Laos;* Richard S. Nixon; pp1/2
[376] *Scope of US Involvement in Laos;* Richard S. Nixon; p5
[377] *London Daily Telegraph* of 30 October 1969

An agreement was signed on twenty-first of February 1973 between the Lao government and the Pathet Lao. It imposed an immediate cease-fire and ended the American bombing from Thailand, although that was reinstated from time to time until April to counter cease-fire violations. Reconnaissance flights from Thailand ceased in June. The following month the parties signed a final form of the February agreement, and under it the new coalition government was to come into power at the end of October 1973.[378]

The effect of this exposure to foreign influence, and to serious fighting beyond all of its borders brought about, or at least accelerated, a change in Thai life-style and of Thai values. It brought the lure of the city, vast increases in investment in infrastructure, easier methods of travel, and more money in the pockets of some individuals. Commercial outlooks changed as also did those of morality. The population was soaring from eighteen million in 1947 to thirty-four million in 1970. It was to reach forty-four million in 1980 and has been estimated at over fifty-five million by 1990. So rapidly did it grow that the average age of the population dropped to the upper teens. Strong growth in the middles classes brought about a substantial movement in employment from the civil service to commercial and industrial fields. The increased numbers and lower average age, together with the development of wider horizons, brought about new elements of population which autocratic rulers would have done well to note. The younger generation, better educated, questioned the dominant role in the Thai economy of Japan and America, and also questioned the role of Thai troops in Vietnam. Rural dwellers became more and more conscious of their relative poverty.

Thanom moved Thailand closer to its neighbours. March 1965 saw the signing of a border agreement between Thailand and Malaysia with acceptance of the principle of hot-pursuit.[379] In 1967 there came the establishment of the Association of South-East Asian Nations (ASEAN), an intra-regional alignment consisting of Thailand, Malaysia, Indonesia, the Philippines, and Singapore. ASEAN was to prove a useful forum for regional discussion, with numerous agreements on complementary rather than competitive development.

[378] *The Ravens*; C. Robbins; p x and *In a Little Kingdom*; Perry Stieglitz; pp195/7
[379] *Thailand's Foreign Relations 1964-1980*; Corinne Phuangkasem; p13

Whilst its most notable developments have been economic, it was the intention of foreign minister Thanat Khoman that ASEAN would principally be a political body with a common defence policy, particularly where Indochina was concerned.

In the midst of all the domestic and foreign turmoil there was a strange happening. Easter weekend, 1967, brought the disappearance of the silk king of Thailand, Jim Thompson, a disappearance which was to become an international mystery. It was a disappearance about which everyone in Bangkok developed a theory. Whilst not in the mainstream of Thai history *per se*, no commentary on this period can ignore it entirely. A précis of events and a further theory offered to the author is included later. The mystery remains.

In 1968 the new constitution, originally commissioned in 1959 by Sarit, was at last promulgated, reinstituting the bicameral legislature of 1932, with an elected lower house and an appointed Senate. It gave the military a virtually unchallengeable control of the political machine with a legislature of seventy-five per cent appointed senators. The military flaunted it as an emblem of constitutionalism while at the same time looked upon it as an instrument to extend its own power.[380] The Democrats, led by M. R. Seni, opposed the constitution and sought a genuinely democratic instrument which would, *inter alia*, exclude the military from politics.

In elections held in February 1969 the government gained a majority, but Thanom gradually became impatient with the slow progress of legislation through the Assembly. In November 1971 he staged a military coup against his own government, rid himself of the National Assembly, banned political parties, and restored military supremacy. It was a good old-fashioned Thai coup. For the remaining period of his premiership Thanom ruled with a National Executive Council, a body which drew its power from martial law. This all built up a head of steam through a generation more politically aware than ever before. Thailand itself was changing and no longer were its people so willing to subordinate themselves to the whims of the

---

[380] *Portraits of Thai Politics*; Jenton K. Ray; p34

military masters. Collectively, peasants, workers, and students sought participation in government. They also sought the removal of American armed forces. Both Thanom and Praphas were now approaching the mandatory retirement age from the Army, but were still anxious to keep hold of power. Their likely successor, Thanom's son, Praphas's son-in-law, Colonel Narong, was highly unpopular, but he was moving to take over the reins of office. Most importantly, he set out to neutralise the power of General Krit who was his natural rival for total authority.

These were difficult times for the government. A booming economy in the 1960s, created partly by foreign investment but principally by American spending on aid programmes, was followed by a period of falling export revenues and rising import costs. Prices of rice, tin, and rubber exports all fell, while that of crude oil and other imported petroleum products rose sharply in line with the surge in world markets. Rice was a particular problem and the falling price brought trouble from the peasant farmers. A government-determined increase in price, a loss of supply, and the failure of a support scheme dismayed the all-important citizenry of Bangkok. Rapid inflation ensued, and as always, it was the lowest paid who were hardest hit, resulting in pay demands and industrial unrest. The students, frustrated at the lack of political evolution, felt betrayed and took to demonstrations.

In the 1973 military reshuffle, a weary Thanom, in his third extension as supreme commander, sought to relinquish his office in favour of Praphas. Praphas, however, realising his own unpopularity, saw his personal power extended by keeping Thanom in post and was in no hurry to change it for a more precarious power. In September, Thanom appointed General Krit Srivara as commander-in-chief in place of Praphas. In so doing he indicated his own intention to retire in 1974, leaving Praphas as his successor. In view of the events to follow, Krit took up his post in the nick of time on the first of October 1973.

American forces in Thailand had numbered about fifty thousand in 1969, thirty-two thousand by mid-1971 but were up to forty-five thousand again in 1972. But it was not solely the removal of American forces which was targetted by demonstrating students. Nor were the demonstrations entirely spontaneous. Thirayudh Boonmi of Chulalongkorn University and his associates had been discussing both the possibility and the methodology of student demonstration for some months prior to October. In the view of the organising group, the principal problem to be attacked was the lack of democratic evolution and thus the target was the new constitution. Feelings ran high against Praphas and Narong. Thanom was looked upon more favourably but was also seen to be too weak to control his henchmen.[381] The student body had the good fortune at this time to have strong leadership, not only from Thirayuth but also from Sombat Thamrongthanyawong and, importantly, the forceful Seksan Prasertkun from Thammasat. Also from Thammasat came a leading lady of the cast, Chiranand Pitpreecha.

Ex-foreign minister Thanat supported the students' call for all American troops to go. The American-financed Thai military contingent, serving under American command in Vietnam, had been withdrawn in 1972. American bombing of Cambodia had ceased by August 1973 by direct order of the American Congress and there was now no external call for troop retention. Only three thousand six hundred men and a hundred planes were earmarked for withdrawal.

Apart from a revision of the new constitution and the matter of repatriation of American forces, throughout June and July there had been confrontations with Praphas over the detention of thirteen students, including Thirayuth, for their critical stance and for producing a newsletter criticising the government. Despite constraints, the press allied itself with the students but the dialogue called for was refused. Although Thanat again on ninth of October spoke forcefully in support of the students, Thanom and Praphas saw the protests not as a demand for a change in policy but as a plot against the government. Two days later some fifty thousand students and sympathisers gathered at Thammasat University and a delegation was sent to Praphas calling for the release of Thirayuth and the twelve other demonstrators. Praphas refused. Instead, as a ploy, he offered a new constitution within twelve months. The ploy failed to work and by the time the government realised its own misjudgement, it was too late.

During the student committee discussions, some thought was given to approaching General Krit to ask for his support of the student

---

[381] Discussions in Bangkok with Dr Seksan Prasertful and Arjarn Thirayuth Boonmi, 27 and 29 November 1993

complaints, but on further reflection the committee viewed him as too close to Thanom to be sure of the outcome of such an approach. The students also had a philosophical problem. Whilst they knew for certain the style of government which they did *not* want, their lack of experience and maturity prevented them from formulating proposals for an acceptable alternative. They had a vision of the democratic society which they sought, but they lacked the necessary worldly-wisdom to put it into practice. They were, in 1973, essentially idealists. The Communist Party, which until then was still a rural party, played no part in this uprising — indeed, as both Seksan and Thirayuth have recalled, the 1973 students barely understood the basic principles of Marxism.[382]

By nightfall on twelfth of October the demonstrators, following the Thammasat lead, had risen to a hundred and fifty thousand. Nothing like this had been seen before in the history of Thailand. It was perhaps more remarkable that students were in the lead, contrary to their Buddhist upbringing of deferring to their elders. On thirteenth of October King Bhumibol sent first for Thanom and Praphas and then for the student leaders, but the damage was done. On Sunday fourteenth of October there were estimated to be half a million demonstrators on the streets of Bangkok, but with the King's assurance that their demands for a new democratic constitution would be met, most attempted to leave the streets. Police attempts to control their movement brought confrontation and full-scale riot.

By now the students sought nothing less than the end of the Thanom/Praphas regime.[383] Tear gas and machine guns came into use from the police and blood was shed. Students burned the police headquarters. Some Army elements brought in tanks and gunships to fire on the demonstrators around Thammasat University. Fortunately, in 1973, gunships were not as lethal as they were to become later, but to students with zero firepower, they were already terrifying. Narong was known to be in one of the gunships but he has denied that he, personally, opened fire on the crowd.[384]

---

[382] Discussions in Bangkok with Dr Seksan Prasertful and Arjarn Thirayuth Boonmi, 27 and 29 November 1993

[383] *The Balancing Act*; Joseph J. Wright Jnr; pp205/8 and *Far Eastern Economic Review*; 22 October 1973

[384] *Nation*; 14 October 1993

At six o'clock that evening the government resigned. At seven-thirty the King went on television and took the unprecedented step of announcing his appointment of Dr Sanya Dharmsakh as prime minister. Late that day Praphas and Narong wanted to blast the demonstrators, only to be met with the rebuke from General Krit Srivara that *"these young people are our children; they want democracy. We cannot shoot them".*[385] There was an attempted coup by Narong and elements of the deposed regime and a call for Thammasat to be bombed, which both the Air Force and the Navy refused. The coup was forestalled by Krit directing the 1st Army to take over responsibility for law and order on the streets of Bangkok. Later that same night, Praphas and Narong fled to Taipei and on sixteenth of October, Thanom, at the request of the King, left the country to live temporarily in America. The death toll was thought to be between one hundred and two hundred, with more than a thousand wounded. It was the end of a strong-arm regime which Sarit had created and which Thanom, or more properly Praphas, had perpetuated.

General Krit refused a Field Marshall's baton and also rejected an appointment as supreme commander of the Armed Forces. It was a wise move. In those turbulent days, he needed to maintain his source of power, the Army, and this was best done by retaining the appointment of commander-in-chief.

Thanom had been seen not as one of the arrogant and greedy prime ministers, but mostly as a kindly man. Handsome, with silvery hair, and possessing a great degree of charm, he was respected as the leading figure of the day throughout the Army, but his political grip was fragile. He was well meaning but weak in allowing himself to be dominated by Praphas, who followed the ruthless pattern of Phao. In the eyes of some, Praphas was an even more reprehensible character than Phao, whilst others see that as hardly possible. Thanom enjoyed the pomp and glory of office and of the Field Marshal's baton. On eleventh of January 1964 he had become a Field Marshal, Admiral of the Fleet, and Marshal of the Royal Thai Air Force. In the end he wearied of the pressures of office but he himself has claimed that the

---

[385] *Far Eastern Economic Review;* 22 October 1973

Cabinet would not let him go.[386] Praphas did not weary of office, neither did he weary of the material gains associated with them. With Thanom as prime minister, Praphas was not only his deputy but also controlled the powerful Ministry of the Interior. A gross man of a somewhat sinister appearance, he was an able speaker and a man of limitless ambition. For nearly ten years he was Army commander-in-chief as well as being in command of central security. He controlled the electricity and water authorities in the Bangkok area and a number of rural developments. Early in 1973 he was promoted to the rank of Field Marshal. Like others before him he ensured that his Army duties did not interfere with his extensive commercial operations, resulting in delegations of duty which were to the eventual benefit of General Krit. Nevertheless, Praphas's control of politico-military affairs and his natural decisiveness combined with his over-commercial behaviour made him a formidable force in the land. *"At that time every rein of power led to the hands of Field Marshal Praphas. To conduct any business, executives recall, one had to cut in Praphas. He sat on the boards of nearly a hundred enterprises"*.[387] Thailand was fortunate that the independently minded Krit had moved into a position of power to save the people from a continuation of the excesses of Praphas's ambitions. But while Praphas has been seen as the principal exploiter of the people and the oppressor of the students, the final responsibility must rest with Field Marshal Thanom. Legally exonerated of the charge that he ordered the violent crackdown on the students, he nevertheless held the ultimate authority and thus was ultimately accountable to the people.

Mass people-power and individual student heroism had forced the hand of the military and terminated the oppression of the Sarit-designed regime. Thailand had been a land where strongmen moved across the surface of a well entrenched military-bureaucratic élite which was unchallenged in its rule. Now it entered on a period of relative democracy. On fourteenth of October 1973, a civilian government took office under a new, if somewhat reluctant, prime minister, Dr Sanya Dharmasakti, a President of the Supreme Court

---

[386] *Far Eastern Economic Review*; 12 March 1964 and 1, 22, and 29 October 1973; and *Bangkok Post*; 14 October 1993
[387] *Far Eastern Economic Review*; 28 April 1978; pp24/5

until 1969, then Rector and Dean of the Faculty of Law at Thammasat University and President of the King's Council.[388]

In Paris, the exiled Pridi Banomyong was reported as waiting for a call to return, but the call never came. He continued to live in Paris for the remainder of his life, his home becoming a place of pilgrimage for Thai students. There he could look back on his past work: *"I had the duty to save my country, its independence, integrity, and sovereignty. My conscience is at ease"*.[389]

---

[388] *Thailand: a Short History*; David K. Wyatt and *Far Eastern Economic Review*; 22 October 1973

[389] *Far Eastern Economic Review*; 1, 22, and 29 October 1973 and 26 December 1980

238

CHAPTER TEN
A Flirtation with Democracy

There was just a sniff of democracy in the air. It was troublesome
but it was a brave attempt. It lasted just less than three years, from
fourteenth of October 1973 until sixth of October 1976. The prime
minister, Dr Sanya, had been appointed by the King and not by any
military grouping, a demonstration of the King's growing authority.
Sukich Nimmanahaeminda, who had previously supported Sarit, took
office again, this time as deputy prime minister. Exerting its authority,
the government froze all of the assets of the Thanom/Praphas clique.
In the following February it disbanded the eight-year-old Communist
Suppression Operation Command, later replacing it by the Internal
Security Operations Command (ISOC). As a further step, Sukich
called for all military personnel to be excluded from government.[390]
Chatichai became deputy foreign minister and in January 1974 went
off to China to see his old family friend, Prime Minister Chou En-lai,
to develop relations based, at last, on an acceptance by Thailand of the
People's Republic. At the same time he hoped to arrange a
fifty-thousand-ton diesel oil deal at friendly prices. He did.[391] But the
new freedoms brought new problems and by the end of the year there
was already widespread labour unrest and mass rural demonstration.
Intellectuals decided that the time had come to publish tracts and other
writings and there were moves to advance political instruction in the
villages. Labour unions and peasant associations were formed. *"The
1973 students,"* one of their leaders has recalled, *"found no time to
develop their theories of a new democracy. They were inundated with
requests for aid from depressed groups of peasants farmers and factory
workers. In providing that aid, they allowed themselves to be seen as
leaders in a period of increasing unrest".*[392]

On seventeenth of December 1973 the Speaker of the National
Assembly, Major-General Siri Siriyothin, issued a list of almost two
thousand five hundred people whom the King, with advice from his
Council, had nominated for the task of electing a two hundred and

---

[390] *Far Eastern Economic Review*; 12 November 1973 and 21 January 1974
[391] *Far Eastern Economic Review*; 14 January 1974
[392] Discussions in Bangkok with Dr Seksan Prasertkul; 27 November 1993

ninety-nine-strong temporary assembly. Under the chairmanship of the revered Prince Wan Waithayakorn the nominees completed their vote on nineteenth of December with M. R. Kukrit leading the field with one thousand and fifteen votes. Only fifty-three military officers were elected and of these, twenty-eight had already retired from active service.[393] The function of the chosen two hundred and ninety-nine was that of a temporary legislative assembly. It was required to accept, amend, or reject a new constitution which was being drafted by a group appointed by the prime minister and which was led by Kukrit.

M. R. Kukrit's draft was completed by eighth of January 1974 and had it been passed into law it would have been the most liberal in Thai history. But it was put before the temporary legislative assembly which was made up principally of bureaucrats with an active dislike of liberalism. On fifth of October of that year the legislative assembly approved an entirely different draft. It killed Kukrit's proposals for an elected Senate and reverted to an appointed Senate with powers which exceeded those of the elected House of Representatives. The student body damned the new Constitution as repressive and merely designed for the privileged classes.

The student body was in a mood for demonstrations. With Sombat and Thirayudh again to the fore, it argued that the privileged classes and constitutional repression were barriers to its own ideas of democracy. So was the occupation of Thailand by American forces. A particular target of student anger was the American ambassador, William Kintner, a one-time CIA operative, who strongly supported CIA activities in South-East Asia. Kintner was also resented by the Thai government for his interference, through the CIA, with State affairs, and for being hand-in-glove with the Thanom/Praphas clique. Although there was presidential support for the CIA as a medium of foreign destabilisation, America eventually eased the pressure and withdrew Kintner.

Student protest continued but gradually it became counter-productive, setting off accusations that the student body itself was communist inspired and that it had been infiltrated by the Soviet agents. In its turn, the military came under attack from allegations that, to cover evidence, it had burned captured communists in oil drums. Statements of communist infiltration of the student body prior

---

[393] *The Thai Young Turks*; Chai-Anan Samudavanija; p30

240

to the 1973 protestations have little if any substance. There is evidence from members of the Communist Party that the fourteenth of October affair took the Party by surprise and it deliberately withheld support. It did not then have an urban intellectual base but it moved rapidly to remedy its failure. Over the years 1973 to 1976 it made steady progress so that when October came round again in 1976, the students were not the starry-eyed idealists of 1973.[394]

In May 1974, Sanya formally resigned his premiership and re-shuffled his government. He was still able to avoid a major military appointment thanks to the influential General Krit who gave him his full support. Krit did, however, ensure that the Army was protected by choosing the new minister of defence. Violence broke out again in the middle of the year, this time in Bangkok's Chinatown and for a few days a state of emergency was enforced. Just as he had protected the students in the previous October, so General Krit moved to combat Sinophobic chauvinism. In the following months, the steadying hand of Krit was seen by foreign observers to hold the Sanya government together amid waves of political unrest.

Legislation in October permitted the formation of political parties. With Khuang retired, leadership of the Democratic Party fell upon M. R. Seni while his brother, M. R. Kukrit, with Boonchu Rojanasathien, founded the Social Action Party. The Soi Rajakru clan, led by Pramarn, were to be found in the Chart Thai Party with support from Chatichai, then deputy minister for foreign affairs. Whilst General Krit's name was associated with a party he remained discreetly in support of the prime minister. The parties were essentially 'Thai-style' parties, not formed in the European mould of the political left and right but reflecting principally styles of management ranging from the dictatorial to the democratic.

On the streets, anti-American pressure increased. Although substantial cuts had been made in American forces, Thailand remained the site of the largest concentration of American air-power anywhere in the world. Unrest was compounded by the sudden reappearance in December of Field Marshal Thanom, resulting in Krit being recalled from a foreign tour. After two days, Thanom was expelled for illegal entry.[395]

---

[394] *The Rise and Fall of the Communist Party of Thailand (1973 to 1987)*; Gawin Chutima; pp22/25
[395] *Far Eastern Economic Review*; 20 September 1974 and 10 January 1975

On the Thai/Laos border communist insurgents were active and there were reports of Pathet Lao pushing across the Mekong in support. The Army still followed the policy of search and kill, which it had learned from the American command in Vietnam, and the results were equally disastrous when applied in Thailand. There was severe criticism of the alleged indiscriminate suppression of the insurgency and of its ruthless nature.

Dr Puey Ungphakon, one-time Seri Thai and Governor of the Bank of Thailand, then Rector of Thammasat University, made a plea for democratic processes to be advanced. He called for press freedom and for a serious approach to solving the economic problems of the people. He sought to limit the insurgency, which he claimed was not all communist inspired, and asked for discussions to be given a chance in preference to the search and kill policy.[396] He was concerned that freedom had been stultified for so long that the Thai people had forgotten how to live freely, without being burdened by overcentralised regimentation.

Not everywhere was there insurgency mayhem. Out in the 2nd Army Region, General Prem Tinsulanonda, in 1973 its deputy commander, began to organise villagers to defend themselves against the insurgents. He also gave them a degree of freedom of movement and gained their trust. Following this pattern, the Security Command established the Thai National Defence Volunteers, trained not only in basic military skills but also to a limited extent, in the principles of democracy and civic duty. In other areas, the search and destroy policy continued throughout the quasi-democratic period. It was not until the residual elements of the Thanom regime were removed from military policy-making and the new men, typified by Generals Prem and Chavalit, emerged at the top of the structure that new policies brought new results.[397]

The elections in January 1975 were held amid demonstrations and continuing street disturbances. The result, as was to be expected, was indeterminate, and M. R. Seni formed a left-of-centre coalition. Chatichai opposed him for the appointment of prime minister but was defeated by an overwhelming majority. On twenty-second of February the King formally appointed Seni to be prime minister. It was a

---

[396] *Far Eastern Economic Review*; 3 December 1973 and 11 February 1974
[397] *From Armed Suppression to Political Offensive*; Chai-Anan Samudavaija; pp177/180

government without a future. On twenty-first of March it collapsed and Thailand's infant democracy was looking fragile.

———————

Seni was succeeded as prime minister by his brother, M. R. Kukrit Pramoj, leading his Social Action Party. M. R. Kukrit was recognised as a man of outstanding intellect. He was also a man of many parts, politician, philosopher, author, and a most effective newspaper columnist. He had been a member of the National Assembly, its Speaker, minister in a number of governments, and was a long-time influential leader in political thought. A product of Oxford University, England, in the leisurely atmosphere of the 1930s, he entered Thai politics in the post-war era of pacifism and liberalism. Being by birth a royalist and by instinct a democrat it was predictable that in the Thailand of those days he would spend most of his time in opposition.

The Pramoj brothers, with their royal ancestry, had not welcomed the power of the left-of-centre Pridi. Kukrit had been no more reconciled to the domination of affairs by Phibun and attacked him, often bitterly, for his failure to introduce a more democratic regime, an attitude which on one occasion resulted in his arrest. Whilst the rule of Sarit and his successors restricted political activity, it did not crush Kukrit's approach to a more liberal society. By the time of the 1973 uprisings, he was a natural leader of broader views on social justice. He played no significant part in the uprisings. With the collapse of the Seni government, his leadership of the Social Action Party and political supremacy brought him to the office of prime minister. It appeared almost to be an unnatural appointment: his career and his skills were at their peak when he was in opposition.

M. R. Kukrit was able to cobble together a coalition of some seventeen parties with a right-of-centre balance.[398] His immediate backing came from his own Social Action party and the Chart Thai. For giving his party's support, Pramarn, the Chart Thai leader, was appointed deputy prime minister and minister of defence. Kukrit's policy tended towards greater independence and non-alignment, less pro-American and less anti-communist. Relations with China and Laos improved. Generally, Kukrit followed a consistent core policy, that of pursuing independence and bending like rice in the wind to the

———————————————

[398] *Thailand; A Short History*; David K Wyatt

necessary changes to keep to this. That he was able to hold so complex a coalition together for almost a year despite the turmoil of South-East Asian strife was a measure of Kukrit's political skill.

Despite the problems of the coalition, he established formal diplomatic relations with China and made some progress in demanding the withdrawal of American forces from Thailand. With other ASEAN heads of government he agreed on the phasing-out of the South-East Asia Treaty Organisation, thus reducing American influence in the area. He successfully held off political challenges from both the Army itself and from the military-oriented Chart Thai party of Pramarn and Chatichai. The Chart Thai defeated him, however, when he attempted to impound South Vietnamese planes flown to Thailand after the surrender of Saigon. He was not able to control the backdoor activities of the military through its chief-of-staff, Kriangsak, neither could he gainsay American forces which violated Thai sovereignty to recapture an American ship taken by the Khmer Rouge. This latter incident brought the students back on to the streets but with little effect.[399]

Relations between M. R. Kukrit's government and Cambodia were made difficult by the rise to power in the latter country of the China-backed Khmer Rouge. A Paris-educated school teacher, Saloth Sar, learned his communism in the France of the 1950s. Like Pridi before him in 1932, he built up a network of like-minded left-wing connections among his countrymen within student circles. With an ambition to overthrow the Cambodian feudal way of life and to give power to the peasant population, he gave up a teaching post in Phnom Penh and in 1963 fled to the jungle. There, with Chinese help, he successfully created the Khmer Rouge guerilla army. He changed his name to Pol Pot: he became a rabid left-wing extremist. By 1975 he had launched the Khmer Rouge on a campaign which resulted in the capture in April of that year of the capital, Phnom Penh. He imposed his own extreme ideas on the populace. He abolished money, burned libraries, and forcibly removed the city's population into the countryside to form agricultural work units. Executions were carried out on flimsy pretences and many died through the sheer inhumanity of a three-year reign of terror.[400]

[399] *Far Eastern Economic Review*; 2 May 1975 and 8 August 1975; *Bangkok Post*; 25 April 1983; and *The Balancing Act*; Joseph J. Wright Jnr; pp236/7

[400] *The Independent*, London; 26 October 1991

During 1975 there were outbursts of student demonstrations in Bangkok and Chiang Mai. There were strikes by workers and calls from the peasant population for agrarian reform. The cry from the students was against *"the evils of colonialism"*,[401] neither French nor British this time but American. There was continuing pressure for the withdrawal of all American forces from bases in Thailand. This general unrest disturbed the Thai élite so that it, in turn, demanded a much tougher approach to government. But the elected government was split by disagreements and vested interests. General Krit Srivara, as Army commander-in-chief, rejected a return to the days of brute force and coups d'état. Vigilante groups appeared in the form of the 'Village Scouts', the 'Nawaphon' and the 'Red Gaurs'. Urban and village landowners and manufacturers turned to unofficial methods of repression.

The Nawaphon, or Ninth Party, was so named in an attempt to associate itself with the ninth king. It had a reputation of being formed from ideological stormtroopers of the *Kristalnacht* brand. It was formed in October 1974 after political unrest which was associated with the celebration of the first anniversary of the 1973 students' revolt. Its members were a destabilising influence but claimed, as was usual, to be the protectors of the monarchy, Buddhism, and territorial integrity. Their banner was labelled 'New Society' but their support was for right-wing elements of the military which were emerging, particularly under Saiyud Kherdpol, the head of ISOC, and General Sant.

The popular Village Scouts were patriotic fanatics and were generally accepted as being close to the Palace, even to the extent of having Palace protection. They were active in the villages as an anti-student, anti-communist, and anti-democratic force which also gained for itself an unenviable reputation for cruelty. They were organised from an American model of South Vietnamese village defence forces, and while theoretically non-political, they were used by the military.

Thirdly, there were the Red Gaurs, founded by Major-General Sudsai Hasdin from extreme right-wing elements of the emerging middle class. The Gaurs included street hooligans, drop-out ex-students, and veterans of Thai units who had fought for America in Indochina. Their training had strong CIA connections. From mid-1974

---

[401] *The Thai Young Turks*; Chai-Anan Samudavanija; p23

onwards they were able openly to carry guns and explosives, immune from police or military arrest.[402] Noted for their cruelty in beating and mutilating demonstrators, they were always capable of lobbing a grenade or two into a crowd.

The groups suspected student movements of being communist-inspired and they developed a particular target in Seksan Praserkul, who had led the 1974 anniversary rally. He was alleged to have collected weapons with a view to killing the King. The Red Gaurs, claimed by Sudsai to be twenty-five thousand strong, moved in to protect the King at a ceremony held close by Thammasat University where, they alleged, snipers would be active.[403] The student leaders were certain that there was a plot in existence, instigated by dissatisfied right-wing generals to harass and eliminate them, together with leaders of the peasant and labour movements. Provoking a disturbance, or perhaps even a riot, would permit a harsh military response. The politicians were powerless to prevent it but Krit dampened down some of the more extreme activities and kept the *agents provocateurs* partially under control.[404]

Both in the cities and in the jungle, Thailand had become a dangerous place for activists. Some fled the country. It was a sound move for, as the troubles intensified, numerous students met their death at the hands of the Red Gaur and the Nawaphon.[405] In 1975, Thirayuth fled to the jungles of Laos and northern Thailand. He joined the communist-led insurgency movement and eventually became secretary-general of the United Thai Patriotic Front until the break-up of the movement in 1980. Seksan and Chiranand also feared for their lives. With help from the Chinese Embassy they and four others fled to Paris and from there on to Beijing. After preliminary discussions, the group was moved to the Hanoi area where it was thoroughly trained in jungle warfare, infiltration tactics, and the creation of party group and cell structures. Individually, they were fed into the active

---

[402] *Political Repression In Thailand*; London University Euro Committee for Solidarity with the Thai People; pp81/3
[403] *Far Eastern Economic Review*; 25 July 1975
[404] Discussions in Bangkok with Dr Seksan Prasertkul and Arjarn Thirayuth Boonmi, 27 and 29 November, 1993
[405] *Far Eastern Economic Review*; 12 March 1976

Chinese-armed party organisation by way of Laos, reaching the jungle forces in October 1976 and fighting with them until late 1980.[406]

Despite troubles on the streets, Kukrit made an important step forward in Thailand's relations with China. On the first of July 1975, with Chou En-lai, he signed a communiqué in Beijing undertaking to *"review and strengthen further the traditional close and friendly relations"* between the two countries, and by so doing ended twenty-six years of virtual non-communication.[407] At the same time, links with Taiwan were severed and the dual citizenship of the Chinese living in Thailand was terminated. Both Thailand and China looked to increase exports to each other. While China undertook not to use force to resolve any future differences, it retained the right for itself to support any popular movement which acted against oppression. The step forward was substantial but not of giant proportions. It did little to resolve the Thai government's problems with the internal communist movement which was then on the increase in the north-east of the country, urged on by the Pathet Lao and Vietnamese combined military command.

Street troubles from the city spread to the large farming population and when Kukrit dropped charges against a number of farming leaders, the police themselves mutinied. With law and order breaking down, General Krit called for a state of emergency to be declared, but Kukrit would have none of it. It was a critical time of the year for the civilian government, for with the annual military changes due in October and General Krit retiring, power was expected to move from the direct Army command to overall forces headquarters where Admiral Sa-Ngad would hold the reins as supreme commander with General Kriangsak Chomanan as his second-in-command.[408]

The turn of the year brought no relief for M. R. Kukrit. The 1975 world rice harvest had been plentiful and the market weak. Steeply falling prices resulted in a country-wide peasant farmer revolt. Kukrit's response was to put up the internally controlled price of rice by fifty per cent, the consequence of which was strike action by workers in the cities. Fomenting the city disturbances, the Nawaphon

---

[406] *Far Eastern Economic Review*; 12 March; 1976 and discussions in Bangkok with Dr Seksan Prasertkul and Arjarn Thirayuth Boonmi, 27 and 29 November, 1993

[407] *Far Eastern Economic Review*; 11 July 1975

[408] *Far Eastern Economic Review*; 28 August/5 September/3 October 1975

called for the dissolution of the National Assembly and for direct rule by a military council.

A no-confidence vote in the Thai National Assembly on twelfth of January 1976 forced M. R. Kukrit's resignation as prime minister. His government had always been fragile and its hold on the country limited. It was the final straw when General Krit, although in retirement, made it clear that the military would not support a Cabinet reshuffle but would remain out of politics if there was a dissolution of the Assembly and fresh elections. Kukrit headed a caretaker government to arrange for April elections and then, despite the limited authority which is accorded to caretakers, it turned on America and its forces of occupation. On fourth of February, minister for foreign affairs Chatichai summoned Ambassador Whitehouse and set out terms which were to apply to American forces from twentieth of March. There was to be no further interference with the internal affairs of Thailand's neighbours; all US facilities and personnel were to be under Thai control; all future US/Thai military agreements were to be limited to two years; and the status of all US technicians was to be approved by the Thai government. Whitehouse, not surprisingly, was shocked. The American response was simply that it would not accept an ultimatum of that nature and counter-proposals were countered by further proposals in the time-honoured fashion. Anti-American slogans on the streets of Bangkok were accompanied by suggestions that America would encourage a coup d'état. On twentieth of March the Kukrit caretaker government ordered all American forces, other than two hundred and seventy advisers out of the country. For the first time in twenty-five years, America would have no substantial presence in Thailand.[409]

The election campaign was violent. It was interspersed with bomb-throwing and with shootings, mostly of left-wing elements. Risk to law and order increased when General Krit died of a heart attack in April and there was no strong military heir-apparent. With his retirement from the Army at the age of sixty-three, Krit could have been expected to take a vigorous interest in political affairs. He had already helped the fragile democratic process along its way with his

---

[409] *Far Eastern Economic Review*; 16 and 23 January and 2 April 1976

rejection of Thanom and his support of Dr Sanya. He had prevented any military excesses. After the 1973 uprising he was appointed to be director of peacekeeping with powers over military, police, and civil affairs. He was not at one with M. R. Kukrit and was behind the no-confidence vote in January 1976 which brought Kukrit down. Krit had been a career soldier until the last few months of his life. He followed the usual pattern through Chulachomklao Academy and then spent most of his time with his regiment in the Bangkok political area. His corporate interests in some fifty companies brought him substantial wealth and the ownership of a string of racehorses. He had played important roles in support of both Sarit and Thanom, and some saw him as equally to blame for the state of the nation as were his superiors. He had at one time been seen by the student movement as the natural rival for power of Narong, and very much to be preferred. Nevertheless, he remained for that movement one of the ruthless men of power, and rich from the proceeds.[410] Eventually Krit dissociated himself from the Thanom/Praphas excesses. He ensured their dismissal by his actions of bringing troops on to the streets and taking over control of law and order in Bangkok. His actions constituted a coup against the Thanom regime but he did not strike out for overt power for himself. In any event, the prompt action of the King in appointing Dr Sanya as prime minister would have forestalled such a move. In the political field he had been deputy minister of defence in 1969 and minister of industry in 1972. He could have been expected to have had a long and possibly distinguished political career, with some part of that as prime minister. By such events are the destinies of nations changed, and as a result, his death removed the one man who might have prevented the ensuing Thammasat massacre.

Seni's Democratic Party took office again on twentieth of April 1976 although it held only forty per cent of the seats. A new coalition was constituted of Chart Thai, Social Justice (with which Krit had been associated), and Social Action, the latter despite M. R. Kukrit's surprising loss of his own Assembly seat. The emphasis was to the right-of-centre in its likely form of management, but it also contained a left-of-centre element from the more liberal wing of the Democrat party itself. Again, differences within the coalition brought attacks from both the political extreme left and the extreme right, and there

---

[410] Discussions in Bangkok with Dr. Seksan Prasertkul and Arjarn Thirayuth Boonmi, 27 and 29 November, 1993

was a more general view that Seni, an extreme royalist, lacked the common touch. Political assassinations were frequent and harassment by the police of left-wing parties was commonplace. Acts of violence became more frequent and villages were attacked and burned. There was a general breakdown in law and order. To the Thai élite, the farmer, labour and student movements, and particularly student activities associated with Thammasat University itself, had all been infiltrated by communists.

Bangkok's Thammasat University was the brainchild of Dr Pridi Banomyong when, in the mid-1930s he looked for an educational unit to increase the availability of capable administrators in the new constitutional monarchy. His new university was formed from the Law School of the Ministry of Justice and the Faculty of Law and Public Administration of Chulalongkorn University. It was officially opened on twenty-seventh of June 1935 with Dr Pridi as its Rector, an appointment which he held without interruption until he left Thailand in 1947. It eventually developed on Anglo-American university lines.[411] It was, in the 1970s, and it remains, a natural centre of Thai socio-political thought. In its time, Thammasat has had other roles. In 1944/5 it served the British Army as a clandestine headquarters and the hiding place for its staff. It was Pridi's temporary headquarters at the time of the February 1949 attempted coup and it was deeply involved in student militancy at the time of the 'Manhattan' incident in 1951. Some foreign observers had no doubt that in the mid-1970s there was an unacceptable level of communist influence. Even the Rector, Dr Puey, accepted that for the previous two years there had been attempts to infiltrate his students but he considered the numerical success to be small.[412] It was almost certainly stronger than he realised during the time that the Communist Party sought to recover from its failure to exploit the 1973 troubles.

Early in October 1976, Field Marshal Thanom returned from exile and his return was the spark which inflamed the nation. Although allegedly he was preparing for a monastic life, his return whipped up fury among the students, and this was particularly noticeable at Thammasat. On fifth of October, a photograph was published in Bangkok newspapers of an alleged hanging in effigy of Crown Prince Vajiralongkorn. In fact, the incident was nothing of the sort.

---

[411] *Pridi Banomyong*; Vitchitvong na Pombhajara; pp107/8
[412] *Puey Ungphakorn, A Siamese for all Seasons*; Komol Keethong Foundation; p123

Thammasat Dramatic Society had enacted a parody on a brutal hanging at Nakorn Pathom of two Electricity Authority workers who had pasted up posters directed against the return of Thanom. From the photographs taken of the actors and published in the following day's newspapers, a fourth-year student bore a resemblance to the Crown Prince. In one newspaper, the *Dao Siam*, the resemblance was remarkable, creating the suspicion that the actual photograph had been doctored for political purposes. Accusations of *lèse majesté* followed. The result was repeated broadcasts from an Army-controlled radio station for patriotic citizens to kill the communist students at Thammasat. Some commentators, including M. R. Seni's biographer,[413] put the remnants of the Phao faction behind this outburst but Chatichai has denied that the Soi Rajakru clan was in any way involved.[414] The Soi Rajakru version is that the Village Scouts were principally responsible for the initial stages, and their action arose from a genuine belief that at least three members of the Seni government were communists.[415] On sixth of October there was an attack on Thammasat by the Red Gaurs, augmented by police, the Nawaphon, and Village Scouts, on the pretext that students were firing at the police, a pretext that was later denied by a major-general of the Border Patrol Police.[416] All indulged in an unforgivable orgy of violence against the Thammasat students, some of whom were hanged, others shot, others soaked in oil and burned alive, while large numbers were savagely beaten.[417] The government was incapable of handling the situation and M. R. Seni resigned as prime minister.

In the Thammasat massacre the official student death toll was given as between forty and fifty, but an independent burial society put the figure at well over three hundred. Another three thousand students were arrested and in the next few months, numerous academics, workers, students, and some politicians were added to the numbers, bringing the total to between four and five thousand. Of them, nearly

---

[413] *Alone on a Sharp Edge*; David van Plaagh; p199
[414] Discussions in London with Major-General Chatichai Choonhavan; 1 July 1991
[415] Discussions in Bangkok on 27 November 1993 with Major-General Chatichai Choonhavan and Khun Kraisak Choonhavan
[416] *Political Repression in Thailand*; London University Euro Committee for Solidarity with the Thai People; p29
[417] *Puey Ungphakorn, A Siamese for all Seasons*; Komol Keethong Foundation; p70; and *Thailand: A Short History*; David K Wyatt; p302

three thousand were detained on the grounds of being a danger to society.[418]

To this day the Thammasat massacre is deeply imprinted in the memories of Thai citizens. Not all saw the need for the repression and this violent aftermath in the same way. To some, without approving of the excesses, it was simply a step on the road to the repudiation of communism with which their neighbouring countries were being afflicted. The students themselves were accused of being in league with Vietnamese communists and there was a degree of truth in the accusation.[419] To the disapproving, it seemed a small price to pay in view of the atrocities being perpetrated on the other side of their borders. Intellectuals came under suspicion. Dr Puey Ungphakorn, the Rector of Thammasat, fled the country in fear of his life and opted for voluntary exile in England. Many of the younger elements took to the jungle to join active communist guerilla units and the leaders of the earlier student uprising, or they crossed the Mekong into Laos and Cambodia.

There were some, not only Thais but also foreigners living in the country, who came to the conclusion that one dose of democracy was enough for the people of Thailand. It was an unsuitable foreign doctrine. Whatever the reaction of individuals, one thing was certain: democracy was off the agenda in Thailand for many years. The call was for unity through 'Nation, Religion and King', a usual call in times of difficulty but in practice a euphemism for military rule.

During the early part of the short period of democratic government, affairs across the Mekong in Laos were quieter than usual. On second of April 1974 a coalition government came into existence with Souvanna Pouma as prime minister and with Sisouk na Champassak in his Cabinet as minister of defence. Pathet Lao leader, Prince Souphanouvong, after his long absence in the northern provinces and in gaol, returned to Vientiane and became Head of the National Consultative Political Council. On twenty-third of July, Souvanna suffered a heart attack. Headlining him as 'an Indispensable Laotian' *The New York Times* explained, *"Prince Souvanna Pouma is the indispensable man who alone is believed able both to hold the*

---

[418] *Far Eastern Economic Review*; 22 October 1976
[419] *Far Eastern Economic Review*; 22 October 1976

coalition government together, and to make it work.... But unless the Premier makes a rapid recovery, Laos will soon be heading into the unknown".[420] Souvanna recovered and in September went to France to convalesce. In October he was back to a tumultuous welcome and, to the surprise of many, the coalition had held together in his absence. It was a temporary hold.

South-East Asia was on the boil. The early months of 1975 saw renewed and then intensified activity on the part of the Pathet Lao and North Vietnamese in Laos. The war in South Vietnam was coming to an end and Saigon fell in April. In Cambodia, Prince Sihanouk, who had been dispossessed in a CIA-backed coup in 1970, was still absent. The Khmer Rouge, under the leadership of the Pol Pot, were in control from 1975 and the Cambodian holocaust was in full flow. Fleeing west out of and across Laos were Chinese, South Vietnamese, Laotian, and Cambodian refugees, all heading for the safety of Thailand. They added to the tens of thousands who had previously crossed into Thailand from the west since 1962 from the scourge of General Ne Win's brand of socialism in Burma.

The Hmong particularly suffered. They had fought for, and had been abandoned by, the French and now, like the peasant fighters of South Vietnam, they were being abandoned by the Americans. The Hmong population in Laos, made up of a number of ethnic groups, was at one time estimated at three hundred thousand. Great numbers of the combined group rose to the aid of America during its Indochina wars and were welded into a loyal and brave fighting force which became known as America's 'Secret Army.' Many of the CIA who had worked in Laos had become dedicated to the cause of the Hmong and suffered guilt and self-recrimination when American policy dictated that the CIA should move elsewhere.[421] The ten-year secret war was now over. Many thousands of the Hmong left their country for ever. Over one hundred thousand became refugees in America. Of those who were left behind, many suffered terribly in the second half of the decade at the hands of the Vietnamese-dominated Laotian government.

Souvanna held on to his post for a short period until eventually the Pathet Lao took over government of the country. Out of the shadows

---

[420] *The New York Times* editorial 23 July 1974, cited in *In a Little Kingdom*; Perry Stieglitz; p203
[421] *Thailand: A Short History*; David K. Wyatt

crept the man of real power, Kaysone Phomvihane, who was to dominate Laos until his death in 1992. It was not long before the 're-education' camps were established in the north of the country to become, in their turn, death camps. At the end of 1975, Prince Souphanouvong became the President of the Republic of Laos but Kaysone held the reins of power. The Laotian King and Queen and the Crown Prince were all removed from Luang Prabang and sent for re-education to the camps, where they died. Souvanna Pouma refused to flee the country and spent the rest of his life under house restraint. Occasionally he was allowed to visit France, but he always returned to his native land. He died there in January 1985. Thailand, flooded by refugees, was now virtually surrounded by active communist governments.

After the Thammasat massacre the Thai military once more stepped in. With the end of the short period of Thai democracy — a relative description — the military junta, led by Admiral Sa-ngad Chaloryu, supreme commander, Royal Thai Armed Forces, but with General Kriangsak as the true man of power, formed the National Administrative Reform Council and the Revolutionary Party. At the instigation of the King, Thanin Kraivichien was installed as prime minister. General Kriangsak and General Serm na Nakhon, the Army commander-in-chief, were members of the Reform Council. The Council was not intended to have merely a temporary role and it announced that it would be sixteen years before there was to be any further risk of democracy.[422] In the meantime, the Council would support the government, counter communism, prevent corruption among officials, and ensure fair dealing by middlemen with the farmers. It all sounded like an echo from the past

The National Administrative Reform Council grouping only won the race for supremacy by a short head. It had seized power at six o'clock in the evening whereas a second group, led by General Chalard Hiransid, a classmate of Chatichai and supported by the Soi Rajakru's Chart Thai party, had planned for ten o'clock that same evening. Chalard was dismissed from the Army and took up temporary residence as a monk in the temple which Field Marshall

-----

[422] *Far Eastern Economic Review*; 22 October 1976

Thanom had earlier patronised.[423] It was becoming a popular place for military retirement.

The coup was seen by the military to have been precipitated by a threat to national security and the very survival of the country. Kriangsak also saw that it was necessary to demonstrate that there continued to be some form of democratic government. He considered that military officers had shown themselves to be disinterested in personal power by their handover within two days to a civilian prime minister and within sixteen days to a civilian government as a whole. The National Administrative Reform Council was to give up its legislative function when the National Assembly was appointed at the end of November, after which the Reform Council would become advisory. It was not, of course, intended to be merely advisory — it was to be the ultimate power in the land.

Thanin Kraivichien was the son of a Chinese merchant. He was educated at Thammasat and London Universities and continued his studies of law at Gray's Inn, England. He returned to Thailand in 1954 and later became a judge of the supreme court. He was a friend of Queen Sirikit and respected as a man of integrity. Thanin was appointed to be a member of the National Administrative Reform Council and took up his appointment as prime minister on eighth of October 1976. He announced that there would be no elections for four years.[424] He put aside his liberal education, and his rule, though short, was oppressive. It infuriated not only the civilian population but also the military which had sponsored it. The four-year ruling found no favour with aspiring local politicians and the regime soured international opinion over the violation of human rights. While trade unions themselves were not banned, all strikes and stoppages were declared illegal, as also were federations of trades unions. The Communist Suppression Act of 1969 had been extended by military decree of the Reform Council through a post-October 1976 constitution. Under the extension, most criminal felonies were put under the jurisdiction of military tribunals: there was no right of appeal and no legal representation. The International Commission of Jurists strongly criticised Thai courts-martial proceedings as a *"serious*

---

[423] *Puey Ungphakorn, A Siamese for all Seasons*; Komol Keethong Foundation; pp86 and 117

[424] *Far Eastern Economic Review*; 22 October 1976

violation of internationally accepted fair trial procedures".[425] There were widespread protests from Japanese and American politicians and from Amnesty International. American secretary-of-state, Cyrus Vance, spoke out against *"cruel and inhuman or degrading treatment or punishment, arbitrary arrest... and denial of fair trial"*.

Blamed for an aggravation of the insurgency throughout Thanin's rule was the ministry of the interior under Samak Sundaravej. Strongly pro-American and a virulent anti-communist, Samat had earlier parted company with the Seni government over his continuing contacts with the exiled Thanom.[426] Reports of frequent political murders, and incidents of torture and imprisonment were quite naturally laid at the door of his Ministry. Relationships with neighbouring countries deteriorated and in December 1976, Samak forecast that the Vietnamese were making preparations to invade Thailand.[427] There were suggestions that ASEAN might be converted into a military alliance, but in other ASEAN capitals such a suggestion was quickly put down and the comment made that if Thailand had military problems it must solve them. Some saw the move partly as a sabre-rattling gesture of Thanin's fanatical anti-communism, others as a reflection of Samak's own political ambitions.[428] Such behaviour only intensified the insurgency problem rather than helping to cure it. It added to the thousands of students and academics who had already joined the communists in the jungle.

Student leaders joining the Maoist-led communists were involved in the formulation of a powerful endorsement of its party line, making stirring appeals to other students by way of its clandestine radio, safely sited in Yunnan. The appeals were particularly against the CIA's alleged control of the sixth of October bloodbath and its support of Thanin. Also bitterly attacked was Thanin's repressive rule, and in this protest the students were supported by complaints from the American ambassador and from EEC countries. Not all Army commanders believed that brutal oppression was the only way forward. General Saiyud Kerdphol sometimes despaired of his own military subordinates. *"When I see operational orders specifying 'Kill*

---

[425] *International Commission of Jurists;* press release of 28 June 1977
[426] *Far Eastern Economic Review;* 15 October 1976
[427] *Political Repression in Thailand;* London University Euro Committee for Solidarity with the Thai People; pp17/23
[428] *Far Eastern Economic Review;* 24 December 1976

the communists' as the only objective, I feel sad that some of our field commanders still have so much to learn".[429]

On twenty-fifth of November 1976 the King opened a new three-hundred-and-forty-member National Assembly, operating under a new constitution and under a speaker, chosen by secret ballot, but who just happened to be the Reform Council's nominee. The Assembly was to have a four-year term with a right to propose bills only with the approval of a Cabinet-dominated committee and even then, not bills concerning finance, which were the prerogative of the Cabinet. It could vote on Royal decrees but only after the decree had been promulgated, a procedure which made a nonsense of the rights of the Assembly. It would have no say in relation to prime minister's Orders which could be made under sweeping powers. At a press conference Thanin said that Thailand would develop *"a form of democratic socialism as practised in England and Denmark... with some modification to suit the Thai way of life".*[430] It would of course develop nothing of the sort. It was merely indulging in democratic posturing.

Early in January 1977, Field Marshal Praphas re-appeared upon the scene and although he claimed that he had only returned to live his life out in his native land, his re-appearance was viewed with some misapprehension. In the previous August he had made an eight-day visit, keeping out of sight but causing extreme embarrassment to the Seni government. It had been believed at that time that he had deliberately been brought in by some elements of the military or by the Chart Thai party to de-stabilise the Seni coalition government, of which Seni's Democrat party and Chart Thai were the principal members. He remained an embarrassment but he was no longer a threat: *"a paper tiger"* was M. R. Kukrit's expressed view.[431]

The Army became more and more disenchanted with the Thanin government, but it was still in search of a politically motivated new leader. Part of the disenchantment was caused by Thanin's determination to stamp out the narcotics traffic, a policy which brought him into collision with vested military and civilian interests. To prevent mysterious disappearances of captured product, Thanin ordered the public burning of crops and stocks, with an accredited

---

[429] *Far Eastern Economic Review*; 19 November 1976 and 16 September 1977
[430] *Far Eastern Economic Review*; 10 December 1976
[431] *Far Eastern Economic Review*; 27 August 1976 and 4 November 1977

chemical analyst present to certify the content. Pressure increased for crop substitution, a policy which was possible only because in Thailand the poppy growers themselves were paid so little for the raw opium.[432] Bangkok governments had previously been tolerant and America had, in those days, closed its eyes to traffic from the KMT remnant and from the Shan rebels. The provincial police were known to be compromised but with Thanin's out-and-out declaration of war upon drugs, the Border Patrol police moved in, seizing large quantities from the Shan United Army led by the Sino-Shan, Chang Shee-fu.

On twenty-sixth of March 1977, General Chalard Hiransiri, presumably refreshed by his temple devotions and his subsequent appointment as deputy chief-of-staff, made another attempt at a coup. The plot was based on fragile planning and support: it backfired badly. Kriangsak and Serm were apparently being tipped off regarding developments, and they were thus able to counter moves before any became effective. In the early stages, General Arun Thavatasin, an officer close to the Palace and who was then commanding the key Army units, was shot and killed by Chalard. The attempt was harshly put down, with summary executions and imprisonment. On twentieth of April, on the instructions of the prime minister, Thanin, and with the support of his Cabinet and the military but without resort to trial, Chalard himself was shot.[433] Chalard had been known to be ruthless, ambitious, and rich. As a commander of Thai forces in Vietnam he had lost no opportunity to improve his financial position. In later years he had linked his future to the Soi Rajakru clan and had been involved in earlier uprisings. Chatichai and the Chart Thai were said by some to be behind the attempt.[434] M. R. Seni has restricted himself to saying that Chalard was 'close to' the Chart Thai party although Dr Puey, speaking earlier in America, was not so reticent. The speedy execution of Chalard and the omission of any public trial certainly prevented him naming any of his associates.[435]

M. R. Kukrit meanwhile, although remaining leader of the SAP, had been concentrating on anti-government journalism. His bold, sometimes even savage, writings were now directed at Thanin and in

---

[432] *Far Eastern Economic Review*; 11 February and 15 Apr 1977
[433] *Far Eastern Economic Review*; 8 April 1977; and *Political Repression in Thailand*; London University Euro Committee for Solidarity with the Thai People; pp23
[434] *Far Eastern Economic Review*; 8 April 1977 and local discussions
[435] *Alone on the Sharp Edge*; David van Plaagh; pp169/179

them he emphasised the dissatisfaction which prevailed in ruling circles. In April 1977, following the Sarit pattern and only a few days after the execution of Chalard, Armed Forces supreme commander, Kriangsak Chomanan, visited America for medical treatment. Still closely following the Sarit pattern he returned on twentieth of October and directed an immediate military takeover Three days after the takeover, the Reform Council voted General Kriangsak to be prime minister. On eleventh of November he was confirmed in his appointment by the King. M. R. Kukrit, having helped in putting Thanin to the sword, spoke out against any new attempt at democracy for a period of at least two years. If elections were to be held too soon he argued, "... *the Democrats will win again and my brother will again become prime minister, and God help us"*. After this expression of brotherly love he called for the reform of the ownership of land, of price support, the development of small councils and of labour unions.[436] It was not to be so. Democratically elected government was out of fashion and once more the military was back in power.

---

[436] *Far Eastern Economic Review*; 18 November 1977

CHAPTER ELEVEN
Prem: By Invitation

With the flirtation with democracy over, the first backlash of the military resulted in its domination through the Reform Council. The burning of poppy crops was put aside and Thailand settled down to what might have been expected to be a quiet overlordship in the well-established format.

Kriangsak Chomanan, the new prime minister, rose from obscurity. Born seventeenth of December 1917, the third of seven children of a provincial civil servant, he entered the Military Academy in 1934. Commissioned in 1940, he spent much of his early career on active service as a platoon leader in the Indochina War and then as a Company commander in the Shan States. After a period as a staff officer he took command of an infantry battalion, a part of the 21st Combat Team. 1952 saw him fighting in Korea and receiving an American citation for gallantry. By 1973 he was a General and deputy Chief of Staff of the Armed Forces, taking over as Chief of Staff in 1974. On the first of October 1977 he became supreme commander of the Armed Forces, a post which he continued to hold for a year after his appointment as prime minister.[437] He had the reputation of being a comparative liberal but that reputation was also alleged to be tarnished by published reports of involvement with narcotics traffic during his years as military liaison officer with the Kuomintang wandering armies.[438] The allegations were not proven.

Kriangsak's rise to political power was helped by the spontaneous creation within the middle ranks of the military of the 'Young Turks'. The classes at Chulachomklao Military Academy were numbered from the time it adopted the American West Point curriculum, and in some instances class loyalties were long-lasting. From time to time they have broken into political issues. The so-called Young Turks were a self-appointed military pressure group established as the Young Military Officers' Group. The group was formed in 1973 by six Class 7 Army officers of whom the most prominent were Major Manoon Rupekajorn and the devout Buddhist, Major Chamlong

---

[437] *Who's Who in Thailand*
[438] *Far Eastern Economic Review*; 7 October and 25 November 1977

Srimuang, later to be secretary to General Prem, then Governor of Bangkok and eventually leader of a new political party, Phalang Dharma. The group remained quiescent until the October 1976 massacre, after which it chose to increase its numbers, reaching fifty by 1980. An early recruit at that time, Major Prajark Sawangjit, was also destined to hit the headlines.

The young Turks, as a group, were not involved in the disgraceful affair at Thammasat. Many of them fought with American forces in Laos and all at one time or another fought in Vietnam. Many were members of the Senate. They saw themselves initially as a secret society, formed out of the confusion and disorder of the 1973 to 1976 democratic period, with the objective of establishing a disciplined form of order and stability. The group was independent of any other right-wing movement and, as all others, supported Nation, Religion, and King. The group brought pressure to bear on the Seni government to reduce American forces stationed in the country, but while so doing, to retain the American ammunition and two key radar stations. It held back forces under various members' command to permit the 1977 takeover under Kriangsak's leadership. While the group may have seen itself as a form of King Arthur's Knights of the Round Table, pure in thought and with only the highest motives, it was in practice a highly improper grouping, aiming to act collectively if necessary against its military superiors or elected representatives.

These Class 7 officers were essentially power brokers looking for quick and effective action in remedying the nation's ills through the traditional Thai route of coup d'état followed by strong military leadership. In Prajark's words: *"We were closely united, all of us determined in our pursuit of the same objective: to solve the nation's problems"*. In Manoon's, the Group was *"a force which the unjust both within and outside the Army would fear"*.[439] Needless to say, their seniors disapproved. As one of them put it, these were soldiers stepping out of line. During the period of Kriangsak's absence in America, there had been rumblings from the group but they had been silenced by General Serm.[440] In October 1977 they were out in force to support Kriangsak and to intervene in government affairs. Once his appointment had been confirmed they demanded that a strategy be put

---

[439] *The Thai Young Turks*; Chai-Anan Samudavanija; pp25/38
[440] *Far Eastern Economic Review*; 24 June 1977 and *The Thai Young Turks*; Chai-Anan Samudavanija; p34

in place "*to defeat communism, which can only come through an essentially political victory by democracy... not a Westminster democracy but Thai-style where everyone feels he has a say*".[441] Irrespective of their concept of a 'Thai-style' democratic process, it was certainly a discerning comment on Westminster-style democracy.

Domestic problems bedevilled Kriangsak's short spell in office. Attempts were made to ease some of the drought and poor harvest problems of the north-east but a World Bank report put nine million Thais living in absolute poverty while great wealth was accumulated by a few privileged family groups. Successive governments were seen by the World Bank to have been inactive over the problem, and difficulty was experienced in discerning the direction of policy. Even where development plans were discernible, there was little evidence that they governed the action of government departments.[442]

Although there were promises of elections by April 1979, repression continued throughout 1978 and left-wing interests saw Kriangsak as a more clever oppressor than Thanin. Political prisoners remained incarcerated and operations against guerilla forces were conducted with even greater savageness. Kriangsak's government had not lasted a year before he decided upon a reshuffle. He completed it by August, well before the annual military appointments which would result in his retirement as supreme commander. His problem was General Serm. Serm was already commander-in-chief of the Army and would succeed Kriangsak as forces supreme commander. It was, for Kriangsak, too much power to be held against him in one hand. He therefore allowed Serm to occupy the supreme command but removed his Army power-base by promoting General Prem Tinsulanonda to be Army commander-in-chief, at the same retaining him as deputy minister of the interior. Kriangsak saw Prem as his loyal friend and supporter, and by juggling appointments he had split the most likely opposition to his own premiership. He also moved Generals Saiyud and Sant to the forefront.

A wide-ranging bill was introduced to grant an amnesty to all associated with the 1976 Thammasat riots. The bill allowed eighteen students remaining in gaol to be freed, whilst those who so wished could return from the jungle or foreign countries. It also pardoned all

---

[441] *Far Eastern Economic Review*; 25 November 1977

[442] Extracts of World Bank Report published by *Far Eastern Economic Review*; 1 December 1978

involved with the atrocities such as the Village Scouts, Red Gaurs, and the Nawaphon.[443] Because of mistrust and fear, offers of the amnesty to students and others who had fled the cities brought little response.

New elections required a new constitution and, as with earlier military governments, Kriangsak had no intention of losing control of affairs. A new bill tabled on fifth of October 1978 allowed for the King to appoint the members of the upper house of the Assembly. He would receive recommendations for the appointments from the outgoing prime minister. There was an outcry from politicians when it was seen that, under a transitory clause, the new constitution perpetuated military rule for the next four years. As elections were then scheduled for twenty-second of April 1979 it was a neatly placed time-bomb ticking away under the prime minister-to-be during the early months of 1983. The April elections resulted in Social Action being the numerically strongest party with eighty-three seats with Chart Thai holding thirty-one, the Democrats thirty-two, and the newly created Prachakorn twenty-nine. Whilst Kriangsak had a virtually certain majority through his manipulation of the appointed senators, he needed a degree of support from the elected members. That support would be at a premium. His trust of elected politicians was reflected in his comment, *"Even when you buy their vote you can't depend on them"*.[444] His second government was in practice only a Cabinet reshuffle and the opposition, led still by M. R. Kukrit, set about the task of endeavouring to demonstrate that a while a degree of democracy existed, Kriangsak was *not* the man to run it.

Economic conditions worsened and the ruling and commercial classes were soon looking elsewhere for a solution to the country's growing problems. In its relationships with trade unions, the Kriangsak government was no better than that of Thanin. Collaborationist unions were encouraged, but martial law limited genuine union activity. Worker protests took the form of go-slows, short spell walk-outs, and working to rule. The murder of union officials, imprisonment, disappearances, arbitrary dismissals, and police harassment continued. But Kriangsak played his political cards better than Thanin and soon secured American endorsement of his

---

[443] *Far Eastern Economic Review*; 5 August to 29 September 1978
[444] *Far Eastern Economic Review*; 18 May 1979

regime from President Carter, bringing with it a renewal of American economic and military aid.[445]

In foreign affairs, Kriangsak revived Kukrit's policy of good relations with China, reversing Thanin's fierce anti-communist stance. With China fostering Thai-Cambodian friendship, tensions eased, although incidents still occurred. Relations with Russian-backed Vietnam and Laos were more difficult but Kriangsak hosted Russian ministers. He visited Burma. He was moving Thailand gradually away from a mere pawn in the American game-pattern towards a piece in its own right on the international chessboard. In time, tension eased with Laos and in 1979 Kriangsak signed a peace treaty with the extreme Leninist prime minister, Kaysone Phomvihane. It was historic in concept after the relationships over recent decades, but peace treaties do not necessarily produce lasting peace. This was no exception. There was frequent crossborder sniping in the years following the signing and, almost a decade later, one brief and bloody encounter. After that, relations improved. Kaysone became President in August 1991 and shortly before his death in November 1992, he made a 'live-and-let-live' visit to Thailand to heal old wounds.[446]

Despite harshness to many within the country, Kriangsak established a level of international goodwill by the Thai contribution to human rights and by harbouring refugees from neighbouring countries. Some one hundred and fifty thousand were living, or perhaps just existing, in the Thailand eastern border country, having arrived from Vietnam, Cambodia, and Laos, whilst in the western lands there were ever-changing numbers of Karen. Many of the Hmong were given a new life in America but the Thais complained that only the skilled were taken, leaving Thailand to cope with the unskilled and the unwanted.[447] It is doubtful, however, whether the goodwill would have been so forthcoming had the international community had full access to all of the camps.

Many of the Hmong among the refugees were forcibly repatriated to Laos to face a policy of genocide. In the second half of 1975 the

---

[445] *Political Repression in Thailand*; London University Euro Committee for Solidarity with the Thai People; pp20/21 and 47/57
[446] London *The Times*; 23 November 1992
[447] *Far Eastern Economic Review*; 22 July 1977

Pathet Lao and their Vietnamese masters had introduced their long-term policy to destroy the Hmong. The Hmong had fought against them first for the French colonial power and then for the CIA's private army. A reign of terror began with the use of lethal agents being sprayed from the air over their isolated mountain villages. Red, white and blue-green rain brought sickness, agony, and death to humans and to their animals. Crops and fish died and the fields became infertile. Villagers who refused to surrender found their salt and rice supplies poisoned. Above all, the dreaded yellow rain was sprayed over the villagers. Most died within a few hours, yellow water oozing from their bodies. Others were hunted by planes and showered with poisoned darts, similar to, if not the same, as the 'microjet' rocket introduced into South-East Asia by America in mid-1961.[448] Among the captured, some were used for medical experimentation. The terrorisation of the Hmong went on for well over five years, with mutual recriminations over the source of the lethal agents between the USSR and the American governments.

An investigation by United Nations observers in October 1981 was superficial and there were suggestions that some of the team were apparently more interested in shopping in Bangkok than investigating in the mountains. The team tamely accepted a refusal of entry into Laos and settled for visits to refugee camps in the north of Thailand. As a result, inconclusive evidence was submitted. Was not America concerned about the fate of the former CIA mercenaries? When Pulitzer prize-winner Dr Jane Hamilton-Merritt, who had methodically examined the allegations in Laotian villages, appeared before the American Senate Foreign Relations Sub-Committee on Arms Control, only one senator thought the matter sufficiently important to justify attendance.[449] Who was to blame for the continuing atrocity? America has strenuously denied that the lethal agents used were left over from its Vietnamese defoliation programme. The Pathet Lao blamed the Chinese, but it has been determined that the yellow rain was a deadly mycotoxin derived from grain fungus fusation, a naturally occurring poison in the USSR. It has also been observed in Afghanistan, thus circumstantially at least connecting the usage in Laos to the most likely source, the Pathet Lao

---

[448] *Newsweek*; 21 August 1961 and *The Furtive War*; Wilfred G Burchett; p63
[449] *Bangkok Post*; article by Dr. Jane Hamilton-Merritt, 7 March 1982

and Vietnamese. Hard evidence was difficult to come by as the gas neutralised very quickly after use.[450]

While the Hmong were being subjected to these ruthless attacks, Kaysone and his Pathet Lao leaders in Vientiane were turning their attention to the problem of financing their regime. It was not long before they resorted to the traditional source. Poppy growing, which had been banned in the earlier days of morally inspired communism was legalised, and from 1977 Laos became a major narcotics pedlar. All opium was to be sold to the state. Laotian Army commander General Ouane's own heroin chemist, Iem Norasing, and a Thai heroin criminal on the run, Poonsiri Chanysak who was then living in Laos on a Chinese passport, were courted and provided with cover-up facilities, diplomatic passports and a licence to import acetic anhydride.

The use of part of the Vietnamese port and airport at Da-nang had been given to the Pathet Lao by their masters to enhance their trade and with it to reduce the dependence of Laos on poverty-stricken Vietnam. The facilities proved most helpful to the Laotian leaders. Da-nang was used to refuel aircraft which could then head out towards Hong Kong for offshore drops of heroin for the world market. The port also gave access from which small boats could rendezvous with offshore shipping on its way to markets in Europe and America. The Vietnamese government was far from happy at these moves which offended its own moral communism. It closed down the Laotian facilities and hastened only slowly in the construction of Highway 9, designed to bring additional Laotian traffic to Da-nang.

None of this prevented trafficking through Thailand. Several sentences of twenty-years or more put away a few of the traders. A more salutary lesson was given when a careless agent had been caught red-handed and, on Prime Minister Thanin's instructions, was summarily executed in a Thai prison. Poonsiri later fell foul of the law in Laos through large-scale corruption and was gaoled in Vientiane. There was no pressure for his extradition to Thailand, it being assumed generally there that he knew too much. Thai diplomats were

---

[450] *Bangkok Post*; article syndicated from *The Australian*, by Nicholas Rothwell; 25 October 1981

too polite to implicate Kaysone but Thai police intelligence had no doubts of the Laos government's deep involvement.[451]

In parallel, cruelty beyond measure was still being inflicted on the gentle Cambodians. From 1975 to 1978, Pol Pot massacred well over one million Cambodian inhabitants before being forced away from his killing fields back into the jungle by the USSR-backed Vietnamese Army. Either success or arrogance or both had gone to Pot Pot's head and he had launched a number of cross-border raids into Vietnam. It was a mistake which brought a savage response. In 1978 Cambodia was occupied by Vietnamese troops, and the Khmer Rouge retreated to the jungle and to refugee camps inside the Thailand border. A puppet Vietnamese regime was established in Phnom Penh. Thailand felt itself under severe threat from this Vietnamese invasion and with the full support of ASEAN it backed the regime of Pol Pot, hated as it was, to retain the Cambodian seat in the United Nations.

The Vietnamese adventure was not to the liking of either China or America, both seeking to limit the influence of the USSR in South-East Asia. They connived to remove the Vietnamese from Cambodia, using the Khmer Rouge as their instrument. Through the medium of a friendly Thai military they armed and supplied the Khmer Rouge, and despite their disgust at its earlier rule, continued to acknowledge it as the legitimate government. In 1979, China made a limited incursion into Vietnam. It was a war which lasted only sixteen days but was waged at a cost of sixty thousand dead, another seventy thousand wounded, and the devastation of a corner of Vietnam. The ferocity with which it was fought resulted in a total of less than two thousand prisoners of war.[452] It split the communist bloc with Russia, Vietnam, and Laos on the one side, and China and Cambodia's Khmer Rouge on the other It was a war which confused communists in Thailand. Steeped as it was in Chinese dogma, the Thai Communist Party moved to the China-Cambodia axis. So did the Thai military but for reasons of security and profit rather than ideology.

---

[451] *Far Eastern Economic Review*; 9 January 1981 and *Bangkok Post*; 7 February 1988 article by Alan Dawson; and *Drugs, the US and Khun Sa*; Francis W. Bellinger; p58

[452] *China's War with Vietnam*; 1979 K. C. Chen; p114

From May 1979 to eleventh of February 1980 General Serm, then supreme commander of the Armed Forces, was deputy prime minister in the second Kriangsak Cabinet. General Prem, who had followed Serm as Army commander-in-chief, was deputy minister of the interior in the first Cabinet up to May 1979 and then moved forward to be minister of defence in the second Cabinet. He was to retain it for the third. He therefore held a key role in the event of any subsequent attempt at a take-over of government. M. R. Kukrit, having helped to see off Thanin, followed up by conducting a news column attack on Kriangsak's administration. The development of government policy was not to the liking of that experienced politician and he accused eleven ministers of the government of *"mismanagement, ineptitude, nepotism, and personal corruption"*.[453] A notable exclusion from the attack was the minister of defence, General Prem. He was still something of an enigma to the opposition, both within and without the Assembly, and he remained quietly on the sidelines during the months of attack. Away from the elected members, the government also came under attack from its appointed Senate in the form of Young Turk activists Chamlong, Manoon, and Prachat. But again, not General Prem. Prem had controlled the October forces promotion and at the end of the round he was seen to be in a strong enough position to overcome both Kriangsak and commander-in-chief, Serm, if he so chose. A number of his supporters had been moved upwards in the fire-power divisions, including among them several Class 7 Young Turks. More important were the movements of his close ally, General Sant, to be deputy commander-in-chief, and of Major-General Arthit to command the 1st Division of Royal Guards.[454] Whilst it has been questioned if these moves were made with the deliberate attempt of displacing Kriangsak, there were no obvious immediate changes.

Kriangsak's was not the only government in trouble. The times were not easy for governments worldwide. The second world energy crisis was in full swing, bringing with it inflation to both city and countryside. Above all of this, Thailand faced a refugee problem of immense proportions. Behind the refugees was the Vietnamese Army which in mid-1979 had nearly ten divisions deployed close to the Thai borders. Whilst the Vietnamese denied any aggressive intentions against Thailand, they were frequently chasing Khmer Rouge fighters

---

[453] *Far Eastern Economic Review*; 26 October 1979
[454] *Far Eastern Economic Review*; 12 October 1979

across the borders and into Thai refugee camps. A more fearsome problem for the Thai Army of a technical nature was that it had nothing that could dent the Vietnamese armour, whether it came at them directly through Cambodia or indirectly when used with the Pathet Lao. Whilst the equipment was adequate to protect the regime within the border, it was not adequate for cross-border confrontation. Kriangsak appealed to America for help and in response, heavy weapons and fighter-bombers which had been ordered some three years earlier under a defunct US grant-aid scheme were rushed to Thailand.[455]

In mid-1979, with the refugee problem mounting, the Thais turned on the Cambodian refugees, expelling tens of thousands on the grounds that if it did not take positive action, millions more would follow across the river.[456] The government appealed to the United Nations for assistance as feeding its refugees became a greater and greater burden. It was a burden aggravated by Khmer elements who were smuggling women and children into the camps and food out from the camps to their struggling army. At the end of the year, in a complete U-turn, Kriangsak announced that, to prevent the death of the Khmer race, Thailand would again open its border to the Cambodian refugees. The largest refugee camp in the world was built and some two hundred thousand refugees were housed. The fear remained that another million might follow. Allies applauded the generosity, but humanitarian ideals at the top of the Thai regime and applause from onlookers were not enough. The eastern border of Thailand was becoming submerged in a flood of human debris, and at the operational level, shortages brought about black-marketing and corruption. There was also an increase in the control exercised in the camps by Khmer Rouge cadres.

Mounting pressures on the government in the early months of 1980 came from industrial strikes. Imported oil prices soared and brought inflation, which in turn spread outwards into other commodities and services. There was general discontent with Kriangsak's government. A further reshuffle of government ministers in the second week of February gave a temporary strengthening when Air Marshal Siddhi was persuaded to take the Ministry for Foreign Affairs. Air Marshal

---

[455] *Far Eastern Economic Review*; June–October 1979
[456] *Far Eastern Economic Review*; 22 June 1979

Siddhi Savetsila, a Second World War Seri Thai, was to grace the Foreign Ministry for over a decade. Further pressure now came from the Class 7 Young Turks, who were promoting a no-confidence attitude within political parties and demanding absolute rule by the military. At the same time, Kukrit led opposing members of the Assembly in attacks upon the prime minister. Kriangsak was prepared to call it a day. On twenty-eighth of February, he and General Prem made a joint visit to Chiang Mai to discuss the position with the King. On twenty-ninth of February Kriangsak resigned, *"in order to maintain democratic rule within the parliamentary system"*. To Members of the Assembly he said, *"We have no time to play around. Because of your never-ending interference it has gone beyond my capability to carry out my administration,"* and with that he strode out of the Assembly at the head of his sixteen-day old Cabinet. [457]

General Prem had been quietly moving out of the shadows of office. Despite his known dislike of politics, and more so of politicians, he had taken to addressing public meetings. At lectures at both Chulalongkorn and Thammasat Universities he had carefully separated his personal views from those of the Cabinet itself. The Young Turks began to move their support behind him and he found himself able to create a coalition government, as he termed it, *"on behalf of the King"*. The coalition was of Social Action, Democrat, and Chart Thai parties, but the most senior of their leaders, M. R. Kukrit, declined a post within the new Cabinet on the grounds of his age. Others saw it as more a matter of his pride. Kukrit would play second fiddle to no one. Prem kept Siddhi at his Foreign Office, Chatichai was given the Ministry of Industry and three party leaders were made deputy prime ministers. Pramarn, as head of Chart Thai, was to oversee agriculture, Dr Thanot Khoman, a previous Foreign Minister and a Democrat, was to oversee foreign affairs, whilst Boonchu Rojanasathien, the co-founder with Kukrit of Social Action and one-time president of the Bangkok Bank, was to oversee economic affairs. Additionally, General Serm, the supreme commander, was given the overview of security.

---

[457] *Far Eastern Economic Review*; 14 March 1980

Although himself an unknown quantity in politics, Prem was well placed with his first selection and he maintained his hold on the military by retaining not only his appointment of commander-in-chief but also the defence portfolio. The Class 7 Young Turks now switched their full allegiance from Kriangsak to Prem under whom many of them had served and who had maintained a close relationship with them. He was instinctively their idol of the moment, the true professional soldier of integrity. One of them, the devout Buddhist, Chamlong, was made the prime minister's military secretary.

Prem Tinsulanonda followed the usual career pattern of military prime ministers although he did not enter the Military Academy until he was twenty-one. A cavalry man, he spent a year at the American cavalry school in the early 1950s after commanding cavalry/tank companies and regiments. By 1955 he was a Major and an instructor at the Thai Army cavalry school. He was later appointed to command the school. In 1974 he was appointed to command the 2nd Army area and became commander-in-chief of the Army in 1978. His power base was thus in the élite element of the Thai Army, the cavalry.[458] He was a "soldiers' soldier", a devoted nationalist almost to the degree of being xenophobic, yet he dealt easily with the many foreigners whose duties brought them in contact with him. He was intolerant of mediocrity and highly professional throughout his military career. His appointment to be commander-in-chief of the Army had been a critical step in the eventual solution of the communist insurgency. Both Prem and his director of operations, General Chavalit, had practical field experience of fighting insurgency and knew the futility of the past policy based solely on 'search and kill'. Prem was able to mould a stratum of senior officers to accept new thinking and new methods. By the time Prem had taken over as prime minister, Generals Chavalit and Harn Leenanond had produced for him a full draft of a policy statement and within a few weeks Prem had signed it, marking a radical change in military doctrine.

The prime minister's order, No. 66/2523,[459] saw the Communist Party of Thailand as manipulating the changing world situation to its own ends. It was developing a revolutionary war and hoping to rely not merely on jungle-to-jungle co-ordination but also to support its revolution, town to jungle. In the protection of the Nation, Religion,

---

[458] *Who's Who in Thailand* and *Bangkok Post*; 9 January 1987
[459] *The Military in Thai Politics 1981-86*; Suchit Bunbongkarn; translation on pp90/3

and King concept, General Prem required the administration of the country to take into consideration the welfare of the people in resolving economic, political and social problems. Reflecting President John F. Kennedy's inaugural speech, the call was for the Thai people to be instilled with a sense of idealism which encouraged sacrifice of personal interest for common good, The bureaucracy was to be reformed to make it more efficient in serving the needs of the public. The prime task of the military was the defence of the realm and of national independence.

This was a sea-change from the policy of the past when the primary role of the military had been cast as that of the defence of the regime. Collectively, the prime task was to defeat communism in the shortest possible time by waging a continuous political offensive and turning the military struggle into a peaceful struggle. Throughout the struggle, political actions were to prevail and military actions were to be supportive of such political actions. Within the operations, social injustice was to be eliminated, corruption prevented, and exploitation of the people done away with. Officials were called upon to be just and uniform in dealing with people of all walks of life. Surrendering or defecting communists were to be treated as fellow-countrymen, not as enemies. Great importance was attached to the breaking of any link between town and jungle. The prime minister's Order analysed a number of possible communist tactics, gave instructions on how they were to be countered, and finally countermanded any conflicting instructions issued by his predecessors. Despite its many merits, Order 66/2523 had one unfortunate interpretation. The Thai military found in it a number of words which not only drew attention to its political role but also, in its opinion, legitimised that role.

Two years later, Order No 65/2525,[460] effective from twenty-seventh of May 1982, reinforced Prem's policy. The objective of the second order was *"to promote true faith and understanding that sovereignty rests with the people"* and to destroy all forms of dictatorship. In so doing, there was to be established a society which was democratic under the leadership of the Monarch. Prem's objective was a society in which people could live with dignity, in happiness, and with personal and material security, free from exploitation. State decision-making at all levels was to be speeded up; civil servants were rebuked for lacking in the sense of duty and idealism. They were

---

[460] *The Military in Thai Politics 1981-86*; Suchit Bunbongkarn; translation on pp94/9

instructed to root out corruption and to prevent their fellow civil servants from *"acting as lords and masters of the people"*. Democratic organisations were to be formed among the farmers and workers. Students were to be allowed to conduct all the proper university activities, including political activity, and to be given opportunity to participate with government in joint efforts to resolve practical problems. The mass media was given qualified freedom. Those promoting democratic aims would be encouraged and backed while those who were not would be subject to curtailment and legal action. The armed forces were called upon to have a correct understanding of democracy and to support it.

The Prem/Chavalit approach to solving the insurgency problem appears to have been derived more from the principles enunciated by Sun Tzu than to the Westmoreland concepts which had operated in Vietnam, where Chavalit had served. The first of Sun Tzu's fundamental factors was that of moral influence, of bringing harmony between a people and its leaders. An early operational requirement was that captives must be cared for and treated well. Queen Sirikit spoke of the need of the soldiers not only to make an area safe but also to understand their humanitarian role.[461] Resistance to communism in Thailand was seen as a direct defence of Buddhism, and the King himself looked upon Buddhism and the discipline that it involved as an essential feature of his life and kingship.

This enlightened approach by the Prem government was timed to perfection. The students and intellectuals who had taken to the jungle proved in the longer term to be disastrous for the peasant-led Communist Party. An immediate effect of the oppression of the 1960s and 1970s, especially the late 1970s, had been to enhance the Party's strength and provide it with a much-needed homegrown intellectual base some three thousand strong. But before long, clashes of both personality and ideology occurred between the energetic, educated intake and the diehard, blinkered Chinese-influenced peasant base. The clashes became more complex and crossed the boundaries of urban against rural, peasant against intellectual, party against newcomer, and eventually, leaders against followers. Disagreement followed by disillusion spread throughout the entire movement and even divided the old Party leadership. Confusion was inevitable and

---

[461] *The Soul of a Nation*; BBC post-production script, written by Leo Aylen, produced by Bridget Winter; II pp24/5

this was aggravated by outside rifts between Russian-led and Chinese-led communism, particularly as it affected South-East Asian countries. The Prem initiatives, and particularly so the first, 66/2523, when combined with the natural attitude of forgiveness which springs from the Buddhist faith, offered a way home for large numbers who had fled from their studies and careers. They had wilted under the hardships of jungle life and defections soon became common. The defections spread to members of the Party who had been in the jungle long before the student influx, and the effect was such that over a period of five years the Communist Party of Thailand had lost all that it achieved in the previous forty.[462] Sun Tzu-theory had been shown to be a practical reality.

The interval between the two Prem directives belonged to the Class 7 Young Turks. In the spring of 1981, they once more sought to use their power, first to change government policy, and when that failed, to change the government. The first of April 1981 attempt to remove Prem was the most serious of a number during his time in office. Its beginnings were in an inter-party squabble over a controversial oil deal. The two major parties of Prem's coalition at that time were the Social Action Party with eighty-two seats and the Chart Thai with thirty-eight seats in the three-hundred-and-one-seat National Assembly. The first of these was led by former prime minister, M. R. Kukrit, and deputy prime minister, Boonchu Rojanastien, who was also at the time a Board member of the Petroleum Authority of Thailand (PTT). Chart Thai was chaired by Phin's son-in-law, Major-General Pramarn, who was also a deputy prime minister, with Chatichai as Prem's minister of industry. In the spread of government appointments, as behoves a coalition, the deputy minister of industry was Visit Tansacha of Social Action. Also watching events closely was the Democrat Party led by deputy prime minister Dr Thanat Khoman.

Early in February 1981, Boonchu and Visit were in Indonesia to negotiate for crude oil. During their absence, Chatichai flew to Saudi Arabia, also in search of an oil deal, and was somewhat taken aback to find that two telexes dated eighth and ninth February had been sent

---

[462] *The Rise and Fall of the Communist party of Thailand (1973 to 1987)*; Gawin Chutima; pp22/23

from Jakarta directly to the Saudis to say that he, Chatichai, was not empowered to commit Thailand to such a deal. The telexes were in the name of Visit and Boonchu although it subsequently materialised that they had been sent by Visit without Boonchu's knowledge. Chatichai was obliged to have Prime Minister Prem telex the Saudi government to establish his authority to negotiate.

Chatichai returned to Thailand and was reported as saying that his oil deal would benefit Thailand much more than a black market deal that other anonymous people were trying to clinch. Charge and countercharge of commissions flew around Bangkok, and despite an attempt at mediation by M. R. Kukrit, the problem was eventually dumped on the desk of the prime minister. In the clash which developed between Social Action and Chart Thai, opposition parties called for Prem's resignation, and then the Social Action party threatened to resign from the coalition.

An interesting twist to the situation was given by the publication of a PTT letter dated thirteenth of December 1979 (this was during the period of Kriangsak's rule) and signed by a PTT deputy-governor. It was addressed to the Saudi agency, Petromin, and called for sixty thousand barrels per day of Saudi light crude. While the letter stipulated an initial period of twelve months, its tone implied a likely extension, and all dealings were to be handled by an offshore company, Thai Yuen Yong Trading (Hong Kong) Ltd, with offices in that colony. It also had Thai connections. Visit claimed that this deal was a source of dispute between Social Action and Chart Thai and that its overall price of thirty-six US dollars per barrel included an unresolved four-dollar per barrel royalty payment or commission, a commission with which the prime minister and Boonchu had already expressed disapproval. It was in connection with this particular deal that he sent the telexes. The prime minister made a personal statement on television. He saw the whole matter as a misunderstanding and considered it closed. Visit tendered his resignation. Prem's military secretary, Col. Chamlong, at first refused to accept it. The government needed to be kept together and the people expected Prem's regime to reflect the honesty and integrity with which Prem himself was undoubtedly personally credited.

Subsequent published facts showed that there were two separate oil deals in the making. Chatichai, with an expert team, was in Saudi Arabia to finalise the transfer of sixty-five thousand barrels per day of crude oil from a government-backed private contract to a direct government-to-government contract. Concurrently, Thai Yuen Thong Trading (Hong Kong) Ltd., a broker with which PTT had dealt previously, had offered PTT a deal involving sixty thousand, not sixty-five thousand, barrels per day of Saudi Crude at the posted price, then about thirty-two US dollars per barrel, plus four dollars per barrel commission. In the absence of its governor, PTT referred it to the deputy minister, Visit. Visit maintained that he knew nothing of the Chatichai team's mission. This was strange, to say the least, because not only was one of the team his own minister but also another was a senior civil-servant of the ministry staff. The broker, suspecting some form of double-dealing which would result in the loss of the commission, demanded to know from Visit what game the Thai government was playing. PTT claimed it acted on instructions given to it by Chatichai. Through apparent lack of communication within the Ministry and between the Ministry and PTT, and because of the similarity of the numbers, the telexes were sent and accusation and counter-accusation flowed. At the end there was no absolute proof of what was to happen to all of the commission which would have totalled over eighty-seven million US dollars per annum.[463] Oil deals do not usually come close to toppling a government. This one did.

Oil negotiations were not the only problem. There had been disputes within the coalition over sugar, over the desirability and location of a soda-ash plant, over the price of paddy, and concerning the overall problem of inflation. An advisory committee, principally of academics but chaired by General Sant Chitpatima, the deputy commander-in-chief of the Army, offered the prime minister alternative approaches to solve the economic dilemma but not much notice was taken of its recommendations.

At this point the Democrat Party decided to leave the coalition, thus allowing or even forcing a reshuffle. Then it changed its mind, allegedly at the request of General Prem.

The Social Action party through its leader, M. R. Kukrit, launched a bitter attack upon the prime minister and at this there were rumblings from the Army. An attack upon the prime minister who

---

[463] *Bangkok Post*; February 20 1981 by Suneesa Hancock, Business Editor

remains commander-in-chief of the Army was an attack on the Army itself. Nevertheless both the supreme commander, Serm, and the commander of the vital 1st Army indicated that the Army would not interfere.

On fifth March there were mass resignations as the Social Action party quit the coalition government. Other ministers also offered to resign to give Prem a free hand, but not the Chart Thai ministers who held on to their portfolios. A desperately needed reshuffle took a few days with parties negotiating with the prime minister to get the best posts. The commander, 1st Division cancelled all leave for battle units in and around Bangkok. Ultimately, General Prem decided to exclude the Social Action party, maintain the Chart Thai in power but without allowing it to increase its hold, bring back the Democrat Party, and most important, as he had been urged by General Sant's committee, to bring in a large number of technocrats and business men. While such an arrangement might save the day, it could only bring about a degree of tension to have Social Action, the strongest political party in the National Assembly, in opposition to his government.

Elements of the Army did not accept the new look and the Class 7 power brokers moved in, with Colonel Manoon Roopkachorn prominent. This time they set out to remove Prem. On the first of April, deputy Army commander Sant, who had previously been considered a close friend of Prem, was persuaded to lead their group. It took over key installations in Bangkok. Sant was backed by General Vasin Isarangkul, the commanding general of the 1st Army and therefore the controller of Bangkok. Colonel Manoon commanded the 4th Cavalry Regiment, and another high-profile fellow Young Turk, Colonel Prachak, the 2nd Infantry Regiment. Colonel Chamlong, despite at an earlier stage of his career being a leading Young Turk, dissociated himself from Manoon and Prachak and remained loyal to Prem. Reluctantly persuaded to support the uprising was General Serm na Nakhon, the supreme commander, the persuasion being carried out at gunpoint. Another reluctant participant in the Revolutionary Council was police-general Montchai Phankongchuen. Montchai had tasted revolution some eight years earlier, and this time he escaped and made his way to Khorat from where he ordered all police forces to remain loyal to Prem. Naval and Air Force commanders named as supporters of the coup carefully kept away. A contingent sent out to capture the minister of industry, General Chatichai, were far too slow. He had skipped out of trouble in his private plane and returned only when it was all over.[464]

In conformity with past practice, a Revolutionary Council was established to usurp the authority of the prime minister. The press was told that it would be shut down if it did not conform to the requirements of the new masters. Radio stations were obliged to confine their programmes to public announcements and martial music. General Sant announced that he was the head of the Revolutionary Council with General Vasin as his deputy; Colonel Manoon was appointed Secretary-General of the Council. General Serm was said to be divested of his post and to be an adviser to the Revolutionary Council. General Prem was said to be retired. The Revolutionary Council dismissed Major-General Arthit Kamlang-ek from his post within the 2nd Army for refusing to obey their decrees.

A long statement was issued to justify the takeover. It spoke of weakness of the leaders, political problems arising from inter-party rivalry, the failure to solve economic problems, an increase in the rate of crime, and of corruption in high places. The lot of the ordinary people was to be improved but there would be drastic punishment for people associated with crimes of public disturbance, narcotics, child labour, prostitution, trade in weapons of war, and for those caught cheating the peasants. No one was to promote any policy which was contrary to the tripartite base of Nation, Religion, and King. It all sounded very familiar: just the usual Thai coup routine.

Troops were positioned to resist any opposition which might come from the North-East while others were dispersed throughout Bangkok in a show of strength. Guard detachments were put on the Grand Palace, General Prem's house, and the principal radio stations. A small detachment was posted near Thammasat University. During the day, the Revolutionary Council reinstated General Serm as supreme commander and appointed General Sant as Army commander-in-chief to replace Prem. General Serm, however, was by then already in contact with General Prem and the 2nd Army.

The National Assembly was recalled and the 1978 constitution declared to be in force but with elected, not appointed, members. Leaders of all nineteen university students' unions were invited to

---

[464] Discussions with Major-General Chatichai, Bangkok; 26 November 1993

attend and to offer their opinions on how best to solve the country's problems. The students did not come. The Revolutionary Council sent emissaries to explain their position to the King. It also broadcast its respect for its former commander, General Prem, and regretted that he had not listened to proposals it had wished to make to solve the country's problems.

One of the allegations which had been made against General Prem in his position as prime minister was that he was indecisive. It was not an allegation to be made against General Prem in his other role, that of commander-in-chief. At the beginning of the coup he had been detained in his house and an attempt by Major-General Arthit to get him out by helicopter was aborted. Arthit then phoned the palace, and when eventually able to speak to Queen Sirikit, he suggested that General Prem be summoned to the palace, an order that the rebels would not be able to refuse. The Queen summoned the prime minister to the palace but the rebels did not respond immediately to the command. The Queen phoned a second time saying that if the rebels did not permit General Prem to leave, she would personally come and collect him. In the confusion this forthright command produced, Prem slipped out of the house and made his way to the palace. The King then summoned the plotters to the palace for discussions with him, but Sant had other plans. Prem, with the King, the Queen and members of the royal family, left Bangkok and flew to the Khorat headquarters of the 2nd Army.

Arthit was made Director of National Peacekeeping with authority to issue orders to all Navy, Army, and Air Force personnel. In this he was supported by Major-Generals Chavalit and Harn. Radio links allowed Prem to broadcast to the nation and on second of April he was already on the air to announce his continuing authority. Planes of the Royal Thai Air Force which had stayed loyal to Prem backed him up by dropping leaflets. Further support for Prem came from the Queen herself with a message broadcast from the Khorat radio station calling for those of good intentions towards the country to cease the contest and to unite to protect the country from external aggression.[465] Meanwhile elements of Arthit's 2nd Army moved on Bangkok.

On second of April, General Kriangsak, the former prime minister, arrived in Khorat in an attempt to mediate between government and rebels, suggesting that the rebels be pardoned and

---

[465] *The Thai Young Turks*, Chai-Anan Samudavanija; p92

allowed to keep their appointments. Arthit sought unconditional surrender but he was under instructions from the King to avoid bloodshed if possible. Prem undertook that the plotters would receive a just trial and that troops returning to barracks and disarming themselves would be pardoned. Kriangsak returned to the principal plotters bearing these tidings. Arthit meanwhile moved reinforcements into Bangkok. By dawn on third of April marines and Navy personnel had been moved into the centre of Bangkok and troops were moving up from Chonburi. By ten o'clock in the morning of third of April, all major objectives were taken and by midday the rebels were disarmed. The attempted coup was over.[466]

Most of the plotters were rounded up but the ringleaders had fled. Twenty-eight Young Turk officers were dismissed from active service without pension. Manoon went to Germany. Sant, having first sought asylum in America, was given asylum in Burma by the Karen. On fourth of April, the prime minister returned to Bangkok accompanied by his military secretary, Colonel Chamlong. Within twenty-four hours the press was enjoying its new-found freedom and radio stations were back to normal.

Arthit Kamlang-ek had grasped a rare opportunity to show his worth and he made the most of it. He was a people's general and his popularity stemmed back to the Phibun era. A man of humble origins, he followed the traditional route through the Chulachomklao Military Academy but without distinction. He then served with the Thai contingent in Korea. He had been a captain at the time of the demonstrations which led eventually to the downfall of both prime minister Phibun and his police general, Phao Sriyanon. In immediate command of troops on the Makkahawan bridge in the heart of Bangkok, he had prevented bloodshed in that very nasty confrontation. Prior to General Sarit's arrival, he had calmed the anxiety of his troops and stopped any trigger-happy reaction. He went on to serve with the Thai force under American command in Vietnam. Prior to his sudden change of fortune, he had spent much of his army career in the provinces.[467] In that dramatic April, Lieut-General Arthit was appointed to command the 1st Army, and with that appointment he

---

[466] General Arthit Kamlang-ek's speech after he had been promoted to First Army commander, published in *Bangkok Post*; 24 May and confirmed in part in embassy discussions

[467] *Bangkok Post*, mid-April 1981

became the master of the Bangkok area and the central plains. In the September Army reshuffle he became a full general and in the following October 1982, commander-in-chief of the Army.

The collapse of the Young Turks' coup brought to greater public notice not only Arthit himself but also, among others, Major-General Chavalit Yongchaiyudh and Major Harn Leenanond. Chavalit was not from the Army élite units, the cavalry and artillery, nor even from the infantry, but from the unfashionable Corps of Signals. A Chulachomklao Class 1 graduate who had fought under American command in Vietnam, he was an army intellectual and pursued his career through the planning channels of the Army. He was a military analyst and was astute in his political perception. He was a member of the 'Democratic Soldiers' movement, a military faction associated more with military strategy than direct command, and the thinking of that movement influenced his own approach to the solution of the communist problem. With Harn he had played an important role in the formulation of Prem's orders 66/2523 and 65/2525. He had been secretary to Prem when the latter was minister of defence in 1979, moving on with him to be an adviser on political and military affairs.

Harn, a contemporary of Arthit's, was also deeply involved in the counter-insurgency strategy. He had worked with Prem in Khorat with the 2nd Army, and after the attempted coup was trusted with the 4th Army region in the south of the country. Here his problems were not only those of insurgency but also the residual problems arising from the activities of the Communist Party of Malaysia, which frequently retreated across the border. At the same time he was required to deal with the continuing problem of the south, the Muslim dissidents. His successful pursuit of peace in the south did not benefit him as it brought him into conflict, as a possible rival, with Arthit who later forced his resignation from active service.[468]

With Class 7 making all the running, another closely-knit class, Class 5, strongly opposed to their juniors' methods, had temporarily been pushed into the background. Class 5 included a number of later power usurpers, among them the Class president, artilleryman Suchinda Kraprayoon and his brother-in-law, Issarapong Noonpakdee.

---

[468] *The Military in Thai Politics 1981-86*; Suchit Bunbongkarn; p21

They remained in the background, but allegedly not supporting the coup route, waited their time. In the meantime they moved closer to Generals Arthit and Chavalit, the principal power men of the Prem premiership, thus assuring promotion which would put them in positions of power on a later occasion. By 1984, Class 5 members held the critical army divisional commands. No coup could succeed without the support of their fire-power.[469]

Perhaps the saddest figure of the whole of the April Fools' Day affair was the supreme commander, General Serm. Serm had the reputation of a "gentleman soldier". He was a product of both Chulachomklao and the British Staff College, Camberley, and had commenced his career with the artillery. Born in 1920, he had by 1976 become Army commander-in-chief. In 1978 he became supreme commander of the Armed Forces, but at the same time General Prem took over as Army commander-in-chief, an appointment which removed from Serm a strong power base. In 1979 he was appointed to be a deputy prime minister by Kriangsak and held that position in the first two Cabinets of the Prem government. He retired from the Army in September 1981 after his reluctant involvement with the attempted coup.

Prem moved to unite the Army and normalise the situation. A Royal decree was proclaimed on fifth of May 1981 granting an amnesty to all but eight of the plotters, those eight including Sant and Manoon. On eighth of June, the National Assembly passed an amnesty bill to pardon the eight. Despite this, nearly forty Young Turks were dismissed from the Army. They were to remain in the wilderness for five years.

Within Bangkok an interservice unit against international terrorism, the Capital Security Command, was established. The intention was that it would only operate in times of emergency and that the command would operate above all three services. Realising its possibilities, Arthit grabbed control of it when he was 1st Army commander and kept hold of it throughout his career. When Chavalit succeeded, he too kept direct control of the Capital Security Command. It ran its own television station and supervised a number of non-military tasks. Under General Arthit it also settled a few major strikes, on at least one occasion with the help of tank support. Eventually it became a source of power that could be abused and, as

---

[469] *The Military in Thai Politics 1981-86*; Suchit Bunbongkarn; p24

282

so often happens when power is abused, it became unacceptable. The Capital Security Command reached the state of unacceptability in May 1992 following anti-military protests. As a result, its role was terminated in July of that year.

Early in 1983, a special parliamentary session was called to amend the 1979 constitution, the ticking time-bomb. With the life of the government coming towards the end of its four-year term, a new government would be elected under changed provisions. The election was not due until June but revisions to the constitution were already due to be implemented on twenty-first of April. Under the new constitution the voting powers of the Senate would be limited and serving military and civil servants would be barred from holding political appointment. Furthermore, election to the National Assembly would be based on provincial voting lists not on the existing multiple constituency, single-candidate voting system. The effect was twofold. It gave political parties a much greater possibility of obtaining, through block votes, a majority in the assembly. This would avoid, or at least minimise, multi-party coalitions with the ministerial appointment complications. It also curbed the power of the Senate and thus the Army. While these provisions were already in the constitution, they were under suspension until twenty-first of April 1983.

The Army and in particular its commander-in-chief, General Arthit, required the National Assembly to extend the suspension for at least another four years. The Army used the Social Democratic Party to sponsor the recall of the Assembly and to put forward a bill to give effect to the necessary extension. Threatening noises had come from the Army in January when the commander of the 1st Army warned that *"if nothing was done and chaos results, threatening security, the Army will have to conduct exercises"*.[470] M. R. Kukrit's Social Action party were strongly opposed to the Army being given a renewal of its privileges and they offered an alternative which accepted just the change in the voting system. Immediately before the house was due to vote on the first reading of the bill, General Arthit made a nationwide television appearance to stress the need for the full amendments to be

----

[470] *Bangkok Post*, 13 January 1983

accepted, and on nineteenth February the Assembly dutifully completed the first reading, rejecting Kukrit's amendment. The third reading was not due to take place until mid-March, and for the third reading the bill had to receive the positive vote of more than fifty per cent of all members. Thus abstentions would count as a vote against the bill. Feelings ran high. One Assembly member even threatened suicide if the Army's amendment went through and he ordered his coffin. A student campaign against military dictatorship was planned with Thammasat University in the lead.

The article-by-article second reading was completed by the end of February. Early in March, Army assistant chief-of-staff, General Chavalit, although speaking in favour of the amendment, gave an assurance that whatever the result of the third reading the Army would respect it. He also denied that the intention behind the amendment was for General Arthit to take over the government. An injunction seeking to declare invalid the results of the first and second readings was rejected by the civil court. The final vote was to be taken on sixteenth March, and Army supporters would require the two hundred and sixty-four votes to carry the day.

That morning, M. R. Kukrit announced that his Social Action party would not vote. The Democrats followed suit. For the leadership of the party this meant that each could control its members, so that there was no breaking faith with party policy during the secret ballot. At the critical moment the Chart Thai, having voted for the amendment during the first and second readings, decided to support its Social Action and Democrat coalition partners. It voted against the amendment. Among the Senators it was believed that members of the Navy and Air Force, together with retired civil servants and academics, all voted to reject the amendment. All sought to avoid military dictatorship. By ten votes, the amendment fell.

The refusal to make changes meant that the June election would involve the electorate picking a block of candidates from a single political party from an electoral district which encompassed a whole province. The government would then be chosen by the party gaining the most seats. Party members, whether or not elected MPs, could be a member of that government but a civil servant or a military officer was barred from government unless he retired from his service. The Senate would no longer be permitted to vote on important national issues, monetary bills, or constitutional matters.

A half-hearted attempt to reinterpret the rules of the count was attempted but failed. Arthit, supported by former prime minister Kriangsak, lashed out at the influence of Kukrit and his newspaper over people's thinking but then said that he would not raise the issue again. It was not that M. R. Kukrit was alone in his attack on the amendment. Before he had entered the fray, the prime minister's one-time military secretary, Colonel Chamlong, had attacked it with an almost religious fervour. Now the suicidal Democrat MP, who had been fasting for the seven days before the vote, was able to eat and to sell the coffin he would no longer need.

Theoretically the matter was closed, and the House Speaker closed the special session of the Assembly on nineteenth of March. Voting at the next election in June would take place in accordance with the unamended constitution. Although the Army, both through Arthit and through Chavalit, had said that it would not interfere with the result, many wondered.

Prime Minister Prem did not wonder. Without consulting any party leader, he went to the King, dissolved the Assembly and scheduled elections for eighteenth of April, three days before the new rules, to which the Army objected, came into effect. He foresaw that, with the disputes already in place and an election on the new rules only two months away, either a military coup or some other trouble would arise, bringing serious consequences to the country and possibly a breakdown in law and order. Prem considered that the people would be happier with the system they understood, voting for people they knew and favoured. He was also wise enough to know that whereas the Army had been snubbed by the defeat of the constitutional amendment, he had now handed it a strategic victory and thus removed the immediate fear of another coup d'état.[471]

There were sardonic cries from the political parties and from the press, but Prem, with the support of the King and an open declaration of loyalty from Arthit, had bought time. The electorate, with no experience of voting for party policies rather than for men with whom it was familiar, did not have to be re-educated in a matter of two months. There was, however, a disadvantage. The decision meant the continuation of the coalition system, as no party was likely to obtain an overall majority under existing procedures. This was what the Army wanted. Economic leader, Boonchu Ronjanastien, resigned

---

[471] *Bangkok Post*, from January to March 1983 and local discussions

from his party, deciding to take no part in any further coalition government. The coalition system would not allow him to carry out the economic reforms for which he had argued and which he considered to be essential for the future prosperity of Thailand.

There were still problems ahead. Under the existing rules, anyone could run for membership of the Assembly without belonging to a political party. Three days after the election, all would be required to be members of one of the registered political parties. Thus it seemed that some members would be legally elected as members of the National Assembly, only to find themselves disqualified three days later when the unamended constitution was due to come into force. Some were sure that the problems would come to nought. There is an old Thai political acceptance that, irrespective of the law, if everyone agrees that something is legal and no one objects in principle, then the action will be taken to be legal.

Hectic electioneering took over for a few weeks. A bomb went off near the Democrat party offices whilst another near to the Social Action headquarters was accidentally defused by a teenager. Kriangsak decided to move back into the political scene by establishing a party of his own, the National Democratic Party. Speaking to crowds of thousands, M. R. Kukrit took up the call for greater democracy and he was now joined on the Social Action platform by the respected foreign minister, Air Chief Marshal Siddhi. Kukrit challenged the Army to keep out of politics and rejected any idea of his party joining a coalition. Boonchu announced that he was ready to co-operate with the military if they took over, provided they gave him a free hand with the economy to put the country right. One foreign observer saw the line up as Social Action against the Army, and openly forecast that, in the event that there was a coalition, led by Social Action but under Prem, there would be a revolt by Arthit and the Army. This forecast was no doubt based on what was obvious to the man in the street, that there was a steady deterioration in the Prem-Arthit relationship. Not all the military saw the position that way. The supreme commander assured the country that the military would not reverse the decision of a general election. As background noises to election fever, tremors of an earthquake were felt in Bangkok and bloody fighting was taking place across the Mekong, close to the Thai/Cambodia border, between invading Vietnamese and the Khmer Rouge.

Despite the introduction of a number of smaller parties, floating members decreased and with the total seats contested increasing from three hundred and one to three hundred and twenty-four, the majors increased their representation. When the shifts from party to party had settled, the vote of both Social Action and Chart Thai had increased, the former to ninety-two and the latter to seventy-three. The Democrat party also stepped its vote up to fifty-six, leaving approximately one hundred votes spread among the other contestants. The struggle was on for seats in the Cabinet and with them, the usual expectation of spin-off wealth. In M. R. Kukrit's words, *"Politicians in Thailand are not easy to befriend, or to make contact with, or to please.... What they want is position and money"*.[472] Kukrit, as leader of the party with most votes, called upon General Prem to accept the post of prime minister and to lead a coalition of Social Action, Chart Thai, and Democrats.

It was unlikely that such a grouping, opposed as it had been over the previous three years to Army interference with government, would prove popular with the powerful Arthit. Much would depend on how a new government would view the previously aborted amendments to the Constitution. First to throw a hat into the ring was Chamlong, always a strident opponent of the amendments, pointing out that the vote of the people was strongly against supporters of the amendment. The Army had its friends. The original proposers of the amendment, the Siam Democratic Party, dissolved itself and merged with the Chart Thai. This merger, together with other members who drifted towards power and opportunity, gave that party one hundred and eleven seats, and with it the first opportunity to form a government. Given the support of numerous small parties, it could govern and leave the Social Action party in opposition. This would allow Chart Thai to put into place the amendments which the Army sought. Once this had been done it would have a high degree of support within the Senate and also the support of the civil servants.

The military proposed an alternative coalition incorporating the Chart Thai, Social Action, and Prachakorn Thai parties, but added a condition that such a coalition must undertake to bring in the previously rejected constitutional amendments. That was an unacceptable condition to Social Action, and M. R. Kukrit rejected the proposal. Conflicting noises came from the Chart Thai who now spoke

---

[472] *The Military in Thai Politics 1981-86*; Suchit Bunbongkarn; pp36/37

of a coalition with Social Action, although the leader of that party had already said that he would not enter such a coalition. This move was outflanked when General Prem himself told the deputy leader of the Chart Thai, Chatichai, that he was not prepared to head such a coalition.

On twenty-sixth of April 1983, Prem announced that he was finished. He had been prime minister long enough and had no ambition to continue. He was washing his hands of politics and even more so of politicians. Prem could not get a free hand to form the Cabinet of his choice and he was not prepared to continue unless he was given it. The same day there came a softening in attitude on the part of Social Action. M. R. Kukrit urged Prem to continue. He openly admitted that he thought any alternative would doom the country and would result in a coup d'état. He then agreed for his Social Action party to join in a coalition government under General Prem and offered to support the amendments to the Constitution required by the military to enable a new government to survive. By taking this stand Kukrit also prevented Chart Thai from being the lead element in a new government. The Prachakorn Thai party, with an eye on a new winner, moved swiftly to dissociate itself from any coalition led by Chart Thai. The more cynical saw the military behind the move, with General Prem's sanction. The military wanted to keep Prem as prime minister and he was prepared to continue, but only if his conditions were accepted. He wanted to choose some members of his new cabinet from outside the political parties.[473]

The following day, General Prem changed his mind. The appeal from M. R. Kukrit had borne fruit and this, together with moves in high places in the military and among other political leaders, led him to believe that he would get the freedom he required. On thirtieth of April the name of Prem Tinsulanonda, backed by all parties, was put before the King by the Speaker of the National Assembly.

It took the prime minister seven days to complete his government. Kukrit's party were given fifteen seats, the Democrats nine, Prachakorn Thai six, the National Democrats three, and there were ten non-politicians, hand-picked by Prem. Prem kept the Defence

---

[473] Discussions with Major-General Chatichai; 26 November 1993

portfolio for himself. Siddhi, now a member of Social Action, continued at the Foreign Ministry. With the growing importance of the development of the country's energy, that portfolio was controlled by two non-politicians, men who were dedicated to the interest of the nation and not to personal gain, Suli Mahasanthana in the prime minister's office and Dr Chirayu Isarangkura in the Ministry of Industry. Both were to concentrate their efforts over the next few years with considerable success in this all-important field. The Chart Thai party, which thought it was playing the Army card by omitting Social Action and Democrats from a coalition, had misjudged badly and was left in the wilderness, a misjudgement which cost Pramarn the leadership of the party. The constitutional crisis had been overcome. Prem could face a further four years in office with a Cabinet acceptable to him personally, and Thailand would benefit from the calmer, low-profile management style which he had brought to Thai politics.

On the first of October 1983, General Arthit Kamlang-ek reached the peak of his service career. The annual reshuffle of the services resulted in his being appointed supreme commander of the Armed Forces, at the same time retaining his posts of Army commander-in-chief, director of peace-keeping forces, and director of internal security operations command. His meteoric rise just two years before his scheduled retirement made him only the fourth military strongman to hold both the appointments of supreme commander and commander-in-chief, the other three being Field Marshals Phibun, Sarit and Thanom.[474] Speculation was rife on how long it would be before Arthit would seek to take power from Prem. Moving upwards behind him was General Chavalit, who became deputy chief-of-staff of the Army.

Whilst the period 1981 to 1984 had reflected strife between the military and the party politicians, the Prem-Arthit friction became more obvious by the middle of 1984. Lieut-General Pitchit Kullanavij led a group of senior officers in requesting the prime minister to extend Arthit's term of office by two years, a move which strengthened Arthit's challenge of Prem. In August, Pichit supported

---

[474] *Bangkok Post*, 23 July 1983

the application of the dismissed Young Turks for reinstatement in the Army, a move known to be contrary to the wishes of Prem as well as both Chavalit and Suchinda's Class 5 group. The Young Turks, not surprisingly, expressed support for an extension of Arthit's service, but in doing so, two of them managed to have themselves arrested for possession of lethal weapons. Pichit then tried to get through the National Assembly the constitutional amendment which it had previously rejected and which would have allowed serving officers to hold government posts. It was a way of expressing the military's strongly held view that it was the only institution which could produce capable leaders. In November 1984 Arthit used the medium of television for a blistering attack on the Prem government for its devaluation of the baht, and called for the move to be cancelled and for a Cabinet reshuffle. Prem, backed by the Palace, stood firm. Arthit relented but he had lost face by this unsuccessful forthright attack.[475]

Early in the morning of ninth of September 1985, there was a further attempt to overthrow the Prem government and again the principal conspirator was Colonel Manoon Roopkachorn. Aided by his brother, Wing Commander Manas, he succeeded in bringing about five hundred troops from the Fourth Cavalry Battalion and the Air Force security force on to the streets of Bangkok. For coups, big names are needed to support the claims, and this time it was former supreme commander and deputy prime minister, General Serm, together with General Yos Thephasdin and former prime minister, General Kriangsak. Later, they were to claim that they were only involved through coercion. It was indeed surprising to find men of such experience as Kriangsak and Serm apparently throwing in their lot with Manoon in such a hare-brained scheme.

The attempt was made when the prime minister was away in Indonesia and the commander-in-chief, General Arthit, was in France. There was no threat to the monarchy as the King and Queen and most of the Royal Family were at a Palace under the protection of the 4th Army. The Crown Prince was in Italy. Deputy commander-in-chief Thienchai and Army chief-of-staff Chavalit moved fast to mastermind a tactical response. In this they were helped by the fact that eleven of the thirteen divisions of the Army were commanded by Major-Gen Suchinda and his fellow Chulachomklao

---

[475] *The Military in Thai Politics 1981-86*; Suchit Bunbongkarn; pp41/3

Class 5 generals who, as a group, had openly stated their opposition to the use of the coup route as a means of solving national problems,[476] a democratic philosophy which they appear to have forgotten six years onwards. The prime minister was back in the country by the evening and General Arthit flew in the following morning. The attempt was lost within a little over twelve hours.

Manoon, who had been heavily involved in the 1981 "April Fools' Day" attempt, had been pardoned for his behaviour, but General Prem had refused to grant his request for a return to active service. Manoon had graduated from Chulachomklao Academy where he had been a father figure and a leading member of the volatile Class 7. He had previously commanded both the 4th Cavalry Regiment and concurrently the 4th Cavalry Battalion, this latter appointment giving him access to tanks in the Bangkok area. After the failed April 1981 coup he had fled the country and only returned when a Royal pardon was to be granted. He again came to public attention in September 1984 when he was taken into custody by the police for allegedly having been involved in a plot to assassinate General Prem, an allegation which was later extended to include as victims of the plot General Arthit and even the Queen. He had been freed on Arthit's intercession. He had returned to Thailand from a visit to America only a few days before the attempt, to lead officers who had previously served under him, presumably thinking that the absence from the country of both the prime minister and the commander-in-chief provided him with an ideal opportunity.

The plotters ran into trouble very early in their attempt. Whilst they easily captured Radio Thailand, they were thwarted as they moved to capture the pro-government 1st Army Division radio station. At this point, violence broke out with rebel tanks shelling the area of the station. Five people, including two foreign journalists, were killed and some fifty to sixty people injured. By midday, government forces had recaptured Radio Thailand, denying the rebels access to propaganda, and then turned the full force of the media back on them. An ultimatum to all rebels to lay down their arms by three o'clock that afternoon or face a court martial was accepted. Rebel troops surrendered to the 1st Army and by four o'clock Manoon and his brother were on the run.

---

[476] *Bangkok Post*; 28 September 1985

To avoid further bloodshed, Manoon was given safe passage to Singapore from where he moved on once more to Germany. Manas headed for a hideout on the Thai/Burma frontier and later for Burma. The three senior generals were not arrested but were put under voluntary house restraint. Added to their numbers the following morning were two Air Marshals. By sixteenth of September, warrants for a total of thirty-three coup suspects had been issued. The following day, twenty-five, including the former prime minister, Kriangsak, and General Serm, were charged with treason. Two weeks later arrests were numbered at thirty-nine, with ten still on the run.

The coup trial formally opened on twenty-fifth of October and all the defendants pleaded not guilty. A request for a secret trial was rejected by the court and early in January it started to hear evidence. The principal witness was Air Chief Marshal Praphan, who had virtually been dragged from his bed on the night of the coup. He had been taken to the headquarters of the rebels. He had met Manoon there and also noted that General Serm was in charge. General Kriangsak arrived later. Praphan had been held at rebel headquarters throughout the period of the rebellion. He had noted than none of the generals present had been held at gunpoint, and when the end came he had personally authorised a plane to take Manoon off to Singapore. It seemed as if the trial would be over at an early date but months later it was still drifting spasmodically through the court. A suggestion made towards the end of January of an amnesty for all concerned to clear the matter out of the way was rejected by the prime minister.[477]

If for some of the Class 7 Young Turks failure seemed an inevitable result of their ambitions, for one of their number came a moment of success. Chamlong Srimuang ran as an independent candidate for the post of Governor of Bangkok. A man of the highest integrity, a devout Buddhist, and a frugally-living vegetarian, his candidacy caught the imagination of the Bangkok voters. They gave him an overwhelming victory.

There were further Army requests for an extension of General Arthit's term of command but Prem was having none of it. On twenty-eighth of March 1986 he rejected the requests and on twenty-fifth of May, to settle the issue, he sacked Arthit as Army commander. Arthit retained the figurehead appointment of supreme

[477] *Bangkok Post*; 25 October 1985 to January 1986

commander of the Armed Forces, but he was cut off from his influential power base.

Prem's turned to his friend, General Chavalit, for support and he succeeded Arthit as Army commander-in-chief. In the August, Chavalit made a bid to unite factions within the Army. He took the surprising step of appointing former prime minister, Thanom, and his henchman, Praphat, as advisers. He then persuaded Prem to agree to the reinstatement of twenty-eight Young Turks, who had been dismissed from active service following the 1981 attempted coup.[478] Residual pockets of communist insurgents who came out of the jungle were pardoned, and the new Army commander sought to have them reintegrated into Thai society. He followed the earlier Prem policy of having them treated essentially as Thais, not as communist prisoners of war.

With success against Thai insurgents during Prem's term of office came the parallel pressure to introduce crop substitution to the hill-tribes and the surrendering Hmong. From the mid-1970s onwards, genuine efforts had been made to wean the hill-tribes from opium growing and with it the slash-and-burn cultivation. There was support of various United Nations agencies in addition to national development schemes. An initial problem arose in persuading people to grow in sufficient volume a fifty-cent commodity in place of a limited fifty-dollar commodity and to provide them with an assured market against competition from the lower lands.

Heavy subsidies were essential, some of which came from the government itself but more from the United Nations and American anti-narcotic agencies. Cash subsidies were of virtually no use and help was provided in the form of food, house-building materials, medicines, water and road infrastructure, seeds of fast-yielding crops, together with education for the young, and training in skills for the not-so-young. The mass surrender of Thai communists in 1982 was accompanied by a surrender of arms and stocks of opium in exchange for the help which would make life possible in the more difficult terrain. Opium production was not stopped completely. The hill-tribes

---

[478] *Bangkok Post*; 30 August 1986

were still permitted to grow sufficient for local medicinal purposes and to satisfy the older, incurable addicts.

King Bhumibol himself refused to punish the opium-growing hill-tribesmen as lawbreakers. Instead he was concerned to persuade them to grow alternative crops which could become more profitable. He has launched numerous projects in support. *"All the project can do is, not to stop, but to improve the situation,"* he has said. *"It is that, so that so many people here, many of them hill-tribes, they have friends, they have relations all over the route from Yunnan to Tibet and down to our country here. It's a long way and they walk. They have communications, very good communications. Apart from what you can see in the mountains, there is something you cannot see. It is the spirit of these people. They come and go and they say that there is the King's project. They are better than the information service of Bangkok... we have the opium or narcotics problem... it is only one aspect of the problem, or say the task we have. The other task is to give these people a better way of life."* [479]

The opium issue was not simple. One of the great advantages of an opium crop was that it did not need any sophisticated infrastructure. There were no roads, canneries or similar processing plants to prepare it for the market. Certainly its conversions to heroin or morphine base required a primitive processing hut, but the investment was in the chemist's skill and stocks of chemicals, not that of high, front-end finance or complex mechanical engineering. To critics of opium production, the Hmong have said, *"Opium does not go looking for money. Money comes looking for opium".* President Nixon declared that the only effective way to end heroin addiction was to end opium production and the growing of poppies. As late as 1992, at a narcotics conference in Texas, an American senator was arguing that the solution to the elimination of the drug problem on the streets of America was the eradication of the poppy crops in the Golden Triangle. Both were, of course, wrong. Demand will always create supply and if not among the Hmong and other hill-tribes, then elsewhere.

Local problems arose within the eco-system because many of the crops substituted in the higher lands needed a greater quantity of water than opium, and diversion of water to this end robbed farmlands in the

---

[479] *The Soul Of a Nation*; BBC post-production script, written Leo Aylen, produced by Bridget Winter; II pp50/55

lower valleys and plains. Some of the problems were not even merely local as the crop markets were international, bringing about the problems of prices, subsidies, and quotas. There was no future in pouring money into crop substitution projects and then denying the new producers the market for the output. Despite these very real problems, progress, if slow, was made as the falling output of opium from Thailand itself demonstrated.

Out of the interest in the welfare of the hill-tribes came a more general interest in the countryside and with that interest, the military grasped at new opportunities. It saw itself as the agency to provide assistance to the people, thus improving relationships with them and at the same time allowing the people to view the Army as its ally. It moved into rural road construction, water supply, crop improvement, education, and medical care. It was a policy of a government within a government. Some of the civilian élite saw it as occupying the military and keeping them out of politics.[480] They were wrong. This was itself high politics. Added to the training of National Defence Volunteers and of the Military Reservists for National Security, the Army was not only able to gain a wider band of support but it also had a captive audience for indoctrination in its own peculiar attitude to democracy.

Meanwhile, outside Thailand's borders, a third Indochinese war had been developing. It was essentially a war by proxy, limited in scope and inter-communistic, between USSR/Vietnam on the one side and China/Cambodia on the other. A North Vietnamese puppet government headed by Heng Samrin had taken power in Phnom Penh. The sympathy of ASEAN in general and Thailand in particular was with China and the Cambodians, although there were some strong reservations on recent government behaviour. America took a similar line. But it was the Thai government which had the problem.

Thailand's eastern and north-eastern border had been a continuing source of trouble to successive governments. The policy of the communist government of Laos in the mid-1980s of encouraging opium and heroin production bothered the Prem government. Whilst some of be product was exported from Hanoi, much of it still made its way out through Thailand. Added to that the Thai government was

[480] *The Military in Thai Politics 1981-86*; Suchit Bunbongkarn; pp49/51

already counting its refugee population in hundreds of thousands.[481] The escape across the borders of refugees from Cambodia and from Laos, the establishment of refugee camps, and the political hijacking of control of the camps by rebel forces was to go on for over a decade. The very presence of such camps, despite United Nations attempts at supervision, involved cross-border politics. An emerging nation does not necessarily look kindly upon refugees from its rule, particularly when they announce that they are fleeing from a repressive regime. In the first ten years of Pathet Lao government in Laos some ten per cent of the population fled the country, sparking retaliatory border raids by armed groups on camps or small illegal settlements. Thai villagers became involved and the Border Patrol Police were frequently called upon to repel such incursions. Complaints by Thailand to the United Nations were ineffective.[482] Limited incidents of this nature were of little importance in the catalogue of international troubles at that time.

Changes in the USSR brought a new policy for South-East Asia and reduced support from that nation for political adventures by Vietnam in Cambodia. Without the support of the USSR, Vietnam could no longer afford extravagant occupations and its troops were withdrawn to within its own borders over a period of time in the late 1980s. A new regime, which had itself at one time been part of the Khmer Rouge, took over government. Prince Norodom Sihanouk returned to join the fray. Thai support resulted in the outline of a four-part coalition rule which would permit a limited return of the Khmer Rouge. While Pol Pot, living in Thailand under the protection of the military and with the full knowledge of America, took no obvious part in this agreement, he was known to be in touch with the Khmer Rouge representatives. That America had, at that time *"publicly winked"* at China's support in exile for Pol Pot was disclosed by President Carter's security adviser.[483]

At Prem's instigation, ASEAN revised its approach and sought to end the backing by China of the Khmer Rouge. It also sought to end the interference in South-East Asia affairs in general, and in Cambodia in particular, by both China and the USSR. ASEAN had by

---

[481] *Bangkok Post*; 26 September 1987
[482] *Bangkok Post*; 17/19 June 1986
[483] American Presidential Advisor, Zbigniew Brzezinski, 1979, quoted by John Pilger, London *The Observer*; 6 October 1990

this time developed a firm policy of attempting to create within South-East Asia a neutral zone of peace, free of manipulation by major powers. To many in Thailand, peace would bring huge trade opportunities from which Thailand, or more specifically its entrepreneurial élite, would prosper.

The Thai elections of 1986 were notable for the large sums of money expended in pursuit of votes and thus power. The ultimate aim of many a Thai politician remained unchanged, that of a commercially attractive Cabinet post. Party financiers were particularly anxious to be appointed so that they first recouped their electoral outlay and then moved into profit. It was no wonder that military cliques held politicians in contempt and sought their own form of government. Unfortunately, with rare exceptions such as Prem himself, despite its frequent criticisms of the body politic, the Army was no better itself when opportunities were open to it. Following elections in 1986 there were soon allegations against ministers' activities, particularly aimed at those within the Chart Thai party. Communication, construction, port management, and logging contracts proved to be the principal targets, but the government survived votes of censure both in October 1986 and October 1987. Prem kept his distance from the sparring politicians but his reluctance to continue in office became more and more apparent. By June 1988, a major re-shuffle seemed inevitable.

General Prem had other ideas. Instead of a reshuffle he dissolved the government and resigned, thus forcing another election. With that election in July 1988 and with the Chart Thai party again being the leading party, a Chatichai-led coalition, with Prem as the invited prime minister, seemed to be on the cards. On twenty-fifth of July, Chatichai declared that he had no wish to become premier and that he would serve under Prem. Prem declined and Chatichai was left to ride the tiger.

The end of Prem's period in office came unexpectedly to most people, including his successor. Prem had begun to look iike the permanent holder of the premiership, invited and not elected, as he chose not to dabble in politics. In 1983 he had declared his intention to stand down, only to be renominated. When he was persuaded to take up the reins of office in 1986, it was known that he wished to be in office for the auspicious occasions of the King's sixtieth birthday, the all-important completion of the sacred Fifth Cycle, in December 1987. It was hoped that he might also stay in post for the celebrations which would take place when King Bhumibol became the country's longest serving monarch in July 1988. That achieved, the unelected General Prem, always a King's man, refused an invitation to be prime minister for a fourth term.

It was a shrewd move. Not only was he walking away from the task which from time to time he had expressly stated that he disliked, but he sensed that the populace was getting restless with a non-elected head of state. There were also threats of personal attacks upon him in the National Assembly by discontented members but he would have ridden them out, had he so chosen. In simple terms, Prem knew that he had had enough and left office while still at a peak of a highly successful career. He may also have seen a number of problems looming with Chatichai's Chart Thai party being the strongest after the election. Chart Thai had a reputation for the protection of vested interests and was reputed to have spent heavily during the election campaign to secure its strong representation. The money would have to be recouped, and ministerial positions leading to the award of government contracts to related or friendly companies might be the recognised route. Even under Prem's leadership, Chart Thai party ministers had been involved in controversial agreements.

Despite this, Prem's had been a remarkably successful premiership and although undemocratically appointed himself, he promoted democratic thinking and behavioural patterns. Indeed, in his consideration of the Thai people in general, he has been the country's most distinguished 'Thai-style' democrat. Much of the administration of his policies was taken away from politicians and implemented through his group of non-partisan technocrats, dedicated to their country's reputation and overall success. General Prem inspired the respect of the King he loyally served, the majority of the ministers who served him, and of the military. He was fortunate in the latter years of his rule in having General Chavalit Yongchaiyudh as his Army commander-in-chief, a man who also thought that the time had come for democracy in Thailand. It is also fair to say that despite his later apparent attempt to dominate the government, General Arthit served Prem well in the first few years of the premiership. For a period of time the all-pervasive influence of a domineering military had been diluted and Thailand prospered. Foreign investment increased rapidly. The threat of communism was removed. All was not as calm as it appeared on the surface but Prem had a knack of avoiding some of the more difficult issues that confronted his country and his administration. On a number of occasions he was seen to adopt an old-fashioned British tactic of 'when in doubt, appoint a committee'. His principal critic, M. R. Kukrit, has referred to the Prem era as one not of stability but of stagnation. But if much was left undone, much was achieved. His outstanding achievement was probably his carefully thought out approach to the insurgency problem. The effect of his policies upon the insurgents was substantial and their estimated strength fell from a peak of eleven thousand in 1979 to less than two thousand by 1984.[484] The back of the insurgency threat was broken by Prem within the first four years of his premiership and was virtually eliminated before he left office. The Prem era will also be remembered for the increasing prosperity of a wide section of the growing urban commercial class, bringing with it a vast increase in foreign-financed projects of peaceful intent. However, in his last year in office, the newly-established middle class, the labour groups, and the students were all becoming restless. If he had accepted the further term, he would no doubt have brought many problems upon himself.

It is interesting to consider briefly General Prem's political stature in relation to that of Field Marshals Phibun, Sarit, and Thanom. Each was involved in a different stage of the evolution of post-Second World War Thailand. Each played an important role but in an entirely different way.

All were dedicated nationalists. Field Marshal Phibun leaves the foreign observer primarily with an impression of adroitness, in the manner he preserved his personal power by riding his two tigers; ruthlessness, in relation to those royalists who crossed his path; intimidation, of the Chinese community; and of weakness, in allowing his regime to be dominated by men of greed. Sarit was sufficiently ruthless in his personal handling of power to avoid political weakness and had no need for adroit handling of subordinates. He did much to modernise the Thai forces and, importantly, to bring the monarchy to

---

[484] *From Armed Suppression to Political Offensive*; Chai-Anan Samudavanija; pp195/216

the fore. But he falls below the standards of greatness because of his personal greed and moral indiscretions. Thanom was strong enough to extend the Sarit regime for almost a decade. He took full advantage of the American need for bases to pursue its wars, both official and unofficial, and some elements within Thailand benefited substantially from the flood of dollars which became available. On the other hand, his weakness in failing to control the excesses of his immediate subordinates ensured that only few of the nation's rapidly growing population shared in the new wealth. This, in part, allowed communism to take a strong hold in the rural areas: savagery was the principal weapon of response.

Prem had the advantage that the American wars in South-East Asia had been terminated and that the sad errors of those wars had come to light before he took office. He had a better understanding of the communist insurgency threat than any other Thai leader and was capable of dealing with it. His period of office was several years after the student uprisings when Thailand had witnessed the first fragile shoots of democracy. A discrete and private man, he was held in high regard as a 'soldiers' soldier' and for his personal integrity. He became the paradox of an unelected democrat, indispensable to the politicians of the day but never seeking office. Prem's method of enforcement of policy was entirely different from that of Phibun, Sarit, and Thanom. He was firm but tolerant, leading from the front to deal with problems, even if more slowly than some might have wished. Like Sarit, he was a 'King's man' but to Prem the leadership of the King was always paramount. Like Sarit again, he did not allow his subordinates to get out of hand. He did more to contain the drug trade than any of the other three, and although unable to defeat it, he made substantial progress in limiting its effect on a more stable and prosperous nation. Future analysts of Thai history are likely to review him kindly.

How wise is the man who knows when enough is enough. Edmund Burke has said that an individual who is intoxicated with power can never abandon it. That intoxication may well be a recognisable trait in others, but Prem knew and understood the limitations of political power. At the end of July 1988, General Prem Tinsulanonda announced his firm intention to quit — and quit he did. A grateful King appointed him to his own Council and bestowed upon him The Ancient Auspicious Order of the Nine Gems.

CHAPTER TWELVE
Exit the Kuomintang, Enter Khun Sa

With the ageing of the KMT 'lost army', the way was open for enterprising Shan groups to step in to satisfy the market for opium and its derivatives. Some of the groups had formal origins founded on a search for freedom from the cruel oppression of the Burmans to whom Britain had handed over its former colony. Among them were the Shan State Army and the Shan United Revolutionary Army, but more important were the Communist Party of Burma and the Shan United Army. Each had evolved during the years which followed the Shan uprising of 1959 and the continuing conflict with Rangoon. The emergence of new leaders was unintentionally assisted by the government itself with the establishment over the period 1963 to 1973 of the local defence forces — the Ka Kwe Ye. The government did not pay these forces but permitted them to move opium freely along government routes. Some concentrated on working closely with the KMT troops while others chose to fight the KMT for control of the trails through the mountains and with that control, the free movement of opium.

The Shan State Army was formed by the Mahavedi of Yawnghwe, the widow of the first Union President of Burma. Its army chief-of-staff was Bo Moherng and its chief-of-operations, Bo Gunzate, a skilled guerilla tactician and strict disciplinarian. Its origins were in the dissident students of Rangoon University, and its formation owed much to patriotic idealism. It developed to a force of more than four thousand at its peak and from 1969 to 1972 Chao Tzang Yawnghwe, the son of the Mahavedi, was its commander. In 1975 there was a brief honeymoon between the Shan State Army and the Communist Party of Burma, but this pragmatic affiliation clashed with the idealism of the State Army's beginnings and many of the original student members defected. In 1978 the State Army broke away from the communist core and re-established itself under one of its founder members, but it was no longer a force of great importance.

Moherng had not trusted the student affiliation and in 1968, with the support of General Li Wen-huan of the KMT 3rd Army, he had formed the Shan United Revolutionary Army, later renamed the Tai Revolutionary Army. The association with the KMT was unlikely to

Prime Minister M.R. Kukrit Pramoj.
(The Nation)

Prime Minister General Prem Tinsulanonda.
(The Nation)

Prime Minister General Chatichai Choonhavan.
(The Nation)

Student leader Thirayuth Boonmi.
(The Nation)

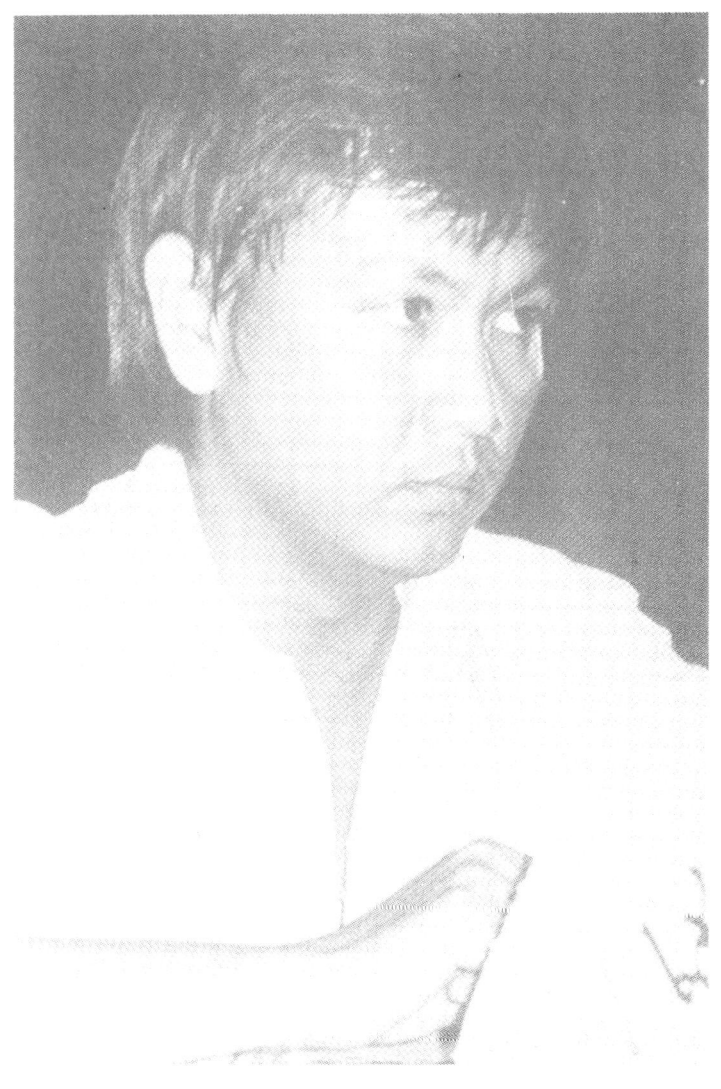

Student leader Seksan Prasertkul.
(The Nation)

Student leader Chiranand Pitpreecha.
(The Nation)

Drug warload - or Shan patriot - Khun Sa (Chang Shee-fu).
(The Nation)

Gathering opium.
(The Nation)

last as Moherng had been a 'white flag' communist. Gunzate, being part Chinese, enjoyed the special confidence of General Li. He moved to Moherng's new formation, became its vice-president with overall command of troops, and consolidated a position on the Thai border.[485]

Moherng then distanced himself from Li Wen-huan, declared himself to be against narcotics and sought to become prime minister-designate of a Shan government-in-exile. By 1982 his Shan United Revolutionary Army had moved to Chiang Dao on the Thai-Burmese border, and although its strength was estimated at between only one thousand five hundred and two thousand, it remained an important supplier of opium to the KMT 3rd Army, despite Moherng's declaration of rejection.

Almost from the outset of Burma's independence the role of the Burmese communists was that of insurgency supported from the early 1950s by Mao's China. By the early 1970s the communists had placed themselves along the Shan-China border areas, a position which gave them easy liaison with the new Chinese government. By their occupation of these areas they forced the KMT troops south towards Thailand, and acquired good poppy-growing country for themselves.

Chang Shee-fu was born in 1932 in Muang Yai in the northern Shan States, the son of a Chinese Haw father and a Shan mother. In the latter part of the 1950s Chang Shee-fu — or Khun Sa as he is more usually called in Thailand — became part of the evolving local defence force. By 1963 he was head of the Loimaw Ka Kwa Ye and had started trafficking in opium. With Ne Win's expansion of his brutal regime bringing about the collapse of the economy, Khun Sa turned against the Burmese. In 1964 he set up the Anti-Socialist United Army, which eventually merged into the Shan United Army. His first group consisted of about eight hundred men, well trained and well disciplined. He established a reputation for ruthlessness and armed his unit by trading opium for guns in Thailand. Where essentially the law of the jungle prevailed, he gained respect from the wilder elements in the mountains. He increased the value of his product by setting up a small refinery and processed raw opium into morphine bricks.

[485] The Shan of Burma, Chao Tzang Yawnghwe; pp131, 172 and 209

His first alliance in 1964 was with the independent Burmese guerilla leader, Bo Deving, but this soon ended in a violent quarrel. In 1965, Sa turned once more to the Burmese Army. With its backing and also with the use of its roads to move his opium, he fought to gain control of the area, destroying Bo Deving's force in the process. By the end of 1966 he was substantially increasing his shipments to Thailand and had expanded his force to about two thousand men. With the KMT controlling some ninety per cent of the traffic he was still only a small player in the game but his trading volume was sufficient to make the KMT sit up and take notice. Success eventually went to Khun Sa's head, and he was rash enough to take on the KMT troops openly with a view to ousting them from the cross-border trade. He bought up large quantities of opium in the northern Shan States and issued his own directives on tariffs which were to be paid by caravans, including those of the KMT, crossing 'his' territory.

The Laotian general, Ouane Rattikone, wanted about sixteen tonnes of opium, partly to pay for strengthening his military force but principally to increase his personal fortune. It was to be delivered safely to Bang Khwan, a small village on the Laos-Thailand border. That part of Laos was CIA country. It was partly from here that intelligence observation of southern China took place, much of it KMT-assisted, until 1971 when President Nixon put a stop to it. Inevitably, two-way movement across the border through Shan territory resulted in a number of opium deals, particularly to the advantage of Ouane Rattikone.

Shan- or KMT-protected caravans brought opium south, returning north with CIA supplies for its listening posts, without risking the hazards of such a journey for Air America helicopters. General Ouane ordered his sixteen tonnes from Khun Sa and Sa had to move the massive caravan that such a quantity entailed across territory which the KMT considered to be its own. Furthermore, if Khun Sa was successful, his profits would permit him to increase the size of his army to about three thousand men which, once drilled and disciplined, would rival the KMT armies. The KMT had a distinct advantage over the Shan, not merely in numbers and fire power but also because for some years previously it had established a string of listening posts of its own throughout Burma. Whilst these, together with those of the CIA, might contribute in some small way to the futile concept of the future invasion of southern China, their principal task was to monitor the activities of any possible rival trader and for the staff manning them to act as local opium brokers.

When in June 1967 Khun Sa's massive three-hundred-mule caravan started to collect its opium, it was soon under close scrutiny. The eventual confrontation was to be the pitched battle of Ban Khwan, some twenty miles north-west of the important Mekong river port of Ban Houei Sai. Here, in this otherwise unimportant logging village, the first major battle for supremacy was fought between Khun Sa's forces and the old KMT armies. At stake was the size of the share of the opium traffic. The caravan was commanded by Chang Chu Chuan, Khun Sa's chief-of-staff. Chang, although a native of Manchuria, looked upon himself as a Shan citizen and was totally loyal to Khun Sa. He had fought against the 3rd and 5th armies frequently during the 1950s. A thousand-strong, heavily armed force made up from both the 3rd and 5th KMT armies ambushed his mile-long caravan outside Kengtung. It was saved by his rearguard cover outflanking and attacking the ambush, allowing Chang and his column to cross the Mekong into Laos on fourteenth and fifteenth of July.

Moving into the village of Ban Khwan, the Shan force dug in and awaited another attack by the KMT. The villagers fled. On twenty-sixth of July the KMT main force arrived. So did a unit of the Lao Army which gave the KMT and the Shan orders to leave the country. The Shan, with custody of over five hundred thousand US dollars worth of opium, refused. The KMT, who needed to destroy the Shan, also refused. On twenty-ninth of July a heavy fire-power battle began. General Ouane now grabbed at a double bonus — to rid Laos of both intruders, even although he had invited one of them, and to get hold of the opium. He positioned a parachute battalion to block the route south. Then he sent in his light bombers to attack both forces simultaneously. Eventually, Khun Sa's force retreated and the survivors crossed the river Mekong back into Burma while the KMT force withdrew northwards, only to be cut off by other elements of the Laotian Army. Protracted negotiations resulted in the payment by the KMT to Laotian forces of a sum of money and the permitted withdrawal of the KMT into Thailand. To the victor went the spoils of war: General Ouane had the bulk of the opium without payment. It would be available for processing in the four or five refineries which he controlled in that part of Laos. The KMT returned to its hilltop retreats without more than a token attempt at disarmament by the Thai

Army. Over two hundred of the participants died in the battle for Ouane's opium.[486]

Whilst the battle of Ban Khwan was at first thought to be the end of Khun Sa, he rode his losses and set about attempting to unite a number of Ka Kwe Ye, with himself as their leader. This brought a determined and protracted effort against him by the Burmese government. The battle of Ban Khwan and the attempt at consolidation of the Ka Kwe Ye had also brought Khun Sa into conflict with the Kokang leader, Lo Hsin-han, an important opium supplier of the KMT. Lo was well connected with the Burmese Army and in the late 1960s, had fought a forty-day battle on behalf of that army against the communists in his own fiefdom. In 1968 a Hong Kong journalist travelling from Lashio to Tachilek in Lo Hsin-han's Landrover noted that whilst other cars were finely combed for all forms of contraband, Lo's Landrover sailed through the army checkpoints without any of the occupants even having to alight.[487]

When in 1971, Khun Sa was arrested and put into a Rangoon gaol, Lo became unofficial leader of all Shan Ka Kwe Ye. He was courted for a while by the Shan State Army with a view to helping it bring international attention to the plight of the Shan. The proposals, which included the termination of opium trading in the Shan States and working with the American Drug Enforcement Agency, came to nothing.

Lo Hsin-han's command was short lived. In 1973, he himself was 'snatched' by the Thai police from Shan territory and without bothering about such trifling details as an extradition order he was transferred to southern Burma and gaoled for seven years. His connections were sufficient to ensure that he was not charged with drug trafficking. There was also a fear that he might name names. While Lo was out of circulation, Khun Sa's soldiery took hostage two Russian doctors and in 1976 exchanged them for Khun Sa's freedom. The way was now clear again for Sa's re-emergence. Before long he was established with a force of some three thousand men in the village of Ban Hin Taek in Thailand's Chiang Rai province. It might be termed a 'fluid' occupation. Numbers rose and fell, and in 1978 Kriangsak ordered Khun Sa out of Thailand. The order was provoked

---

[486] *The Politics of Heroin*; Alfred McCoy; pp 295/7; also local journals July/August 1967

[487] *Far Eastern Economic Review*; 2 August 1990

by Sa writing to the newspaper *Thai Rath*, protesting that he was not an opium producer and that he merely taxed it as it passed through his territory.[488] Most of his force left for a while. Sa was back in occupation before the end of the year.

———

Over a long period, some elements of the Thai government, and particularly the military element, perceived the KMT armies as a barrier standing between Thailand and the possibility of an invading Chinese People's Liberation Army. There was, from time to time, political pressure to take action against them. Thai sovereignty was affronted by the fact that there was a heavily-armed, nomadic foreign army on its soil. There was also always the risk that the Chinese might use the KMT remnant as an excuse for an invasion of Thailand and with it gain access to the great rice bowl of the central plains.

The Army could of course have been used to remove the KMT by force, but this was not an option it relished, as the KMT, with nowhere else to go, was likely to be far more motivated than the Thai Army. It was more familiar with the terrain and was regarded as having developed into a competent fighting unit. Additionally, the large ethnic Chinese community in Thailand, which was only gradually changing its loyalties from Taipeh to Beijing, constituted a fifth-column threat.

In 1973/4, the Thai government was not too dismayed by the alien army's quiet occupation but saw no reason why it should not be made to sing for its supper. General Kriangsak Chomanan, then deputy chief-of-staff of the Thai Army, asked Tuan Shi-wen to use his KMT forces to attack a Thai communist settlement. The settlement was occupied in the main by Hmong tribesmen and located high up on Mount Hwamong in the Chiang Khong/Mae Sai area of Thailand. Kriangsak's deal was, essentially, that if the KMT were able to rid Thailand of this communist settlement, the KMT would be offered a permanent position of an armed auxiliary force and thus allowed to keep its weapons. The deal was accepted and the attack was successful. A mixed force of six hundred men from the 3rd and 5th Armies, under be command of General Tuan Shi-wen of the 3rd, surmounted the considerable problems of the terrain, took the

———

[488] *Far Eastern Economic Review*; 28 April 1978

settlement, and occupied it.[489] Tuan Shi-wen was decorated by the King of Thailand for his loyal services and the combined 3rd and 5th Armies were redesignated as the North Thailand Border Region People's Self-Defence Force with Tuan Shi-wen as its commander and Li Wen-huan as its deputy commander. It had an authorised establishment of one thousand five hundred armed men but there was an important proviso. Arms were only to be issued to the soldiery when authorised by the Thai government. Names die hard. The 3rd and 5th Armies were still so structured and the Thais still cheerfully referred to them as the 93rd Division.

By the 1980s, the original KMT soldiers had grown old. A second generation of generals now commanded the remnants which were integrated into the Border Region People's Self-Defence Force. General Tuan Shi-wen died in 1980 and Li Wen-huan was both old and sick. Thai communist insurgents had firmly established themselves at Mount Khaoya, an inaccessible jungle mountain near to Phitsanulok and overlooking the main west–east arterial road. In February 1981, the Thai government called on the Border Region People's Self-Defence Force to support the Thai Black Panthers, considered in Thailand to be the equivalent of the British SAS, to attack the stronghold which up to that time had been thought to be impregnable. The deputy commander and leader was General Yang Weigang, who as a junior commander had hidden the weapons at the Mae Salong surrender. After a sharp but bitter battle he dislodged the communist forces and occupied the mountain.[490] The KMT was not yet an entirely spent force.

Wishing to avoid offending the government of Burma, China had over the years become unwilling to provide the Communist Party of Burma with the arms and supplies that the latter considered it needed. The communists had turned to the control of opium growing in the area of Burma which they occupied and by the early 1980s were the principal opium growers within the so-called 'Golden Triangle'. The amount of available opium was rising. The crop harvested in the Triangle in 1981 was estimated at six hundred tonnes and the 1982 crop at least seven hundred tonnes, of which only about forty were grown in Thailand. The Burmese communists sold the opium to the Khun Sa's Shan United Army which provided and escorted the

---

[489] *Golden Triangle: Frontier and Wilderness*; Kuo Yi-tung; pp146/7
[490] *Golden Triangle: Frontier and Wilderness*; Kuo Yi-tung; p154

transport and controlled the refineries for processing either to morphine or heroin. It also negotiated the market for disposal of the end product. As the communists were using the arms purchased with the opium revenue against the Rangoon government, they were in practice relieving pressure which the government might otherwise have applied against the Sa and his army. There being no ideological compatibility between the Shan United Army and the communists, the whole of the production, processing, transportation, and disposal was a matter of commercial dealing, thus allowing others to join in from time to time.

Despite Kriangsak's 1978 order, the Shan maintained its foothold in Thailand at the village of Ban Hin Taek which it developed into *"a bustling drug-running centre"*.[491] Ban Hin Taek was far superior to the average Thai village. The old shacks had been removed and new structures built of concrete. It had running water and electricity and a hundred-bed hospital. Above all, it was a prosperous community. Its revenue came not only from opium smuggling but also from its local control of the movement of jade and minerals. A tax or tariff was exacted on the movement of commodities through the wide area of Khun Sa's operations. Other revenue was derived from heroin production in a number of small processing units across the nearby border with Burma. About seventy per cent of the processed output of the Triangle came from these units. The Prem government gave the impression at first of being fairly relaxed about how the Shan behaved, provided they kept their activities out of Thai territory. It was more concerned with the expansion of the control of the Burmese communists who had spread themselves from the Chinese border southwards towards the Thai border, bringing with them the risk, in the late 1970s and early 1980s, of linkage with Thailand's own communist insurgents. That attitude was soon to change.

In mid-January 1982 reports reached the Thai government of an unusually large opium caravan making its way south through the Shan States into Thailand towards the stronghold of Ban Hin Taek. Intelligence reports indicated that the caravan was made up of at least two hundred mules protected by some three thousand Shan United

---

[491] Thailand Narcotics Bureau Annual Report 1991; extracts from Narcotics Suppression Bureau, Bangkok, 30 November 1993

Army men and that it was being led by Chang Shee-fu, Khun Sa, himself. At the direction of the prime minister, interception was mounted on twenty-fifth of January by a Thai force of some one thousand Border Patrol Police supported by ten counter-insurgency planes and ten helicopters. Local hospitals were alerted for reception of the wounded.

Ban Hin Taek was stormed and a small number of Shan troops killed or captured but neither Khun Sa nor his chief-of-staff, Chang Chu Chuan, were taken. The Shan army withdrew the bulk of its support group to a new position some six kilometres away and throughout the second day of the battle there was skirmishing. The greater familiarity of the Shan United Army with the terrain enabled it to minimise the effect of bombing and strafing, but nevertheless there surfaced a request for talks with the Thai government with the usual statement that all that Khun Sa sought was the independence of the Shan States from Rangoon control. In Sa's rear a Burmese force, operating in the area primarily in search of poppy harvesters, moved to cut off his retreat across its border. By the end of the third day there was fighting on both sides of the border. Soldiers from the Thai Army were brought into support the Border Patrol Police. Khun Sa's Shans made a diversionary raid, storming the police station at the Thai border town of Mae Sai. They also set up road blocks on a main road, destroying vehicles and robbing civilians. A number of foreign tourists rafting along the Mae Kok river were seized.

The prime minister was furious at the activities in the north, branding Khun Sa as a common international criminal, a threat to Thai society which would deteriorate under the danger of narcotics, and as an affront to national sovereignty and dignity. American civilians were evacuated south from the Chiang Mai and Chiang Rai districts. The director of Army operations, Major-General Chavalit Yongchaiyudh, moved north to co-ordinate attacks on Khun Sa, whose army had been reinforced by the Shan State Army. Thai attacks forced the Shan northwards.

The government was determined that on this occasion the village of Ban Hin Taek, the bulk of which had been destroyed by the armoured cars and grenade launchers of the Border Patrol Police, was not going to be re-established as a Shan base. It commenced an immediate resettlement plan with Thai villagers, some of whom were occupants of the village before being driven out by the Shan. Other civilians,

Shan and Haw, who had lived in the village under the domination of Khun Sa's men also returned. Two battalions of Thai troops moved in to convert the village to an Army strong point. A closer control was instituted on the movement of opium-associated chemicals, particularly of the essential acetic anhydride. The prime minister, General Prem, and his Army commander, General Arthit, arrived to reassure the inhabitants that the Shan had been driven out for good. The name of the village was changed and peace returned to the area.

The battle for Ban Hin Taek was an important stepping stone in the implementation of Prem's policy. The action had been mounted by the Thai government of its own volition, not under any specific pressure from America. Contrary to the policies of its predecessors, the Prem government had shown that it was no longer prepared to tolerate the lax situation which had prevailed in the northern mountains throughout much of the post-war period. The firmer policy did not in itself point to the end of the movement of opium across its border, nor even to the demise of Khun Sa.

Khun Sa saw Ban Hin Taek from a different point of view. He claimed that the initiation of the attack was prompted by the American Drug Enforcement Agency, not the Thai government, and that the attack had not been pressed home. He described it as a fiasco.[492] However, he now needed a new base, and in the weeks that followed his removal from Ban Hin Taek the Shan United Army began to penetrate the cross-border area of the Doi Lang mountain. Matters came to a head in the last week of July 1982 when a Shan force of some eight hundred men armed with mortars and 75mm guns and, supported on this occasion by a number of KMT soldiers, seized the stronghold of the communist-backed Wa National Army on the Burmese side of the mountain. Had he remained on the Burmese side Khun Sa would not have invited the attention of the Thai armed forces, but by October his troops were seen on the Thai side of the mountain. A small heroin refinery and tax post had been established. Thai border police and troops, supported by aircraft and with the Thai Army commander-in-chief, General Arthit, in close command, attacked the area and destroyed the new positions.[493]

In February 1983 the Thai government had a separate but minor success when a Lahu force which had settled around the border village

---

[492] *New Straits Times*; interview by Kim Gooi; 27 January 1986
[493] *Bangkok Post*; 27/29 July 1982

of Ban Muang Na, ingratiated itself by tipping off the police about the movements of a notorious heroin refiner and dealer, Lao Su. It was a small force which had earlier enjoyed support from Taiwan for its intelligence gathering, but when this ceased, so did funds. Later it allied itself with the Shan State Army and then, when its base at Doi Lang was taken over by Khun Sa after the battle of Ban Hin Taek, it allied itself to Sa and his Shan United Army before it moved on again. Lao Su, a Chinese Haw, had been sentenced to death *in absentia* for trafficking in heroin, morphine, and opium. He had been arrested in August 1977 but in October had walked free from a Bangkok hospital. As a heroin caravan under his command moved out of Burma through the dense jungles around Ban Muang-Na it was ambushed by the Border Patrol Police. Lao Su was killed in the battle which ensued.[494]

No such misfortune befell Khun Sa, whose Shan United Army went from strength to strength. With previous operations principally in the eastern Shan States, he began in 1983 to beef-up his representation in the mountains across the border from Mae Hong Son, which had previously been the recognised territory of the Shan State Army. He also moved another contingent to put pressure on Moherng's Shan United Revolutionary Army. With greater exposure along the Thai-Shan border area, he once more attempted to pose as a Shan nationalist whose primary concern was the freedom of his country from the oppression of the Burmans. It was to little purpose. He lacked credibility and was almost universally looked upon as a drug-running adventurer, commanding a well-disciplined, heavily armed force. In the following months his army came under attack from a number of sources. The Burmese Army attempted to remove him from its side of Doi Lang while the Thai police attacked the south of the area. Elements of the Burmese communist party also ambushed a Khun Sa patrol as each faction vied to control trafficking areas.[495]

The following year, matters between the Prem government and the KMT remnant came to a head. The last of the older generation of warlords, the sixty-seven-year-old Li Wen-huan was a sick man. From the early 1980s, Li had eased himself out of the trade, which was becoming more competitive with the advance of the forces of both his

---

[494] *The Shan of Burma*; Chao Tzang Yawnghwe; p180 and Thailand Narcotics Bureau Annual Report 1991; extracts from Narcotics Suppression Bureau, Bangkok, 30 November 1993

[495] Misc. *Bangkok Post*; August/September 1983

rival, Khun Sa, and of the communists. He settled down in multi-millionaire retirement, but not out of touch, in his fortress-like abode in Chiang Mai. He spent more time there than at his jungle headquarters at Tham Ngob. He had followed the government wishes in taking up Thai nationality under the name of Chai Chasiri. It did not protect him from his past.

On eleventh of March 1984, his house in Chiang Mai was attacked. About one hundred and fifty pounds of explosives in a pick-up truck, parked in the grounds of an adjoining property, wrecked a number of houses and killed his neighbour. Li himself was not injured. The principal suspect was Sa, but another possible reason lay in the jealousy surrounding the local KMT and Chinese Haw community. No one knew for certain how many of the old KMT were still active and how many were second generation. Local estimates put the total at about twelve thousand. Hong Kong sources, very interested in the settlement because of the heroin route through Kunming and the South China Sea to that colony for worldwide distribution, put the actual KMT fraternity at between seven and eight thousand.[496]

The attack in a Chiang Mai suburb was too much for the prime minister. On twelfth of June 1984, the Cabinet approved a crackdown on the local KMT and its 'state within a state'. Full Thai administration was to be imposed on KMT villages. Chinese language schools not conforming to the Thai curriculum were to be closed and all groups were to be disarmed. Theoretically they had already been disarmed over a decade earlier in accordance with the National Security Council ruling of twenty-fourth of June, as ratified by the Cabinet on sixth of October 1970. Thai nationality was to be withdrawn from any previously naturalised citizen guilty of engaging in acts detrimental to the Thai nation, including drug trafficking. Most-favoured-nation treatment of KMT citizens seeking naturalisation was to cease and non-naturalised citizens were to have their movements restricted.

The villages would be required to conform fully with Thai village administration and thus its citizens would be taxable. The attack on the schools was of particular significance as they were accepted as being some of the best in the land. School books were provided from

---

[496] *Bangkok Post*; 25 March, 15 July, and 4 August 1984; and *South China Morning Post*; 24 November 1988; and *The Shan of Burma*; Chao Tzang Yawnghwe; pp203/4

Taiwan and many Bangkok Chinese sent their children north for basic Chinese education as a pre-qualification for later studies in Taiwan itself. The change would result in Chinese being only the second language of choice, with limited time allowed for tuition.[497] Whilst the ruling was easy, the task of conversion met an economic problem. Teachers in the Chinese schools such as the popular boarding school at Mae Salong, the headquarters of the KMT 5th Army, spoke only Chinese and the village could not afford to pay Thai-speaking teachers to work in such a remote area. It would be solved in time. Implementation of the control over the KMT was put in the hands of a new 3rd Army Division named 'Force 327', which had been formed earlier that year (BE2527), charged with the containment of poppy growing. The two issues were seen to be linked. With forecasts of a bumper opium crop in the Triangle for the 1984/5 growing season, Force 327 had plans to wipe out large areas of poppy fields within its reach and would thus be in close contact with numerous KMT villages.

One of Prem's continuing problems was whom he was to trust to destroy poppy fields before they were cropped, rather than to arrive conveniently just after cropping and, for publicity purposes, merely burn already-milked poppies. As late as 1991, the head of Thai Office of Narcotics Control Board, Police Major-General Chavalit Yodmanee, admitted that he did not use local police in his attempted prevention of narcotics activity because some of the officers were involved in the business.[498] The police were not without reported successes and from time to time raided and destroyed heroin-producing plants along the border. Typical of such raids was that in early August 1988. The producing plant was known to have been operating from twenty-sixth of July and the names of the Chinese chemists were also known. A night march and a dawn attack by a force of a hundred police on the plant, which was protected by some thirty guards, resulted in the total destruction of the unit together with stoves, stocks of acetic anhydride, and even boiling opium. Despite a thirty-minute gun-fight, not one of the offenders was either killed or

[497] *Bangkok Post*; 13 and 24 June 1984
[498] *Bangkok Post*; 24 May 1991

captured.[499] A similar raid by the same command in November of that year involved a forty-strong police force, another night march and dawn raid, this time against a unit protected by twenty guards. It also resulted in the destruction of the unit, together with a hundred kilogrammes of semi-processed heroin, acetic anhydride, and ether. On this occasion the police had been searching for some months for the unit, which it knew to be financed by a KMT group. Despite a twenty-minute gunfight, again not one of the offenders was killed or captured.[500] It was this type of raid and result which led the Drug Enforcement Agency's Washington establishment to allege that the Thai Army was not keen to confront its problems. It was not a remark designed to commend itself to the Army commander, Chavalit, who was moved to say only that he saw no point in arguing with a Washington desk-bound expert on jungle warfare.

While Prem was containing, although not defeating, the opium activity within Thailand, the northern states of Burma were becoming even more active than before. With the removal of Khun Sa from Thai territory and his ousting of the Wa army from Doi Lang, northern Burma saw a whole series of shuffling and reshuffling of the pack of minority groups and armies and with them, an occasional visit from the Burmese Army. In mid-May 1984, Burmese troops in an anti-narcotics drive reached as far as one of Sa's temporary outposts and reported the destruction of five heroin factories, a claim that was regarded by embassies in Bangkok as wildly exaggerated. In March 1985, war in the Shan States flared up again, with an attack on Khun Sa by a combined force of the KMT and the Wa National Army, with Karen elements in support. The battle lasted throughout the month but at the end of the day, Sa was left as the master of the battlefield. A number of Wa tribesmen defected to him.[501]

In July 1986, Moherng decided on a publicity effort for his Tai Revolutionary Army and with a great display of morality, burned seventy kilogrammes of opium product which he had captured the previous month from a communist convoy. He then announced that he was finished with all drug trading and attempted to set himself up again as head of a free Shan state. The financing of his operations became a critical matter, but Moherng was confident he could achieve

[499] *Bangkok Post*; 6 August 1988
[500] *Bangkok Post*; 24 November 1988
[501] *New Straits Times* article by Kim Gooi; 29 January 1986

314

this by taxation of minerals or by developing Shan mineral wealth itself.

Moherng's alleged withdrawal from the opium trade coincided with Khun Sa's increasing influence along the Thai border from the Salween in the west to the eastern Shan States. He had recently solved a chemical supply problem: his new route for the important acetic anhydride was via India and he did not need Moherng. Despite that, in September 1984 Sa approached Moherng to form an alliance of Shan units. In view of his seniority, Moherng would be considered the head. In October there were premature reports of an agreement.[502] By March 1985, agreement had been reached to combine Moherng's Tai Revolutionary Army and Khun Sa's Shan United Army to give a force of about twenty to thirty thousand and to form the Muang Tai Army under Sa's leadership. It was heavily armed and was anxious to acquire Russian surface-to-air missiles.

Moherng was accepted as the President of the Tai Revolutionary Council but military power remained with Sa. Each maintained his own headquarters and close support staff. Thus there was established a force full of contradictions, the president of which declared himself as being against drugs and an army chief who, despite his own occasional claim that he was only a Shan freedom fighter, was recognised as the most important of all the drug warlords. The Muang Tai Army was also recognised under the title of the United Tai Liberation Army, the objective of which was to fight Ne Win's Burmese government. With that objective, it would require a continuing flow of arms and supplies. How were they to be bought? The answer lay in the usual practice of the mountains — opium.[503]

New leaders emerged in the mountains of Burma with an interest in the opium trade. Three brothers, Wei, formed a new group, associated with the communist elements of the Wa, to challenge the Muang Tai Army for opium control. The autumn of 1986 saw a combined force made up from the Wa National Army and communists. It attempted to oust Khun Sa from Doi Lang,[504] and by mid-February 1987 the attack had been developed into an all-out joint offensive. On eighteenth and nineteenth of February, Burmese troops overran outposts across the border from the Thai town of Mae Hong

[502] *Bangkok Post*; 21 October 1984
[503] Misc. *Bangkok Post*; December 1985
[504] *Bangkok Post*; 17 Sept; and *South China Morning Post*; 22 October 1986

Son. Over the next few days the Thai 3rd Army and Burmese Army forces moved against the Muang Tai Army on Doi Lang, resulting in claims that Khun Sa's army had been driven back further into Burma and nine of its outposts had been overrun. Large areas of poppy fields and a number of mobile heroin processing plants together with stocks of raw material and chemicals were also said to have been destroyed. In early March, Khun Sa again came under attack and was reported to be moving his processing plants into Laos on the banks of the Mekong. On nineteenth of September 1986 the Thai government issued a warrant for the arrest of Khun Sa on charges of *"participation in the killing of officials... in the exercise of duty"*.[505] In March 1987, Prem publicly declared his intention to drive Khun Sa out of Thailand permanently and to bring pressure to bear on trafficking through Thailand. He also intensified the Mekong river patrols in an attempt to prevent opium smuggling from Laos which, at the same time, limited illegal movement of an expanding production of Laotian marijuana.

Despite the various pressures upon him, Khun Sa continued not only to survive but also to prosper. Over the years there had been various rumours concerning his health and survival. At the beginning of 1984 and then in his fifty-first year it was reported that he was seriously addicted to heroin. In March his illness had become diabetes to the extent that he was bedridden. Reports of diabetes flourished again in October 1984 together with a suggestion that he had undergone plastic surgery. His death was reported in January 1985. Like rumours of Mark Twain's death, it was greatly exaggerated. In mid-1987 the freedom fighter-cum-drug warlord put on a major display at Homong for selected journalists. Moherng also attended to take the salute of new recruits to the Muang Tai Army.

Just as there were no absolute borders in this part of the world, so there were no absolute truths. The American Drug Enforcement Agency's view of Khun Sa was straight-forward. He was a villain, a drug warlord, and a Burmese rebel. He was a criminal to be brought to justice, although it was accepted that the removal of Sa would have only a temporary effect, if any, on the flow of opium and its derivatives from the area. Viewed from a neutral standpoint the Agency's whole task was futile. While there remains a demand for drugs, there will be a supply. The economics of supply and demand of

---

[505] Thailand Narcotics Bureau Annual Report 1991; extracts from Narcotics Suppression Bureau, Bangkok, 30 November 1993

commodities always lean to the demand side, and until that is eliminated or at least seriously restricted in the western world, Khun Sa and his eventual successors will flourish.

Khun Sa's argument was that he was the genuine freedom fighter for the Shan people, or the Tai as he frequently referred to them to curry favour south of his border. He argued that he was fighting communism in the guise of the Communist Party of Burma, which was true except that his motives were not those of ideology. He claimed that the KMT troops were the refiners of Burmese communist opium, and because they were permitted to live in Thailand and could not be attacked, he was made the scapegoat. He described the Drug Enforcement Agency as a bunch of foreigners, encouraging the rumours of his involvement to continue their own rich life-style of big cars and mistresses in Thailand. From time to time he proclaimed his freedom-fighting role and offered, at a suitable price, to co-operate with Washington to stamp out all drug-related activities in northern Burma.

In 1986, Washington went as far as sending a representative to discuss the subject of drug suppression but, after hearing Sa's Shan-freedom requests, the initiative faded and both the American and the Thailand government have chosen to reject Sa's approach.[506] The Burmese military junta took no steps to pick up such an offer and there may have been good financial reasons why it preferred the status quo.[507] American allegations that the junta itself was involved in developing outlets through Rangoon were vigorously denied, a denial which was contradicted by one of Khun Sa's deputies, Khuensai, who admitted that heroin was moved out through Rangoon because *"it is easy to bribe Burma officials"*.[508] To a visiting British journalist, Khun Sa vigorously argued his case as a freedom fighter against the repression of Ne Win and offered his views of the Drug Enforcement Agency, protesting, *"Nobody thinks about the human rights of my people"*.[509] The most well informed judge of the situation at the time was no doubt General Prem. The Thai prime minister's view had been

---

[506] Thai-Yunnan Project Newsletter dated Sept 1990 quoting interview with Khun Sa published in *Khaw Piset* of 30 July 1990

[507] *Asia* Magazine; 12 July 1987 and *New Straits Times*; interview by Kim Gooi; 28 January 1986

[508] *Bangkok Post*; 14 June 1990

[509] *London Observer*, article by Andrew Drummond, May 1988 and subsequent discussions

indicated as long ago as seventeenth of July 1980 by his indictment of Khun Sa on a number of counts including insurrection against the state, the possession of firearms without permission, and illegal immigration. On twenty-first July 1981 a reward of half a million baht (twenty thousand US dollars) was offered for the arrest of Khun Sa.[510]

In March 1989 came mutiny among the Burmese communists with the hard left leaders, mostly Burmans, fleeing to China, where they were put under house arrest. The uprising started with the local leader in the ethnically Chinese Kokang group and was followed by a rebellion of Wa hill-tribesmen who formed the bulk of the Communist Party's armed force. Parts of that force, one a Shan-dominated brigade and another a Chinese-led group acting independently, broke away. Pressure on the government of Burma was reduced, allowing it to work on the principle of divide and conquer. If that were to be successful, it would then be in a position to try to take on the Khun Sa's Muang Tai Army. It turned to the retired Kokang opium warlord, Lo Hsing-han, to try to bring the Kokang group on to the government side but the move had little effect. An alternative open at that time was for one or more of the defecting groups to join the National Democratic Front, a move which might have added substantially to that body's negotiating power with the military.[511] The Burmese military, however, had its own ideas for stifling the opposition of the Democratic Front.

With the advent of the Chatichai government there was great concern at the rate of deforestation in Thailand. The ecological disaster which was brewing was not, however, confined to vague national borders. The concern should have embraced the much wider area of Cambodia, northern Laos, and northern Burma. Thai home-based logging contracts were cancelled by the government and the companies forced to look beyond their borders for their raw material. There was substantial government interest in this decision as a number of its members had logging investments. Visits, both official and unofficial, were made to neighbouring Burma and new road patterns were to be observed. A major road had to be constructed into

[510] Thailand Narcotics Bureau Annual Report 1991; extracts from Narcotics Suppression Bureau; Bangkok; 30 November 1993
[511] *Far Eastern Economic Review*; 1 June 1989

the prolific forests of the Shan States and observers were not slow to comment that logs would be only one of the commodities likely to be passing down it.

The official contracts of the Thai logging companies for the rich hardwoods of Burma, particularly teak, were made with the Burmese government. On top of this, contractors found that they had to pay Khun Sa about one-third of the price of the timber for protection and as a tariff on its movement through his domain. Additionally, roads could not be constructed in Shan territory without money, labour, and protection. This was also supplied by Sa, who, apart from his taxation of the outgoing product, occasionally retained the road-making equipment.[512] In January 1990, a United Wa Army force overplayed its hand by attacking a Muang Tai Army post controlling a logging route. A Muang Tai force from Doi Lang and commanded by Sa's right-hand man, chased it into Thailand. Thai villagers, including KMT remnants, fled and Sa's army withdrew, leaving the Thai Border Patrol Police to remove the unwanted Wa.[513]

In February 1990, there were further outbreaks of fighting as Wa soldiers who had left the Burmese communist forces and were now commanded by one of the Wei brothers, Wei Chio Long, attempted to establish outposts in preparation for an attack on Doi Lang. Muang Tai forces attacked the self-styled United Wa State Army. Thai forces were put on the alert along the border to keep the fighting out of Thailand. The Wa had an early commercial success as the attack enabled them to move opium past the battle zone to the Laos border for processing. Skirmishes continued to be reported throughout the year and into 1991. In March of that year each of the two combatants continued to prophesy the defeat of the other. Sa was confident because he believed that the Wa lacked continuity in the supply of ammunition: his confidence was misplaced and the Wa were still battling on some two years later. According to the Wa they were able to buy supplies from the Burmese Army, which also obliged with an occasional air raid on the Muang Tai Army but not too close to Khun Sa's recently acquired surface-to-air missiles.

The Thai Army, fearing that the warring parties would move south over its border, joined in the fray. In late March and early April it pounded the southern areas of Doi Lang with mortars and helicopter

---

[512] *Bangkok Post*; 11 August 1989, 12 April 1990 and others
[513] *Bangkok Post*; 20/21 January 1990

gunships. It captured a number of mortar positions from each of the warring parties, pushing both of them well back into the Shan States. Sa meanwhile was at Homong, his personal base in a high valley, about sixteen kilometres from the Thai border. From this vantage point he was able to continue to control and tax the movement of jade, mined in the northern states of Burma, and the more recently developed logging activity.[514]

Khun Sa attempted a follow-up of the Washington 1986 contact by writing directly to the White House. (It was a tactic which he was to attempt again with the Clinton administration in a letter dated first of October 1993). His letter was timed to coincide with a visit of Prime Minister Chatichai in May 1990 and he offered drug suppression in exchange for the independence of the Shan States. There was no response either from Washington or Bangkok.[515]

Sa went ahead to strengthen his hold over the Shan States some months later by displacing Bo Moherng as president of the Tai Revolutionary Council in a bloodless coup, and in July Moherng died of cancer. One of Sa's uncles was moved into the senior post, thus in theory leaving Sa himself as only commander of the Muang Tai Army. The word 'revolutionary' was then removed from the title of the Council and eventually it became the Tai United Committee. In September 1991, Khun Sa took personal control of it and became its president.

While Sa remained the dominant force along the Thai-Shan border throughout the early 1990s, he was not entirely free from misfortune. Hong Kong was one of the principal outlets for opium, morphine, and heroin from South-East Asia and from there much of the product went onwards to America. In June 1990, four allegedly top men from his drug ring were arrested in a joint operation between the Hong Kong police and American and Thai narcotic agents. Among them were two of Sa's relatives, one of whom was known to be an operator in the Mae Sai district of Thailand while the other handled European marketing.[516] Hong Kong was undoubtedly more successful in its anti-drug activities than were governments in South-East Asia. Earlier, in the 1970s, it had some spectacular successes when in late

---

[514] Bangkok Post; 18/19 February 1990; and Bangkok Post Weekly, 5/12 April 1991
[515] Thai-Yunnan Project Newsletter dated September quoting interview with Khun Sa published in Khaw Piset of 30 July 1990
[516] Bangkok Post Weekly; 1 June 1990

1974 to early 1975 and again in mid-1976 the authorities made major gains against the trafficking rings . In 1974 the principal drug ring "godfather", Ng Sik-ho, was arrested and in May 1975 he was imprisoned for thirty years. Mid-1976 had seen the capture of large stocks of hard drugs.[517] Worse for Khun Sa was the collapse of the Bank of Credit and Commerce International. The Bank had a worldwide reputation of laundering drug money and when the Hong Kong branch was closed down by the government of that British colony on seventeenth of July 1991, Khun Sa was reputed to have lost several millions of dollars.[518] There was a further setback for him when another of his principal agents, Lin Chien Pang, was trapped by American Drug Enforcement Agency officials when he arrived in Thailand without papers on deportation from Malaysia. January 1993 saw Lin in a New York courtroom.[519]

Price figures for opium and heroin abound in various publications, but most of such figures are imprecise. One or two principles are certain. The growers in the mountains receive very little, but even with that, the amount still makes the crop more attractive to grow than many of the practical alternatives. A general figure for raw opium in the mountains in 1966/7 would have been about thirty-five to fifty US dollars per kilogramme. It stayed fairly constant into the early 1980s and by the end of the decade the growers were still only receiving about fifty dollars. Thus a family of four working members, growing and harvesting about twelve kilogrammes as a unit, would have received, over this period, an income of about four hundred to six hundred US dollars for each annual crop. In some cases the income recorded was as low as one hundred and twenty dollars. The period border price for a kilogramme of opium was about one hundred and fifty dollars while the Thai city price, Chiang Mai or Bangkok, was in the region of two hundred and fifty to three hundred. The price could be seriously affected by such problems as lack of rainfall at the right time.

Convoying opium had its own rates. For a medium-sized convoy of, say, eighty mules carrying about four thousand kilogrammes of

---

[517] *Far Eastern Economic Review*; 27 August 1976
[518] *Bangkok Post Weekly*; 26 July 1991
[519] *Bangkok Post Weekly;* 19 March 1993

raw opium, the convoy value might be about two hundred thousand US dollars. A small Ka Kwe Ye, or other escorting body, averaging two trips per year and without much leverage, would expect to be paid a fee equal to about ten per cent of the value of the opium handled, and for this it would provide collection and transportation, as well as the all-important route knowledge and armed escort. A strong Ka Kwe Ye, such as Kokang or a force such as the Muang Tai Army, would seek up to fifty per cent of the value. The return journey would bring additional revenue, depending on the value of the supplies or military hardware carried.[520]

The skills required to produce high-grade No. 4 heroin, about ninety to ninety-nine per cent pure, had reached the Thailand and Shan mountains by late 1969, brought about by the ever-increasing demand which arose from the build-up of American troops in Vietnam. Chinese master-chemists from Hong Kong were brought into the border areas. A Congressional report published in Washington in May 1971 quoted that forty thousand American troops in South-East Asia were hooked on heroin.[521] During 1970 the American authorities in Vietnam became more and more conscious of the growing addiction and by October of that year the heroin epidemic was fully developed, with seemingly unlimited supplies available from the Triangle. The problem was not merely one for America and its overseas troops. Over sixty per cent of heroin seized in Europe in the mid-to-late 1980s had its origins in Triangle opium.[522] The publicity given to the attempts, sometimes successful, of the Thai Border Police to shut down heroin processing plants only reflected a small part of the problem. The chemists moved on, the chemicals were re-routed and other processing plants established, frequently outside the permissible area of Thai operations.

The range of figures for heroin were wider than for opium because of market location, demand, and purity. As the amount of processing in the mountains or along the Mekong increased, it was the price of heroin that mattered. On its way to Bangkok and thence to the world markets, dilution would be common. Prices in the mid-1980s for

---

[520] *The Shan of Burma*; Chao Tzang Yawnghwe; pp128 and 150 and United Nations (London) library documents

[521] Congress Report quoted by London *Guardian* 25 May 1971

[522] *The Politics of Heroin*; Alfred W. McCoy; p245 and United Nations Commission on Narcotic Drugs — Report of the 33rd session, February 1989, Document E/1989/23 — E/UN.7/1989/21 p24

No. 4, the purest heroin, varied on the streets of New York and Amsterdam from as little as a hundred thousand to a hundred and twenty thousand dollars per kilogramme for diluted, and up to one million dollars for ninety per cent pure. It had not always been as high. The demand which had built up during the Vietnam war collapsed between 1976 and 1977. In April 1976 No. 4 heroin in Bangkok was priced at about two thousand five hundred dollars per kilogramme. One year later it was down to one thousand two hundred and fifty, although it was still fetching nearly nine thousand US dollars in Hong Kong that year and seventy-five thousand dollars in New York.[523] There was a fall in price in the second half of 1982 as a result of Khun Sa's increasing his production of heroin to pay for his losses after the battle of Ban Hin Taek, but trafficking groups then slowed down collection to force the price back up again. By the end of the 1980s it was reported at one million six hundred thousand dollars per kilogramme in New York, while the FBI put the figure at as high as two million six hundred thousand.[524] A 1993 New York street valuation by the American Drug Enforcement Agency put the figure as low as a hundred thousand dollars for Khun Sa's high-grade 'Double-U' Globe brand.[525]

Despite the volatility, at any of these prices the traffickers and middlemen were making a killing, in more ways than one.

With opium being a major source of revenue for a number of leading Thai citizens, and particularly some of the military and police, Thai production had been encouraged, and for many years remained high. Although it had been Sarit who had shut the opium dens, the personal wealth which opium brought made it a product under close control. The arrival of KMT forces had expanded opium production in Burma from about forty tonnes in 1945 to four hundred tonnes by 1962. From bases in Thailand the KMT continued to send caravans north to collect the opium harvest and to export it through friendly channels in Thailand. By 1970 the KMT caravans controlled almost thirty-three per cent of the world's total opium supply and had a

[523] Figures edited from *Far Eastern Economic Review*; 15 April 1977 and 14 September 1979 and United Nations library, London
[524] *Bangkok Post*, 23 February 1989
[525] US Drug Enforcement Administration conference at headquarters of Thai Narcotics Suppression Bureau on 4 August 1993 reported by Bangkok Post Weekly 13 August 1993

growing share in South-East Asia's heroin trade.[526] At the height of Thanom's power, in 1967, Thailand was producing about a hundred and forty to a hundred and fifty tonnes of opium. After the temporary democratic experiment of the mid-1970s and production running at between sixty an seventy tonnes, it was Thanin, in 1977, who began the all-out attack on opium growing. Thanin's bonfire of opium was far from popular with some of the military, and certainly highly unpopular with their KMT friends.

It was left for the arrival of Prem as prime minister, with the strong support of General Chavalit, to attack the northern poppy fields, a policy made easier by the increasing availability of helicopter gunships. The Thai output dropped dramatically. In 1981/2 the crop was down to little more than fifty tonnes while in the following years, it settled nearer to the thirty tonne mark. By the time General Prem decided that he had enough of office, opium production in Thailand itself was less than thirty tonnes. The problem remained of trafficking opium from other sources.

Demand will always bring forth supply. As the Thai opium production fell away, rapid increases in both Burma and Laos more than compensated for its decline. Through the decade of the 1980s the need for funds to purchase armaments for domination in Burma resulted in a massive increase in growing and production. The 1983/4 crop from that country alone was calculated at nearly four hundred and fifty tonnes, but even such a large output was dwarfed by the crops in the latter part of the decade which shot through the thousand-tonnes barrier. In Laos, the communist Pathet Lao government encouraged poppy growth to assist in developing its economy, a lesson the Lao had learned from the French colonialists some fifty years or more earlier. The 1987 and 1988 crops for the Triangle as a whole each reached one thousand to one thousand two hundred tonnes while over the period 1989 to 1991 the annual yield increased to between two thousand and two thousand four hundred, tonnes. Of these, the Thailand effective production remained steady at below thirty tonnes, reflecting an ever-improving eradication policy.[527] The 1992/3 estimates for the Triangle were slightly less at under two thousand tonnes of which about one thousand five hundred

---

[526] *The Politics of Heroin*; Alfred W. McCoy; p127
[527] From Statistics provided by Narcotics Suppression Board, Bangkok, 30 November 1993

were expected to come from Burma, twenty-five tonnes only from Thailand, and the remainder from Laos.[528]

For the KMT 'lost army', the 3rd and 5th and their various aliases (but which remained in the thoughts of many as the legendary 93rd), the road was reaching its end. By the late 1980s the aged army was a spent force, and whilst remnants of its second generation dabbled in lesser activities its primacy as an opium trafficker had been lost, outgunned and out-fought by the Shan, the Wa, and the Hmong. Most of its families had merged with the village life of northern Thailand. Some still clung to an old loyalty which could be seen in the structure and decoration of their family houses. But their day was past. It was no overnight demise and perhaps the passing might have been reflected in a First World War British marching song which declared that old soldiers never die, they only fade away.

Whether KMT soldiery or the Shan rule the opium trails, the problem will continue unchanged. The poppy remains a source of great wealth as well as of corruption, violence, degradation, and death, but the answer to the problem it brings is not to be found in the jungle mountains which form the foothills of the Himalayas. Neither will it be found within the ever-changing governments of Thailand. The problem is of consumer demand throughout the world, and so must be the solution.

---

[528] Thai Northern Control Office cited by Bangkok Post Weekly of 29 January 1993

CHAPTER THIRTEEN
A Struggle for Democracy

The election of twenty-fourth of July 1988 resulted in the Chart Thai under the leadership of Chatichai winning eighty-eight seats to become the most successful party. Chatichai saw the result as leading to a coalition with a party line-up of Social Action (forty-nine seats), Democrat (fifty-two), Rassadorn (twenty), and United Democratic (five), giving a total of two hundred and fourteen seats out of the three hundred and fifty-seven of the new Assembly, all under the premiership of General Prem. Samak and his Prachakorn Thai attempted to find an anti-Prem solution based on Social Action, Democrat, and General Arthit's small party with eighteen seats, thus excluding Chart Thai. It failed. Taking its first step on to the political scene the Palang Dharma party, led by the one-time Bangkok Governor, Chamlong, won fourteen seats. In the background Army commander-in-chief, General Chavalit, friend of the outgoing premier, waited and said nothing.

Misjudging Prem's positive intention to wash his hands both of politics and more so of politicians, Chatichai made a positive declaration that he did not want to take the premiership. He was convinced that a government led by himself would last no longer than three months, a belief that was echoed by many in Bangkok at that time. With Prem maintaining his refusal, Chatichai had no alternative but to form his own coalition. He then offered an opinion that he could form a coalition that would last the four-year term and that the military would not *"step over the boundary of their responsibility"*. While Army commander Chavalit offered the backing of the military, Armed Forces chief-of-staff, General Sunthorn, voiced a contrary opinion. He saw the change as unfortunate, a view that was supported by Samak and Arthit.

On fourth of August, Chatichai received the Royal Assent to his premiership, thus fulfilling the wish that his father, Field Marshal Phin, had expressed long before. His appointment was not so readily approved by his own son, Kraisak, to whom he had in the past referred as 'my socialist son'. Kraisak, a lecturer in political science at Kasetsart University, had totally disagreed with his father's association with rightist movements. He has accused his father of leaning too much towards the industrial aspects of national prosperity and discounting the human and environmental aspects. He wished that his father would put a brake on the accumulation of capital by the developing middle class who were *"riding in Mercedes Benzes at the expense of their workers"*.[529]

There were three notable features in the Chatichai Choohavan regime — its coming, its going, and the wealth alleged to have been accumulated by some of its Cabinet members.

The Choonhavan family, which heads the Soi Rajakru clan, is of Sino-Thai origins and has frequently been referred to as being very rich, although it is not the richest in the land. There are reported to be extensive commercial interests within the country and property interests in Switzerland. On his mother's side, Chatichai's origins go back to Hainan, and the commercial expertise of the family has been strongly Chinese-oriented. He has, since its inception in 1980, been a founder member and president of the Thai-Chinese Friendship Association. He was born on the fifth of April 1920, the only son of Phin Choonhavan. When he was a boy of twelve he was by his father's side at the time of the 1932 coup d'état. He held the horses and waited at table on the military as they trusted no one who was not 'one of us'. In later years, he looked back upon the 1932 group as split simply into two parties: the military, which maintained strong support for the continuance of the Royal Family, and the civilian, which he has described as *"leftist with a communist element led by Pridi"*.[530]

His military career had followed the traditional route into Chulachomklao Royal Military Academy from 1938 to 1940, and on completion he saw active service during the Second World War in Indochina and the Shan States. Subsequently he saw service in the Korean War. In 1953 he was appointed by Phibun to represent the Thai government on the United Nations' four-power commission to examine the KMT problem in Burma. That same year, when Prince Sihanouk of Cambodia, in exile, was treated *"with cold reserve"* by the Thai government, it was Chatichai who took him into his home. The two became firm personal friends.[531] He was soon a full colonel and in 1954 became the youngest acting Brigadier-General in the Thai

[529] *The Nation*; 28/29 July 1988
[530] Discussions with Major-General Chatichai Choonhavan, London; 1 July 1991
[531] Discussions with Major-General Chatichai Choonhavan, London; 1 July 1991

Army, a situation which cannot have been other than helped by the fact that his father was a serving field-marshal and the commander-in-chief. He became personal chief-of-staff to Prime Minister Phibun. There were visits to China where he had the delicate task of moving Thailand more into line with the *de facto* situation of the government of China. Here his Hainan ancestry and the family friendship with Chou En-lai stood him in good stead.

He was assistant commandant of the Armoured School at the time of Sarit's coup and from there was virtually exiled on Foreign Office overseas appointments. He has himself described his position as that of a *'circumstantial ambassador'* [532] and it was not until 1972 that Thanom brought him back as deputy minister of foreign affairs, a post which he also held within the Sanya government.

It was during the time of the latter appointment, on twenty-ninth of December 1973, that there was a dramatic interlude in Bangkok, removed from the everyday troubles of South-East Asia. The Palestinian "Black September" terrorist movement captured the Israeli Embassy in Bangkok. They took six hostages. Chatichai attempted to negotiate a bloodless settlement and with it the release of all hostages. He submitted himself as hostage in exchange for the Israelis and was held until a final solution was negotiated. It was an act of great personal courage and one which fortunately proved to be successful. He was promoted to Major-General and deservedly awarded the Bravery Medal.

January 1974 saw Chatichai off again to China to discuss with Chou En-lai the future development of trade between the countries and to develop a 'one-China' policy. The improvement in relations between China and Thailand owes more to his efforts than to those of anyone else. His friendship with the Chinese premier involved a strange mixture of political philosophies but its roots went much deeper into Chinese hospitality, not philosophy. In the days of the terrible hardships during the 'Long March', Chatichai's family had fed the starving marchers while at the same time totally disagreeing with their objectives. When M. R. Kukrit became prime minister in 1975, he chose Chatichai for his minister for foreign affairs.

Chatichai was now taking politics seriously, perhaps as a diversion from his first love, golf. In 1975, with his brother-in-law Pramarn, he formed the Chart Thai party and became MP for Nakhon Ratchasima,

---

[532] *Bangkok Post*; 29 July 1988

a constituency which has supported him up until the time of writing. With the M. R. Seni government in 1976 he became minister for industry, a post which suited his commercial instincts. His direct involvement in that October in the crushing of the Thammasat students is frequently questioned but it is an involvement that he, personally, has stoutly denied.[533] Being a good member of the Soi Rajakru clan he did not overlook his commercial interests and in 1977 he established a number of companies in the fields of investment, oil, and manufacturing under the 'Erawan' logo.

He was out of political office during the Thanin and Kriangsak governments, having declared himself to be unhappy with the way in which power had been attained and the damage which he believed had been done to Thailand's image abroad.[534] In March 1980 and until 1983 he was again minister of industry in the first three Prem Cabinets, and during that time he became leader of the Chart Thai party. With its strong representation in the coalition, that party leadership automatically brought him a post as a deputy prime minister in the last two Prem Cabinets, thus closely following in his father's political footsteps. He was a deputy prime minister and leader of the strongest party in July 1988 when Prem decided that enough was enough.

It was unlikely that Chatichai would have an easy run as prime minister. In recent years he had been looked upon as a playboy minister who enjoyed the good life. Granted, he had an easy-going style which would help him through difficult Cabinet sessions but he was neither held in such respect as General Prem nor wielded the clout of a one-time Army commander-in-chief. The coalition took several days to settle itself, with trade-offs and face-saving much to the fore. It looked unwieldy but the new prime minister was, however, helped in the early days by the knowledge that he had the support of both Air Chief Marshal Siddhi, who would be looked upon favourably by foreign governments, and of General Chavalit, who had promised to keep the Army out of politics, a promise which he kept until his retirement from his post. The critical factor was likely to be how the Chart Thai party ministers behaved themselves when in office. If they allowed their well-known commercial instincts to run

---

[533] Discussions with Major-General Chatichai Choonhavan, London; 1 July 1991
[534] Discussions with Major-General Chatichai Choonhavan, Bangkok; 26 November 1993

away with them, then the Chatichai premiership was likely to be short. *"I promise justice and fairness in my performance as prime minister to resolve business problems"*, the new prime minister declared.[535]

It was a critical time in the country's history. Its first attempts at democracy in the mid-1970s under elected prime ministers had failed. Once again the democratic theory was to be put to the test. Cabinet ministers and individual members of the Assembly, whether members of the coalition or fated to be cast in opposition, had new responsibilities and each would be required to accept those responsibilities in the searching light of modern media coverage. The Cabinet ministers in particular should have realised that in the modern world and with a better educated citizenry, there would be no place for the blatant corruption of the pre-Prem years.

A slight confusion arose within his first forty-eight hours of office with the arrival in Bangkok of the British prime minister, Margaret Thatcher. As she was not a lady to be put off lightly, Chatichai dodged the onerous task of discussions with her by delaying the announcement of his Cabinet and persuading Prem to conduct her visits. The delay was not solely due to her visit. A complex coalition government of the brand that Chatichai was forced to make to get the backing of the Assembly took almost two weeks of horse-trading. Not all the political parties could be satisfied, and above all he had to look after his own Chart Thai interests first, whatever the public perception of some of its members. Despite criticisms which had previously been made over questionable business-related contracts, the party was allocated posts which gave it a strong grip on government affairs.

There was little optimism that the Chatichai government would survive more than a honeymoon period. Public criticism of the choices made by the new prime minister was swift. Within Thailand came the comment: *"Judging by their past performance, certain new Cabinet members appear to fall short of the rigorously high standards the public has a right to expect of them. This raises the question of just how much hope it is realistic to place in the new administration."* Informed Hong Kong published comment was no better. Having suggested that there was little inspiration in the choice of Cabinet

---

[535] *The Nation*; 5 August 1988

members and despite noting the call of the military and the Thai business élite to give the government a chance to prove its worth, it went on, *"Little regard was given to competence or qualifications in choosing the Cabinet. Instead, influential personalities and wealthy party sponsors were named to several important posts. Among them were some veteran politicians with controversial past records. "* [536]

A far from hopeful early sign was a declaration by Chatichai to restrict the activities of the National Economic and Social Development Board and to replace it by a think-tank of his own creation. This was formed from a number of bright young men, including his own son, Kraisak. Many were creative thinkers and were appointed to give advice directly to the prime minister, an arrangement which was predestined to bring the group into conflict with appointed heads of ministries.

He resolved the outstanding problem of the accused officers in the 1985 rebellion, including Kriangsak, Serm, and Manoon, by providing for a general amnesty for all political prisoners. The amnesty brought about the release of communists as well as generals.

The new prime minister's views on Indochina were, however, full of hope. One of his earliest comments after he had been formally appointed was that he intended to *"turn Indochina from a battleground into a trading market".* [537] Any worthy contribution he could have made to such a cause would have been welcomed almost worldwide. When the time came to put such a policy into practice, questions were raised as to who primarily benefited. Whilst some progress was made in private deals within the Laos and north-east Thailand orbit, there was a major stumbling block to any progress with Cambodia: it was Washington. America had been humiliated by its defeat by the peasants of Vietnam and it had neither forgotten nor forgiven, despite public utterances. The fact that it was the hated Vietnamese who freed their fellow peasants of Cambodia from the horrors of the Pol Pot regime was treated as almost unforgivable. The Khmer Rouge was given discreet American support, using the Thai military, as had become customary practice. Some eighty-five million US dollars has been admitted as the degree of monetary support between 1980 and 1986, with Washington operating through its 'Kampuchean Emergency Group', an alleged humanitarian agency which was placed in the

---

[536] *Far Eastern Economic Review*; 18 August 1988
[537] *Far Eastern Economic Review*; 18 August 1988

American embassy in Bangkok. This group overtly was distributing aid to the refugee camps along the Thai border, but covertly was ensuring that the aid went through the Khmer Rouge-dominated camps to their active bases. Some twelve million dollars of food was moved on the directions of Washington, through the Thai Army to the Khmers, for the benefit of some twenty thousand or more guerillas. Some fifty CIA agents were at one time employed in running the support operation from Thailand. Throughout the 1980s, Washington paid the bills for supporting the coalition forces which were resisting the Vietnamese occupation. In practice the support was of the Khmer Rouge.

Despite its declaration of innocence, Britain was also involved when its élite undercover force, the Special Air Service, was brought in to train a Sihanouk-operated unit which in turn worked closely with the Khmer guerillas. The words 'genocide' and 'atrocity', although justified in reference to the Khmer Rouge, were dropped from United Nations' documents by the late 1980s as the Western countries sought for some form of compromise which would allow them to wash their hands of the Cambodian dilemma, without admitting that they were indirectly supporting Pol Pot.[538]

It was within this political environment that the incoming prime minister of Thailand sought to replace a battle area by a trading area. In 1989 he called for a regional conference as a first step to isolating the Khmer Rouge. Hun Sen, the leader of the Phnom Pen government, who had himself earlier rebelled against the extreme cruelties of the Pol Pot regime, visited Chatichai in Bangkok. The National Assembly sought the expulsion from Thai soil of Khmer bases, without which Pol Pot's regime would wither. There was no conference. There was, at the critical moment, a visit from an American under-secretary to remind the Thai government that there were trade privileges which were not sacrosanct. The Thai military continued to protect the Khmer Rouge and the tragedy that was Cambodia continued, despite the signing of agreements.[539]

Not all was darkness. It was in Thailand that the first steps were taken towards a Cambodian solution. Hun Sen had previously been opposed by Thailand, but in Chatichai's reasoning, Hun Sen commanded sufficient support in Cambodia for a policy change to be

---

[538] *The Guardian*, London; 6 October 1990; article by John Pilger
[539] *The Guardian*, London; 6 October 1990; article by John Pilger

made. The four-part coalition approach as a solution to the Cambodian problem, with Sihanouk as king, first saw the light of day in the house of General Chavalit and it was then put forward covertly to United Nations officials. In the meantime, because of relationships with China, it was necessary for overt arrangements to support the Khmer Rouge to remain in force. Even before a treaty was signed, Thai traders were on the move and were among the early investors.[540] An agreement to four-part coalition rule in Cambodia was eventually signed in Paris under the auspices of the United Nations on twenty-fourth of October 1991. It looked full of problems but by late September 1993 its new National Assembly voted for Sihanouk to be King and for a power-sharing government. Sihanouk was by then seventy, with a mild stroke behind him and treatment for suspected cancer ahead of him.

Questions of opium and heroin movement were never far below the surface of Thai administration and matters came to an embarrassing head in August 1989 when America issued a warrant for the arrest of Thai assistant police inspector-general Vech Pechborom for conspiracy to import drugs into America. The charges were comprehensive and listed importing heroin into America, distribution within Thailand knowing it to be for importation to America, and possession with a view to distribute. All of the offences were alleged to have taken place between May 1984 and October 1985 and specifically in November 1984. The principal allegation was that he allowed couriers to pass through Bangkok's Dong Muang airport on their way to America. Vech was a Major-General commanding a Police Patrol and Special Action Division, an anti-terrorist unit, at the time. It was later admitted that the warrant had been issued on the evidence of only one drug trafficking suspect and in any event it had no validity in Thailand.[541] Whilst the alleged events took place before the Chatichai era, and were strenuously denied, the indictment gave greater credulity to current allegations that some police and Thai officials were still involved in drug trafficking.[542] Later that same

---

[540] Discussions with Major-General Chatichai Choonhavan, Bangkok; 26 November, 1993

[541] *Bangkok Post Weekly*; 3 and 6 August, and 7 September 1989

[542] *Bangkok Post*; 7 September 1989

year, a local police chief in Chiang Saen was sacked for involvement in heroin imports from Laos, brought in by Chinese Haw merchants through Mae Sai and Chiang Saen.[543]

Not all was failure; there were also substantial successes. February 1988 had seen the biggest haul to date in Thailand when police at Bangkok port, Klong Toey, seized one thousand two hundred and eighty kilogrammes of No. 4 pure heroin, and in the first three months of that year the hauls exceeded the whole of those made in 1987.[544] Increased surveillance in the Bangkok area only forced some of the traffic south so that it made its way through Phuket to Penang and Singapore. Early in 1989, officials working in collaboration in fifteen countries, including Thailand, broke a major drugs ring, the king-pin of which was a seventy-one-year-old New York liquor store dealer. The centre of the ring was in Hong Kong and there were also Thai attachments.[545] Some four years later police surveillance in Mae Hong Song resulted in the seizure of three hundred and sixty kilogrammes of Khun Sa's high grade 'Double-U' brand heroin.[546]

In December 1989, America filed an indictment in a Brooklyn Court against Khun Sa. The indictment stemmed from the February 1988 drug seizure but it only became public knowledge in March 1990 because of unspecified 'sensitive issues'. It was known that America had sought the aid of both Thailand and Burma in capturing him but the Burmese government warned against any violation of its sovereignty, making it quite clear that it would not condone a 'snatch'. The US Drug Enforcement Agency claimed that Sa controlled some ninety per cent of the heroin production in the Triangle,[547] a far cry from the days when the young Chang Shee-fu had to bow the knee to the renegade Chinese 'lost army'. It was not hard to deduce the reasons for the lack of co-operation from the Burmese military junta — too many incomes might be at risk.

If there were to be a Noriega-type attempted snatch of Khun Sa, Washington might well find itself in trouble. Its failure in Vietnam would presumably have made it realise that it was not equipped with

---

[543] *Bangkok Post*; 8 October 1989
[544] *Bangkok Post*; 15 March 1988
[545] *Bangkok Post*; 23 February 1989
[546] US Drug Enforcement Administration conference at headquarters of Thai Narcotics Suppression Bureau on 4 August 1993 reported by *Bangkok Post Weekly* 13 August 1993
[547] *Bangkok Post*; 17 March 1990

the troops necessary for intense jungle warfare. It would have had to use a Thailand base which would have caused internal difficulties in that country. It would certainly provoke reaction from China and possibly from Vietnam. It was unlikely that it could persuade the Thais to do its dirty work. Such an action, when discovered, would again provoke hostility within Thailand itself as well as from Burma. The KMT remnant was by now too run-down to be recruited for such service, and in any event the threat of removal of Thai nationality would dampen the ardour of most of the residents of Mae Salong. To persuade the Burmese Army to undertake the task would require a one-hundred-and-eighty-degree turn as America had already withdrawn aid from Burma because of the involvement of some of its military in the drug business and because of its total disregard for human rights.

Thailand had remained the drug trafficker's favourite route to the Western consumers, but China had become a major if unwilling partner with secondary routes leading to Hong Kong for distribution. Thai police were successful in Chiang Rai when in late 1989 they arrested Na Ts'ai K'uei, one of Sa's top men in moving drugs. The Royal Canadian Mounted Police, working with American and Thai narcotic agents, were also successful in infiltrating and arresting traffickers in Vancouver. These small triumphs did not satisfy Washington. Airing its frustration, the American Drug Enforcement Agency, which had been subsidising the Thai police to the tune of some three million US dollars per annum, was moved to comment in the spring of 1990 that out of the hundreds of buildings which had been built in Bangkok in the 1980s, there were more than just a few built from heroin money.[548]

In October 1990 there were rumours of Chatichai resigning his premiership after differences within the Chart Thai party itself, where there was a call for Pramarn to replace him leader. There was trouble over a major telephone contract. On fifth of October the prime minister announced that he was certainly not going to resign but that he was contemplating a reshuffle of the Cabinet. General Chavalit, by then in retirement from the Army, was approached to join the government but declined. An Opposition request to recall the

---

[548] *Bangkok Post*; 20 May 1990

Assembly to discuss corruption in high places was refused. There were student demonstrations against alleged corruption, with the telephone contract very much to the fore. Army chief Suchinda Kraprayoon warned that whilst the military still considered the government legitimate, it would not be able to continue its support if the people would not accept the government's authority.[549] A comment from this source would have come as no surprise. No sooner had Suchinda been made Army commander-in-chief in 1990 than he was making critical noises on the running of the country. It was very much a case of coming events casting their shadow before them.

In December came the reshuffle, with Chatichai's Chart Thai party receiving five out of six positions in the prime minister's office. One appointee was his nephew, the rising Chart Thai star Korn Dabbaransi and another an old colleague, General Harn. Of the ministries, Chart Thai were given defence, interior, finance, and industry and thus controlled the commercial aspects of government. It had the look of a last desperate throw, or as the retired General Chavalit described it, *"a second-hand Cabinet"*.

In late January and early February 1991, controversy arose from another quarter. There were a number of sudden changes at the top of branches of the police force and allegations made of a cover-up since 1984 of an assassination plot. The plot was first rumoured to have been against key national figures, two of whom were soon identified as General Prem and General Arthit. There were hints of a third unidentified figure being a member of the Royal Family. A proliferation of unsigned leaflets suddenly hit the streets of Bangkok, making damaging accusations and counter-accusations against separate groups. They indicated a power struggle in the making between the prime minister and those close to him on the one side, and the Class 5 generals, of whom Army chief Suchinda was the leader, on the other.

The temperature rose when the premier's son, Kraisak, and the recently pardoned Manoon became involved. On fifth of February Manoon and Kraisak filed formal complaints with the Crime Suppression Department that they were being defamed by allegations of involvement in the assassination attempt.[550] Fuel was added to the fire when it was learned that a Class 7 Young Turk and Phalang Dharma member of the Assembly, Colonel Bulsak, was prepared to

---

[549] *Bangkok Post Weekly*: 19 October 1992
[550] *Bangkok Post Weekly*; 15 February 1991

testify about the assassination attempts. He was held in police custody 'for his own safety'. He had given a video-taped interview to the police concerning those implicated. It was then disclosed that testimony by two supposed communist defectors had named the third target as H.M. Queen Sirikit.[551]

The plot had been to kill the Queen, the prime minister, and the Army commander-in-chief at the Queen's Cup football tournament on twentieth of October 1982. Chatichai insisted that the police speed up the investigation as he was well aware that the attempt to discredit his son, Kraisak, was a part of a deliberate plot by some elements within the Army to smear him personally.

Other events overtook the investigations and moved swiftly to a climax. On twentieth of February, Prime Minister Chatichai, who himself held the post of minister, announced that he had appointed General Arthit Kamlang-ek to be his deputy at the Ministry of Defence. Already a deputy prime minister by reason of being a coalition party leader, Arthit was moving to a position of political power, a move which had been expected of him before Prem had fired him as Army commander. He would retain the portfolio of a deputy prime minister and, more important to the military, Arthit and Chatichai would oversee the promotions and reshuffles of the military commanders in the annual review in the following September. The previous Army commander, Chavalit, was already an active politician with his own supporting party, and although opposed to Chatichai, he was a man to be watched. Thus the Class 5 generals who held the principal fire-power posts were being hemmed in by retired but experienced military men who had played the game years before them. They would also need to take account of the popular and respected Class 7 Major-General Chamlong who led his own political party, the Phalang Dharma. Without doubt, everyone would need to keep a close watch on Manoon, who had always had a high political profile.

While the reason for the appointment of Arthit was given as being necessary to ease the burden of work on Chatichai, it was a highly provocative move and Chatichai, an experienced political campaigner, must have known that. It can therefore only be construed that he felt the appointment essential in an attempt to bolster his personal position. He had already been at odds with the top military when he, quite

---

[551] *Independent on Sunday*, London; 24 February 1991

properly, reprimanded the brutal rulers of Burma, or Myanamar as it had become, and also distanced Thailand from the Khmer Rouge. A number of top military were involved in lucrative logging contracts in Burma and would be looking forward to similar arrangements in Cambodia if the tripartite opposition, dominated by the Khmer Rouge, had a greater say in the country's affairs.[552] The prime minister had already discussed with the principal military officers the question of the replacement of three of his ministers who were seen blatantly to be feathering their own nests, although the solution proposed by the military was not acceptable to him. Their approach had been to require a repeat of the Thanom tactic of the prime minister conducting a coup against his own government and having done so, scrap the constitution and rule by dictatorial, military-dominated council. Adopting the same stance that he had taken in 1976, Chatichai would have none of it, being himself an elected representative.[553]

He now knew that a coup d'état by the military to remove him from office was virtually inevitable. With his son, Kraisak, and other close advisers, options open to him were carefully considered. Chatichai could grasp the nettle and sack Army commander-in-chief Suchinda and supreme-commander Sunthorn. If he did so, he risked his own assassination and bloodshed on the streets. If he left both of them in place and removed a number of second-tier generals from key units, the prospects were better. Chamlong Srimuang added his personal appraisal of options open. In his view the government might just survive with the second option, provided that key fire-power officers were removed from nominated cavalry and infantry units. He believed that such removals might create internal division within the military and whatever bloodshed occurred would result from internecine strife.

Eventually, Chatichai, with the full support of his family, decided against both of these principal options and left himself with the unenviable third — to let the attempt run its course. He hoped by this choice to avoid blood on the streets of Bangkok and in this he was successful. Neither he nor anyone else could have foreseen that he had only postponed it by one year.[554] The moment of truth came within

---

552 *The Economist*, London; 2 Mar 1991
553 *Bangkok Post Weekly*: statement by Kraisak Choonhavan; 8 March 1992
554 Discussions with Major-General Chatichai Choonhavan, Bangkok; 26 November, 1993

three days and the military staged its first successful coup for twelve years, led by supreme commander Sunthorn Kongsompong, but with Suchinda as the power broker. It was the seventeenth attempt since June 1932.

It was a quiet affair and hardly noticed. On twenty-third of February, the streets of Bangkok were clogged. The prime minister had travelled as far as the airport on his way to see the King at his winter palace at Chiang Mai. There, with General Arthit, who was to be sworn in to his new office, and with others, he was taken off a plane and arrested. While the military accused the premier of undemocratic behaviour and running the country by private cliques in a tyrannical manner, it was without doubt the appointment of General Arthit which forced its hand, Neither side trusted the other. All branches of the military were solidly behind the coup but the cavalry was not privy to the plan because of the close connections which Chatichai maintained with the armoured units. It was put simply by an academic: *"It was like watching a piece of rotten fruit — everyone was expecting it to fall and no one is sad now that it has".*[555]

The announcements, which are the hallmark of the military in Thailand, followed, although observers close to the political centre knew that it was the Arthit appointment which was the ultimate cause of the coup.[556]. A National Peacekeeping Council was established to usurp the power and authority of the government. Martial law was declared. The 1978 constitution was abolished. The National Assembly was shut down. Political gatherings of more than five people were prohibited, a news censorship imposed, and radio and television stations were permitted to transmit only the programmes from the military's own stations. Permanent secretaries of ministries took over responsibility for the day-to-day running of affairs, subject to the policy of the Peacekeeping Council. Groups of editors, bankers and labour leaders were summoned for instruction. Hoarding and profiteering were forbidden.

Some people worried. In the time which had lapsed since the military deemed coups to be fashionable, Thailand had changed. For two decades it had seen its gross domestic product increase by an average of nine per cent per annum. In the Chatichai era, it had been

---

[555] *The Economist*, London; 2 March 1991
[556] Confirmed by Air Chief Marshall Kaset Rojananil, one of the coup leaders in *Manager Daily* 27 January 1993 cited *Bangkok Post Weekly* 5 February 1993

a spectacular 11.7 per cent.[557] Now, tourist agents saw an immediate drop in arrivals. Hotels worried over cancellation of bookings. Aircraft companies were concerned about the load factor of Bangkok flights. The Board of the Stock Exchange of Thailand and countless investors became immediately concerned over the future of share values.

Some people were relieved. To the executive director of the American Chamber of Commerce the coup was *"a great leap forward to a better, Thai-style democracy"*.[558] It was a strange, or possibly naïve, view, coming from an official representative of a leading democracy. How often the expression 'Thai-style democracy' is used for dictatorial behaviour! A number of academics believed that the government had pushed the military too far and action of this nature was inevitable. Others felt that confrontation should have been avoided. To some people in the street, the government was corrupt and the military action was justified, if not long overdue. Others regretted that Thailand's democratic processes had been reversed and inevitably asked whether or not the people themselves would benefit from the change.

To the most knowledgeable of all critics, M. R. Kukrit, again leading the Social Action party, it looked a better organised coup than those in the early 1980s and he saw little chance of interference with long-term democratisation. He had been very concerned with the Chatichai government's interference with the police investigation of the alleged plot. *"The Chatichai government had acted as if it were above the law and the Constitution, and as if this country belonged to Mr Chatichai and the Rajakru dynasty"*.[559] Unfortunately for Thailand, he was to concern himself no longer. After fifty years in politics, Thailand's foremost politician decided to quit the leadership of the Social Action party and in so doing brought to an end his most distinguished and devoted political service to his country. He was

---

[557] *The Financial Times*, London; 19 May 1992
[558] *The New York Times*; 27 February 1992
[559] *Bangkok Post*; 24 February 1991

fearless in his criticism of governments and his integrity was beyond question.

On the evening of the coup, perhaps as a diversion but principally as part justification of its cause, the military released the video-taped interview with Colonel Bulsak. The tape had been made on eighth of February in the presence of police officers, and in it Bulsak named his fellow Class 7 military graduate, Manoon, as the plot leader. The plot was said to be not only against the government of General Prem and his Army commander, Arthit, but also aimed at the overthrow of the monarchy. Later, doubt was cast on the method of interview and one senior police officer described it as 'staged'.[560]

Manoon once more left the country and did not reappear until November 1992, waiting until after Suchinda had been forced to resign and the election of the democratic alliance had taken place. Already stripped of his military rank, he then surrendered himself to stand trial before the Criminal Court.[561] It was to be a trial which would drag on and on: in the course of it there were allegations of six other attempts on the life of General Arthit and another on the life of General Prem. In the end, the chief prosecution witness, Class 7 Colonel Bulsak, failed to provide the necessary weight of evidence and indeed frequently failed to arrive at the Court to give his evidence. To the obvious delight of his Class 7 supporters, Manoon walked out of the Court, a free man.

Whether or not the Class 7 Young Turks have cards to play in the future remains to be seen. A future judgement of history is likely to see them, Chamlong excepted, merely as an unsuccessful group of dissatisfied officers with questionable judgement. Their one success may have been to help the transfer of power from Kriangsak to Prem, but it is virtually certain that such a transfer would have taken place without their being involved. Their concept of the role of the military was anachronistic and their ultimate contribution to good government in Thailand was zero.

Allegations of corruption in the outgoing government were rife and its levels, even for Thailand, were claimed to have reached spectacular heights. General Suchinda described the government as

[560] *Bangkok Post*; 24 and 27 February 1991; *The Nation*; 27 February 1991
[561] Journal *Lak Thai* quoted by *Bangkok Post Weekly*; 20 and 27 November 1992

democratic on the surface but comparable to the crony-capitalism of the deposed Philippine president, Marcos. To substantiate the claim of corruption, the Council ordered all banks to disclose details of the accounts of a number of the members of the previous government, including Chatichai himself. It then set up a kangaroo court to assess the movement of wealth through the hands of those included. As a sop to the general public, income tax and fuel prices were reduced. A strict censorship plan was proposed but dropped within twenty-four hours.[562] The first group of citizens to feel the wind of change were the members of the state industry unions. The Peacekeeping Council decided that state unions should never have been allowed to form and that they would be disbanded.[563]

A successful coup is one thing but governing a country is another. The National Peacekeeping Council, through Suchinda, promised elections and a new constitution within six months. Apart from in the takeover and in the ultimate downfall, the individual military officers of the Council proved to be an irrelevance, a mere hiccup in the passage of Thai progress. A caretaker government was needed but with the Council retaining overriding powers. Great care was needed in its selection as the first outside reaction had been from America which had deplored the coup and cancelled sixteen million dollars worth of aid. Japan left its aid intact. The King became concerned and called upon the military junta not to let the people down. Nevertheless he endorsed the takeover by confirming the appointment of General Sunthorn Kongsompong as chief of the National Peacekeeping Council.[564]

It is, perhaps, for its choice of caretaker prime minister and government that the military of those days should best be remembered. Whilst its objective was a new constitution which would leave the military with ultimate power but yet be acceptable to the people, it had first to deal with the everyday running of the country. It opted for a caretaker government of non-politicians although some had previous experience of government affairs. While there were avowals from Suchinda that the caretaker government would not be hindered by the military,[565] no one doubted where ultimate power would rest.

---

562 *The Economist*, London, 2 March 1991
563 *Bangkok Post Weekly*; 29 March 1991
564 *The Nation*; 27 February 1991
565 *Bangkok Post*; 27 February 1991

342

It was something of a surprise that the Council recommended the King to invite Dr Anand Panyarachun to become the caretaker prime minister although it was noted that, within a provisional constitution, the Council retained the power to dismiss him.

Dr Anand was a member of a Thai élite family which for generations had served as government officials. He was both an experienced diplomat and an experienced businessman. He was widely respected in both private and public circles. He was born in the year of Pridi's coup d'état. Educated first in Bangkok, he went on to Dulwich College and Cambridge University, England. Rapid promotion followed his joining the Foreign Ministry in 1955 and twelve years later he was appointed to be ambassador to Canada as well as permanent Thai representative at the United Nations. He retained the latter appointment when he was moved south to become ambassador in Washington, where he served from 1972 until 1975. His assistant military attaché was the young Major Suchinda. As permanent secretary to the foreign ministry for two years, he ran into trouble in 1976 with the new prime minister, Thanin, who went as far as accusing him of communist leanings. Cleared, he moved to be ambassador in Germany, but after only one year he gave up the diplomatic life for commerce. His services were much in demand. He soon held directorships or chairmanships of a number of leading companies in Bangkok. At the time of his invitation to become premier, he was the executive chairmen of Thailand's leading textile group. His appointment was to prove acceptable in the world's capitals, an important factor when considering the continuing need of foreign investment in Thailand.[566]

Anand declared that he would pick a Cabinet of men of integrity and it soon became clear that he did just that. He was himself sufficiently respected to attract to him many brilliant men from all walks of life who would not have soiled their hands on the politics of the Chatichai government. He was still bedevilled by the military in its overseeing role. As his deputy prime ministers, replacing heads of political parties, he brought in the former chief economic planner, Dr Snoh, a one-time police chief and son of a former prime minister Pol. General Pow Sarasin, and also the one-time legal adviser to prime minister Prem, Meechai. Pow's brother, Arsa, took the post of foreign minister while the industry portfolio went to Thailand's

---

[566] *The Nation*; 3 March 1991

premier nuclear physicist, Dr Sippanondha Ketudat. But the National Peacekeeping Council was not to be excluded, and within the thirty-five-member Cabinet, the key post of minister of the interior, responsible for arranging the next elections, was allocated to the Army deputy-commander in chief, General Issarapong. Apart from the military, it was a Cabinet of technocrats and specialists. Given a free hand, it might have developed into one of the best governments in post-war Thailand.

The King having given his approval of the Cabinet on seventh of March, the former prime minister and colleagues were released on ninth of March. Three days later Chatichai left for one of his London homes.[567] He announced his intention to steer clear of politics in the future. Many doubted such an intention, knowing his love of the intrigue of which Thai politics is constituted. The principal members of the National Peacekeeping Council were present to bid him farewell — or possibly to make sure that he left. That same week General Arthit, released at the same time as Chatichai, decided that a holiday abroad might be good for his health.

Chatichai and his family returned from London on eleventh of April, allegedly only for the purpose of his receiving a decoration from the King. He was met by a Council representative and whisked off to his home in Soi Rajakru. A few days later he returned to London. On sixth of June, although still in exile, he was again nominated as leader of the Chart Thai party. He was not away for long. In his absence he had been accused, with others, of becoming rich too quickly during his period of office. In Chatichai's case it might have been more accurate if the allegation had been rephrased to convey that he had added to his existing wealth too extensively. By mid-August he was installed back in Soi Rajakru, this time for the purpose of replying to the charges.

His return also coincided with the time of the year when the annual military reshuffle was under way and thus a time when careful thought was being given to any dissent within or with the Peacekeeping Council. It was also the time when, despite the independence being given to the caretaker government, General Suchinda was refusing to rule out the possibility that he, Suchinda, might become prime minister after the election.[568] There was a feeling of unease over

---

[567] *Independent on Sunday*, London; 10 March 1991
[568] *The Economist*, London; 21 September 1991

Suchinda's position and, within a few weeks, Suchinda himself considered it essential to make a positive statement that neither he, nor the ambitious Air Force chief, Kaset, would be prime minister after the election had been held. Few believed that he would not try.

Thailand, or specifically Bangkok, had changed since the days of the 1973 and 1976 disturbances. By 1991 it was not merely a question of risking a student revolt on the streets. Students now formed only part of the opposition to dictatorship. There was now also a better-educated and well-read professional, commercial, and politically conscious generation watching the progress, or the lack of it, being made towards a greater spread of democracy. Many were the students of the seventies. There was a much stronger and more outspoken academic body than during earlier troubles. People looked to the military to produce a liberal solution within a new constitution and not for a harking back to the days of Sarit and Thanom.

In November, the logging issue came back into public notice when the extent of Thai interests in log importation from Burma was disclosed. Some forty-one firms were listed and the top eight were dominated by current and recently retired military officers, together with various relatives and also by Chart Thai members of the Assembly and their financial backers. Despite the abuse of human rights taking place in that country, Thai financial interests took a clear priority. This was a far cry from the origins of the Thai interest in Burmese logs when, under General Prem, cordial relations were sought with Burma, and government-to-government contracts cemented that relationship. At that time there had been a mutual concern to act jointly against communists and, *inter alia*, the log trade helped the relationship.

With the publication of a draft of a new constitution, commercial interests in Bangkok were put on the back burner. Some fifty thousand people took to the streets to protest at a draft which clearly intended to maintain the power of the military, whatever the result of the elections. The National Legislative Assembly, which had been responsible for the draft, took a quick step backwards. It removed from its draft the power of the military-dominated Senate to elect the prime minister as well as its right to take part in budget debates and in other important bills. Nevertheless, retention of powers of the Senate to censure the government and thus force its resignation were retained. The amended constitution still had sufficient teeth to reinforce the military coup d'état of the previous February. At this point King Bhumibol intervened. Using an address to wellwishers on the occasion of his sixth-fourth birthday, he pointed out that within the draft constitution, the fifteenth since 1932, "...*any regulation could be changed if it proved unacceptable or impracticable*".[569] Thai politicians and military understood their King. Only on rare but vital occasions in his long reign had he involved himself directly in politics, but the statement gave a clear indication that His Majesty did not approve of some parts of the draft even although he had put his signature to it on ninth of December.[570] The question in the minds of many people was whether or not the Class 5 generals would heed the warning. They did not. They were looking for a long stay in power. As so often occurs, wisdom was rejected by the knowledgeable.

With an election somewhere over the horizon, some of the political parties ran into problems of their own making. General Chavalit's New Aspiration Party showed signs of fragmenting over a choice of tactics. Although he had given up the leadership, Chatichai started to campaign openly on behalf of the Chart Thai party which the Soi Rajakru clan looked upon as its own child. Much of his campaigning was, however, against the Peacekeeping Council and its kangaroo court which had frozen much of his wealth together with that of other senior party members. Military support was given to a newly formed party, the Samakkhi Tham, which was to be its tool in the post-election period.

The March 1992 elections over, the usual bid for power within the coalition began. The Chart Thai, Social Action, Rassadorn, and Prakachorn Thai parties joined the Samakkhi Tham to form a coalition and the nominal leader of the Samakkhi Tham party was to be put forward for prime minister. At this stage America, unhappy with the trend of events, took a hand. It publicly confirmed that it had refused to issue a visa in July 1991 to the prime minister designate because of his suspected ties with drug trafficking. The incident which had given rise to the American suspicion was based on a visit to Laos, followed shortly after by a visit to America in October 1990. America declared the information not to be actionable at present but *"It is the kind of*

---

[569] *Bangkok Post Weekly*; 13 December 1991
[570] *The Economist*, London; 4 January 1992

information that can be used in seeking an indictment". Demonstrators were fetched from a number of northern provinces to demonstrate in front of the American embassy against outside interference in Thai politics. America stood firm and the coalition had a problem. To the outside observer it was a distinctly odd stance for America to take on a specific case after presidents from Ford through to Bush himself had expressed satisfaction with the co-operation each had with Thailand in countering narcotics. *"Let's be frank about it,"* said Fred Dick, a retired regional director for the American Drug Enforcement Agency in Bangkok. *"We have had other interests in Thailand more important than drugs. ...nobody is interested in looking under any rocks"*.[571]

The coalition's problem did not last long. It took General Suchinda only a few days to make his move, despite his previous statement that he would not accept the post of prime minister. On seventh of April he suddenly discovered that, sorrowful though he was at having to go back on his word and swallow his pride, he *was* prepared to accept an invitation from the coalition to fill the appointment, *"for the sake of the country"*.[572] More simply, through him, the Class 5 generals were determined to prevent both their previous commander-in-chief, General Chavalit and the Class 7 man of integrity, Major-General Chamlong, from being elected into the top office.

Suchinda's attitude in senior posts made it perfectly clear that, as so many of his predecessors, he believed in the absolute right of the military to dictate the role of government in Thailand. He was more fortunate than most in that he came to military power at a time coinciding with unacceptable behaviour on the part of a number of members of the Chatichai government. Despite that advantage, he had not realised the extent to which Thailand had changed. His manoeuvres to enable him to have ultimate power were amateurish and showed a grave lack of sound judgement, for which many innocent Thais would pay with their lives.

He moved into power owing many favours to military colleagues and to coalition politicians who had supported the electoral dominance of the Samakkhi Tham party. It was not a recipe for stable government. The new constitution obliged Suchinda to give up his

---

[571] *Bangkok Post Weekly*; 10 April, quoting UPI, and 17 1992
[572] *Bangkok Post Weekly*; 17 April 1992

military posts and leave the Army. Despite the ambitions of the Air Force commander, Air Chief Marshal Kaset, who now took over the role of supreme commander, Suchinda had no problem in covering his back as it was arranged that his classmate and brother-in-law, General Issarapong, would succeed him as the head of the Army.

Anti-government demonstrations began almost immediately and share prices on the Bangkok Stock Exchange slumped. Indeed, so quickly did the demonstrations begin that Suchinda had the doubtful privilege of having his position challenged before he had made any statement of policy. To the surprise of many, when the Cabinet was announced on seventeenth of April, it included a number of the politicians against whom 'unusually rich' allegations had been made. The earlier American veto had little effect as the former prime minister designate now appeared as one of the deputy prime ministers. The Soi Rajakru clan also held a number of senior appointments. The price which Suchinda had to pay to satisfy his ambitions was beginning to show.

The size of the demonstrations increased. It was clear that there was an overwhelming desire among the middle class city dwellers for an end to military domination. They also sought increased participation in a form of government which was accountable to the people. On twentieth of April the numbers on the streets were estimated at forty to fifty thousand, protesting at the undemocratic appointment of Suchinda. Banner slogans became bolder: *"WE, THAI PEOPLE, AREN'T AFRAID OF FASCIST SUCHINDA"*. Some demonstrators carried video cameras, the pictures from which would be useful as evidence in the future.[573] Political commentators went as far as suggesting that whilst it was evident to anyone that the new government was not in the same league as that of Dr Anand, it may have been even worse than that of Chatichai against which the coup had originally been mounted.[574]

On fourth of May, Chamlong Srimuang announced that his Palang Dharma elected party members would not attend the assembly and that he himself would go on hunger strike against the Suchinda regime. There were by now an estimated hundred thousand people on the streets, and the coalition government parties agreed that the constitution would be amended to ensure that all future prime

---

[573] *The Economist*, London: 16 May 1992
[574] *Bangkok Post Weekly*; 1 May 1992

ministers would be chosen from members elected. Within a
background organisation, Thirayuth Boonmi, a leader of the 1973
student uprising, was anxious to ensure that earlier mistakes were not
repeated. From his past experience he concluded that success might
come from a temporary easing of the pressure on the military and he
conveyed this thought to Chamlong. On ninth of May, Chamlong
ceased his hunger strike and told the assembled masses to go home.
Further protest meetings were called for on seventeenth of May if the
amendments to the Constitution were not forthcoming.[575]

They were not forthcoming. The people were unhappy and
returned to the streets by seventeenth of May, and that evening the
government declared a state of emergency. By nineteenth of May the
numbers on the streets were put at a hundred and fifty thousand and
the military started a crackdown. Many of the troops employed were
from outside Bangkok, the peasant element of the Army. In the
following four days the clashes were bloody, and estimates from
hospitals gave the first casualty list as fifty killed and large numbers
wounded. It later became clear to outside, independent observers that
the Suchinda government had planned well in advance to put down the
demonstrations by violent means. Police forces were apparently
prevented from using non-lethal crowd control equipment and resorted
early to intentional firing directly at unarmed demonstrators. Many in
the crowd were shot at close quarters and some shot in the back while
trying to escape. Hundreds were arrested, among them, Thirayuth. No
members of the security forces were recorded as killed or wounded
from gunfire during the period of the crackdown. Testimony was
given that the Capital Security Command was responsible for orders to
troops to arm themselves to crush pro-democracy demonstrations.[576]

America stepped up its pressure on the Thai government to find a
peaceful solution. On eighteenth of May, Chamlong was arrested
along with other protest leaders. The Bangkok stock exchange suffered
its largest daily fall, some nine per cent of its total value. There were
warnings from foreign governments that their companies would think
twice before putting new investment into Thailand. Shops closed. By
nineteenth of May there was a run on banks and on gasoline

---

[575] Partly from discussions with Arjarn Thirayuth Boonmi, Bangkok, 27 November
1993

[576] 'Bloody May', a report by Physicians for Human Rights and Asia Watch; October
1992 and Bangkok Post 1 July 1992

stations.[577] Foreign nationals were advised to stay away and tourist figures dropped. Airlines suspended flights. Despite heavy-handed suppression, the crowds burned down a police station, the state lottery building, and the government public relations department.[578]

There was a strange silence from the palace. The worst of the news and pictures were being kept from the King, as well as from his people, by the military's manipulation of television programmes. Even international channels were denied their customary access to local stations. There was a suggestion that troops outside Bangkok who were loyal to the former prime minister, Prem, and through him to Chamlong, were to march on the capital.[579] News was difficult to smother, and away in Paris the Princess Maha Chakri Sirindhorn was seeing pictures of the suppressive and bloody nature of affairs. So did Crown Prince Maha Vajiralongkorn, on a visit to South Korea.[580]

King Bhumipol was informed and moved swiftly. On the evening of twentieth of May, he summoned Prime Minister Suchinda to the palace and required him to bring Chamlong with him. In the presence of Chamlong and former prime minister General Prem, the King, in front of television cameras, berated Suchinda for the troops firing on the Thai people. Chamlong was released from arrest and immediately appealed for calm from the assembled crowds. Suchinda agreed to require the Assembly to amend the constitution. The King instructed both Suchinda and Chamlong to seek the advice of two of his own counsellors — the former prime ministers Dr Sanya and General Prem. *"You, especially you two, General Suchinda and Major-General Chamlong, must turn towards each other and not confront each other in order to solve this problem. In the end people no longer know why they are fighting. All they want is to win and this is dangerous."* [581]

The night curfew remained in force and some protesters still manned barricades. An amnesty allowed the release of over three thousand protesters from gaol. The end of the violence appeared to be in sight, but it was not yet over. Bangkok moved into an uneasy calm.

World public opinion had turned against the Thai military. Thai ambassadors in distant countries were summoned to be told of the

---

577 *Bangkok Post Weekly*; 29 May 1992
578 *The Financial Times*, London; 20 May 1992
579 *The Economist*, London 23 May 1992
580 *Bangkok Post Weekly*; 29 May 1992
581 *The Financial Times*, London; 21 May 1992

dismay and disgust at the firing by the Army on unarmed civilians. American and Australian troops were withdrawn from joint exercises. There was, for a few days, a fear that Thailand would go the way of Burma, resulting in the clock being put back thirty years. Warnings to citizens of European countries continued in force, although there was no move to cut political links.

On twenty-fourth of May, Suchinda gave up his fight to stay in power and resigned from his unelected office of prime minister. As Sarit had done before him, he first of all ensured that a Royal decree had been obtained, granting an amnesty to both military and civilian participants in the riots. In getting such a decree he had in practice sown the seeds of further problems. There was immediate opposition to the amnesty from academics and from students, soon to be supported by the press. Senate investigations into the whole affair were set in motion. In resigning, Suchinda spoke of the whole event: (it) *"has left deep scars in the minds of the Thai people, and on the economy which will take time to recover to its former shape"*.[582] It was the incalculable damage to the economy which brought the greatest pressure on Suchinda. All of a sudden, Thailand was no longer the darling of South-East Asia. Too many people had an interest in the bright and blossoming expansion for a coup to be welcomed, although they had tolerated the removal of the Chatichai government, which they perceived to be corrupt.

Suchinda was not the only casualty. Chamlong declared that he himself would not consider any request to be prime minister. There can be no doubt that in his hungerstrike and in his speeches he had over-committed himself to the uprising. He surrendered the leadership of the Palang Dharma party. He set his sights on remaining a member of the Assembly and in continuing to fight corruption in high places. It was a sad development: the Thai political scene had lost a leader of integrity, but he had left himself virtually no way back.

The military closed ranks behind its new leaders, vowing to keep *"...the Army spirit from being trampled on anymore"*.[583] It would need such solidarity because, as an army, its attitude and its culture had become anachronistic. The Thai people, seemingly always ready to forget and forgive, had been gravely offended, and memories of the October protests of 1973 and 1976 were revived. The goodwill that

---

[582] *Bangkok Post Weekly*; 5 June 1992
[583] *Bangkok Post Weekly*; 5 June 1992

the Army had been carefully nurturing — principally under Prem, Arthit, and Chavalit — had been shattered in an unthinking and unforgivable display of lack of discipline and crude violence. People from all walks of life had risen gallantly, not merely against an individual but against the principle itself. Whilst the focus of protest had been in Bangkok, the call for change was nationwide. It was particularly in its breadth of protest that the 1982 uprising differed from that of 1973. It had the support not only of students but also a strong leavening of both industrial and rural workers. Its support was more mature in its representation, partly because the 1973 students were now in their forties. It seemed that for once in its modern history, the Thai civilian population had spoken with one voice. Thailand would never be quite the same again.

With the departure of Suchinda, it was now up to the coalition politicians to find a new solution. They certainly wished to avoid another election with all the personal expenses which such an event would incur. Furthermore, having grasped office from which most would expect to recoup the costs of the previous election, with interest, they were unwilling to face the likelihood that a new election would almost certainly favour the parties of democracy which, during the unrest, had been prominent on the side of the people. There was also the question of the unpopular amnesty. The politicians determined that the matters should be resolved by electing a prime minister from within their own ranks and they decided on the newly elected leader of the Chart Thai party, Air Chief Marshal Somboon Rahong. This would have been acceptable to the military in the circumstances in which it now found itself, as Somboom was the protégé of Kaset, the supreme commander.

On the evening of tenth June, having reached its decision, the top military brass gathered at Somboon's house in celebration, and Somboon, in full formal dress, awaited the summons from the palace. It did not come. Instead, the celebrations were interrupted by a telephone call from the palace. Somboon's services were not required. The King, having perceived the risk of a return to past problems, made an unusual political move. Ignoring the new constitution which had passed into law only that day and which restricted the appointment of prime ministers to elected politicians, he recalled Dr Anand. The recall was only of a temporary nature, with terms of reference to act as caretaker and arrange a new election.

Anand took office again and summoned a Cabinet made up principally of the ministers who had served him well on the previous occasion. They were neither politicians nor associated with the political parties. It was a return to 'clean' government. The pro-military political coalition tried desperately to avoid a dissolution of the Assembly and with it the new election. It did not prevail.

Anand believed in open government and had the personal courage to declare publicly his intention for his short second term of office. He saw his task as *"returning sovereignty to the people"*. He saw the need for decentralisation, believing many of the elected representatives to be more capable of dealing with local issues than national. This had also been Chatichai's view and the 1991 coup had killed off a bill which the then government had been keen to push through the Assembly. But Anand was only too conscious of the need to solve the problem of a proper role for the military in relation to the political and bureaucratic framework. *"In the past sixty years,"* he said *"we merely dealt with the symptoms of the malady and we either did not have the courage or didn't have the vision to try to undertake some structural adjustments... I hope that by the time I leave I will have begun a process of structural reform."*

He was clear that he wished neither to destroy nor discredit the Army, as the faults of the past sixty years did not lie entirely with the Army but with the Thai system as a whole. *"...we have either given or we have acquiesced in the acquisition of this very high profile role of the Army. I think we need time to think, to ponder seriously, whether certain roles they have been given or they have acquired on their own are really the roles that should belong to them."* He was aiming at the process of *"demilitarising the political process and decommercialising the armed forces."* He realised, however, that open debate about the role of the military or about its power was alien to its culture. He was not looking for punishment of the military, requests for which he put aside as a Western attitude.

Its principal, immediate task was the restoration of confidence in the Thai economy and to revive the important tourist industry. As a non-elected prime minister with a non-elected Cabinet, he did not see his role as making too many changes. He was very conscious of the non-election problem and he himself had begged the King to find an elected man rather than reappoint him.[584] The King eventually informed him that he had no option but to nominate him, Anand, as prime minister.

A first structural reform came quite soon. On ninth of July, Anand's government revoked the prime ministerial order which had set up the Capital Security Command. In one stroke, he had removed the structure upon which the military depended to take upon itself, without any request from government, the use of its forces in a peace-keeping role. The Command itself had been set up in detailed form by General Arthit in 1981 after the April Fools' Day attempted coup, and successive Army commanders had kept a tight personal hold on it. Internal peace-keeping thus reverted to the police.

The next move came on thirteenth of July with be decision by the Cabinet to remove Thai Airways International, the country's flag-carrier, from the control of the Royal Thai Air Force. Whilst the reason given was the conformance with stock market requirements, the move was consistent with the policy of 'decommercialisation' of the armed forces. Under previous practice, the Air Force chief, on appointment, automatically became the chairman of the company. It was a brave decision, as the existing chairman was not only the head of the Air Force but also the supreme commander, Kaset. There were mutterings from Kaset that the military might think about another coup but that comment provoked swift responses, first from Prime Minister Anand that a coup d'état was an act of treason, and then from the leader of the Democrat party that treason was still punishable by execution.

It was at this time that the former prime minister, Chatichai, made a reappearance on the political scene. Written off by many after he gave up the leadership of the Chart Thai party, he now became involved in discussions for the replacement of the party leader as Somboon, after his rejection by H.M. the King, had resigned. He declined to appear at a meeting where the selection was to take place and in his absence his brother-in-law, Pramarn Adireksarn, was once more elected, thus keeping the party leadership within the founding families of the Soi Rajakru clan. By now, however, financial control was very much in the hands of its secretary-general, Banharn Silpa-arch. While Banharn's reputation had been slightly tarnished by

---

[584] *Bangkok Post Weekly*; interview with Dr. Anand Panyarachun; 10 July 1992

his close personal association with Suchinda,[585] his wealth would allow him to repolish it for a future attempt at party leadership with possibly greater things to follow.

There had been differences within the grouping for some time over the leadership and this new move allowed Chatichai to take the step he had been planning since his ousting in the 1991 coup. He formed a new party, the Chart Pattana, or National Development party, as a vehicle to make a come-back into Thai politics and to put up candidates at the forthcoming election. With the Chart Pattana, there would be no stigma like that attached to the parties which had formed the pro-military coalition under Suchinda. It was an audacious step. Less than eighteen months earlier he had been ousted from the highest political post in the land, placed under arrest by a military leadership which was itself now disgraced, and escorted from the country. He had been accused of an unseemly increase in his personal wealth by the kangaroo court set up by the military leaders and he had yet to clear his name in the Thai courts of law. It was going to be a long haul, and after he and others had persuaded the courts of law that the attack upon wealth was unconstitutional, he still had to reckon with a dedicated taxman.

He let it be known that he favoured the leader of the Democrat party, Chuan Leekpai, as the next prime minister. By doing so, he placed his new party carefully into a position that a Democrat-led coalition, looking for support, might invite the Chart Pattana to join it, either on the first round following the election or possibly at a later date if it ran into problems with another partner. His move from Chart Thai to Chart Pattana was followed by some twenty to thirty members of the Assembly, with his nephew and heir-apparent, Korn Dabbaransi, in a key role. Support came from another group of members led by his former deputy prime minister, General Arthit Kamlang-ek. A senior Democrat became secretary-general of the party. Perhaps even more important was the support immediately tendered by a number of the very rich, both private and corporate.[586]

Leopards do not change their spots. Still a believer of converting South-East Asia from a battleground to a trading area, Chatichai was already backing commercial dealings between Thai businessmen and the Khmer Rouge. He was also prepared to state publicly that if he

[585] *Bangkok Post Weekly*; 17 and 24 July 1992
[586] *Bangkok Post Weekly*; 24 July 1992

were in the next government, he would encourage such trade as a perfectly normal business. He made a three-day visit to Cambodia and subsequently addressed a seminar in Bangkok on the possibilities of trade across the border and of the possibility of joint-venture in the oil and gas fields.[587]

Prime Minister Anand moved again. On the first of August he transferred the supreme commander of the armed forces and three senior 'fire-power' Army generals to positions of lesser responsibility, thus reducing the threat of a possible coup against his caretaker government. To replace them he made appointments of soldiers more concerned with military matters and less with commercial. He then went on to remove military appointees from the board of directors of the Expressway and Rapid Transit Authority of Thailand. On the same day, eighteenth of August, he made changes in the Telephone Organisation of Thailand to facilitate an investigation into possible corruption.[588] A follow-up to this was the announcement of new elections to take place on thirteenth of September. Dr Anand was now near to the end of his short, reluctant, term of office. His courageous changes were not liked by all and in his limited spell of power he had created unforgiving enemies.

It was described by a foreign newspaper as *"Thailand's day of the angels"*.[589] The elections of thirteenth of September brought a narrow victory for the anti-military, democratic parties. Out of a possible number of three hundred and sixty seats in the lower house the grouping obtained one hundred and eighty-five votes between them, the Democrat party scoring most with seventy-nine. Palang Darmha took forty-seven seats, Chavalit's New Aspiration party fifty-one, and the Solidarity party a mere eight. It was a very thin margin; but it was a margin that could hold office. The Chart Thai party obtained seventy-seven seats and was thus only narrowly prevented from forming a coalition, while Chatichai's new Chart Pattana party notched up sixty. The names of these two parties were linked with heavy vote buying, which was true to form.[590] Had the Chart Thai party gained another three votes, there is no doubt that Chatichai would have thrown in his party's lot with it, to give a basic one

---

[587] *Bangkok Post Weekly*; 11 September 1992
[588] *Bangkok Post Weekly*; 28 August 1992
[589] *The Economist*; London: 19 September 1992
[590] *The Economist*; London 19 September 1992

hundred and forty votes on which to build a coalition. Now, he was obliged to move to the sidelines, hoping no doubt for a government split which might well bring an invitation to support the new prime minister, for which support Chatichai would no doubt require a rewarding position. It seemed to be a last desperate throw of the dice for power. He must either gain favour from the new government or seek to lead an opposition coalition if the government came under pressure.

Within weeks of the new government being formed, it repealed the amnesty granted to those involved in the May disturbances. The number of missing rose to over two hundred. The military, however, had the last laugh, as in November of that year the Constitutional Tribunal ruled that the Amnesty Executive Decree could not be overturned retroactively and the martyrs of the uprising and their families and friends were left without redress. Suchinda and his military had pardoned themselves and, against all common sense, those guilty of the crime could not be prosecuted.[591]

Among some citizens there was still hope for better days to come. *"This time,"* wrote a hopeful observer, *"we are going to have democracy along the British pattern."* So be it, but the British pattern often leaves much to be desired.

---

[591] *Bangkok Post Weekly*; 20 November 1992

CHAPTER FOURTEEN
The Path of a King

A unanimous vote in the National Assembly on the night of ninth of June 1946 proclaimed Bhumibol Adulyadej, son of Prince Mahidol Adulyadej and descendant of the great King Chulalongkorn, to be His Majesty King Rama IX. Shortly before midnight that same day he ascended the ceremonial throne in the presence of the nobility and the political controllers of his land. Fourteen years had passed since the coup d'état which had replaced the absolute monarchy by that of constitutional monarchy. Eleven years had passed since King Prajadhipok, Rama VII, had abdicated and five since he had died in exile in England. Only hours had passed since the tragic death of King Ananda, Rama VIII, Bhumibol's elder brother.

King Bhumibol was born on fifth of December 1927 in Massachusetts, USA, where his father was living while studying for a doctorate of medicine at Harvard University. When he succeeded to the throne, the young King knew little of his own country. He was to learn little of the practical side of it over the next five years, which he was to spend completing his education in Switzerland. After his investiture, for his own safety, he was kept under close protection and on fourteenth of August left the country. So great were the fears for his safety and such was the lack of trust of each other between groups within the Kingdom that a British plane and British military escort were provided. The plane having arrived at Don Muang airport, it was placed under twenty-four-hour British military guard and floodlit at night for greater security. The British crew were forbidden by that country's ambassador to leave the airfield and refused permission to eat in any bar or restaurant before take-off.

There were occasional political visits to Switzerland from Bangkok. Pridi visited the young King in February 1947. Phao and others visited in connection with evidence for the trumped-up trial of the three palace servants. However, it was not until his return shortly after the 'silent coup' in November 1951 that Bhumibol's years of kingship effectively began. Even then, with the dominance of the Phibun regime, there was little place for him in the affairs of state. His brother's reign covered a decade. During part of it, Thailand had been occupied first by Japanese forces and then by British Indian troops who were temporarily stationed there while removing the Japanese. There had been little effective sovereignty, although King Bhumibol himself has viewed it as a period when the role of kingship truly changed. Whatever view is taken of that decade, it is sad but true that King Ananda will always be remembered for his death rather than his life. King Bhumibol will always be remembered for his life. Whatever the cause of Ananda's death, the result was that Thailand lost a king who might have been a good king, but in his place gained a king whom history is likely to judge as being the greatest king in the two-hundred-year-old Chakri dynasty.

King Bhumibol married his beautiful Queen Sirikit in April 1950 when she was eighteen. They had met first when she was only fifteen, a time when her plans were to be a concert pianist. They had become engaged following the serious car accident involving the King in which he lost the sight of his right eye. The formal coronation took place on fifth of May 1950. Bhumibol was crowned as King and with consecrated water from the royal conch, he anointed his Queen to raise her to sovereign rank. He pronounced the Oath of Accession, *"We will reign in righteousness for the benefit and the happiness of the Siamese people".*[592]

The King's years of introduction to his new role began quietly at the end of 1951 and it was not long before ruling groups benefited from the fall-out of his charismatic personality. He had to accustom himself to a position entirely changed from that of the earlier Chakri kings. The privilege of patronage, and with it the control of commercial monopolies, had moved from the monarchy to the political rulers, and King Bhumibol's return to Thailand coincided with a time of unscrupulous operators in that field. He remained a source of prestige, revered by the common people and aloof from the factions of rival power groups. Foreign ambassadors found much in him to admire. He was a slim, tall, and gracious young man with a delightfully dry sense of humour, and he came to be looked upon by foreign embassies as a symbol of hope for the future of Thailand.

The Thai monarchy was and remains vital to the stability and well-being of Thai society, a source of legitimacy of government and a representation of unity, culture, and tradition. The absence of an adult king for some sixteen years had left a vacuum in the role of the monarch. After his return, the young King had little influence on the

---

[592] *Chakri Monarchs*; English Version by Dr Duangtip Somnapan Surintatip

consolidated position of his prime minister, Phibun. He was allowed to attend a number of ceremonial occasions of no great consequence and his public appearances brought him popularity. During a visit to Isan it became clear how greatly he was esteemed by the people and enthusiastically received by them.[593]

This was not Phibun's aim, but the reception helped the King to develop a strong interest in farming and to take great pains to help the under-privileged farmers. In a speech to the students at Kasksat Agricultural University he beseeched them *"to use your particular field of knowledge for the betterment of all of those engaged in agriculture, who are like the backbone of our country"*. By 1960 he had developed a non-profit-making farm in the grounds of his Bangkok residence, the Chitralada Palace, at which he researched milk production and distribution as well as rice seeding and milling. Demonstrating the practicability of his work, he moved on to husk-grinding for use as fuel or fertilising and to fish farming.[594]

Phibun was not able, totally, to shut out the King from contact with the Thai élite. The King held in his hand a commodity which Phibun could neither stifle not replace: prestige. He founded a school within his Bangkok residence for nobility and commoners alike. He founded charitable trusts to which donations could be made, thus enabling the wealthy to 'make merit' in Buddhist fashion. The foremost of these trusts he named after his elder brother, The Ananda Mahidol Foundation, with the objective of granting scholarships for medical students to study abroad. In so doing, he linked it to the Harrow- and Harvard-educated Prince Mahidol Adulyadej who was not only the father of the two kings but was also looked upon as the father of modern medicine in Thailand. Prince Mahidol's pioneering work in northern Thailand had eventually cost him his life from an illness contracted during his duties. In 1965, following his father's vocational interest, King Bhumibol modernised the centuries-old Corps of Royal Physicians and turned it into a mobile unit capable of travelling with him on extended visits to the provinces. From being a unit to take care only of the monarch and his family, it developed to treat over one thousand patients per day, working with Border Patrol Police, Red Cross Society, and Ministry of Health doctors for the

---

[593] *Thailand and the Fall of Singapore*; Nigel J.Brailey; pp193/5
[594] *Chakri Monarchs*; English Version by Dr Duangtip Somnapan Surintatip

benefit of the rural poor. It was financed from the privy purse. A dental unit followed.[595]

Police General Phao and his CIA advisers saw merit in using the prestige of the King. The Police Aerial Reconnaissance (Resupply) Unit and the Border Patrol Police were required not only to be loyal to Phao but also expressly to the King. As Phao gradually eliminated Army recruitment for his specialised forces, so the influence of former personnel from the Navy, essentially the 'royal' service, increased. In 1953, Phao moved the Reconnaissance Unit's headquarters to a site adjacent to the King's Hua Hin palace, the proximity designed to indicate a special relationship. There was nothing to suggest that the King was particularly impressed, the principal objective obviously being the enhancement of Phao's own position.

With the removal of Phibun and the advent of Sarit, the position of the monarch changed radically. To improve the image of his government, Sarit harnessed the services of the young King Bhumibol and his popular Queen. The King had given qualified support to the Sarit regime in its early days and, after years of the isolation of the monarchy, moved gradually into the area of important domestic ceremony. He opened the great hydropower dam to which he gave his name. He attended ceremonial parades, which brought him closer to the military establishment which would stand him in good stead in later times. He made numerous visits to the provinces. Did the visit of his King have any significance for the lowly peasant, far from Bangkok? *"It has great meaning and merit for the village... they feel a sense of gratitude. The old people feel that they can now pass on to the other world as a result of having seen the King and Queen before they die. The loyalty to the Royal Family will rise in the village, our love for them will increase having seen them with our own eyes. ...he is a real live person and therefore it takes on great personal meaning."* [596]

One interpretation of the Sarit coup of 1957 was that it was an attempt to stop criticism of the throne, reflecting Sarit's wish that the

---

[595] *Chakri Monarchs*; English Version by Dr Duangtip Somnapan Surintatip
[596] *Soul of a Nation*; BBC London, Post Production script; producer — Bridget Winters: Part II p47. A village headman offering an opinion

King be revered and above the law.[597] It was a generous interpretation as Sarit's strike for power had strong personal motivation. Sarit's attitude to his sovereign was without doubt one of great respect and his assurance of loyalty after the 1957 coup led to an early indication of the King's own attitude and delicate wisdom. Acknowledging the acceptability of the proclamation wordings, particularly with regard to the safety and interests of the nation and of the need to encourage progress, he required Sarit to implement them faithfully and honestly. He made it clear to Sarit within that reply that his support was dependent upon implementation for the benefit of the people.

Despite his own moral weaknesses, Sarit was a King's man, and was the prime minister who gave the King the opportunities which led in the years that followed to a fullness of kingship beyond anything Thailand had previously known. When, in the following year, illness struck Sarit, there were flowers from the King to wish him well and he "*prayed for his quick recovery*". When, in Sarit's absence, Thanom held the partial elections of March 1958, the King chose to praise him for the correct and honest manner in which the elections had been carried out.[598]

With Sarit's return and the new coup of October 1958, resulting in the establishment of the Revolutionary Council, one of the first messages from Sarit was to the King:

One institution which the Revolutionary Council will never allow to be changed is the institution of the monarchy, representing the nation as a whole. The Revolutionary Council will stand firm in preserving this system and have promised the people in various proclamations regarding this point. I would like to give your Majesty personal assurances that the new constitution will preserve this particular feature.[599]

In return, the King signed a decree granting an amnesty to all who took part in the 'revolution', and the following day he reminded the newly-formed Revolutionary Council that it should act for the good of the nation.

The members of the 1957 and 1958 coup groups were in a different position from the 1932 group. They were educated in Thailand, away from the more liberal attitudes of the European

---

[597] *The Sarit Regime*; Thak Chaloemtiarana; p221
[598] *The Sarit Regime*; Thak Chaloemtiarana; pp180/183
[599] *The Sarit Regime*; Thak Chaloemtiarana; p199

universities. They had no personal connections with the overthrow of
the monarchy in 1932 and took a more traditional view of the status
and role of the monarchy. Thus they sought to use the throne as a
source of legitimacy for their regime. A conscious effort to promote
the popularity of the King himself, and to involve him to a greater
extent in military and ceremonial matters, also gave respectability to
the regime. The King took to presenting flags to the military and, in
so doing, enhanced the occasion. On his birthday anniversary, fifth of
December 1959, the 21st Infantry Regiment became the palace guard
and Queen Sirikit became its honorary colonel. The King became
honorary colonel to the 1st Infantry Regiment, the 11th Infantry
Regiment, the 1st Engineers Regiment, the 1st Cavalry Regiment, and
the 1st Artillery Regiment.

Elaborate foreign and domestic tours gave prestige not only to the
Thai royal family but also to Sarit and later to his successor, Thanom.
Sarit, realising his own social limitations and lacking Phibun's
sophistication, saw the advantages in the King representing the nation.
Exposure of the King to both a domestic and a foreign public reduced
the international criticism of the repressive regime at home. In the
period late 1959 to early 1960 the King toured Vietnam, Indonesia,
and Burma to a very favourable reception. From mid-1960 to January
1961 the King's visits were wide-ranging through America, Britain,
West Germany, Portugal, Switzerland, Denmark, Norway, Sweden,
Italy, Belgium, France, Luxembourg, and Holland. From then on,
until Sarit's death in December 1963, the King continued his visits,
adding Malaya, Pakistan, Australia, New Zealand, Japan, and the
Philippines to the list. Such a hectic schedule was seen by the King as
a royal duty on behalf of, and for the benefit of, the people. He is
recorded as saying before one long tour:

*"We would like to thank the people for understanding and
supporting our trip... without the acquiescence of the people we
would not have been able to go. We shall carry out our
duties... to demonstrate to foreigners that we are friends, and
willing to co-operate with them."* [600]

The graciousness of King Bhumibol and Queen Sirikit brought
Thailand more and more to the notice of those foreigners, especially
in America where the treatment was particularly lavish. The King and
Queen gave all of the people they met an impression of a civilised and

---

[600] *The Sarit Regime*; Thak Chaloemtiarana; p401

sophisticated country. Sarit himself could not have achieved this and was wise enough to realise it. An end-of-tour welcome in Bangkok was an elaborate occasion but carefully staged to show that ultimate power rested with the government, not the crown. In his turn, the King was careful to ensure that the public saw him as being above political issues, and the effect was to give his words added authority. Earlier, his refusal to be dictated to by Phibun and his outward show of this by his boycott of the twenty-fifth Centennial Buddhist Celebrations had helped to discredit the Phibun/Phao regime, and Sarit had not been slow to use the divide as one of his excuses for the 1957 coup.

With his careful avoidance of matters political, other than always to urge governments to give consideration to the good of the people, the King's 1961 New Year's Day address to the nation was something of a surprise. In it he gave outspoken support to Sarit's government policy, both domestic and foreign, in a manner very helpful to his prime minister.[601] The King then repeated his support the following year and added a need for national unity and opposition to communism, a subject he was to adopt for a number of years. By a continuing emphasis on internal security he gave an impression of supporting the military and police in their policies.

In a speech to the King on the occasion of his birthday celebration in December 1959 Sarit said:

"Your majesty is very far-sighted and is genuinely concerned with the development of the country. ...you have advised and cautioned myself and others to carry out our duties faithfully for the development of the nation and happiness of the people. ...I would like to ask your royal indulgence to state to you from the bottom of my heart that your subjects have realised your great kindness, and will revere you within our hearts. Your visits to the countryside have swayed the hearts of your people towards unity within the nation." [602]

In fact, it was Sarit himself who proved to be far-sighted when he went on to say:

"...Your majesty is a King who will go down in our history as one who is truly loved and respected by the people."

---

601 *The Sarit Regime*; Thak Chaloemtiarana; pp403/404
602 *The Sarit Regime*; Thak Chaloemtiarana; p408 citing Sarit's speech during the parade to celebrate the King's Birthday 7 December 1959

Following Chakri Kings before him, Bhumibol was to maintain freedom of worship throughout the land. With Muslim unrest and lack of integration in the south, the King and Sarit met the problem head-on. They first arranged for a large delegation of Thai Muslims to have an audience of the King, thus allowing the Muslim community to speak face-to-face with a man for whom it had respect, for the King had not neglected the disciplines of his own faith. After that first approach to him, the King, while always remaining a devout Buddhist, chose to attend Muslim ceremonies associated with the birth of the Prophet.

Traditional Thai ceremonies were revived to emphasise nationhood. The First Ploughing ceremony, the most important of rituals was the first to be revived. The ceremony is founded on Brahminical harvest rites, and dates back to the days of the kingdom of Sukhothai. Whereas in pure Brahmin rites there is a total reliance on the blessing of the seed, King Bhumibol backed up the blessing with modern technology, the sacred seed for the ceremony being selected from his experimental rice farm.[603] Also revived in its full glory was the Buddhist ceremony of 'Kathin', involving the ceremonial procession of the highly ornate royal barges and by the King's gift of substantial value to the temple as his public expression of faith. Presents of robes for monks were made on the occasion of visits to different parts of the country. The King was also persuaded to perform marriage ceremonies among not only the accepted élite but also the expanding commercial and political *nouveaux riches*. By this act he virtually conferred upon them an acceptance within the élite itself, frequently confirming complex business and marital relationships. Good fortune attached itself to him with the discovery of a number of white elephants which, as a matter of practice, were donated to him and which were recognised as symbols of royal power.

At the end of 1963, Sarit was clearly dying and the King made an unusual gesture to his favoured faithful servant. He visited Sarit on his deathbed and wide publicity was given to a photograph of the stricken Sarit taking the King's hand and placing it on his own head, a final demonstration of his loyalty.[604] With the death of Sarit, the King took a step backward from the political field and remained aloof from the

---

[603] *Soul of a Nation*; BBC London, Post Production script; producer — Bridget Winters: Part I pp42/43
[604] *The Sarit Regime*; Thak Chaloemtiarana; p407

incoming regime. If Sarit's unfailing loyalty to King Bhumibol had seemed to some that he was preparing the King for a return to absolute monarchy, then the King deemed it otherwise. He had used Sarit's goodwill to move the throne to a more independent position and had himself enhanced its standing in the eyes of the people. He was now, in Buddhist manner, to follow the middle path of impartiality. It was a path which was to stand him in good stead at times of future crises.

While the Thanom/Praphat regime ruled throughout the 1960s the concern of the King was more for matters external rather than internal, which were primarily the concern of his prime minister. With the communists on the country's borders, with communist insurgency rife within the borders, and a full-scale American occupation of significant installations throughout his realm, the role of the King became more difficult. He himself had no illusions as to where his priorities lay. *"The first thing is security, that is the security of the people. The Thai people have to fight for their freedom, for their independence, so the main thing is to be a good general and then after that, when the country is more settled, is to have law and order, law and administration, and ...at the same time we must have enough food to eat, enough facility for a good home, to have shelter. These are essential things. And then we must have the social order and more things of the heart, that means we must be good people, so that there won't be disorder because people who are good don't create trouble so much. So we must have religion."* [605]

That he was able to surmount his problems depended much on the fact that he both understood the complexities of kingship and was able to analyse his own position. Most of all, he remained concerned about the welfare of the ordinary subject, without representation in high places. He acknowledged that: *"political parties will have their own interests at heart,* (but) *what about those who don't have the power... who are just ordinary people who cannot make their views known? They must look up to somebody who is impartial."* [606] Asked about his

---

[605] *Soul of a Nation*; BBC London, Post Production script; producer — Bridget Winters: Part I p18

[606] *Soul of a Nation*; BBC London, Post Production script; producer — Bridget Winters: Part II p35

duty as a king, King Bhumibol declined any pompous definition. He replied simply, *"I do things that I think are useful and that's all. ...if you asked me what I had in mind, what plan I had, I had no plan. ...we are going to do something that is good."* [607]
Impartiality had become the keystone of his approach to his relationships with the various ruling groups. His power was that of perceived morality. Sooner or later, a time was bound to come when intervention would become essential. That he could intervene effectively was a natural outcome of his earlier disciplined approach to his concept of kingship. As each year passed the weight of his impartiality increased, as did his worldly experience and power of leadership. He was not unaware of the attempt of parties to use him. *"It is quite normal that people will use the King. He's here to be used"*, and he drew a parallel with the Queen of the United Kingdom being used by political parties in her address when she opened a parliamentary session. It was his acceptance of his role that brought about the comment that he was *"a man of the people"*. [608]

There were limits to the way in which he would consciously be used and when, during the 1969 election, Thanom and Praphat's United Thai political party attempted to trade on his good name by claiming that he had great confidence in the leaders, it was immediately denied. The King declared that he would not support along party lines and that he looked for ways of avoiding military intervention. *"In my view there is no necessity for any revolution ...I believe that instead there will be an evolutionary change, in a good way."* [609]

The moment of truth for him arrived on thirteenth of October 1973, following the student demonstrations and with General Krit holding off attempts by Praphat and Narong to stamp out the opposition by violent means. The King first saw Thanom and his Cabinet and, to the surprise of many, permitted a deputation of students to put their case to him. The students left the King's presence confident that the military government would be held to its promises of reforms. The story of the night has already been told. By the early

---

[607] *Soul of a Nation*; BBC London, Post Production script; producer — Bridget Winters: Part I pp12/13
[608] *Alone On The Sharp Edge*; David van Praagh, quoting M.R. Seni
[609] Address given by H.M. King Bhumibol at Prasarnmit Educational College 15 March 1969

morning the demonstrations had turned into a full-scale riot. Narong's calls for Air Force and Navy support were refused and Krit blocked further troop movements.

That evening the King put his crown at risk by a second intervention. Had the prime minister's regime won the day, the King would have been lost and the question of abdication could have arisen. In an act of great courage he went over the heads of the political regime and spoke directly to the people. He had decided to appoint a new prime minister, Dr Sanya, then the Rector of Thammasat university. He referred to the events as a day of great sorrow, the most grievous in the history of the Thai nation. He called for an end to the violence and a return to the Thai way of life. With Krit backing his King by countering all attempts of Narong to revive Thanom's authority, the transition of power took place.

The King's risky intervention was successful and Praphas and Narong fled the country. Thanom left at the specific request of the King. People-power had prevailed with the help of the monarch. Politics in Thailand had entered a new phase. Any ambitious opportunist would in future know that apart from overcoming his natural opposition he would also have to reckon with the King himself. Had the King overstepped the bounds of sovereignty and moved too far into the realms of politics? A considered judgement on that position was later offered by M. R. Seni. *"I came to realise that if His Majesty had not intervened, the country would have gone into anarchy. Due to him — he dared to intervene — the country is not in anarchy."* [610]

The interest which King Bhumibol took in students was not confined to their days of demonstration. He had long encouraged greater education among the hill-tribes and the rural poor. His encouragement extended to the provision of scholarships for local undergraduate study and for overseas post-graduate studies. He attended numerous graduation ceremonies, looking upon the graduates as one of the nation's most vital resources. In an address to students at Chulalongkorn University at their annual 'Law Day', he pointed out to them the incongruity in law as they understood it and reality as

---

[610] *Alone On The Sharp Edge*; David van Praagh; p176

ordinary villagers understood it in relation to a specific incident. *"In a village... people are earning their livelihood in peace and in an orderly manner. They have their own self government... in fact, they are more democratic than if they had a district chief to govern them. But we act as if they were outlaws. ...(We are) charging them with having trespassed on reserved forest lands and driving them out. How should they know that those key areas are in conservation category, since there have been no government officials in the area to tell them so? Yet we can repress those ordinary villagers under an assumption that they ought to know the law. "* [611]

At the end of 1973 the King nominated a list of nearly two thousand five hundred citizens who were to select a new National Assembly of two hundred and ninety-nine. Under the chairmanship of Prince Wan Waithayakorn, the vote was completed on eighteenth December, with M. R. Kukrit the most favoured candidate. With the two brothers, Seni and Kukrit Pramoj, the King had the services of devoted royalists as prime ministers, both themselves descended from the royal line. Kukrit has clearly expressed his personal view of the position of the King within society. *"The Monarch, I would say, is the soul of the nation. The King is more than a ceremonial head. ...first of all, he is the head of the clan, he is the father of a very big family of Thais... and he is the source of Thai culture. Everything emanates from him. Good manners, way of living, the sort of thoughts and the way of thinking which we regard as the best of Thai thinking. Even the Buddhist religion to us seems to emanate from the King and the Monarchy. "* [612]

It is a view generally held by the traditionalist Thais. Whereas a western monarch holds himself out as a servant of his God, a Thai King has no such problem. He knows that he is accepted as divine. But in December 1975 his call was for earthly virtues. In his birthday speech at the taking of the salute of the Royal Guard the King's request was for loyalty and for the need to stand up to internal and external threats to the country's sovereignty and freedom. [613]

After the brutal treatment of the students at Thammasat university in October 1976, the King was once more obliged to demonstrate his

---

[611] *Political Conflict in Thailand*; David Morell and Cha- Samudavanija; pp67/8
[612] *Soul of a Nation*; BBC London, Post Production script; producer — Bridget Winters: Part I p23
[613] *Far Eastern Economic Review*; 2 January 1976

authority. The Kriangsak-controlled take-over of power was not to the liking of the King, and at his instigation Thanin was installed as prime minister. Again the question arises: did the King tread outside the bounds of sovereignty, and why did he then back the military, although he had not done so in 1973? M. R. Seni has found a reason in the continuation of peaceful rule. *"The King did not turn about — he was always for law and order. The end result, in both 1973 and 1976, was law and order."* [614] It was also thought that the King was aware in 1973 that some of the leaders favoured the creation of a republic. Thus the King was certainly not going to support such a regime. By 1976, the King was more concerned with the threat of communism and saw the continuation of the Chakri dynasty as safer in the hands of the military.

In an address on December 3 1976, the King put the situation in his own words. *"At a time when our country is being continually threatened with aggression by the enemy, our very freedom and existence as Thais may be destroyed if Thai people fail to realise their patriotism and their solidarity in resisting the enemy. ....accordingly, the Thai military has the most important role in defence of our country at all times, ready always to carry out its duty to protect our country."* [615] It was a reasonable judgement at the time, taking into account the security problems on his country's borders and the treatment of the royal house of Laos.

If the King thus saw his own role, how did the common people see it? From the point of view of students and Bangkok intellectuals, the King could not be held responsible for the events of 1976 but they felt a sense of betrayal by the King in that he had appeared to condone the ending of democracy by the military.[616] It was not the ending of democracy which had been the King's aim. It was an understanding of the changes which had taken place in the student body with the democratic process purists in 1973 having been replaced by a communist-inspired, if not infiltrated, hard core in 1976. The authority of the monarchy is derived from the Sukhothai and Ayutthaya days and is reinforced by the previous eight kings of the Chakri dynasty. When the testing times came in October 1973 and October 1976, the people saw again an apparent old-style kingship, a

---

[614] *Alone On The Sharp Edge*; David van Praagh; p176
[615] *Thailand; Society and Politics*; J. L. S. Girling; p215 citing *Siam Chodmaihet*
[616] *Alone On The Sharp Edge*; David van Praagh; pp176/80

King who led from the front. For a short time the King was the only voice of government, and his firmness, whilst putting his crown at risk, saved his people from anarchy.

Unfortunately, Thanin's performance as prime minister was such that when the military struck again the following year and ousted Thanin, Kriangsak was able to have himself installed as prime minister. The King, earlier that year, had expressed his disapproval of the continuing coups d'état, fearing that Thailand would be looked upon as a *'banana monarchy'*.[617] When the occasion arose — despite the disapproval both of the King and more so of Queen Sirikit, to whom Thanin was a political adviser — the King made no move to help Thanin. On the critical day he refused him an audience but in so doing, he left himself with little option but to confirm the appointment of Kriangsak some few days later. He appointed the deposed Thanin to be a member of his own advisory council.

———————

When the next reshuffle came to pass, the King appeared to welcome the arrival of General Prem. From the beginning, the staunchly royalist Prem found favour with the Palace and with that backing came a new-found political stability in the country. To ensure the continuation of that stability in the early years, the King backed a move to extend Prem's tenure as Army commander-in-chief.

The attempted coup in April 1981 brought constitutional problems for the King, although prime minister Prem's prompt action and Arthit's speedy military moves prevented the spread of trouble. Moving out of Bangkok with Prem and placing himself under the protection of Arthit's 2nd Army was a strong political gesture. On their arrival at Khorat, a supportive message from the Queen was broadcast, favouring the status quo of a Prem government. At the time, Thailand was beginning to enjoy a period of relative stability and the sudden and decisive end to the rebellion was warmly welcomed. The safety and well-being of the King and the Royal Family was of much greater concern to the populace as a whole than a technical problem of political involvement. In any event, after first sending emissaries to the King to explain their reasons, the plotters had been

---

[617] *Far Eastern Economic Review*; 4 November 1977

given a chance of an audience of the King before he had left Bangkok but they had rejected it.

Commenting on the pattern of coups d'état in Thailand, the London *Financial Times* said that there was a curious predictability about them. With rare exceptions, coups merely signalled a change in the ruling clique. *"Behind this curious predictability is the steadying hand of the monarchy. The King, who is revered as almost divine by the people, will, when necessary, step in and quietly restrain extremism. In this he is supported not only by his own authority and the Buddhist ethic but also by the realisation among the ruling élite that to flout the rules is to endanger the fragile structure on which they all depend."* [618]

King Bhumibol again spoke out about disputes between senior statesmen and the military when it came to his birthday speech in December 1984. He stated frankly that the disputes were against the country's best interests, leaving no doubt in anyone's mind that the Palace wished to see General Prem remain in post. [619] The comment had the immediate effect of cooling down General Arthit's supporters.

As the mid-1980s approached, thoughts had turned to the all-important anniversary of fifth of December 1987, when the King would reach the age of sixty and have completed the auspicious Fifth Cycle of life. In 1986, General Prem had been persuaded to take up the reins of prime ministerial office with less reluctance than on earlier occasions. He was known to wish to be in office for the King's birthday and to remain in office until the celebrations which would take place in July 1988, when King Bhumibol would become the country's longest serving monarch. This he did out of loyalty to, and respect for, his sovereign. Prem left the political scene within the month of the second great occasion.

In such an exalted role as that of a God-King, is there not absolute loneliness? Can family ties and love of one's people fill the void created by the denial of an equal? King Bhumibol himself does not accept loneliness as a problem. In the 1980 interview he responded to such an enquiry: *"I'm not lonely and I have work to do... The way of*

[618] *Financial Times*, London 24 April 1983
[619] *The Military in Thai Politics*, 1981-1986; Suchit Bunongkarn; p42

*doing work is to have some concentration and some peace, and then
one can think more clearly. It is a way of preparing myself to be able
to do whatever circumstances will have me do."* [620] He was, of
course, blessed by supportive members of his family. H.M. Queen
Sirikit herself was a tower of strength and she frequently accompanied
the King on his working tours. Her promotion of the Supplementary
Occupations and Related Techniques Movement, which was designed
to find extra income for impoverished but able farmers in the post-rice
harvesting season, paralleled the King's own concerns for the peasant
element of his realm.

Looking back over his reign to date, the King himself is seen not
as the instrument of the modernisation of Thailand but rather a
catalyst. It is surprising that the monarchy survived the Phibun era.
Once it had done so, the King maximised the advantages presented by
Sarit, to the extent that he could then remain above the unsavoury
elements of the Thanom/Praphas rule. With the first emergence of a
shaky democracy in the mid-1970s his role entered its catalytical
phase, a phase which could adapt itself to the solution of political
problems.

With the arrival on the scene of Prem, the monarchy gained in
both strength and popularity and the King was able to move with
greater ease both in and out of politics without being tainted by it.
Perhaps a more difficult problem for him in recent years was the
acceptance of the removal of Chatichai, a staunch royalist at heart, by
a military coup, a means which the King abhorred. In a little over a
year, the King again demonstrated his power when, quite summarily,
he instigated the removal of Suchinda, refused to accept the
appointment of Somboon, and overruled the politicians by appointing
the non-elected Dr Anand.

Throughout his reign, King Bhumibol has witnessed the continual
comings and goings of both political and military leaders, in some
cases the two materialising as the same person. He has observed the
antics of get-rich-quick politicians and their blatant corruption. He has
witnessed the evolution of a political structure which has struggled
towards a more democratic style, only to see it fall by the wayside as
an impatient military stepped in, then to become equally corrupt in its
turn. Perhaps it was this scene of continual change that shortly before

---

[620] *Soul of a Nation*; BBC London, Post Production script; producer — Bridget
Winters

his sixtieth birthday anniversary, brought from him the remark, *"The water of the Chao Phraya river has to flow on, and the water that has flowed on must be replaced."* [621]

---

[621] *The San Francisco Examiner*; 1 February 1987

CHAPTER FIFTEEN
Alpha or Omega?

Over the fifty years since the outbreak of the Second World War there have been repeated attempts to democratise the Thai form of government. There has been an undercurrent of thinking that, given some form of democratic government, many of Thailand's political ills would be cured. Almost inevitably, attempts to introduce it have withered away or have been chopped off at the roots by military intervention. Sarit's allegation that Western democracy was an alien culture was only too true. He had seen in it the cause of Thailand's political instability because it ignored the characteristics of the Thai people themselves. He sought a unifying authority as a focal point for national development. Sarit was, of course, arguing for his own dictatorial powers. Despite his reverence of the monarchy he did not look upon the King as the unifying element, although that is what the King essentially came to be.

An early attempt at the introduction of democratic principles by Pridi, with the help of M. R. Seni and Khuang, was killed off by Phibun's 1947 coup. A second, an apparent late conversion of Phibun himself after his visit to America and Britain, failed even to get off the ground. Democracy needed not only universal suffrage but also nationwide education. It was natural therefore that the more important moves of the 1970s were led by students, particularly from Thammasat and Chulalongkorn Universities. Lacking continuity of leadership as do all student movements, these heroic and sacrificial uprisings were doomed to failure. But a small first step on the road to the democratic principle was taken. At least the students of the day had thrown off the allegation that Thais were politically apathetic.

Seksan Prasertkul put his jungle experiences behind him, took a doctorate at Cornell University, USA, and became a political writer, lecturer, and eventually Dean of the Faculty of Political Sciences at Thammasat University. The leading lady of student rebellion, Chiranand Pitpreecha, also left jungle warfare behind and, married to Seksan, took a doctorate in history at Cornell. She became one of the country's leading poets, winning the South-East Asia 'Writers' Prize' in 1989.[622] Thirayuth Boonmi gave up his co-ordinating role in the jungle and returned to the city. He has become a respected *arjarn* at Thammasat's Faculty of Sociology and Anthropology, and whilst he wisely kept himself off the streets in the 1992 uprising, he was involved in its methodology and once more in his career suffered the indignity of arrest. With their contemporaries they represent the children of democracy, and are now among the mature element of Thai society which in the late 1980s and early 1990s must become the reasoning critics of government policy and behaviour.

In 1973, the Thai people sensed that the student movement was important, that it had a genuine role to change society, but that it lacked definition in its purpose. Chaturon Chaisaeng, a medical student of Chiang Mai university and chairman of that university's 1976 student group, who himself fled to the jungles after the 1976 cruelties, was in due course elected to be a member of the National Assembly. Reviewing, in October 1990, the student movement he was to comment,[623] *"...(not) even the echelons of seasoned, respected academics, learners, and veteran politicians, no one has come up with a clear proposal of how society should change."* Thus, while the students may have acted as a pressure group and indeed as a think-tank, there was quite naturally a lack of experience from which to think through the solution. Political leadership needs more than just theory.

In 1973 there was a wide spectrum of opinion that knew that change was essential. But to what, and on behalf of whom, within the bounds of realism? Chaturon described the student revolt as a *"vehement sentiment in defiance of the status quo."* So be it, but the *status quo* both before October 1973 and after October 1976 was not dissimilar. It was that of a people held in check by a military overlordship which arrogantly saw itself as the statesmanlike saviour of the nation. In the mid-1970s, defiance of the status quo led to the jungle, to a flirtation with communism, and eventually for most, to disillusionment. In his later comments, Chaturon spoke of the lessons of 1976: *"We have been through events to force significant social changes built upon a systematic, uniformed set of thoughts. We failed.*

---

[622] *Bangkok Post Weekly;* 1 October 1989
[623] *Bangkok Post Weekly;* 26 October 1990; Interview with Chaturon Chaisaeng, one-time Chart Thai MP for Chachoengsao Province, later for New Aspiration party

...we've learnt our lessons that even now, we can't find the absolute answer." He himself offered no long-term specific answer to Thailand's problems, merely that it became a question of proceeding to the extent that any current system would allow. *"We persevere on how to make the system less imperfect, make it develop towards the ultimate goal of being an effective tool to solve problems."*

In practice, there could be no absolute answer to a system that was inherently flawed. Similarly there was no clear answer to where the Thai student movement would go from the days of its 1970s suffering. It became frustrated, its youth spent in unfulfilled dedication which in itself led to years wasted in the jungle and in resettlement after that trauma. Unknown to Chaturon at the time of his statement, it was heading for an even more bloody conflict in the May days of 1992.

Where Sarit led in his thinking, or more likely Witchit's thinking, so inevitably, Thanom and Praphas followed. For over fifteen years democratic principles were consigned to the dustbin of history. After the brief democratic attempts of the 1973 to 1976 period they were put back there with the rise of Kriangsak and more recently during the short-lived rule of Suchinda. What progress can be detected in the brief intervals? Some, but not much. Unfortunately, there was no man of sufficient stature and democratic principles who could come forward to face election and lead the struggling coalitions to success. Windows of opportunity opened and closed. M. Rs. Seni and Kukrit led coalitions to the right and to the left of centre with different management styles. But the circumstances cried out for a democratic giant, a liberal Sarit, if such a contradiction had been possible. To many, it was a matter of regret that Dr Puey Ungphakorn did not accept the invitation to attempt to lead a government, but it is a matter of speculation whether or not he would have had sufficient backing to advance the country to a greater extent than the two royalist brothers. It is highly improbable because Thailand in the 1970s was not ready for democracy.

Neither was it yet ready in 1992. Endeavours of leaders, however highly principled, are not sufficient. Democracy is a philosophy of the human spirit which gives freedom to the people. It assumes that man himself is the world's principal resource and that his intelligence will enable him to satisfy human needs fairly from the other resources around him. It needs to be accompanied by sustained efforts to further the cause of human dignity. It is founded on discipline, not merely for leaders and governments but also for peoples themselves. As an ideal form, which it seldom if ever achieves, democracy involves decisions being taken as closely as possible to the citizen. To reach the necessary democratic standards of self-discipline and the essential supporting integrity, which are the foundations of democratic thought, requires decades of learning and, even more important, of understanding. In principle, it needs leaders of courage who are prepared to move the decision-making towards the citizen and in doing so, give up already held central power. That is a lot to ask of a person who has already, through dint of effort, acquired that power. In the past, and despite its own high principles, democracy has tended to produce leaders in many countries and blocs who have minimised consultation and reduced the size of the ruling circle.

Despite the endeavours of many well-meaning citizens, it is doubtful that Thailand will have a sustainable democratic government for decades. There is a need for free, untainted elections leading to not only sustainable government but also sustainable opposition, an opposition which must, if needed, be capable of replacing the government of the day. It is a difficult concept to introduce into a society of the extremes of rich and poor, of the highly intelligent educated bureaucrat and the exploited peasant farmer whose problems are aggravated by a strong control of the product of his labour by a partly-alien trading class. There remains a great cultural gap between Thailand's rural and urban sectors and it will not disappear in a mere decade or two. There is room in Thailand for the early development of the democratic process at local and provincial level, so that a small town or countryside community is able to see the result of the process at a stage that it can understand, away from the more dubious 'big-city' party management.

Attempts to dismiss democracy as a Western product resulted in requiring a 'Thai-style' product to develop for home consumption. Sarit's view was enshrined in the expression that in Thailand a tree *"was supposed to grow mangoes and bananas, not apples and grapes."* In words attributed to Thanom, in 1965, Sarit's revolution *"abolished democratic ideas borrowed from the West... (for) ...a democratic system which would be appropriate to the special characteristics and realities of the Thai ...a Thai way of*

Democracy. " [624] Sarit's revolution has been compared to that of De Gaulle or of Ne Win, although it is unlikely that De Gaulle would have been flattered either by the comparison or by the specific coupling. But what *is* the "Thai way of democracy"? To many foreign observers the statement alone to a contradiction in terms because democracy, as understood in the West, has never prevailed in Thailand. The expressions "benign dictatorship" and "benevolent despotism" are contradictions in themselves although they give an impression of a form of government not too dissimilar from the last years of Thatcherism in Britain in the late 1980s.

The problem that many Thai military leaders have had with Western democracy is simply that it *is* democratic, or substantially so. In the past the military has been unable to live with or even to tolerate this. An Army Radio '20' announcement of the Revolutionary Council on thirty-first of August 1965 asked, *"The question is how to make party conflict beneficial to our democracy. ..one way is to stipulate in the constitution that there should be executive supremacy over parliament. This would mean that elections would not greatly affect the formation of a new government."* [625] There was no follow-up to suggest why anyone should bother to hold an election in such circumstances. The use of the word 'democracy' in such a context is ridiculous in the extreme.

Thoughts on home-fashioned democracy have been developed over decades by the military and have been features of Chulachomklao Military Academy teaching. In a speech at the Academy, General Arthit spoke of *"duties beyond regular military functions... aimed at preserving national security, educating people to understand the democratic form of Government."* [626] General Chavalit, at a press conference, spoke of the period after the removal of the communists, when strategy would invoke the *"...eradication of social injustice to establish absolute democracy in the country".*[627] Again, General Chavalit on the principle: *"...the army will fight against ill practices and injustices in the political, social, and economic spheres... in order to build, as the Thai people always wish, a perfect democratic system*

---

[624] *The Sarit Regime*; Thak Chaloetiarana; citing Army 'Radio 20' of 17 August 1965
[625] *The Sarit Regime*; Thak Chaloetiarana; citing Army 'Radio 20' of 17 August 1965
[626] *The Military in Thai Politics, 1981-6*; Suchit Bunbongkarn; p65 note 1/33
[627] *The Nation*; 18 October 1984

of government... " [628] But the democratic concept remained unclear. The essential element of such teaching continued to be the right of the military to judge whether or not changes in style, content, or personnel of government were necessary and for it to take such action as it deemed appropriate.

The power of an individual soldier has come from personal promotion within the military, a power sometimes enhanced by the Chulachomklao Academy class structure. Financial rewards have come principally from individual involvement in commercial enterprises, sometimes legally as directors of boards of companies, frequently Chinese or Thai-Chinese, sometimes from less savoury enterprises. The powerful men of the early post-Second World War decade set the example by their 'patronage' of major banks which had been established with Chinese expertise. The Soi Rajakru clan influence extended over the Bangkok Bank, the Bank of Ayutthaya, the Thai Commercial Bank, and the Agriculture Bank. Phao's assistant Phinit, controlled the Bangkok Bank of Commerce. Sarit's Sisao Deves clique exercised influence over numerous banks which included the Union Bank of Bangkok, the Bank of Asia, the Provincial Bank, and Thai Military Bank. [629] Military influence over banks has to some extent been reduced, at least in theory, by the 1979 Banking Act which limited individual shareholdings. Like the 1978 Public Liability Companies Act, and many other matters of a controlling nature in Thailand, it is frequently ignored and at the beginning of the 1990s needed reinforcement by further legislation of an enforceable nature. In the state-owned industries, the armed forces have established control over their particular interests, an earlier example of which was the Royal Thai Air Force control, or controlling influence, over Thai International Airlines.

Perhaps the problem for the military and many others in Thailand springs from a reluctance to lose face. To foreigners it is noticeable that many Thai tend to dislike the responsibility of decision-taking: criticism is equally disliked and frequently resented. It is a feature which has to be overcome. A major principle of democracy rests in the right of the individual citizen to have the unfettered right without fear of retribution to criticise governmental and other bodies of a

---

[628] *The Military in Thai Politics*, 1981-6; p68 citing speech by General Chavalit Yongchaiyudh, Army Commander in Chief
[629] *The Thai Young Turks*; Dr Chai-anand Samutavanija; pp16/17

380

public and ruling nature. An extension of that right is the natural freedom of the press. Two of the great modern democracies, America and Britain, have spelled out this position within their law when protecting the critical citizen from being sued in libel and defamation by the all-powerful State. In 1923, the Supreme Court of Illinois ruled that the City of Chicago, as an entity, could not maintain an action for damages for libel against a citizen. It ruled: *"The fundamental right of freedom of speech is involved in this litigation ...every citizen has a right to criticise an inefficient or corrupt government without fear of civil as well as criminal prosecution. This absolute privilege is founded on the principle that it is advantageous for the public interest that the citizen should not be in any way fettered in his statements, and where the public service or due administration of justice is involved he shall have the right to speak his mind freely."* [630] The proposition was endorsed in a similar case by the Supreme Court of the United States. [631]

In Britain, in a much later hearing, a ruling of the House of Lords, it was held: *"It was of the highest public importance that a democratically elected governmental body should be open to uninhibited public criticism, and since the threat of civil actions for defamation would place an undesirable fetter on the freedom of speech, it would be contrary to public interest for institutions of central or local government to have any right at common law to maintain an action of damages for defamation."* The British judgement was based on the common law of England and Wales, but it was also noted within the ruling that reference to the European Convention for the Protection of Human Rights and Fundamental Freedoms would have brought the same result. [632] This perception of freedom to criticise and to be criticised, readily acceptable as fundamental to true democracy, is a high hurdle for proud military men to jump, but to fail to do so is to eliminate a claim of democratic principle.

Not surprisingly, the perception of the importance of the role of the military in civilian affairs has been best expounded by military

---

[630] *The Times* of London; 19 February 1993; reporting Britain's House of Lords' judgement and citing City of Chicago v Tribune Co, 1923-139 NE86

[631] *The Times* of London; 19 February 1993; reporting Britain's House of Lords' judgement and citing *The New York Times* v Sullivan 1964-376 US 254, 277

[632] *The Times* of London; 19 February 1993; reporting Britain's House of Lords' judgement in the case of Derbyshire County Council v Times Newspapers Ltd and Others

writers, frequently in army journals. Initially concerned with corporate stability, the thinking moved onwards to the need for national political leadership and control of the economy. Politics, as a subject, was seen first as the affair of the cities as distinct from the nation as a whole, but from the late 1950s onwards, love of the nation itself was seen to be the prerogative of the military, whose members then saw themselves, rather than the politicians, in the role of statesmen. The military saw the politicians as being concerned only with the next election, a view with which they would no doubt find a lot of sympathy from Western voters. The distinction between politician and statesman is important in the Thai military thinking, bringing, as it does, an assumption of a right to lead the nation.

The convoluted thinking of the military is reflected in a statement from the National Defence College in 1964 when there was a call to include the military in politics because "... *it is imperative that the military should be relied upon as an institution to suppress unstable forces.*" Later, comparing soldiers to monks owing to the alleged purity of their hearts, a 1970 National Defence College paper, calling upon history, offered, "*It is no surprise that only the best soldiers could become Kings in ancient times. As a corollary, it should not be a source of wonder today that the prime minister is for ever a soldier.*" [633] There appears to have been no reflection in Thai military thinking of the concept of "*government of the people, by the people, for the people*". The military was to take a leading role in politics, judge what was an unstable force, and then put it down. Its continuing ostrich-like attitude was hardly the stuff of democracy, and even today the attitude remains only just beneath an eggshell-thin surface. The principle that a peasant and a field-marshal have equal rights before the law has to be swallowed.

Ten years on in the Spring of 1980, a leading Thai political analyst argued that over the previous forty years the military had been so strongly represented in the government of the country that it had no cause to be hostile to government *per se*. In view of its role, it could not be treated only as a professional group. It was principally a political group, making use of the coup weapon as a means of participating in politics. In so doing or merely because it had the

---

[633] *The Sarit Regime*; Thak Chaloetiarana; p377, quoting Colonel Charung Prakobwannakit

power so to do, it protected its status within the legislative process and was enabled to expand its power.[634]

A further ten years on, little had changed. After his coup against the elected Chatichai government and having established the National Peace-Keeping Council, General Suchinda, then Army commander-in-chief, warned politicians not to push for a more democratic constitution. Deputy commander-in-chief, General Issarapong, spoke up in support of his brother-in-law, *"Political parties,"* he said, *"should concentrate on their responsibilities and should not waste time criticising the National Peace-Keeping Council and government"*.[635] He offered no comment on what the true role of a responsible political party should be if it was to be denied criticism of government. In an attempt to muzzle critics of his regime, Suchinda went on to criticise the Press, requiring it to conceal 'bad things' in the interest of the country.[636]

There is a proper role for military forces of all arms in a democracy, particularly when the country has neighbours which from time to time make hostile gestures or are perceived to be developing a position to make such gestures. That role is, however, one of disciplined subservience to the elected political power. It is not one which offers support to individual corporate structures or engages in commercial undertakings. It is not one that needs the support of privately controlled media. Its budget is of a size which the political authority determines to be necessary for the nation's external military hazards. It is not a budget to cover canal and river improvements or for the 'greening' of huge tracts of the country. Those are civilian tasks which a government can contract-out in line with its purpose and its current prosperity. There is a role for the police distinct from that of the army on which it will call, usually only in times of civil emergency and when the situation is beyond the control of the police force. The roles are complementary and this is reflected in the fire-power of each. There have been many outstanding army and police officers in Thailand who have appreciated this distinction, but regrettably it has been those who had no wish to understand it who have dominated the less fortunate periods of recent history. The need

---

[634] *Bangkok Post*, April 1980; article by Dr Chai-anand Samutavanija
[635] *Bangkok Post Weekly*; September 13 1991
[636] *Bangkok Post Weekly*; September 13 1991 — reporting a speech at the Reporters' Association of Thailand

for the military as the provider of external and internal security has massively diminished but many of its principal members have failed to perceive it, and this has been particularly noticeable among the high-profile military class cliques. Confusion has arisen because elements of the Army, particularly, have from time to time seen its role not as the defender of the realm but as the defender of a regime.

Had it not been for the interference of Washington in the immediate post-Second World War period, advised by inexperienced American OSS operatives, the Thai military might have been contained within its proper role. Much of Washington's problem arose from the OSS lack of background intelligence and knowledge of local history. Its activities became the subject of wide comment. One, referring to the lack of fundamental background, was particularly to the point. *"If they were ignorant of all of this, they had no right to be called an intelligence agency. If they were not, a large question mark must hang over the South-east Asian Branch of the OSS, particularly in regard to the actions of some of their personnel in the weeks immediately following the Japanese surrender. "* [637] Elsewhere General Douglas MacArthur refused to have the OSS in his Pacific Theatre. He was concerned that their loyalties were too frequently divided and some of their major conclusions were projected on inadequate field intelligence.[638] From the postwar Indochina theatre of operations came the view that the Americans were *"playing the anti-colonial and anti-white game (and) helped to pave the way for Asiatic communism. "* The question was posed as to why the OSS, *"so rich in men of valour"* sent such *"short-sighted amateurs".*[639] Throughout South-East Asia the OSS appeared to be running around like loose cannon on a gundeck.

The longer-term effects of OSS mismanagement or incompetence outside Thailand were worse than within. When end-of-hostilities spheres of influence were divided by the Allies, Britain was allocated Burma, Malaya, Singapore, Thailand, Indonesia, and North Borneo. All remained anti-communist despite the attempts that were made to subvert them. America was allocated China, North Vietnam, Laos, and subsequently, South Vietnam. All turned to communism: it may

---

[637] *The First Vietnam War*; Peter M. Dunn; p15, note 27
[638] *The First Vietnam War*; Peter M. Dunn; p81; note 25
[639] *The First Vietnam War*; Peter M. Dunn; pp41/4 quoting M. Jean Sainteny, Commissaire de la Republique

be presumed not to be entirely by coincidence when the OSS was so noticeably obsessed with anti-colonialism that it would back any uprising. Unwittingly, it was digging the graves of a generation of Americans just being born.

If the OSS had a role for which it should be particularly commended, it was for its far-seeing recruitment of young scholars who, under the leadership of Kharb Kunjara, became part of the Seri Thai, making their way across the age-old opium trails of southern China, the Shan States, and Laos. Their successful journeys provided a key link with America, sustaining the particular interest of that great nation in their homeland. It was an interest which was to intensify with the passing years, although principally in self-interest rather than in the interests of Thailand. While many of those scholars, with other Seri Thai colleagues attached to the British SOE, achieved success in post-war Thailand, their contribution might have been infinitely greater if Pridi had fulfilled the expectations of the Western Allies. Without him they were leaderless. Not even Adun could stem the tide of the OSS-encouraged military usurpation of power.

The role of free-world super-power and policeman brought an arrogance to the American personnel who became embroiled in South-East Asia and this in itself made logical judgements difficult. When the errors of the Eisenhower/Dulles domino theory were perceived, it was Senator John F. Kennedy who attacked both the policy in South-East Asia and the concealment of the truth from the American people. On sixth of April 6 1954 in a speech in the American senate he said: *"To pour money, materials, and men into the jungles of Indochina without at least a remote prospect of victory would be dangerously futile and destructive. ...I am frankly of the belief that no amount of American assistance in Indochina can conquer an enemy which is everywhere, and at the same time nowhere; an 'enemy of the people' which has the sympathy and support of the people."* [640] Nothing was learned, and when Kennedy himself became President his government was entrapped in the jungle mountains of South-East Asia. Despite his own earlier doubts he was unwilling to heed the advice which President de Gaulle offered him in May 1962, *"For seven years we wasted our time there. If you want to get bogged*

---

[640] *The Furtive War*; Wilfred G. Burchett; p59 note

down in that one — go ahead." [641] *The New York Times* also took up the issue. It pointed out that, for American soldiers, there would be a lack of motivation and ability to endure, added to unbelievably tough conditions of jungle warfare against an illusive but dedicated enemy.[642]

Four years later, de Gaulle returned to his theme. *"....there is... no chance that the people of Asia will subject themselves to the law of the foreigner who comes from the other shores of the Pacific, whatever his intentions, however powerful his weapons. In short, as long and cruel as the ordeal must be, France holds for certain that it will have no military solution."* [643] Many years passed before the lesson was finally learned, that a war of the people was not the same as orthodox confrontation. It was fortunate for Thailand that after others' earlier mistakes, Generals Prem and Chavalit, with their greater understanding of local conflicts, appreciated the distinction. Communism was contained and then beaten back within Thailand.

Unfortunately for President Kennedy and for his successor, Lyndon Johnson, they were the inheritors of a flawed theory, the concept of monolithic communism against the falling dominoes of South-East Asia, of which Thailand was the key state to be saved. Others, closer to the conflict and versed in the ways of that part of the world, believed and advised otherwise. An ambassador in Bangkok at that time recorded: *"With John Foster Dulles in charge of US foreign policy, there was much talk of dominoes falling and about doing something to prop them up. Dulles insisted that communism was monolithic, whereas it was pretty clear to us who worked in Asia that it was nationalistic. ...it seemed to me that where the West should draw the line was Thailand, a country which — except for its north-east provinces where food was less plentiful and there was a threat of communist penetration from across the Laotian border — was happy, independent, and self-respecting under a constitutional monarchy, with none of the inhibitions of its colonised neighbours upon which the communists could batten".* [644]

---

[641] *The Furtive War*; Wilfred G. Burchett; p139, citing *Le Monde* of Paris; 31 May 1962

[642] *The New York Times*; article of 25 July 1962

[643] Speech of President de Gaulle on a state visit to Cambodia 1 September 1966

[644] *A Marvellous Party*; p177

He was not alone in his view. When students fled from persecution in the 1970s and joined communist bands, they rapidly came to appreciate the fervent nationalism which pervaded communism in the neighbouring countries. The centuries of history from which the kingdoms developed was much stronger than acceptance of a temporary political philosophy.[645] This same nationalism has shown itself in the individualism of members of ASEAN, an individualism which, if anything, is likely to be enhanced if each of the Indochina states join that organisation.

While Thailand has steered itself away from communism, it is not perhaps a country in which orthodox democracy will evolve. Democracy is not the only political philosophy available, although, with the apparent collapse of Russian communism, it has become dominant. Geographically placed as it is, Thailand has no choice but to learn to live with its intransigent neighbour, China. With its potential for ever-increasing economic expansion, China will almost certainly become more important to Thailand than are either America or Japan. Fortunately for Thailand, China is more of a defensive than offensive power and its limited post-war incursions have been short-lived and not particularly successful. In the event of a dispute it is more likely to finance local insurgency than engage in direct, all-out hostilities. Thailand can take some comfort that it has already survived the insurgency of the 1960s and 1970s, and by the time of the Chatichai regime, it was geared to exporting Thai-style capitalism.

It has yet to reach for some form of stability in practical politics. With paternalism a natural part of the Thai culture, perhaps benign Cabinet rule, if it were possible to construct without corruption, might be more suitable for it than democracy. The successful Prem decade and the second short-lived Anand-appointed Cabinet were not far removed from such a regime. Much depends on the military coming to terms with limitations to its own role. It was thought reasonable that by the end of the 1980s, despite its inherent craving for power, it had drawn a line under history and rejected past forms of dictatorship. It was not to be so. *"In his errors a man is true to type,"* said a Chinese sage, *"Observe the errors and you will know the man."* [646] The Thai military has been, regrettably, a modern proof of an ancient wisdom.

---

[645] Discussions in Bangkok with Dr Seksan Prasertkul and Arjarn Thirayuth Boonmi, 27 and 29 November, 1993
[646] *The Analects* Part IV – 7; Confucius

In the Phibun era, the Thai state had shunned constitutionalism and degenerated into militarism with an emphasis on the cult of personality. While this personality cult continued until the 1970s, the advent of communism forced upon the Thai élite a strong anti-communist ideology in which the trinal concept of Nation, Religion, and King was recognised as a way forward for stable government. The civil and military élites were forced to compromise their status with the rising commercial middle classes. Political parties, in name at least, became a centre of activity in which all citizens, including the Chinese groupings, could participate across a wide field. Unfortunately, Thailand's early years of party politics have left much to be desired. The purchase of votes to guarantee elections has been too generally accepted and as result, politicians elected have sought offices where, at least, compensatory remuneration can be enhanced by spin-offs from the letting of contracts and other practices which are unacceptable in an ethical democratic society.

The politicians have not been alone. While making its justifiable criticisms of the Chatichai government ministers, some of the military were up to the same tricks, enriching themselves from logging and other contracts in both Burma and in the newly developing Cambodia. While Chatichai was thinking positively and calling for the whole of Indochina to be converted from a battle zone to a market place, some of the military were making their own arrangements either with the unscrupulous and degenerate anti-democratic military of Burma to the west or through the equally disreputable Khmer Rouge to the east. It is this type of behaviour which has denied to the military the 'knight-in-shining-armour' role which it attempts to offer for public viewing. Elements of it, distinct from the truly professional soldiers, have an in-built lust for power accompanied by greed.

The opinion of the outside world was perhaps well, if cruelly, reflected in a comment from the United Nations forces in Cambodia when, to constrain Khmer Rouge activity, it was necessary to guard the border between Cambodia and Thailand. The Thai military offered to secure it. *"Asking the Thai military to guard a border is like asking a mouse to guard a piece of cheese"* was the offered opinion of the United Nations.[647] It was an unfortunate comment at a time when the Army, under General Wimol Wongwanich, was making great efforts to improve its culture and the perception of it at home and abroad.

---

[647] *The Times* of London; 2 January 1993

Nevertheless, it was not totally unjustified at a time when close relationships linked the Thai Army to the Khmer Rouge along the border. It was reasonable for the Thai Army to assume that when the United Nations pulled out of Cambodia, it might be left to sort out the mess. Many Thai Army officers who had close links with the Khmer Rouge were no doubt helpful to the communist rebel force while it has clung desperately to small areas of its mother country, particularly to those areas which contain vast tracts rich in hardwood forests and the famous Paili ruby mines. General Wimol's task of rebuilding army morale was considerable. A Chulachomklao Class 5 general himself, he has steered clear of the Suchinda clique and has become an outspoken critic of the involvement of the Army in politics.[648] Fortunately for him, respect for a popular monarchy, and, since its founding in 1975, the movement in share prices on the Bangkok Stock Exchange, have also, to some extent, helped to hold the old-style military in check.

It has been quite a common occurrence in the Western press to find writers of articles on the subject of Thailand, launching forth into generalised statements of the all-prevailing corruption and commercial criminality within that country. It is not difficult to find substantial allegations within Thailand itself. But Thailand is not alone in this problem. Allegations can be levelled equally at most other states, including those in the West which have been so free with their criticisms. There has been a long history of Middle East 'arrangements' running from straight commission agencies to one-sided 'joint ventures'. Japanese banks have reeked of scandal. In July 1991, after a Nomura Securities scandal with gangster involvement, there were a number of cases involving the issue of forged deposit certificates for client transactions to help raise loans.[649] The London *Economist* was moved to comment that, *"Japan is up to its neck in dirt. ...the real Japanese worry is that the supply of scandals will cease. This will be a sure sign that change has been replaced by cover-up."* In the same week the biggest bond dealer in America admitted to massive misdeeds in cornering new American

---

[648] Asiaweek; 13 October 1993

[649] *The Economist*, London; 27 July 1991 and *The Independent* of London

Treasury-bond issues. By that time, gaols already held a junk bond king and notorious financiers and arbitragers.

Internationally, the massive fraud of the Bank of Credit and Commerce International was still unfolding. The Bank was a haunt for drug-runners, including Khun Sa and President Noriega of Panama, fraudsters, money-launderers, arms dealers, terrorists, members of the Mafia, and the CIA.[650] Britain also collected its own crop of financial scandals. An illegal share-support operation resulted in the chairmen of two major companies being committed to prison. A number of operators of illegal insider-dealing, financial advisers, and company directors followed. All of these British misdemeanours were however dwarfed by the sudden disappearance from his yacht off the Canary Islands of the chairman of a major circulation newspaper. Disclosure followed that he was a swindler who had even stooped to raiding the pension funds of his own employees. Early in 1993, the Italian government totally disintegrated under allegations of Mafia-linked corruption, the news of which was followed closely by the disclosure that the self-same government had been merrily defrauding the European Commission of hundreds of millions of dollars. Corruption recognises no political borders.

So what of corruption in Thailand? Some votes at fifty cents to a dollar a time? Such behaviour was not so far removed from an American president seeking votes by selling fighter aircraft to Taiwan and Saudi Arabia to ensure that work would fall in States where votes were needed. Some petty payments for certificates that should never have been signed and a few million dollars from fiddling construction, logging, and other contracts? They all seem relatively small beer when compared with the expert pin-striped crooks in the West. Nevertheless, the extent to which corruption is practised elsewhere can never be justification in itself, and until professional pride and ethical behaviour penetrate the corridors of political power in Thailand, there will continue to be an unscrupulous scramble for personal gain on the part of the few. Beyond that, the ordinary commercial problems will remain, and to them can be added the complexities arising from the trafficking of locally produced narcotics.

Thailand's problems of opium and of the associated derivatives, heroin and morphine, are not yet over. Whilst great efforts have been made formally to move away from the evils of the Phao and Sarit

[650] *The Economist*, London; 27 July and 17 August 1991

days, reducing the production of opium in the Thai mountains to an acceptable level, substantial trafficking of foreign output still takes place. The American Drug Enforcement Agency maintains its presence and in moments of frustration is liable to remind enquirers that it considers that half of the high-rise buildings in Bangkok were financed from opium proceeds. No one doubts that the capital structure of more than one bank owes its foundation to that commodity. Bangkok has many rich men who would prefer not to say where their family wealth originated. Klong Toey port continues to be raided for drug parcels, sometimes successfully. It remains one of the great outlets of the Triangle produce as well as Mekong-basin-grown marijuana. Futile theories of reducing the addiction in the West by stamping out the supply continue to be voiced outside Thailand but the West will have to solve its own problems by stamping out demand. While there is demand there will *always* be supply. Such is the commercial balance of all commodities and opium, heroin, and marijuana have been no exception. If opium is not grown in the mountains of the Shan States and Laos, then it will be grown somewhere else. That production has been reduced in Thailand itself has been in part due to the crop substitution programme and part due to the drift to the cities where more attractive work has become available.

If the huge opium crop from the Shan States is to be reduced, as some wish, then Burma has to rid itself of its corrupt government and the influence of Khun Sa has to be diminished. Whilst he is frequently depicted as an uncouth bandit, visitors credit him with well-developed qualities of leadership — flamboyant, but a man of charisma. All peoples have a right to self-determination and he has sought to have accepted the principle of, *"full autonomy in internal administration of... the Shan States"*. The actual words are not his. They were written by Britain in 1947 in the Treaty with Rangoon, a treaty which has studiously been ignored by successive Burmese governments. His own words are directed elsewhere in reference to the world drug problem. *"I grew up in the Shan State. I know the harm of opium. We can control our children. If you cannot control yours, it's your problem."* [651]

He is uncomfortably right. Only the consumer countries can cure this problem by eliminating demand. There are at this time enormous

---

[651] *New Straits Times*; 28 January 1986

sums of taxpayers' money being spent in an effort to eliminate supply, bringing the allegation from Khun Sa that the Drug Enforcement Agency fakes arrests and burns soap-powder disguised in drug packing to justify its existence and life-style.[652] In the five years to 1991, American aid to Thailand for activities related to narcotics law enforcement and crop control exceeded sixteen billion US dollars.[653] The sums spent on deterring potential consumers — the only measure with a chance of success — are, by comparison, piggy-bank money.

The danger from the use of narcotics is at least as great as the danger from rampant nuclear energy, and with present attitudes it may yet prove to be greater. Its elimination cries out for the building of a world which people seek to live in, not to escape from. As far as the Shan States go, perhaps America will have to swallow its pride again and exchange a policy of indictment for one of constructive discussion. It could learn a lesson from the dissolution of the former British Empire, where many of the first generation of great leaders of the emerging countries had at some time been in British-run prisons or had lived with a price on their heads. All disputes and wars one day reach a position where the two sides have to speak to each other. If Jew can speak to Arab, can no one speak to the Shan?

Time will change the Triangle narcotics supply pattern, but it will not in itself eradicate it. The remnant of the Kuomintang army, so powerful in the drug trade, has grown old and the younger generations lack the enthusiasm and motivation of the old 'lost army.' By 1992, even Khun Sa at the age of sixty was speaking of retirement but he was not inactive. In 1991, reports filtered through of deals with the Karen to provide soldiery and weapons to help the Karen in their struggle against the Rangoon government and of the attempted purchase of unused American arms left behind in Vietnam.[654] By June 1992, Sa was reported as having relinquished all of his commands and become an ordinary Shan citizen. But Khun Sa was not destined for simple citizenship. A little over a year later he was being described as president of the Shan State Restoration Council, and he was calling for the implementation of the 1947 Treaty with Britain. With it came the

---

[652] *Bangkok Post Weekly*; 27 August 1993
[653] Thailand Narcotics Bureau Annual Report 1991; extracts form Narcotics Suppression Bureau, Bangkok; 30 November 1993
[654] *Bangkok Post Weekly*; 13 March 1992

natural demand which such a move would bring in its train, the independence of the Shan States.

The state-sponsored output from Laos will only cease when there are marketable alternative products from that land-locked country. Again, Laos in its turn is likely in time to turn to America for help, and not unreasonably so in view of the unpardonable harm done to it through the CIA, with Thai support, during the 'secret war'. The problems of Laos continue to affect Thailand, first through refugees and the camps which were established for them and then as recently as mid-1991, through an incident involving the dreaded 'yellow rain', the mycotoxin, which drifted into a corner of the land to kill and injure Thai citizens.[655]

The refugee camps on Thailand's eastern border, first established out of sympathy and charity, became a Thai nightmare. The exodus from the communist-controlled Indochina countries started in 1975. By 1989 there were nearly four hundred thousand refugees. Of these, over one hundred and fifty thousand had arrived in the first five years of Pathet Lao rule. While the Lao are a people with whom the Thais of Isan readily identify, sympathy and charity wear thin over time. On the argument that many of the refugees were there on economic, not political, grounds and that others were known to be Khmer Rouge sympathisers, there to keep a watch on other refugees, a new 'pushback' policy was introduced in 1985. The policy has resulted in the death of many of those forcibly returned. The Thai assertion that it only provided 'first asylum' was understandable but such an assertion contravened international law. By 1992, the United Nations' High Commission for Refugees had taken a positive lead in reducing the numbers of Cambodians in the Thai camps and had become responsible for their reintegration into their homeland. It was a problem with no easy solution if human rights and humanitarian principles were to be observed. It is a problem which will continue to arise worldwide as long as other nations fail to give sufficient help to small countries such as Thailand which are incapable themselves of carrying the refugee load.[656]

---

[655] *Bangkok Post Weekly*; 14 June 1991

[656] *Forced back and Forgotten*; Lawyers Committee on Human Rights, New York 1989; and *Khmer Rouge Abuses Along the Thai-Cambodia Border*; Asiawatch; 1989

In 1992, Thai capital was being rushed into developing Cambodia, ahead of the peace process. At first, much of it went into bricks and mortar, but there was soon a darker side which involved itself in narcotics development and in the rape of great forests and mineral wealth. *"Thailand is the golden gate to open Indochina"* Chatichai had said. Thailand was already the developed air-transport hub of the Indochinese region and had extended its banking and financial services industry into welcoming neighbouring countries. Its currency was stable and accepted in the lesser-developed countries. Soon, however, the major Thai investments were seen to be in sleazy bars and fast-buck enterprises. Get-rich-quick traders were making Chatichai's golden gate look like nothing more than a massage parlour door.

Much of the new investment in the countries of the former Indochina has been Asian, with little Western influence. Perhaps that is for the good. Looking back over the history of South-East Asia for the last one hundred years, it is reasonable to question whether or not it would have been a happier place if the colonial British and French and the quasi-colonial Americans had stayed away. The exploitation of the lands did little for the indigenous population, whose culture pre-dates the European, and thus American as generally accepted, by some three thousand years. Against the will of the populations, their lands were brutally occupied, the opium habit was forced upon them, and the produce of their lands extracted for the benefit of peoples who had scarcely heard of them and had little idea of where and how they lived.

Thailand was not entirely protected from the turmoil that engulfed its neighbours. Whilst it makes much of its reputation of not having been colonised, in practice that was only because neither France nor Britain particularly wanted it. It has tended to throw in its lot with the strongest power of the day, and in many ways profited from this policy. There has been a price to pay in the devclopment of its land and the economic subjugation and exploitation of many of its peoples at the behest of foreigners. It is a price which continues to be paid.

How much has Thailand changed from the early days of Phibun to the fall of Chatichai? It is certainly a much more populous place, yet the grip of the Thai élite on the established structure has changed remarkably little. Everyone who really matters knows everyone else who really matters. Whether overtly or covertly, the military dominate the political scene as it did then. It is easy to come to the conclusion that, at times, the country has exercised poor judgement in its choice of friends. It picked the wrong side in the Second World War and again in the American incursions in Laos and Vietnam. Its links with Pol Pot in Cambodia and in the protection provided for him, contrary to government policy, by some elements of the military can only be considered undesirable, but the connections satisfy numerous vested business interests. The relationships with Ne Win and his successors in Burma have been equally ill-chosen.

Despite the rapid growth of skyscrapers and the development of light industry, despite the glitzy hotels of the resorts and despite the appalling traffic jams and diesel pollution of Bangkok, Thailand's economy remains primarily agrarian, although less dependent on that sector than in the days of Phibun. The agrarian element has had little to do with politics, regarding it as a 'city matter'. The remainder of Thailand's economy is dominated by Western-style industrial powers, particularly Japan and America, despite its efforts to link itself more closely to its ASEAN partners and China. General Chatichai more than anyone, with his inherent ability to spot entrepreneurial opportunity wanted to change Indochina from a Thai battleground to a market place but progress has been hindered by the fact that those countries are still at a low *per capita* gross domestic product in relation to Thailand itself. In addition to their activities in Cambodia, Thai business men have already become the biggest foreign investors in Laos. A Mekong crossing has opened to road traffic with the new Thailand-Laos 'Friendship' bridge. A second may follow. Eight new banks in Vientiane are Thai-owned and Thailand may well achieve through economic progress the influence in Laos which it has previously sought through conquest. The crossing of the Mekong also has greater, if less immediate, trading prospects for Thailand with infrastructure improvements linking it to China.[657]

Thailand can claim that it has retained its political independence and that it lives in the alliance of Monarch, Religion, and State. But true democracy still eludes it as coup and attempted coup follow the old pattern, despite avowals that such a practice is out of date. Although the process of coup and attempted coup has retained an almost gentlemanly form of conduct, the period 1973 to 1976 and the days of May 1992 have shown how explosive the society has become. The insurgency, the demonstrations, labour unrest, and land reform

---

[657] *Financial Times*, London 11 August 1993

agitation of those days have shown a new side of the Thai nature, one that is not portrayed in the travel literature of exotic temples and blue skies.

Political parties remain more personality-based than policy-based. Personal cliques or clans still emerge as the most important vehicles for applying political pressure and counter-pressure but the old élitism of the civil service is in the process of giving way to a new commercial class. High salaries tempt away those once satisfied with power alone. No longer is it necessary to be a senior officer of the armed forces, or a senior civil servant, with income backed up by a clutch of imposed directorships. The new industrial and commercial companies operating in a growing market economy can offer the people of Thailand another way of life, and signs of increased well-being are readily found.

Prime ministers and military chiefs and their supporters have come and gone, but since that early morning tragedy of June 1946, one King has reigned over Thailand. Over the long years of his reign, Bhumibol Adulyadej, ninth King of the Rama dynasty, has progressed with a quiet but sure hand on the tiller to steer his country away from its self-inflicted disasters. Holding himself above the machinations of politicians, both those properly dedicated to the service of their country and those blatantly on the make, he has moved with increasing sure-footedness to dampen-down troubles arising within his kingdom and to improve the lot of the unrepresented poor. He has ruled for longer than any other king within the Rama dynasty. It is eventually for history to give its verdict on his reign, but it would be surprising if history did not judge him to be the greatest of that dynasty.

Despite its apparent avoidance of the worst of the political horrors that have befallen its neighbours, Thailand's materialistic aspirations have left awful scars across its cities. It has been prepared to give up virtually everything for money. In Phibun's days, a hard-headed foreign resident wrote of it, *"The King in his yellow Rolls Royce... parties in flower-perfumed gardens... light bulbs which attracted myriads of mosquitoes, moths and bugs... Siamese boxing... the lovely elephants... peasants working in paddy fields, picking up rice with one hand and catching fish with the other... the graceful Siamese dancing girls... the unequalled good manners of the Thai"*.[658] An equally hard-headed writer, in the days of the Chatichai government, noted a

---

[658] *A Marvellous Party*; Sir Berkeley Gage

different situation. *"Half of Thailand's GDP is produced by Bangkok, a Chinese city in Thai disguise. In Bangkok, traffic now moves at an average speed of less than eight kilometres per hour... it is impossible to quantify how much foreign investment Thailand has foregone because of its overburdened infrastructure, but future growth will clearly be hostage to improvements in the country's physical condition. "* [659]

The Thai identity has been diminished in a welter of foreign fast-food palaces and pop-music culture. Only in the often neglected villages can there be found the calm and peace that was once Thailand, much beloved by discerning visitors. Outwardly, the new Bangkok is air-polluted, traffic-jammed, brash, and sleazy. Yet even there, inwardly, it retains to a considerable degree the strength of the close-knit family society, a strength which, regrettably, the West has mostly lost. Despite the lurid reports of Bangkok life which appear from time to time in Western tabloid newspapers, written apparently by reporters whose thought processes appear to be incapable of rising above the level of their navel, there is an inherent dignity to be found in the family life and its observed proprieties. Therein lies a strength which may yet survive the depravity which the adoption of some forms of Western civilisation has brought.

In the seventh year of his reign King Prajadhipok, Rama VII, wrote: *"We must try to educate people to be politically conscious, to realise their real interests so that they will not be misled by agitators or mere dreamers of Utopia. If we are to have a parliament, we must teach the people how to vote and how to elect representatives who will really have their interests at heart. "* [660]

Over half of a century has passed since then and the problem is still to be solved. It is an agonisingly slow process.

---

[659] *The Economist*, London; 16 November 1991
[660] *The Thai Young Turks*; Dr Chai-anand Samutavanija; p7 citing National Archives, Seventh Reign, Royal Secretarial 6/3

APPENDIX I
The Jim Thompson mystery.

James Hamilton Wilson Thompson was born in 1906, the grandson of an American civil war general of distinction. He joined the Delaware National Guard and after the Japanese attack on Pearl Harbour he was commissioned and posted to the OSS, with whom he operated in the North African and European theatres of war. By 1945 he had moved to Ceylon and was jungle trained. On the very day that Japan surrendered, he was in flight to parachute to the Thai/Lao border for OSS work in that area. The plane was diverted to Rangoon and Jim Thompson arrived in Bangkok in a much less spectacular fashion than he had expected. Within a few weeks of his arrival, he had taken over the post of OSS station chief, after which he set up a temporary American consulate.

Both demobilised and divorced in 1946, he spent two decades developing the Thai silk trade beyond any previous conception. He improved the commercial distribution network for the existing products, developed higher quality and more marketable products, and then reorganised the small-scale production operations to meet the growing market. Not everyone was on his side. His success created jealousy among his competitors. In his early years he had become a close friend of Pridi and number of his Seri Thai supporters. Many had disappeared during the era of Phao's police suppression. He held strong anti-colonial views, particularly of the French return to Indochina. Local works of art graced his Thai-styled home which became a centre of social life in Bangkok. He was joined at his table by the Thai élite, foreign ambassadors, and many from the growing commercial activity. He was described by a British ambassador as a most interesting person, tall, slim, rather reserved, and artistic, a gentleman by birth, in behaviour and in appearance. He was a respected member of the Siam Society and in 1962 King Bhumibol appointed him to the Exalted Order of the White Elephant.[661]

Despite certain frictions over some part of his art collection, Thompson was a much loved, highly regarded man to whom many went for advice. It was to provide commercial advice that he left

---

[661] *The Legendary American*; William Warren

Bangkok on the Thursday before Easter 1967 with his friend of many years, Connie Mangskau, and journeyed via Penang to the Cameron Highlands of Malaysia en route for business discussions in Singapore. Connie, one of the great international characters of Bangkok, was the daughter of a half-Thai, half-Chinese girl who was said to have been the most beautiful girl in all of Thailand. She had eloped with an Englishman and Connie was born in Chiang Mai. Connie became a nurse and married Norwegian Fridtgof Mangskau when she was only eighteen. Widowed at the age of twenty-three, she was a wartime prisoner of the Japanese and after the war, developed an internationally-known antiques business. The two of them stayed that weekend with Dr Ling, a Chinese from Singapore, and his American wife. Golf and dinner on Saturday were followed by church and a picnic lunch on the Sunday before, at the request of a restless Thompson, they returned to Dr Ling's cottage to retire. Thompson did not retire. He left the cottage at about three o'clock in the afternoon and was never seen alive again.

Thompson meant to return. He was a chain smoker, but his cigarettes were left in the cottage. He needed regular medication but his pills were also left in the cottage. He was a man among old friends in the middle of a specifically arranged journey. A search that night revealed nothing. The next day, Easter Monday, the official search began, initially with a few local policemen. By nightfall nearly one hundred people were involved. Thompson's company were informed and from there, information reached US General Edwin Black, an old military friend. General Black sent a number of American helicopters which searched for nearly a week. By Tuesday twenty-ninth of March, there were over three hundred policemen and thirty jungle aborigines involved. A reward of ten thousand US dollars was offered. Soon that became twenty-five thousand dollars, a large enough amount to tempt any local inhabitant.

There were no trails; there were no signs of clothing; there were no wheeling vultures. Some weeks later a British jungle expert, Richard Noone, who was at that time with SEATO, went with chosen companions to discuss the disappearance with local tribesmen. He was away some forty hours, after which he declared that he was convinced that Thompson had not been in the jungle. On seventh of April the official police search ended. On thirtieth of August that same year, Thompson's seventy-four-year-old sister was found murdered at her home in America. Her dogs raised no alarm. Nothing was stolen. The case was not solved.

Jim Thompson's disappearance brought to the Malaysian highlands a surfeit of seers and magic men of all colours, races, and creeds. A witch doctor was convinced that he was being held by evil spirits under a tree in the jungle. Another placed the tree in Cambodia, to which country Thompson had gone by plane, or perhaps by sea. He had been captured by communists to be brainwashed and cast in the role of a defector. He was posing as a fortune-teller in a market-place. He was a house guest of Pridi in China. He had been captured and put aboard a Norwegian boat bound for Hong Kong. He had been killed by a poisoned blowpipe dart. One theory had him captured by a frustrated love-sick aborigine woman from one of the local tribes, although why in that state she should pick on a sixty-one-year-old man is hard to imagine. In October 1967, a British officer of the Gurkha regiment, financed by an American journalist, spent a week in northern Cambodia, following up a seer's vision.[662] No trace was uncovered.

Less far-fetched theories suggested that he had fallen down a ravine, been caught by mistake in an animal trap, kidnapped by a convoy of Thai police cars, and that he had been abducted because "once an agent always an agent". Eventually the Malaysian police, who certainly did not like this happening in one of the country's prime tourist areas, were convinced that the absence of clues ruled out his being either killed or injured within the vicinity of the cottage, that the absence of demand ruled out any ordinary kidnapping, and that such an abduction would have required perfect timing, organisation, and discipline. To the Malaysian police it could only have been carried out by communist insurgents.[663]

In some embassies at the time, the view was held was that it was most likely to have been death in some form of animal trap, although there was respect for Richard Noone's expert opinion. A second theory had him abducted and murdered by jealous competitors.

Looking back across time and distance, it is to easy to discount the more weird and wonderful theories of witch doctors and seers because none were to produce any answers. Incursions by Thai police or jealous Thai businessmen into a foreign country to carry out a simple

---

[662] *Bangkok Post*; date missing
[663] *The Legendary American*; William Warren

murder are illogical for their unnecessary complexity. Businessmen in Thailand have proved themselves quite capable of removing rivals by the medium of the 'motor-cycle murder' where the pillion rider shoots the victim and the driver quickly hides the getaway in the legendary Bangkok traffic confusion. Its frequency is almost high enough to make it appear a variation on competitive tendering. If the highly regarded, expert evidence of Richard Noone had not been available, the ravine or animal trap theory would have seemed probable and to some people, including Connie Mangskau, it was the *only* acceptable answer. The Malaysian police view of a communist strike is convenient and not too damaging to the interests of tourism. As with the jungle options it would account for the absence of clues in the vicinity of the cottage.

However famous the individual, and Thompson was without doubt famous, the massive efforts of General Black, whilst praiseworthy, seem to the casual observer to be somewhat excessive. It had been twenty-one years since Thompson had taken off an American uniform. In practice, was it excessive? The intelligence officer of a Gurkha battalion in charge of some three hundred men who searched for a week has said that although their own particular task was carried out with thoroughness, the American effort could best be described as all noise and show. He also noted that a highly skilled Malaysian force searched in a manner which convinced him that they knew that Thompson was not there. A young volunteer from a local missionary school found what he thought was a wad of gauze, which could have been used with chloroform or some similar substance. The police, to whom he gave it, treated it as a matter of no importance.[664] The sum total of all of these extensive efforts on the part of American, Thai, and Malaysian resources in search of this eminent Thai citizen failed to show that Thompson was at any time anywhere in the vicinity after he left the cottage.

Many years later an elderly Thai citizen, respected throughout the length and breadth of the land both in the commercial/financial world and in the cultural, spoke of the incident.[665] Jim Thompson had been a great friend of his and a fellow member of the Siam Society. They had dined together frequently and he would have known him anywhere.

---

[664] *The Riddle of Moonlight Cottage*; Article by Charles Nichol in London *Daily Telegraph* supplement, 21 March 1992; pp36-44
[665] Discussions with Dr Kraisri Nimmanahaeminda; 26 January 1987

He was confident that Thompson was not a foolhardy man who would have wandered off alone into the jungle. He further discounted any intervention of Thai police or of Thai business interests in Malaysia. It would have been too easy to settle scores within Thailand where a contract hit-man would be available for a mere twenty US dollars.

Over the Easter holiday, he himself was off Penang on a fishery development vessel. He had no doubt whatsoever that a corpse he saw in the sea was that of Jim Thompson. He reported it to the police in Penang and he reported it to the American ambassador in Bangkok. The police took note but he heard no more. The American ambassador quite obviously did not want to know. He disputed the fact and later stated that the body was that of another American but there was no specific identification. Asked how he thought the body came to be in the sea off Penang, the elderly citizen offered a thought that the sudden disappearance and absence of clues in the vicinity of the cottage supported the Malaysian police theory of an initial act of abduction. But the Malaysian communist party was not the only organisation capable of swift and disciplined action — so was the CIA. It was well understood in Thailand that Thompson had become more Thai than American in his life and loyalties. As a one-time station head, might he not have been in possession of information which might prove gravely embarrassing to his previous employers?

There can no doubt of the speaker's authority or of his integrity, and yet there must be a lingering factual doubt. Intelligence information is soon outdated but the behavioural patterns of the CIA in South-East Asia have been such that observers might conclude that any act on its part was not beyond the bounds of possibility. But why murder Thompson after so many years? That is unanswerable — yet the theory is as good, if not better, than others put forward.

402

BIBLIOGRAPHY

Alone on the Sharp Edge   David van Praagh: (published 1989,
                                         DK Books, Bangkok)

The American Influence on the   Fred W. Darling: (paper published
Evolution of Constitutional   1961, Journal of the Siam Society)
Government in Thailand.

Anglo-French Declaration of   C. Jesherun: (paper published 1970
January 1896 and the   Journal of the Siam Society)
Independence of Siam

Anglo-Siamese Secret   Mrs Thamsook Numnonda: (paper
Convention of 1897   published 1965 Journal of the Siam
                                         Society)

Atonement before Absolution   Nicholas Tarling: (paper published
                                         1978 Journal of the Siam Society)

An attempt to fly in the Face of   Nicholas Tarling:(paper published
the Ordinary Laws of Supply   1987 Journal of the Siam Society)
and Demand

Bangkok Top Secret   Sir Andrew Gilchrist: (published
                                         1970 by Hutchinson London)

British and American Influence   Frank C. Darling: (paper published
on Post-War Thailand   Journal of the Siam Society)

The Balancing Act   Joseph J. Wright, Jnr: (published
                                         1991 Pacific Rim Press, Oakland,
                                         California)

Bloody May   Physicians for Human Rights and
                                         Asia Watch (who also published
                                         1992)

Chinese Society in Thailand	G. William Skinner: (published 1957 Cornell University Press, Ithaca, New York)
Chakri Monarchs	Dr Duangtip Somnapan Surintatip: (published 1982 by Office of His Majesty's Principal Private Secretary)
China's War with Vietnam, 1979	King C. Chen: (published 1987 Hoover Press, Stanford University, California)
Devil's Discus	Rayne Kruger: (published 1964 Cassell, London)
Drugs, the US and Khun Sa	Francis W. Bellinger: (published 1989 DK Books, Bangkok)
End of the Absolute Monarchy in Siam	B. A. Batson: (published 1984 Oxford University Press, London)
F. M. P. Phibun Songkhram	B. J. Terwiel: (published 1980 University of Queensland Press, Australia)
From Siam to Thailand	Jorges Orgibet: (published 1982 Kofco (Thailand) Ltd, Bangkok)
Fall of the Phibun Government, 1944	B. A. Batson: (paper published 1974 Journal of the Siam Society)
First Phibun Government and its involvement in World War II	Charnvit Kasetskk (paper published 1974 Journal of the Siam Society)
Foreign and Domestic Consequences of KMT Intervention in Burma. Cornell paper No. 93	Robert H. Taylor: (published 1973 Cornell University Press, Ithaca, New York)

The Furtive War	Wilfred G. Burchett: (published 1963 International Publishers, New York)
From Armed Suppression to Political Offensive	Chai-anan Samudavanija and others: (published 1990)
The First Vietnam War	Peter M. Dunn: (published 1985 St. Martin's Press, New York)
Forced Back and Forgotten	Lawyers' Committee on Human Rights: (who also published 1989)
Golden Triangle: Frontier in Wilderness	Kuo Yi-tung (Bo Yang): (published 1987 Joint Publishing Co., Hong Kong)
The Hmong of Thailand	N. Tapp: (published 1986 Anti-Slavery Society, London)
Hmong and their Language	T. M. Lyman: (paper published 1990 Journal of the Siam Society)
Hmong, Opium, and Haw	Terry C. Grandstaff: (paper published 1976 Journal of the Siam Society)
How We Won the War	Vo Nguyen Giap: (published 1977 Recon Pubns, Ypsilanti, MI, America)
Into Siam, Underground Kingdom	Nicol Smith and Blake Clark: (published 1965 Bobbs-Merrill Co., Indianapolis)
In a Little Kingdom	Perry Stieglitz: (published 1990 M. E. Sarpe Inc. Armonk, New York)
The Korean War	Max Hasting: (published 1987 Michael Joseph, London)
KMT Aggression against Burma	Burma Min. of Infm: (own publication 1953)

King Prajadhipok and the Apple Cart	Nicholas Tarling: (paper published 1976 Journal of the Siam Society)
Khmer Rouge Abuses Along the Thai-Cambodian Border	Asia Watch Committee (USA) (own publication 1989)
Leadership in Power in the Chinese Community of Thailand.	G. William Skinner: (published 1958 Cornell University Press, Ithaca, New York)
Legendary American	Wm. Warren: (published 1970 Houghton Mifflin Co., Boston, America)
A Marvellous Party	Sir Berkeley Gage: (privately published 1989)
The Military in Thai Politics 1981-6	Suchit Bunbongkarn (published 1987 Institute of South-East Asia Studies, Singapore)
My Secret War	Richard S. Drury: (published 1979 Aero Publishers Inc. Falibrook, Ca. America)
Nationalist China Troops in Burma: Obstacles to Burma Foreign relations 1949-61	K. R. Young: (published 1971 as a dissertation submitted for PhD, New York University 1970)
Negotiations Regarding to Cession of Siamese Malay States 1907 to 1909	Mrs Thamsook Numnonda: (paper published 1967 Journal of the Siam Society)
Outrage (Burma)	Bertil Lintner: (published 1989 Review Publishing Co. Ltd, Hong Kong)
Political Repression in Thailand	Euro-Committee for Solidarity with the Thai People: (published 1978 London University)

Politics in Thailand	David A. Wilson: (published 1966 Greenwood Press, Connecticut
Poppies, Pipes, and People	J. Westermeyer: (published 1982 University of California, Los Angeles)
Political Conflict in Thailand	David Morrell and Chai-anan Samudavanija: (published 1981 Oelgeschlager, Gunn in Hain Inc. Cambridge, Mass.)
Pridi Banomyong	Vichitvong na Pombhejara: (published 1979 Institute of South-East Asian Studies, Singapore)
The Politics of Heroin	Alfred W. McCoy: (published 1972 Harper and Row, Singapore)
Portraits of Thai Politics	Jenton K. Ray: (published 1972 Orient Longman, New Delhi)
Puey Ungphakorn; a Siamese for all Seasons	Komol Keemthong Foundation: (own publication 1981)
The Ravens	C. Robbins: (published 1987 Crown Publishers, New York.)
Rice and Reconciliation	Nicholas Tarling: (paper published 1978 Journal of the Siam Society)
Revolution in Laos	Kaysone Phomvihane: (published 1980 Progress Publishers, Moscow)
Rise and Fall of the Communist Party of Thailand (1973-1987)	Gawin Chufima: (published 1990 University of Kent at Canterbury — paper No. 12)
Sarit Regime	Thak Chaloemtiarana: (published 1974 Cornell University, Ithaca, New York)

Siam and World War II   Direk Jayanama: (published Social
                                   Science Association of Thailand)

Source of the River Kwai   Pierre Boule: (published 1967 SOE)

Shan of Burma   Chao Tzang Yawnghwe: (published
                                   1987 Institute of South-East Asian
                                   Studies, Singapore)

Second World War   Winston S. Churchill: (published
                                   1948 Cassell and Co. Ltd, London)

Scope of the US Involvement in   Richard S. Nixon: (published 1970
Laos   Bulletin of US Dept of State —
                                   Vietnam pamphlet No. 113e)

Storm over Laos   Sisouk na Champassak: (published
                                   1961 Praeger, New York 1961)

Soul of a Nation   BBC London post-production script of
                                   1980 TV programme: (written by
                                   Leo Aylen, produced by Bridget
                                   Winters)

The Struggle for Thailand   General Saiyud Kerdphol: (published
                                   1986 S. Research Center Co. Ltd,
                                   Bangkok)

Thai Resistance Movement   John B. Haseman: (published 1981
during Second World War   Center for South-East Asian Studies,
                                   Northern Illinois University)

Thailand and the Fall of   Nigel J. Brailey: (published 1986
Singapore   Westview Press Inc.)

Thailand: A Short History   David K. Wyatt: (published 1984
                                   Yale University Press)

Thailand: Origins of Military   David Elliot: (published 1978 Zed
Rule   Press, London)

Thailand: Modernisation of a Bureaucratic Polity	Fred W. Riggs: (published 1967 East-West Center Press, Honolulu)
Thailand: Society in Politics	J. L. S. Girling: (published 1981 Cornell University Press, Ithaca, New York)
Thailand: Politics of Despotic Paternalism	Thak Chaloemtiarana: (published 1979 Social Science Association of Thailand, Thammasat University, Bangkok)
Thailand and US Relations	A. Ramsay and Wiwat Mungkandi: (published 1988 Berkeley Institute of East Asian Studies, University of California)
Thailand in the United States	Frank C. Darling: (published 1965 Public Affairs Press, Washington D.C.)
Thai in Yunnan	M. Carthew: (paper published 1952 Journal of the Siam Society)
Thailand: A Political, Social and Ecͬ ͺic Analysis	D. Insor: (published 1963 Allen in Unwin Ltd, London)
ͺͺand's Foreign Relations 1964/80	Corinne Phuangkasem: (published 1982 Institute of South-East Asian Studies, Singapore)
The Thai Young Turks	Chai-Anan Samudavanija: (published 1982 Institute of South-East Asian Studies, Singapore)
The Tragic Mountains	Jane Hamilton-Merritt: (published 1993 Indiana University Press)
US National Security Policy and Aid to Thai Police	Thos Lobe: (published 1987 University of South Dakota)

US Foreign Policy in and Thai Military Rule, 1947-77	Surachart Bamrungsuk: (published 1988 DK Books, Bangkok)
US-Thailand Diplomatic Relations during World War II	Sethachuay Vivat: (published 1977 as dissertation presented for Ph.D. at Brigham Young University, Utah)
UN Survey: Report on Economic and Social Needs of Opium Producing Areas	United Nations 1967, which also published
US and Thailand	R. Sean Randolph: (published 1986 Berkeley Institute of East Asian Studies, University of California)
The US and the Coming of the Coup of 1947 in Siam	Thanet Aphornsuvan: (paper published 1987 Journal of the Siam Society)
Vietnam: A Diplomatic Tragedy	V. Bator: (published 1965 Oceana Pubns, New York)
When I Parachuted into Thailand	Wimon Wiriyawit: (English translation 1990 privately printed)